Reproductive Justice and the Catholic Church

Grateful acknowledgment is made to the following for permission to quote from copyright material:

Gwendolyn Brooks, "The Mother," reprinted by consent of Brooks Permissions.
"A Prayer of Accompaniment" and "Prayer to St. Brigid," Catholics for Choice (Washington, DC): www.CatholicsForChoice.org. Used with permission.
Karen Ross, "A Prayer for Times of Reproductive Loss," used with permission.
"The Second Letter to Agnes of Prague," Clare of Assisi, in *Clare of Assisi: Early Documents,* revised and translated by Regis J. Armstrong, O.F.M.Cap. Published by New City Press, Hyde Park, NY, 2006. Used with permission.
Katie Ford, "From the Nursery," from *Blood Lyrics.* Copyright ©2014 by Katie Ford. Reprinted with the permission of The Permissions Company, LLC on behalf of Graywolf Press, Minneapolis, Minnesota, www.graywolfpress.org.
"Prayer for Those Denied Abortion Care," National Council of Jewish Women. Used by permission.
"i carry your heart with me(i carry it in". Copyright 1952, ©1980, 1991 by the Trustees for the E. E. Cumming Trust, from *COMPLETE POEMS: 1904-1962* by E. E. Cummings, edited by George J. Firmage. Used by permission of Liveright Publishing Corporation.
Excerpts from Emily Reimer-Barry, "The Shared Strengths of Catholic Social Teaching and Reproductive Justice," *Conscience*, vol. 44 no. 1 (June 2023). Used with permission.
Excerpts from "Lou's Abortion Story," *Abortion, with love.* Season 2. Episode 24 (December 14, 2021). https://www.abortionwithlove.com/episodes/lous-abortion-story. Used by permission.
"Wise Women Also Came" © Jan Richardson from *Night Visions: Searching the Shadows of Advent and Christmas.* Used by permission.
Excerpt from Elise Erikson Barrett, *What Was Lost: A Christian Journey through Miscarriage* (Louisville: Westminster John Knox Press), 2010. Used by permission.
"This Pregnancy," by Mary Gordon (November 2022). Copyright © Commonweal Foundation, reprinted with permission. For more information, visit www.commonwealmagazine.org.
Jessica Zucker, excerpts from *I Had a Miscarriage: A Memoir, A Movement.* Copyright © 2021 by Jessica Zucker. Reprinted with the permission of The Permissions Company, LLC on behalf of The Feminist Press at the City University of New York, www.feministpress.org. All rights reserved.
Excerpts from Anna Wood, *I've Had One Too: A Story of Abortion and Healing* (Numinous Books, 2021). Used by permission.
Excerpts from *Interrogating Pregnancy Loss: Feminist Writings on Abortion, Miscarriage, and Stillbirth*, eds. Emily R. M. Lind and Angie Deveau (Bradford, ON: Demeter, 2017). Used by permission.
Tilted Uterus: When Jesus Is Your Baby Daddy. Copyright 2019 by Taiyon J. Coleman.
The Face of Miscarriage. Copyright 2019 by Soniah Kamal.
Kamali's *Stillbirth.* Copyright 2019 by Janet Lee Ortiz. Used by permission.
Scripture quotations are from *The Catholic Edition of the Revised Standard Version of the Bible*, copyright © 1965, 1966 National Council of the Churches of Christ in the United States of America. Used by permission. All rights reserved worldwide.

Reproductive Justice and the Catholic Church

Advancing Pragmatic Solidarity with Pregnant Women

Emily Reimer-Barry

A SHEED & WARD BOOK
ROWMAN & LITTLEFIELD
Lanham • Boulder • New York • London

Published by Rowman & Littlefield
An imprint of The Rowman & Littlefield Publishing Group, Inc.
4501 Forbes Boulevard, Suite 200, Lanham, Maryland 20706
www.rowman.com

86-90 Paul Street, London EC2A 4NE

Copyright © 2024 by The Rowman & Littlefield Publishing Group, Inc.

All rights reserved. No part of this book may be reproduced in any form or by any electronic or mechanical means, including information storage and retrieval systems, without written permission from the publisher, except by a reviewer who may quote passages in a review.

British Library Cataloguing in Publication Information Available

Library of Congress Cataloging-in-Publication Data

Names: Reimer-Barry, Emily, author.
Title: Reproductive justice and the Catholic Church : advancing pragmatic solidarity with pregnant women / Emily Reimer-Barry.
Description: Lanham : Rowman & Littlefield [2024] | "A Sheed & Ward Book." | Includes bibliographical references and index.
Identifiers: LCCN 2024008069 (print) | LCCN 2024008070 (ebook) | ISBN 9781538182642 (cloth) | ISBN 9781538182659 (paperback) | ISBN 9781538182666 (epub)
Subjects: LCSH: Human reproduction--Religious aspects--Catholic Church.
Classification: LCC BX1795.H84 R44 2024 (print) | LCC BX1795.H84 (ebook) | DDC 248.4/82--dc23/eng/20240508
LC record available at https://lccn.loc.gov/2024008069
LC ebook record available at https://lccn.loc.gov/2024008070

Contents

Acknowledgments	vii
Introduction	1
Chapter 1: Why Reproductive Justice?: Beyond Problematic Binaries	13
Chapter 2: How Moral Absolutism Undermines Reproductive Justice	43
Chapter 3: The Shadow Side of the Pro-Life Movement: 1973–2022	95
Chapter 4: Structural Change for Reproductive Justice	129
Chapter 5: Complexity and Ambiguity in Women's Experiences of Pregnancy and Pregnancy Loss	161
Chapter 6: The Full Humanity and Moral Agency of Pregnant Women: A Key Claim for Reproductive Justice	193
Chapter 7: Pragmatic Solidarity and Spiritual Supports: Enacting Reproductive Justice as Church	233
Appendix: Poems and Prayers for Reproductive Justice	249
Bibliography	265
Index	279
About the Author	287

Acknowledgments

My writing is situated in revisionist and feminist frameworks for doing Catholic theological ethics, and is deeply indebted to the trailblazing work of post–Vatican II scholars who sought to bring forward the wisdom of the Catholic tradition with attention to moral complexity and pastoral sensitivity. I thank in particular Lisa Sowle Cahill; Margaret A. Farley; Patricia Beattie Jung; Susan A. Ross; Rosemary Radford Ruether; Christine E. Gudorf; Cristina L. H. Traina; Shawnee Daniels-Sykes; Cathleen Kaveny; James F. Keenan, SJ; Charles E. Curran; Edward C. Vacek, SJ; Kevin T. Kelly; Bryan Massingale; and Richard M. Gula. I admire their courage and practical wisdom, especially as change seems to happen so slowly within the Catholic Church, and I grow impatient.

I am grateful for all of the support, encouragement, and critical feedback I have received as this book was in various stages of development. I especially thank the many undergraduate students who have shared their spiritual journeys with me. It would be impossible to name all of the ways that my students' questions and concerns have challenged and inspired me over the years. Structural support at my university made this project possible. In particular, I am grateful for the research sabbatical, faculty research grant, research assistance of Megan J. Peng, and Steber Professorship. I am grateful to colleagues at University of San Diego (USD), especially the faculty who collaborated on the Dialogue after Dobbs events in 2022–2023. Thank you for recognizing the place of reproductive justice conversations at a Catholic campus, and for making space for feminist theologians. The Society of the Sacred Heart, rooted in a charism of sharing God's love with students and with the world, inspires my pedagogy and my writing. Special thanks to the Society of the Sacred Heart of Jesus (RSCJ) sisters at USD.

Speaking engagements provided me the opportunity to test some of these ideas and further develop them in conversation with scholars across the country and around the world. Special thanks to Maria Pilar Aquino, who invited me to give a plenary address at the June 2019 Catholic Theological Society of America convention, to Nichole M. Flores for her powerful and persuasive response to my paper, and to the *National Catholic Reporter* readers who emailed me afterward to share their stories of reproductive loss and hopes for a new way forward in the Church. I am grateful for the opportunity to have presented the Shannon Lecture Series at Nazareth College; the Consistent Ethic of Life lecture at Aquinas Center at Candler School of Theology, Emory University; the Switgall Lecture at the University of San Diego; the Koch lecture at the College of St. Benedict and St. John's University; the Katherine A. Henry '86 Memorial Lecture Series on Women's Health at College of the Holy Cross; a plenary address for the Brazilian Society of Moral Theology; a presentation for the Association of Pittsburgh Priests; a breakout presentation for the *Amoris Laetitia* conference at the Pontifical Gregorian University; the first annual "Respect Women" lecture for Future Church; a presentation for the Complex Social Issues Series at St. Louis University; and a public lecture at St. Mary's College, sponsored by the Center for the Study of Spirituality. To all of the organizers of those events and audience members who asked questions—thank you. The members of my Wabash Center for Teaching and Learning Digital Salon provided a brave space to reimagine new possibilities for transformative work in anti-racist pedagogies and ethics. The members of the Catholic Theological Ethics in the World Church virtual table on reproductive justice and the common good have inspired and challenged me in our Zoom conversations. In particular I want to thank my co-facilitator, Simeiqi He. I'm also grateful for my colleagues at the Society of Christian Ethics and the Catholic Theological Society of America for nurturing my vocation as a theologian over the years. Within those conferences, I experience a deep sense of belonging and I always leave with tremendous hope for our guild.

I thank my Weston prayer group for journeying with me each Lent and Advent season, and the Perry's breakfast club for their friendship and encouragement. I thank my parish community for modeling inclusive discipleship and all of the teachers and coaches at the school who have taught my daughters that there is a place for their voices in the Roman Catholic Church.

Thank you to Richard Brown, Jaylene Perez, Victoria Shi, and Naomi Minkoff at Sheed & Ward for your support at every stage of the publication process. Colleagues were generous with their time and energy, and I want to thank in particular those who have read chapter drafts and/or shared research along the way. Special thanks to Kathryn Lilla Cox, Jill O'Brien, Meghan Clark, Suzanne Mulligan, Julie Clague, Sandra Sullivan-Dunbar, Michael Jaycox, Karen Peterson-Iyer, Margaret Kamitsuka, Susan Ross, Andrea Vicini, Susan Reynolds, Steven Millies, Cristina Traina, Kristin Heyer, Daniel Daly, Todd Salzman, Don Clemmer, David DeCosse, Mary Doyle Roche, M. Therese Lysaught, Natalia Imperatori-Lee, Kate Ward, Karen Teel, Mary Doak, Toddie Peters, Julie Hanlon Rubio, Simeiqi He,

Lisa Powell, Mindy McGarrah-Sharp, Mark Hearn, and the Sheed & Ward anonymous reviewers. I thank Daniel Maguire, Mary Hunt, E. Jane Via, and Richard Penaskovic for speaking to me about their experiences as signatories of the 1984 *New York Times* ad and their hopes for the Church (and academy) today. Special thanks to the women who gave me permission to reprint their testimonies of pregnancy loss, poetry, and prayers.

My dear friends Melissa Browning and Shawnee Daniels-Sykes passed on to eternal life before this book was published, but both in their own ways have inspired and supported me as I sought to develop a vision of pragmatic solidarity with pregnant women. I'm grateful for their friendship and their scholarship. May they rest in God's eternal embrace of love.

From the bottom of my heart, I thank my family. Jay's support meant the world to me as I navigated the ups and downs of the research and writing process. I thank my daughters for their patience when Mom needed to write/edit/read more that day. I dedicate this book to all our daughters—past, present, future—with the hope that (in the words of Cristina L. H. Traina) they will flourish in the midst of finitude.

Introduction

It is time for a new conversation in the Catholic Church about pregnancy and pregnancy loss that centers women's experiences and offers a more dignified and more just framework for reconsidering reproduction and social justice. The risks women take to bring new life into the world are often underacknowledged and underappreciated. And when Catholic women decide that they are not able to continue a pregnancy, they can hear shame-based messages, exacerbating their pain in an already difficult situation. I seek to contribute to a growing body of scholarship in Catholic theological ethics that takes seriously the sinful social conditions in which we live, while also holding Christian communities accountable for enacting our justice-based advocacy today. I am indebted especially to the intersectional coalition of scholars and activists in the reproductive justice movement for their wisdom, courage, and tenacity in calling attention to racism and structural violence for decades.[1]

Loretta J. Ross and Rickie Solinger—two leading figures in the reproductive justice movement in the United States—argue that people who reproduce and become parents require a safe and dignified context for these most fundamental human experiences.[2] Reproductive justice "calls for an integrated analysis" and a "holistic vision."[3] As a social justice movement, reproductive justice is a framework that looks at the multiple layers of structural and personal support necessary for human flourishing, including health care access, housing, safe and affordable child care, education, political structures, healthy environment, and other important factors. Scholars of reproductive justice problematize unjustified coercion of pregnant bodies and detail the oppression of women of color in US history. Access to safe and legal abortion is one part of the broader policy framework that reproductive justice advocates support, but more broadly, reproductive justice seeks to build healthy relationships and communities organized justly so that all people thrive.[4] One can find considerable overlap between the normative claims of Catholic teachings and the goals of the reproductive justice movement, even though

Catholic teachings and reproductive justice scholars have divergent positions on abortion rights.[5]

Abortion is not the *focus* of the reproductive justice movement, but it is an important *part*, and one that is often a stumbling block for faithful Catholics.[6] As such, abortion is a focus of substantial portions of this book. Despite the ways that abortion seems to dominate the headlines, I find when I teach this material that my students are often not aware of how pervasive abortion is in human history and even in US history.[7] Many are also unaware of the breadth of wise and compassionate responses to pregnant women's struggles in the history of the Catholic Church, including moralists' defenses of therapeutic abortions and saints' accompaniment of women facing dangerous, unwanted, or ill-timed pregnancies.[8] While the Catholic Church is often in the headlines in the United States today because of pro-life politics, many Catholics also find themselves ambivalent or explicitly critical of magisterial approaches to this important question. Moral absolutes may make for easy talking points and social media posts, but real life is far more complex. The story of abortion in the United States is a layered story that, from the beginning, involves groups of men and women at conflict over how best to support pregnant women, nurture new life, and establish control over reproduction. It should come as no surprise that faith communities have been part of these conversations since the beginning and that faith communities continue to shape religious beliefs and practices. Religious beliefs about gender roles, marriage, and the purposes of sexual intercourse have deeply influenced political conversations about whether abortion should be criminalized.

I was born after *Roe v. Wade*, the US Supreme Court decision that established abortion as a constitutional right on the basis of privacy, a right that women across the country held from 1973 until 2022, albeit with increasing limitations.[9] I grew up in a White, pro-life, Catholic, Republican household in the deep South. Opposition to legal abortion was as much a religious as a political issue in my community, and my moral values were shaped, for better or worse, in that context, by people who sincerely believed that life begins at conception, unborn children have a right to life, and that all good women want to be mothers. In high school I was active in the pro-life club at my Catholic high school, and I attended the March for Life in Washington, DC, both as a high school student and undergraduate. On those trips our group met with Republican legislators to advocate for restrictions to abortion rights. I sometimes joined groups who prayed the rosary outside of known abortion clinics, and I remember selling bumper stickers as part of a fundraiser that read, "Abortion Stops a Beating Heart." I had one on my car for years. I share this with you because I am personally complicit in the problems that this book identifies. I understand how people of faith in the United States can have a simple (though also heartfelt and genuine) approach to abortion, while not realizing their complicity with structures that harm pregnant women. My Catholic faith is a core part of my identity and has deeply influenced my formation as a person, spouse, parent, teacher, and citizen. But I have also been horrified and saddened at how some Catholics have adopted positions that now seem mean-spirited and contrary to the heart of a gospel message of compassion in the midst of difficult circumstances. Nowhere is this more apparent than when talking about abortion in an election year.

My faith has changed since I marched on Washington as a pro-lifer. I've since also joined other marches, this time on the West Coast, including the Women's March, a march in San Ysidro to protest immigrant detention centers on the border, and Black Lives Matter protests. A number of factors contributed to shifts in my thinking; they include the study of academic theology, my immersion into the messy relationships and the complexities of an unjust world, and my experiences of pregnancy and parenting. Over time, I let go of a faith that tended to frame issues as black and white, with no room for gray. In prayer I began to explore the ways that the gospels highlight Jesus's critique of systems of injustice. I learned wise compassion from the ways that Jesus's preaching in the gospels honored and wrestled with legal traditions within Judaism while seeking to meet the material and spiritual needs of the people in front of him. I explored feminist ways of naming God and thrived in communities that valued women's voices and women's leadership. I began to recognize the economic and racial privilege with which I had grown up, privilege that for many years of my life was invisible to me, and I asked myself what my faith had to do with those experiences of privilege. And I began to see both racism and sexism in the Church as sinful expressions of human dominance in a broken institution. In my wrestling with complex questions about life, death, power, justice, compassion, and mercy, my faith has changed and deepened. My awareness of God is sharpest in times of struggle, heartache, and sadness; in those moments, God is not "out there," but "right here," drawing us into a mystical embrace no matter our situation. All of these shifts in my way of thinking about God, liturgy, and community shaped the way that I began to think about reproduction, the common good, and women's agency. As my faith changed with age, I have become increasingly uncomfortable identifying with the pro-life label.

In the past decade, I have been saddened by the way that some Catholic bishops and politicians have contributed to a toxic political climate by centering abortion in their political discourse. This book is my way of sharing both a critique of their approach to the issue and my hope for a new and different way forward for people in my faith tradition. Building on the scholarship of women from communities marginalized because of race, class, and gender, I demonstrate that the Catholic community can and should learn from the important social justice work led by women of color in the US context. I do so as a White feminist scholar aware of my own reproductive privilege.[10]

I never intended to write a book about women's experiences of pregnancy loss, including abortion. I have been teaching undergraduates at a Catholic university for over fifteen years, and in my sexual ethics course, the abortion unit has been my least favorite module, for many reasons. The issue is complicated. Students arrive with assumptions and prejudices about abortion, feminism, and the church that take time to name and unpack. Many have very little knowledge about sexuality, methods of preventing pregnancy, and the prevalence of sexually transmitted infections. Many young people also carry a lot of pain from the messages they have absorbed from our culture, their families, and their religious communities about their bodies, relationships, and sex. The hookup culture pervasive on college campuses seems to promote the goods of freedom and sexual pleasure, but in practice retains harmful scripts regarding gender, power, intimacy, and mutual care that undermine sexual flourishing for college students.[11] And there are always students for whom the issue of abortion is very personal: they have had an abortion, they took a friend to get an abortion, their partner had an abortion, or they cried with relief when they got their period and realized they were not pregnant after all. Usually if they disclose anything about their personal experiences to me, they do so after the class has ended. By that time, it is too late for me to adapt my language, soften my tone, or speak with special sensitivity about an issue they have experienced personally. My pedagogy has shifted as a result of this knowledge. I know now not to assume anything about a student's sexual experience (or lack thereof) by the way they present in class—the way they dress, the way they talk to their peers, their academic performance, what they say about their faith. Even figuring out how to structure a syllabus and assignments in a trauma-informed way is difficult. How do I teach the material without causing mental anguish? How should a teacher reconcile the reverence for life with the sexism that accompanies Church teachings? What is the best way to teach the material while also helping students to develop their own voices and encourage them to wrestle deeply with these complex questions? Since I do not have complete answers to any of these questions, I never thought I would be in a position to write a book on such complex and morally fraught topics.

The catalyst for this book was a regular Sunday Mass. It was "Respect Life" month and the preaching that Sunday focused on abortion, and only on abortion. I live fewer than twenty miles from the busiest overland international border crossing in the world, and the detention of migrants had been on the news for weeks. I experienced total silence from the pulpit on this humanitarian crisis in our own back yard. I cannot remember a single homily that ever mentioned racism. America had been at war for twenty years in

Afghanistan, and the military industrial complex employs many workers in San Diego. But during "Respect Life" month the focus was solely on abortion. I grew increasingly uncomfortable as the pulpit was used to shame women using pro-life talking points. All of us in the pews were told that as good Catholics we should support legal protections for unborn children. Abortion was described as a mortal sin that prevents a woman from being in relationship with God. Nothing was said about male responsibility for unplanned pregnancies, or about domestic violence, the high cost of housing and child care in our community, or the fact that women who find themselves pregnant may not feel adequately prepared for or supported in motherhood. The homilist did not seem to understand that some women who procure abortion believe that to do so is the most loving decision they can make within their constrained circumstances. In most of the male cleric's homily, the reality of the pregnant woman was invisible. The focus was on the innocent unborn child. For the first time in my life, I got up and walked out of Church. I was angry, but my body expressed my rage through tears. I did not get far from Church, because my kids were singing in the choir—I had to stay on the campus. I found a small garden where a statue of St. Francis of Assisi stood among blooming flowers and chirping birds. I told Francis all about the homily I had walked away from, and asked him for advice. I tried to breathe as I cried and listened to the birds.

What came to me in that moment was the story of St. Francis stripping before his bishop, returning his clothes to his father, so that he was utterly naked and vulnerable, but also stripped of his privilege and ready for a new mission. As I reflected on this story, I realized what a privilege it was for me to teach and write about sexual ethics and social justice while avoiding writing about pregnancy loss (including abortion). I had checked out of something that I found uncomfortable, keeping the issue at arm's length. I had long ago decided that the discourse was hopelessly polarizing and that no good could come from one more person chiming in to this debate. But at the same time, I was struck by the paucity of resources that preachers could access. What if the homilist that morning had actually tried to find materials by a Catholic theologian about women's experiences of miscarriage, stillbirth, and abortion? Was there anything out there?[12] How could I walk out, criticizing his lack of awareness, when my silence as a theologian was contributing to the problem? He had not heard my students' disclosures. How could I expect him to understand? I began to see my responsibility in a whole new light. I told a colleague I would be willing to speak on this issue at a national conference, and this project was born.[13] I had already begun the writing process when the *Dobbs v. Jackson Women's Health* decision was first leaked on May 2, 2022, and then the final argument published on June 24, 2022. By August 19, 2022, abortion bans were in effect in fourteen states.[14] As I have observed some Catholic leaders celebrating the *Dobbs* decision,[15] I have also shared my own concerns about the implications of the decision for women's reproductive health care.[16]

This book employs a feminist and Catholic approach to moral issues related to pregnancy and pregnancy loss. By feminist, I mean a critical and constructive stance that claims full humanity for every person.[17] Feminist methods center women's experiences and move through stages of criticism, retrieval, and reconstruction.[18] Feminist theologians oppose discrimination on the basis of sex; feminism takes a "bias for women, however temporary or prolonged that bias must be."[19] A key feminist principle is that "whatever diminishes or denies the full humanity of women must be presumed not to reflect the divine or an authentic relation to the divine, or to reflect the authentic nature of things, or to be the message or work of an authentic redeemer or a community of redemption."[20]

By Catholic, I mean rooted in the Catholic intellectual and liturgical tradition, with special attention to the principles of Catholic social teachings[21] as well as authoritative teachings of the Catholic magisterium, in conversation with Catholic theologians.[22] As Pope Francis wrote in *Amoris Laetitia*: "The thinking of the pastors and theologians, if faithful to the Church, honest, realistic, and creative, will help us to achieve greater clarity."[23] I will take seriously this invitation to propose a *faithful*, *honest*, *realistic*, and *creative* strategy to move us beyond the impasse in which we currently find ourselves on abortion politics. I had the distinct pleasure of joining fellow Catholic moral theologians in an audience with Pope Francis on May 13, 2022, in which he encouraged us to foster "*a new creativity* to express in the current challenges the values that constitute us as a people in society and in the Church." He repeated: "I emphasize: *new creativity*."[24] A few months after this speech, in an address to catechists, the pope differentiated between the role of a catechist and the role of a theologian. Pope Francis explained that a theologian has a vocation to go beyond existing doctrine because "he is trying to make theology more explicit."[25] When I offer explicit criticisms of magisterial teachings, the work of fellow theologians, or policies of the United States Conference of Catholic Bishops, I do so as a theologian who has a deep and abiding love for the Church, which leads me to seek more adequate formulations in our communal life together. I am glad that my Church teaches that there should always be a presumption against taking human life.[26] But double standards persist in how this Church teaching is applied to a range of issues today.[27] We need a better way forward that addresses the complexity and ambiguity of human reproduction, while recognizing how coercion of pregnant women cannot be reconciled with a Catholic approach to the common good in a pluralist society.

I write this book as a scholar trained in theological ethics. My experiences of pregnancy, childbirth, and motherhood are certainly relevant, though unique to my perspective and positionality. My positionality is undoubtedly shaped by the unearned privileges I have experienced as a White, cisgender, heterosexual, married woman of US citizenship. My formation and education as a young person were shaped by the dominance of White and Eurocentric Catholic theologians. In graduate school I had more exposure to the writings of female and nonwhite theologians. These readings profoundly challenged my assumptions, and exposed many of my blind spots. The research for this book has been significantly shaped by BIPOC (that is, Black, Indigenous, and People of Color) scholars. I am grateful for my conversation partners over the years who have pointed out my privileges and helped me to think differently about my responsibilities in the world. I have no expertise in medicine, US law, counseling, political science, or community organizing. As a lay theologian, I speak *from*, not *for* the Catholic Church.

This book's argument unfolds in seven chapters. In the first, I explain the problems of a pro-life versus pro-choice binary, and argue that a reproductive justice framework is more suited to the complexity of the task at hand. I explain how abortion can be viewed through multiple lenses (moral, social, political, and so on), and I show that a reproductive justice framework is a holistic action plan in alignment with theological anthropology and Catholic social teachings. In the second chapter, I describe magisterial teachings on sexuality and reproduction in recent papacies, noting a moral absolutism that has emerged. I also detail how magisterial moral absolutism impacts sacramental life, political action, and health care policy. In the third chapter, I uncover the shadow side of the pro-life movement since the early 1970s in the United States. I demonstrate that neither major political party in the United States aligns neatly with a consistent ethic of life, and show how other interests (including sexism and racism) also shape discourse about what it means to be pro-life. I then move to more constructive chapters that seek to move the debates forward in important ways. The fourth chapter advocates for structural change and suggests that the reproductive justice movement's key goals advance a Catholic feminist vision for social change. I name concrete structural supports that would create the possibility for more pregnant women to reasonably see a way forward that safeguards both their well-being and the well-being of dependent children, born and unborn. The fifth chapter attends to narratives of pregnancy loss, suggesting that renewed attention to complexity and ambiguity is necessary. The sixth chapter defends the full humanity and moral agency of pregnant women. I name prenatal life as sacred potential human life, valuable in itself, while at the same time positioning the power of the pregnant woman over the prenatal life she carries. The final chapter suggests that the role of the Church is *not* primarily to be a moral teacher but rather a community of support and pragmatic solidarity. Becoming a Church that actually helps pregnant women, including through structural and policy reforms, will demonstrate the Church's support for life.

The United States Conference of Catholic Bishops (USCCB) Statement on the *Dobbs* ruling expressed a goal I share. Catholic bishops write that now is "a time for healing wounds and repairing social divisions; it is a time for reasoned reflection and civil dialogue."[28] I hope that this book can contribute to healing wounds, repairing social divisions, and advancing reasoned reflection and civil dialogue. Women who have experienced pregnancy loss often report isolation and confusion in Catholic liturgies and institutional settings. They deserve a discourse in the Church that recognizes complexity and ambiguity, that holds their experiences as sacred and that recognizes moral growth and support over time as essential to what an ecclesial community is all about. Reproductive health researcher Diana Greene Foster once wrote that "abortion is a medical procedure so controversial it decides elections and ruins Thanksgiving dinners."[29] I look forward to the day when abortion politics does not decide elections or ruin Thanksgiving dinners. I hope this book helps us get there.

NOTES

1. Loretta J. Ross and Rickie Solinger name the "twelve founding mothers of the concept of reproductive justice" and their affiliations at the time (1994): Toni M. Bond, Chicago Abortion Fund; Reverend Alma Crawford, Religious Coalition for Reproductive Choice; Evelyn S. Field, National Council of Negro Women; Terri James, American Civil Liberties Union of Illinois; Bisola Maringay, National Black Women's Health Project, Chicago Chapter; Cassandra McConnell, Planned Parenthood of Greater Cleveland; Cynthia Newbille, National Black Women's Health Project (now Black Women's Health Imperative); Lorretta J. Ross, Center for Democratic Renewal; Elizabeth Terry, National Abortion Rights Action League of Pennsylvania; "Able" Mable Thomas, Pro-Choice Resource Center, Inc.; Winnette P. Willis, Chicago Abortion Fund; Kim Youngblood, National Black Women's Health Project. They also name the women in the 2003 SisterSong plenary and workshop who continued to shape the reproductive justice framework: Byllye Avery, National Black Women's Health Project Founder; Adriane Fugh Berman, National Women's Health Network; Jatrice Gaithers, Planned Parenthood of Metropolitan Washington; Rosalind Palacios, National Latina Health Organization; Dorothy Roberts, Northwestern University School of Law; Malika Saada Saar, Rebecca Project for Human

Rights founder; Eveline Shen, Asian Pacific Islanders for Reproductive Health; Jael Silliman, Ford Foundation; Barbara Smith, Combahee River Collective cofounder. See Loretta J. Ross and Rickie Solinger, *Reproductive Justice: An Introduction* (Oakland: University of California Press, 2017), 277–78, n. 5–7. See also Jael Silliman, Marlene Gerber Fried, Loretta Ross, and Elena Gutiérrez, *Undivided Rights: Women of Color Organize for Reproductive Justice* (Boston: South End Press, 2004).

2. Ross and Solinger, *Reproductive Justice*, 9.

3. Ross and Solinger, *Reproductive Justice*, 69.

4. Ross and Solinger, *Reproductive Justice*, 54–69.

5. Emily Reimer-Barry, "The Shared Strengths of Catholic Social Teaching and Reproductive Justice," *Conscience*, vol. 44, no. 1 (2023): 18–20.

6. Ross and Solinger distinguish between reproductive *rights* (a legal and advocacy-based model), reproductive *health* (focusing on health care services), and reproductive *justice* (an organizing framework that analyzes the impact of social institutions). See Ross and Solinger, *Reproductive Justice*, 68–69.

7. Rebecca Todd Peters and Margaret D. Kamitsuka draw attention to historical accounts of women who sought to end dangerous, ill-timed, or unwanted pregnancies, citing evidence from a Sumerian tablet, Egyptian papyrus, and other ancient texts. See "Introduction" in *Abortion and Religion: Jewish, Christian, and Muslim Perspectives*, ed. Rebecca Todd Peters and Margaret D. Kamitsuka (New York: T&T Clark/Bloomsbury, 2023), 1–17, at 2. Abortion was legal in the United States before the mid-1800s, and legal abortions were performed by midwives and apothecaries before "quickening," when the woman detected fetal movement. Attitudes began to change when the medical profession launched a campaign to criminalize abortion except in cases in which the mother's life was in danger; in those cases, they argued, only a male physician with a medical degree should be authorized to perform the procedure. The all-male American Medical Association was formed in 1847 and sought to control surgeries, childbirth, and pre- and post-natal care. For a thorough history of abortion and the law in the United States in nineteenth century, see James C. Mohr, *Abortion in America: The Origins and Evolution of National Policy, 1800–1900* (New York: Oxford University Press, 1978). Historian Kathleen M. Crowther notes that most historical records of abortion are written from the perspective of men. See Kathleen M. Crowther, *Policing Pregnant Bodies: From Ancient Greece to Post-Roe America* (Baltimore: Johns Hopkins University Press, 2023), 169. For more on the conflict between midwives and physicians see Judith P. Rooks, "The History of Midwifery," *Our Bodies Ourselves Today* (May 30, 2012): https://www.ourbodiesourselves.org/book-excerpts/health-article/history-of-midwifery/.

8. For example, Zubin Mistry suggests that a careful reading of the penitentials in Church history reveals compassion for women who had procured abortion, recognizing extenuating circumstances that mitigated guilt. Zubin Mistry, *Abortion in the Early Middle Ages, 500-900* (Woodbridge, Suffolk: York Medieval, 2015), 160. One of the legends told of St. Brigid (Kildare, Ireland, fifth century) recounts a miracle whereby Brigid "restores the virginity of a young woman," which hagiographers cite as Ireland's first recorded abortion. *The Life of Saint Brigid*, reprinted in Philip Freeman, *The World of Saint Patrick* (New York: Oxford, 2014), 106. St. Hildegard of

Bingen (1098–1117) has been called the first female German doctor, and recorded her knowledge of medicinal plants including one which "makes an abortion to a pregnant woman with a danger to her body, should she eat this plant." John M. Riddle, *Contraception and Abortion from the Ancient World to the Renaissance* (Cambridge: Harvard University Press, 1992), 116–17. These stories highlight how holy women in the Church's history have sought to discern the best way forward in complex and morally fraught situations. See Emily Reimer-Barry, "Four Holy Women Who Model Reproductive Discernment," *US Catholic* (February 2024): https://uscatholic.org/articles/202401/4-holy-women-who-model-reproductive-discernment/.

9. *Roe v. Wade*, 410 U.S. 113 (1973). The trimester framework in *Roe* meant that states could impose restrictions after viability except when necessary to protect the mother's life or health. As states began to impose regulations and restrictions, women's access to abortion became more limited, especially in rural areas and for poor women of color.

10. Caroline R. McFadden writes that White feminists can and should "theorize about reproductive justice from a place that recognizes our racial and imperial privilege." See Carolina R. McFadden, "Reproductively Privileged: Critical White Feminism and Reproductive Justice Theory," in Loretta J. Ross, Lynn Roberts, Erika Derkas, Whitney Peoples, and Pamela Bridgewater Toure, eds., *Radical Reproductive Justice: Foundations, Theory, Practice, Critique* (New York: Feminist Press, 2017), 241–50, at 243.

11. Karen Peterson-Iyer, *Reenvisioning Sexual Ethics: A Feminist Christian Account* (Washington, DC: Georgetown University Press, 2022), 55–79; Jennifer S. Hirsch and Shamus Khan, *Sexual Citizens: Sex, Power, and Assault on Campus* (New York: Norton, 2021), 63–85.

12. There is, of course, but it can be hard to find. Katie Woodruff, a public health social scientist who studies the media's coverage of abortion, found that only 4 percent of articles referred to a real-life woman who experienced an unwanted pregnancy. Sarah Cowan's research found that Americans who do not think abortion should be legal are far less likely to hear about someone's abortion than Americans who support abortion rights, because women choose carefully to whom they disclose their abortion stories. See Diane Greene Foster, *The Turnaway Study: Ten Years, A Thousand Women, and the Consequences of Having—or Being Denied—an Abortion* (New York: Scribner, 2020), 32–33. While scholars with access to university libraries may have access to extensive publications, those responsible for preaching in Catholic Churches do not always have those same resources. Priestly formation and deaconate formation in my Diocese do not require readings in Catholic feminist theological ethics. So even though Catholic feminist, womanist, and revisionist scholars have been writing about these issues for decades in scholarly journals, these are not part of a typical preacher's moral and spiritual formation in preparation for ministry in the Diocese.

13. Emily Reimer-Barry, "Another Pro-Life Movement Is Possible," *Proceedings of the Catholic Theological Society of America* 74 (2019): 21–41. https://ejournals.bc.edu/index.php/ctsa/article/view/11403. See also Nichole M. Flores, "A Response to Emily Reimer-Barry's 'Another Pro-Life Movement Is Possible'—Power, Politics,

and the Pro-Life Movement," *Proceedings of the Catholic Theological Society of America* 74 (2019): 42–45.

14. Sarah Knight, "With Roe Overturned, Which States Have Banned Abortion?" *National Public Radio* (August 19, 2022): https://www.npr.org/sections/health-shots/2022/06/24/1107126432/abortion-bans-supreme-court-roe-v-wade.

15. United States Conference of Catholic Bishops, "USCCB Statement on U.S. Supreme Court Ruling in Dobbs v. Jackson," June 24, 2022: https://www.usccb.org/news/2022/usccb-statement-us-supreme-court-ruling-dobbs-v-jackson, "Society of Jesus in the United States Welcomes Overruling of Roe v. Wade," (June 24, 2022): https://www.jesuits.org/stories/society-of-jesus-in-the-united-states-welcomes-overruling-of-roe-v-wade/. See also Gerard V. Bradley, "Dobbs Decision: A Monumental Moment in the March for Equal Rights for Every Human Life," (June 24, 2022), *National Catholic Register*: https://www.ncregister.com/commentaries/dobbs-decision-a-monumental-moment-in-the-march-for-equal-rights-for-every-human-life.

16. Emily Reimer-Barry, "Miscarriage of Justice," in *Disturbing the Foundations: Feminist Ethicists Respond to the Dobbs Decision* (Catholic Re-Visions Series, Political Theology Network, July 22, 2022): https://politicaltheology.com/disturbing-the-foundations-feminist-ethicists-respond-to-the-dobbs-decision/; "Wisdom from a Reproductive Justice Framework," *Journal of Moral Theology* 12:1 (2023): 131–34, https://jmt.scholasticahq.com/article/66249-wisdom-from-a-reproductive-justice-framework; "A Year after *Dobbs*: What about Maternal Life?" *National Catholic Reporter* (June 29, 2023): https://www.ncronline.org/opinion/guest-voices/year-after-dobbs-what-about-maternal-life.

17. Ahida E. Pilarski, "The Past and Future of Feminist Biblical Hermeneutics," *Biblical Theology Bulletin* 41:1 (2011): 16–23.

18. Anne M. Clifford, *Introducing Feminist Theology* (Maryknoll, NY: Orbis Books, 2000).

19. Margaret A. Farley, "Feminist Theology and Bioethics," in Barbara Hilkert Andolsen, Christine E. Gudorf, and Mary D. Pellauer, eds., *Women's Consciousness, Women's Conscience: A Reader in Feminist Ethics* (Minneapolis: Seabury, 1985), 285–305, at 288.

20. Rosemary Radford Ruether, *Sexism and God-Talk* (Boston: Beacon, 1983), 19.

21. Pontifical Council for Justice and Peace, *Compendium of the Social Doctrine of the Church* (2005): https://www.vatican.va/roman_curia/pontifical_councils/justpeace/documents/rc_pc_justpeace_doc_20060526_compendio-dott-soc_en.html.

22. On the role of the Catholic theologian "to pose new questions in light of changing historical circumstances," see Richard P. McBrien, "What Theology Is and Is Not," *America* (June 8, 1996), 15.

23. Francis, *Amoris Laetitia* (2016): https://www.vatican.va/content/dam/francesco/pdf/apost_exhortations/documents/papa-francesco_esortazione-ap_20160319_amoris-laetitia_en.pdf, 2.

24. Francis, "Discorso Del Santo Padre Francesco ai Partecipanti al Convegno Internazionale di Teologia Morale," Sala Clementina, 13 Maggio 2022, https://www

.vatican.va/content/francesco/it/speeches/2022/may/documents/20220513-convegno-teologia-morale.html (English translation my own).

25. Hannah Brockhaus, "Pope Francis Says This Is the Difference Between Theologians and Catechists," *Catholic News Agency* (November 24, 2022): https://www.catholicnewsagency.com/news/252913/pope-francis-says-this-is-the-difference-between-theologians-and-catechists.

26. Congregation for the Doctrine of the Faith, *Donum Vitae* (1987): http://www.vatican.va/roman_curia/congregations/cfaith/documents/rc_con_cfaith_doc_19870222_respect-for-human-life_en.html. Chapter 2 will elaborate on magisterial teachings.

27. Citing the scholarship of Catholic feminist theologian Christine E. Gudorf, I noted this in my 2019 address to the Catholic Theological Society of America. See "Another Pro-Life Movement Is Possible," 29.

28. USCCB, "USCCB Statement on U.S. Supreme Court Ruling in Dobbs v. Jackson."

29. Foster, *The Turnaway Study*, 15.

Chapter 1

Why Reproductive Justice?
Beyond Problematic Binaries

If we imagine religious and political conflict about women's reproductive decisions today as a debate between two clearly defined sides (i.e., pro-life versus pro-choice), we miss the reality of the more complex and nuanced dimensions of debates about life, death, human personhood, and social justice, especially the racialized dimensions of these debates in US history. This chapter proceeds in five steps in order to lay the groundwork for the unfolding argument of the book. First, I explain the pro-life/pro-choice binary as it is typically understood and point out the limitations of this approach. Second, I explain why I have chosen the terminology that I employ. Third, I defend the claim that abortion is a complex problem by identifying multiple lenses with which we can view and analyze abortion. Fourth, I situate present debates about bodily autonomy within the troubled legacy of enslavement in US history. I conclude the chapter by describing why a reproductive justice-focused method is superior to a binary agenda. By adopting the framework of reproductive justice, and articulating a feminist Catholic approach to abortion in light of the goals of the reproductive justice movement, this book seeks to bridge conversations between theologians, activists, pastoral ministers, and policy experts. My central concern throughout is for the flourishing of pregnant women physically, emotionally, and spiritually. I argue that reproductive flourishing cannot exist without *both* moral agency *and* structural-spiritual support.

THE PRO-LIFE/PRO-CHOICE BINARY

"But are you pro-life or not?" I have been asked this question too many times to count. I usually respond with a question. "What do you mean by pro-life?"

Answers vary, but personal opposition to abortion is usually at the center. Here's what I understand the term to mean.

Someone who identifies as pro-life claims to respect human life at every stage, including at its very earliest stages of development. Since they believe that human life must be protected in utero, they say that the prenate (life in the womb) has a right to life—that is, a right to be nurtured in the womb by a pregnant woman who is thereby compelled to undergo gestation and childbirth. In an effort to reduce abortions, the pro-life movement has sought to end legal access to abortion. They say that abortion is not really health care.[1] Not surprisingly, many pro-life Catholics celebrated the *Dobbs v. Jackson Women's Health Organization* decision that overturned *Roe v. Wade* in 2022.[2] In the media, it is a common practice *not* to use the term pro-life but rather to translate this activism into the descriptor "anti-abortion" or "anti-choice."[3] This translation is frustrating for many pro-life activists, who see their work as constructive and life-affirming.[4]

The pro-life movement is a diverse group of activists, many of whom identify religious motivations for their work. They describe sidewalk counseling at abortion clinics as an attempt to educate patients in the hopes that patients will reconsider their decision. They run pregnancy crisis centers that offer free and/or sliding scale prenatal services (pregnancy tests, ultrasounds, nutrition assistance and supplies, and so forth). They organize protests at clinics and marches to show public support for their work, the largest of which is the March for Life that takes place every January in Washington, DC. They engage in voter education and mobilization efforts in order to elect pro-life politicians, as well as political lobbying and lawsuits to further their political agenda of reducing access to legal abortion at the local, state, and federal levels. Debates within the pro-life movement focus on issues such as: whether and how to align with partisan politics; whether to focus attention on federal or state-level restrictions to abortion; details of abortion bans, including different gestational age limits and penalties for doctors and women who procure abortions; and what other issues (if any) count as "life" issues.[5]

Some members of the pro-life community describe their activism as a "seamless garment" stance that links opposition to legal abortion and support for social programs; "whole life," "seamless garment," and "consistent ethic of life" advocates make explicit connections between support for prenatal life and support for the poor, hungry, incarcerated, undocumented, and other targeted and marginalized groups that face dehumanizing treatment in our society.[6] In this framing, abortion is one of many life-issues, including opposition to the death penalty and assisted suicide.[7] Joseph Cardinal Bernardin is credited with articulating the Catholic consistent ethic of life, which he developed in his 1983 Gannon lecture at Fordham University, in which he said he was "convinced that the pro-life position of the Church must be developed in terms of a comprehensive and consistent ethic of life."[8] He saw the same principle operating in Catholic teaching against nuclear war as in Catholic teaching against abortion: namely, "the principle which prohibits the directly intended taking of innocent human life." Bernardin explained how a consistent ethic of life approach would demand a heroic social ethic that would translate to political and economic positions on tax policy, welfare policy, nutrition and feeding programs, and health care. Bernadin added that "those who defend the right to life of the weakest among us must be equally visible in support of the quality of life of the powerless among us: the old and the young, the hungry and the homeless, the undocumented immigrant and the unemployed worker."[9] Jesuit author James Martin links his own advocacy for refugees, the LGBT community, and the environment to his consistent ethic of life position.[10] Catholic moral theologian Charles C. Camosy describes his position as a "consistent ethic of life" position in which opposition to abortion is one "life" issue among others, though a "preeminent" one.[11]

But many pro-life advocates do not share this wider "whole life" view; Catholic politicians such as Governor Greg Abbott of Texas and Governor Ron DeSantis of Florida are examples of politicians who describe themselves as pro-life even though they support the death penalty and dehumanizing treatment of migrants.[12] A challenge we face when summarizing the pro-life movement is that there is not a single spokesperson or a unified platform for the movement; additionally, there are contradictory policies within the movement itself. We will explore these and other tensions in greater detail in the third chapter.

When people identify as pro-choice, they mean that they are not opposed to the legal right of women to procure abortion (medical and surgical). Importantly, they are not necessarily pro-abortion, in the sense that abortion may not be a choice they would see themselves making. Someone who is pro-choice sees abortion as a legitimate component of comprehensive reproductive health services for women.[13] One often sees the claim that abortions should be safe, legal, and accessible (meaning, not only available to the wealthy but also to poor women, including those on public aid programs). Pro-choice Christians do not necessarily identify abortion as a moral good, but they are not comfortable with pro-life goals of reducing or eliminating women's access to abortion.[14] Coerced pregnancy and motherhood do not align with a pro-choice understanding of women's inherent dignity and equality to men. Indeed, many point out that thinking about women only as baby-carriers is reductionistic. Pro-choice advocates would say that fetal life is *a* value but is not the *only* value at stake.[15]

The pro-choice movement is a grassroots movement in the same way that the pro-life movement is, and is built from a broad coalition. The heart of the pro-choice movement is maintaining women's access to abortion services.

This means operating clinics, coordinating volunteers who serve as escorts to patients seeking care (given that crossing protest lines can make it difficult to seek care), mobilizing support for ballot initiatives, lobbying efforts, initiating legal cases, voting, and fundraising. As with the pro-life movement, there is not a single spokesperson for the pro-choice movement.

Both the pro-life movement and the pro-choice movement engage in similar types of actions, but with very different goals. I recognize that there are people of faith in both social movements, and that this vocabulary has been with us for over fifty years. It may seem difficult to envision a different way, but I suggest that the pro-life/pro-choice binary is of limited value in our current political and theological landscape, for a few reasons. First, the binary is problematic because labels oversimplify. As one research respondent put it: "We stick with labels a lot. They create comfort zones, but they also create barriers."[16] Second, when we use binary language, we imply an "either/or" distinction, but many express that aspects of both positions resonate with them. Sarah Kliff's reporting from 2015 shows that many Americans are not comfortable "picking sides."[17] Third, the liminal space in between these supposedly opposing viewpoints can provide unexplored common ground for people seeking to effect structural change that would safeguard health both for women and for vulnerable children.[18]

I suggest that the Catholic hierarchy should move away from a discourse that only recognizes two sides, one of which is considered true to Catholic teachings (pro-life) and the other of which is described as gravely sinful (pro-choice). In reality, there are elements of goodness in both social movements, and there are elements of evil in both as well. While the rhetoric of the pro-life movement is focused on protecting unborn life, the movement itself is also associated with the use of dark money and anti-democratic strategies.[19] Further, demonizing the pro-choice movement has incited political violence which is surely not "pro-life."[20] And finally, pro-life talking points can foster spiritual harm for women in the pews who agonize over reproductive decision making while hearing shaming scripts from the pulpit. But the pro-choice movement is not perfect either. Its historical ties to the eugenics movement in the United States provide a warning about how social policies regarding the "right" to control one's fertility can be distorted as a "duty" for those who lack social privilege.[21] Spokespersons for the pro-choice movement have been callous in ignoring the value of prenatal life and too often privilege abortion rights over other important aspects of reproduction, including the right to parent in safe and healthy conditions.[22] This problem within the pro-choice movement mirrors problems in White-dominated feminist movements in which the ability of middle-class White women to exercise their "choice" became central, while the holistic well-being of women from marginalized communities was undervalued.[23]

I envision a stronger approach as one that draws on the best of both pro-life and pro-choice frameworks and that moves beyond a stalemate. The framework of reproductive justice "provides a space in which to consider the intersections of social structures such as poverty and institutional violence with social and political ideologies of race, class, gender, sexuality, and citizenship."[24] The reproductive justice movement has the potential to move beyond a binary approach and toward a both/and approach that respects pregnant women's bodily integrity while at the same time attending to the social conditions that contribute to holistic flourishing for vulnerable people.

LANGUAGE MATTERS, BUT IT'S COMPLICATED: TERMINOLOGY DECISIONS

Human reproduction is a complex process.[25] The language that we use to describe human reproduction should be both medically accurate and sensitive to the person whose story we are trying to understand. In discussing pregnancy loss, including abortion, choosing the correct terminology is morally fraught.

Good theological ethics depends on good data from a wide range of sources including embryology, gynecology, obstetrics, and public health. But the scientific/clinical terminology of human reproduction can be confusing to non-specialists. Distinctions between a zygote and fetus matter, but also include details that are not always most relevant in context, and which can obscure other important aspects of a moral dilemma. While the following represents important scientific data, such information is not always of primary importance in a pregnant person's moral discernment.

Fertilization occurs when two *gametes* form a *zygote*.[26] This happens when a *spermatozoon* enters a mature *oocyte*. The DNA of the sperm cell combines with the DNA of the ovum. The zygote divides to create *blastomeres*. When it has sixteen cells it is called a *morula* (about 3–4 days of cleavage). The morula nears the uterine cavity and develops a fluid pocket called a *blastocele*; it is then called a *blastocyst*. About six days after fertilization, the blastocyst attaches to the endometrium and begins to burrow through to use the nutrients of the uterine lining. If implantation is successful, human chorionic gonadotropin (hCG) can be detected in the pregnant person's urine (about ten days after fertilization). Only then would a pregnancy test indicate a positive result, even though this is more than one week after fertilization has occurred. Medical providers calculate *gestational age* by counting from the first day of the last menstrual period, assuming ovulation on day fourteen.[27] The first eight weeks after fertilization occurs (or first ten weeks of gestational age) are referred to as the *embryonic stage*.[28] If implantation is successful, then the beginnings of the central nervous system begin to form for the embryo and cardiac activity begins in what will become the heart at around six weeks.[29] The developing *embryo* is differentiated from the gestating mother but entirely dependent on her body.[30] Clinically the embryonic stage is generally described as the first trimester. The *fetal stage* begins at ten weeks gestational age and lasts until birth. During the fetal stage, organ systems are growing and maturing.[31] The brain continues to grow and develop, the respiratory system differentiates, the urogenital system further differentiates, and the endocrine and gastrointestinal tract develops. Clinically this period is generally described as the second trimester and the third trimester. *Fetal viability* is the date by which a fetus can survive outside the uterus, but this is variable because it depends on the circumstances of a particular birth and the resources of the neonatal intensive care hospital team after birth. A full-term pregnancy usually progresses to forty weeks. According to the American College of Obstetricians and Gynecologists, neonates delivered before twenty-three weeks have a 5–6 percent survival rate; further, "significant morbidity is universal (98–100%) among the rare survivors."[32] Between twenty-two and twenty-five weeks of gestational age, survival depends on various factors, including weight, lung development, the health of the mother, expertise of the caregivers, and resources of the hospital.[33] According to the Society for Maternal-Fetal Medicine's *Obstetric Care Consensus*, rates of neonatal survival to discharge between weeks twenty to twenty-five range dramatically from 23 percent to 27 percent for births at twenty-three weeks, 42 percent to 59 percent for births at twenty-four weeks, and 67–76 percent for births at twenty-five weeks of gestation.[34] Even if the neonate survives, the long-term neurologic impairment can be exceptionally high, so initiating resuscitation and offering life support may be considered futile or not in the best interests of the child.[35] Although most infants delivered between twenty-two and twenty-four weeks gestation will die in the neonatal period or have significant long-term neurodevelopmental morbidity, outcomes in individual cases are difficult to predict, and vary widely from hospital to hospital.[36] The American Congress of Obstetricians and Gynecologists does not recommend trying to resuscitate babies born at twenty-three weeks.[37] At twenty-four weeks, doctors communicate the significant risks to the parent and sometimes resuscitation is performed. Resuscitation is often recommended at twenty-five weeks, even though there is still risk of infant death or disability.[38] But even within these professional guidelines, a wide range of outcomes is associated with periviable (borderline viability) birth.

Many couples experience fertility as a gamble. There are many factors that must be considered when evaluating fertility. A woman is fertile for a limited number of days in her menstrual cycle, known as the fertile window.[39] The timing of ovulation, the quality of cervical fluid, the quality and quantity of egg and sperm, and the stamina of sperm are just some of the factors that influence fertility. In a cycle where ovulation occurs, the chances of conception are between 3 percent seven days before ovulation and 42 percent the day before ovulation.[40] Women who do not regularly track their cycles, or whose contraceptive use disrupts cycle length, bleeding patterns, or quality of cervical mucus, may not even know that pregnancy is possible or has occurred.[41] This brings us to the importance of considering the subjective experience of pregnancy.

Our moral language should reflect the subjective experience of pregnancy, which is influenced not only by medical science but also by a pregnant woman's degree of knowledge, beliefs, hopes, expectations about the future, self-identity, and plans for her future. Sometimes what is happening inside her body is unknown to her—which does not mean it is not happening, but it does mean that it is beyond her scope of understanding. Similarly, many pregnant women are not interested in the medical terminology that correctly explains the stages of fetal development—they speak about the prenate as "a baby," even in its contingent existence.[42] For some, this language facilitates maternal bonding with the "child" in utero and helps the pregnant person to prepare for a transition to a parental role. But using the language of "child" or "baby" can also misinform because it fails to acknowledge the real legal and ethical differences between human life in utero (especially pre-viability) and human life after birth. Because of these linguistic deficiencies, feminist Christian ethicist Rebecca Todd Peters coined the term prenate, which is also used by Sandra Sullivan-Dunbar in her work as a Catholic theologian.[43] "Prenate" is a descriptive and moral category distinct from "child," and is useful because it reflects the contingent nature of human life in the womb. As such, I have chosen to adopt this language most often in this book. My position is similar to Christian ethicist Margaret Kamitsuka's, who argues that the prenate "is not a nonperson without value," but neither is it "a person with the status of an already-born child."[44] In chapter 6 I will further develop this claim, focusing on what it means to say that the prenate has *inherent* value but not *absolute* value. Since my goal is to center the pregnant woman in moral discourse about pregnancy and pregnancy loss, I do not engage fetal personhood debates in depth.[45]

Terminology to describe what is lost after miscarriage or abortion can be equally difficult. Recognizing the fragility of human life at its earliest stages of development can invite caution about using terms such as "unborn child" to describe the products of conception at a very early stage. One reason for this is that miscarriage is common, occurring in 10 to 20 percent of known pregnancies, and early miscarriage masking as menstruation is thought to be even more common, though difficult to detect.[46] Some scientists estimate that anywhere from one-third to one-half of fertilized ova never become implanted in the uterus but are expelled from the uterus during the woman's next menstrual cycle.[47] Over half (some estimates range as high as 78 percent) of fertilizations do not result in live births.[48] Philosophers and theologians have raised questions about the status of early embryonic life as a result of our growing understanding of the high numbers of fertilized ova that do not result in live births; for example, theologian Vincent Genovesi asks: "Can we really claim that such sloughed-off fertilized ova are persons with immortal souls and eternal destinies? Would this not constitute an extravagant or prodigal waste of personal human life?"[49] It is important to hold in tension both the data on the fragility of human life in its earliest stages and the variability of women's subjective experiences of that loss in their bodies, the meanings of which are connected to women's own contexts, hopes, and plans for their future. Many women who have experienced pregnancy loss refer to what is lost as their "baby" or "child,"[50] although many do not, preferring instead to speak of terminating the pregnancy with reference to "tissue," or a "clump of cells."[51] Dr. Willie Parker, a physician who is an abortion provider, uses the terms "products of conception," "fetal tissue," and "fetal remains."[52] *Mizuko* ("water child") is a Japanese term for an aborted, stillborn, or miscarried baby.[53] Rebecca Todd Peters argues that no matter what language one uses, "our words are charged," and we should take great care to be as precise as possible in describing the "moral, physical, developmental, and social uniqueness" of what happens in pregnancy while also avoiding language that creates moral confusion.[54] To that I would add moral anguish and moral injury.[55] Christians accompanying women after pregnancy loss should seek their integral healing, and the words we use should be sensitive to the uniqueness of each woman's testimony and experience so as to contribute to her growth and healing, instead of intentionally fostering shame.

When I use the term "pregnancy loss," I am referring to the end of a pregnancy, whether due to miscarriage, stillbirth, or abortion. Using such terminology can foster solidarity among women who share the experience of pregnancy loss and can also serve to de-pathologize abortion discourse in Catholic spaces. Since medical interventions for miscarriage and abortion can be similar, one way to clarify terminology is to identify specific procedures. Medication abortion has become more common in the United States since the Federal Drug Administration approved mifepristone in 2000; the drug, which can be administered by the patient at home, works by blocking progesterone, a hormone essential to the development of a pregnancy.[56] Medication abortions can also be administered in a clinic setting.[57] Surgical abortions are administered by a provider in a hospital or clinical setting and can take approximately fifteen minutes, although later in the pregnancy the preparation time for the procedure can take hours. A vacuum aspiration (dilation and curettage, or D&C) abortion can be performed to terminate a pregnancy up to sixteen weeks.[58] A dilation and evacuation procedure is less common but required after approximately sixteen weeks.[59] The Catholic moral tradition recognizes that *spontaneous abortion* (miscarriage) happens and incurs no guilt; *indirect abortion* is permissible and incurs no guilt; but *direct abortion* is considered illicit in every circumstance. All three use the term "abortion" but they are not the same, morally speaking, according to authoritative Catholic teachings. One of the strengths of the Catholic moral tradition is its appreciation of contextual analysis in moral discernments; both the intention of the moral agent and the circumstances of the action are significant in determining the moral meaning of the act. So while miscarriage is a different moral experience than direct abortion, both experiences of pregnancy loss share important features.

Language for the pregnant person is also contested. Given my focus in this book on sexism and misogyny as structural harms, I will focus on women's experiences and I do tend to use the phrase "pregnant women" most often, with she/her pronouns. But when I use the phrases "pregnant people" and "gestating person" it is because not everyone with a uterus identifies as a woman. Transgender men, nonbinary people, gender fluid people, gender queer people, Two-Spirit people, and others with uteruses who do not identify as women can have unplanned pregnancies and abortions.[60] Given that patriarchy harms women *and* members of the lesbian, gay, bisexual, transgender, and queer community, there is common cause in seeking to name and disrupt the harmful social scripts in Christianity and in US politics that empower cisgender men over others.[61] At the same time, I do not want to contribute to the erasure or minimization of women's experiences of harm in a patriarchal Church and society by describing them as "people" when many readers see the normative "person" as male. I have chosen to center women in this project, and my language choices reflect that centering.

WHAT KIND OF ISSUE IS ABORTION?

My goal is to situate Catholic discourse about abortion in the wider framework of reproductive justice. Doing so enables us to see that it is not easy to make moral claims about abortion.

Abortion is a *personal moral issue*. No matter your gender, age, religious affiliation (if any), or relationship status, abortion is an issue that you likely have a position on based on your moral values, your understanding of the issues at stake, and your sense of what it means to "do good and avoid evil."[62] Abortion is especially personal if it is a decision you face yourself, or have faced, as a pregnant woman. Many people find that it is unnecessary to disclose their private feelings about abortion in public. For some, it would be considered impolite, while for others, imprudent, given that the issue is often presented as a source of conflict in our society.[63] Abortion is deeply personal, but it is not simply personal.

Abortion is also a *social issue*. We can ask, what kind of society do we want to be a part of? Does abortion have a place in that vision of social life? Thinking about abortion exclusively through the lens of personal decision making (or claiming that it is a "purely private" decision) is problematic because even personal decisions that we make about our bodies have inherent social implications. As individuals formed within social groups, our language, imagination, and understanding of the world are shaped by the communities in which we live. Reflecting on our social location and the fact that each of us is embedded in multiple relationships can further challenge one's sense of moral agency as we come to more deeply understand that we must act within systems that constrain our agency, and we sometimes feel that we have very little control over the choices in front of us.

Abortion is a *political issue*. Catholic arguments on abortion have dominated the public square in every election cycle since 1976,[64] the US presidential election following the landmark Supreme Court abortion decision *Roe v. Wade*. Movements on both sides of the debate are able to energize their bases, including the most extreme voices of the two dominant political parties in the United States, when abortion rights are on the line. Since the 2022 *Dobbs* ruling, abortion has and will continue to be a political issue at every level of government in the United States, but even more so at the state level.

Abortion is a *legal issue*. Ongoing access to legal abortion requires advocates to regularly defend this through complex litigation at every level of the judicial system. Debates continue about whether women should be understood as having a constitutional right to abortion pre-viability (*Roe*) without undue burden (*Casey*) or whether it depends on the state in which one lives (*Webster, Dobbs*).[65] Some legal scholars find the privacy justification in *Roe* to be flawed, instead preferring equal protection justification. Pro-life advocates have used the courts for decades to impose restrictions on services that have as their goal a diminishment of abortion access; these include the requirement for multiple visits with a mandatory waiting period between visits, the requirement that the same medical provider conduct both exams, and required ultrasounds with reading of a script about possible complications of the procedure and information about fetal development, among others. Politics and the law can go hand in hand, as we saw in Texas in 2021 with the passage of Senate Bill 8,[66] which made it illegal for women to procure an abortion if the provider documented fetal cardiac activity. Because of the way the bill was written, it could not be challenged until a private citizen sued an abortion provider (or anyone who "aided or abetted"), thus merging the political and the legal. The fetal personhood movement within legal studies has led to the prosecution of women because they or their newborns tested positive for controlled substances.[67] The *Dobbs* decision began as a state law in Mississippi that banned most abortions after the first fifteen weeks of pregnancy, a departure from the trimester/viability framework in *Roe*. Jackson Women's Health Organization sued Thomas E. Dobbs, the Mississippi health officer with the Mississippi State Department of Health, in March of 2018, and it took four years for the case to make its way through the courts all the way up to the Supreme Court of the United States. Abortion is clearly a legal issue, but it is not only a legal issue.

Abortion is a *human rights issue*. Abortion rights advocates focus on the human rights of the pregnant woman and her access to medical treatments and procedures, arguing that coerced pregnancy is anathema to a person's full human dignity. Anti-abortion advocates focus on the rights of the prenate, claiming constitutional protection of prenatal life as innocent human life. The central tension on this question, as with so many others, is "Who counts as human?" If access to health care is a human right, what counts as health care?[68] Human rights discourse is often a helpful framework, but only if we have further clarity about who counts as "human," which of course is a racialized and contested history and legacy (an issue explored later in this chapter). Scholars also make careful distinctions between positive rights (a society's obligation to ensure that people can exercise their freedoms) and negative rights (a society's obligation to refrain from interfering with people's autonomous decisions and actions).[69]

Abortion is a *medical issue*. When legal, abortions are most frequently medical decisions made by patients who have the assistance of skilled medical practitioners; when illegal, pregnant people resort to methods that can be more dangerous.[70] The Guttmacher Institute, a research institute that advocates for reproductive rights, claims that "abortion is one of the most common and safest medical procedures performed in the United States."[71] The *Turnaway Study*, which followed over a thousand women for ten years after they either procured or were denied an abortion, found "no evidence that abortion hurts women."[72] However "we find many ways in which women were hurt by carrying an unwanted pregnancy to term."[73] Complications from abortion are rare, and continuing a pregnancy is actually far riskier given the crisis in maternal mortality in the United States, especially for women of color.[74] When viewed through the lens of medicine, one would attend to questions of patient care, training of medical professionals, procurement of supplies, and the logistics of providing medical care.

Abortion is an *economic issue*. The most common reasons people seek abortions are socioeconomic—not having the resources to nurture a new baby.[75] Raising children is expensive, and parenting women know well that the responsibility for housing, educating, feeding, clothing, and providing for the needs of a child is not a short-term commitment, nor is it a responsibility that can be accepted lightly. Women who do not believe they can afford to raise a child often also struggle to pay for an abortion. In 2024, a woman without insurance will pay approximately $750 for an abortion procedure in the United States if she lives in a state where the procedure is legal,[76] and four times that much if she must travel out of state; it can be difficult to gather that much money for someone who is unemployed, underemployed, living paycheck to paycheck, or a minor. Poor women are more likely to be delayed in accessing an abortion than non-poor women, and financial barriers contribute to the delay in one-fifth of second trimester abortions, with uninsured women having over six times higher odds of reporting financial difficulties as a reason for delaying abortion compared to insured women.[77]

Abortion is a *public health issue*. When viewed through the lens of public health, we think not about the medical care to individual patients but about the health of populations. This means thinking about how abortion fits into a broader paradigm of reproductive and sexual health. Does access to legal abortion create more stable and just sexual relationships? Would the alternative—including coerced pregnancy for women who experienced unplanned or unwanted pregnancy—facilitate the health of families and communities? The *Turnaway Study* claims that women who are denied an abortion are more likely to live below the poverty level and be unemployed years after being denied the abortion than women who receive their wanted abortion. When we think not only about the rights of contingent fetal life but the well-being of children already born, we begin to see a more complicated picture of how women who seek abortion are navigating a range of responsibilities. When women have a greater degree of control over their fertility, they can make decisions for themselves and their children that contribute to family stability, female empowerment, and poverty reduction.[78]

When we think about abortion through the lens of *gender justice*, we have to attend to the data regarding pervasive sexual violence that women and girls experience.[79] We are also invited to ask about who pays the penalty for sexual "mistakes" or "accidents," and why. Feminist thinkers have long exposed the problems of a double standard morality, that is, different rules for different groups of people (i.e., men and women) in a society that advocates fairness. Feminists argue that women should be able to assert control over their financial security, health, and bodily integrity, just as men do.[80] Further, when decisions affecting women are made almost exclusively by men (political, medical, and clerical), gender justice is absent.

Abortion is a *racial justice issue*. Coerced pregnancy was practiced in the system of chattel slavery when enslaved women had no legal right to bodily integrity and little control over their reproductive decision making. Forced sterilizations of Black, Indigenous, and Latina women occurred in different waves in US history and included sterilization of Black women on public aid without their consent, Indigenous women, women in mental institutional settings, and incarcerated women.[81] Today, abortion restrictions can be viewed through the lens of White supremacy—a White racial minority imposing its will on society using nondemocratic and even violent means. The maternal health outcomes for women of color in the United States are part of a systematic failure to respect the bodies and lives of people of color in a racist country. Numerous restrictions at both the state and federal levels have been implemented that make it more difficult for poor women of color to access abortion services; women in thirty-four states have restricted Medicaid coverage due to the Hyde Amendment.[82]

Abortion is a *social justice issue*. We must ask what kind of structural supports are necessary to raise children and create a culture that values all life. In the Judeo-Christian tradition, justice requires being in right relationship with one another and giving to each their due.[83] We do not flourish alone as singular beings but in a web of relations; our work together requires an active commitment to the common good and to collaboration.

Abortion is a *philosophical and theological issue* because of the kinds of questions that it raises about when human life begins, how to adequately describe and define the human person, and how to know God's will for a particular pregnancy as well as for social policy. The religions of the world do not speak with one voice on the complex issue of abortion, and interpreters continue to debate how best to apply Sacred Scriptures to contemporary social issues.[84]

Any of these perspectives could be the focus of a series of books. My purpose here is to invite cautious humility and honesty about the complex issue of abortion. I have found that the framework of reproductive justice has helped me to step back and conceive of the interrelationship of all of these different perspectives on the issue in a synthetic and productive way. A woman in the United States who faces an unplanned pregnancy has a host of considerations to discern, including medical, theological, spiritual, economic, relational, and vocational. Reproductive justice is a framework that brings together the complexity of all of these perspectives.

PLANTATION POWER THEN AND NOW

Human reproduction is a social good, but it can also be a site of violence. Loretta J. Ross explains, "the right to mother is never and has never been uncontested for black women in the United States."[85] The Catholic Church now strongly condemns the institution of slavery as dehumanizing and contrary to God's divine justice.[86] But it was not always so.[87] In the 1724 *Code*

Noir, which governed life in the Louisiana colonies, the Catholic faith was mandated for all, and a racial hierarchy was imposed.[88] Control over reproduction was central to the slaveholder's ideology of White supremacy: "Children, issued from the marriage of slaves, shall follow the condition [enslaved status] of their parents, and shall belong to the master of the wife and not of the husband, if the husband and wife have different masters."[89] This system persisted at the birth of the nation and as states began to develop their own slave codes. Sociologist Dorothy Roberts explains that the story of the control of Black women's reproductive lives in the United States begins with the experience of enslaved women. "Slave women's childbearing replenished the enslaved labor force: Black women bore children who belonged to the slaveowner from the moment of their conception."[90] This evil system "marked Black women from the beginning as objects whose decisions about reproduction should be subject to social regulation rather than to their own will."[91] Here we must ask whether laws today that regulate women's reproductive decisions fall into these same patterns.

Pro-life Christians in the United States today typically describe pregnancy as a blessing. But when we investigate reproductive history from the perspective of pregnant women in contexts of coercive violence, we see that pregnancy was not always experienced as a blessing or a good gift from God. Historian Jennifer Morgan describes the "alienation of reproductive labor" that enslaved women experienced in the colonial period and through the nineteenth century because of their own sense of being "commodified."[92] Morgan explains the need to hold motherhood and intimacy with some degree of ambivalence in the lives of enslaved women, given the realities of disease, overwork, and the struggle to survive in situations of violence and exploitation. "In that context, the birth of a child would have done nothing to alleviate sorrow; indeed, it would only have made the load heavier."[93] Morgan explains that "emotional attachments exposed one to further abuse"[94] because a male slaveholder saw an enslaved woman's reproductive capacity as part of her value to *him*, even while she had little control over the well-being of her children.[95] To *him*, she was just a breeder. An enslaved woman could not protect her children from harm and could not be assured that she would be able to remain with her children. Morgan writes that "slaveowners' desire to add children to their balance sheet did not carry a corollary of recognition, and women would reap little reward from bearing these children. Having children did not change a woman's economic situation or decrease her work load in the sugar fields."[96] One enslaved woman, Arrabell, gave birth to a daughter she called "Mines," in South Carolina. Morgan explains that in naming her child "Mines," Arrabell appears to have been claiming what was hers, but "even as she staked this claim, she and her child were sold. The next sale may have been the one that irrevocably reminded her that Mines could not actually be hers."[97]

The precarity of everyday life on a plantation made gestation, childbirth, and parenting particularly difficult. Enslaved women in North America in the nineteenth century lost at least 54 percent of their pregnancies to stillbirth, infant mortality, and early childhood mortality, according to plantation records analyzed by historian Richard Steckel.[98] It is thus not entirely surprising that some enslaved women sought to limit their fertility. Maria Merian described how women passed down knowledge about plants that have contraceptive and abortifacient effects.[99] Okra, aloe, snakeroot, cotton root, gum, camphor, and rue helped enslaved women assert some degree over control over their fertility, when they could not claim full control over their lives.[100]

Morgan explains that Carolina slaveowners found that "newly enslaved Africans were the primary means of immediately increasing their own wealth and the size of their slaveholdings."[101] Such a system of domination, exploitation, and control rendered sexuality a site of violence and parenting a site of enslavement. The reproductive decisions of enslaved women were made in what can be described as a situation of constraint, or what historian Emily A. Owens describes as "consent in the presence of force."[102] White women on the plantation, constrained by their gender, were nevertheless empowered within the system of slavery by their Whiteness. Womanist Catholic theologian M. Shawn Copeland describes their "silent collusion" as the White women failed to mount significant resistance to the evils with which they were complicit and they refused to take up solidarity with the enslaved women of the household.[103]

The violations of women's human dignity maintained in slavery were sanctioned by law. As Roberts explains, "the social order established by powerful White men was founded on two indispensable ingredients: the dehumanization of Africans on the basis of race, and the control of women's sexuality and reproduction. The American legal system is rooted in this monstrous combination of racial and gender domination."[104] These dynamics of racial and gender domination in the law have not magically disappeared, even as they have changed by degree over time. Harriet A. Washington's gripping account of medical experimentation on Black Americans shows how pervasive racism has been in the US medical system, as she documents that nontherapeutic experimentation persisted from the eighteenth century to the modern era.[105] Rickie Solinger, an expert in reproductive politics, examines who has power over matters of pregnancy and its consequences.[106] Solinger explains that Native American women in the United States have also experienced egregious injustices. Settler colonial policies aimed to conquer, subdue, and destroy Indian nations and take control of their lands. Scholars of Indigenous history emphasize that Andrew Jackson told troops to kill Indian women and children to complete the extermination of their peoples.[107] In the early years of the United States of America, and during the Western expansion, White leaders repeatedly expressed concern about populating the continent while ensuring that the dominant group remained White. Some nineteenth-century doctors opposed abortion because they worried that White Protestant women would not have enough babies to keep up with other racial and ethnic groups.[108] This concern surfaces again today in claims from White supremacist groups about demographic changes and the threat of a White minority,[109] preoccupation with White birthrates, and even the "great replacement" conspiracy that inspired the shooter who killed ten people of color in 2022 in Buffalo, New York.[110]

Baptist theologian Willie James Jennings describes the "pedagogy of the plantation" as a re-inscribing of power relations of domination and subordination in contemporary institutions, even as we celebrate how far we have come since the time of legalized chattel slavery in the US context.[111] Jennings explains that the "racial paterfamilias" haunts Western institutions today,[112] cultivating in people a "plantation logic" of power relations that is often unacknowledged.[113] Plantation logic does not treat women as ends in themselves but rather as objects that can be manipulated to serve the needs of those in power. In plantation logic, women are breeders whose bodies can be used by others.

Some pro-life activists also draw on the US legacy of slavery when describing their movement as a civil rights movement.[114] In doing so, they claim that until the prenate is recognized as a human person with full legal rights, justice is denied. But when we analyze such discourse from the perspective of the pregnant woman, we can see that her own dignity and agency are obscured in a prenatal-rights-discourse. Abortion bans do not focus on empowering pregnant women to make their own discernments, but rather, focus on restricting their legal options and forcing compliance with pro-life policies. Jennings explains that "desire rooted in control is disordered desire that inevitably forms social prisons that drain life."[115] To the extent that the pro-life movement seeks to use the law to control other people's reproductive choices, plantation logic is at work. We must take seriously Black women's call for reproductive freedom today; today's reproductive justice movement is part of a long struggle for freedom.

It can be challenging to raise these patterns of thinking for further scrutiny today. After all, we are living in a time in which teaching US history has become politicized. White tourists report feeling triggered when they encounter the stories of enslaved people while touring historic plantation homes in the deep South.[116] It is not easy to discuss the rise of Christian nationalism and White supremacist hate groups, but even the US bishops explain the importance of a racial reckoning and an honest account of Catholic complicity in racist social structures.[117] To see what is happening today, we have to be willing to look honestly at the past and recognize how the past continues to shape our present.[118]

REPRODUCTION + SOCIAL JUSTICE = REPRODUCTIVE JUSTICE

Reproductive justice results from combining attention to *reproduction* with *social justice*. As a movement focused on the reproductive flourishing of all, with special attention to marginalized and racialized communities, reproductive justice resists the pro-life/pro-choice binary and has the potential to move us beyond plantation logic.

The reproductive justice movement in the United States officially began in 1994, but it did not appear out of nowhere. The Committee for Abortion Rights and Against Sterilization Abuse (CARASA) was formed in 1977 by women who sought to create a grassroots reproductive freedom movement that moved beyond a single-issue focus on abortion and included sterilization abuse and violence against women. In 1979, Reproductive Rights National Network (R2N2) was formed, which situated abortion rights within a broader social justice and anti-racist context. The National Black Women's Health Project, formed in 1984, was the first women of color reproductive health organization.[119] During the Clinton administration, Black feminists gathered in Chicago to analyze healthcare reform proposals and suggested that the debates were too focused on abortion, neglecting the many other health concerns that members of their communities faced.[120] While such a concept was not new, the women's organizational strategy was. They launched Women of African Descent for Reproductive Justice and began to influence health care reform conversations. Members also traveled to the International Conference on Population and Development in Cairo, Egypt, and learned from the ways that women's groups around the world were drawing on a human rights framework to claim that women's rights are human rights.[121] When they returned, they created a new activism infrastructure that was separate from the pro-choice community's political activism yet broadly connected to ongoing resistance to the intersections of patriarchy and white supremacy. Today, many organizations across the United States are joined under the banner of reproductive justice activism, and most of these are led by women of color; they include SisterSong, New Voices, COLOR (Colorado Organization for Latina Opportunity and Reproductive Rights), Native Youth Sexual Health Network, SisterLove, CARA (Communities Against Rape and Abuse), the Afiya Center, SisterReach, Indigenous Women Rising, Black Mamas Matter Alliance, Birthmark Doula Collective, In Our Own Voice, and SACReD

(Spiritual Alliance of Communities for Reproductive Dignity).[122] There is not a single leader or organization who speaks for the reproductive justice movement as a whole; many scholars contribute to the theoretical work and many more are doing organizing work at the grassroots level.[123]

A central feature of reproductive justice scholarship is the application of human rights discourse to the politics of reproduction. Three rights in particular are often repeated in reproductive justice literature: the right to have a child, the right to not have a child, and the right to parent children in safe and healthy conditions. It is important to note that in reproductive justice discourse these three rights are not separated but are described as interrelated. Celebrating motherhood and supporting mothers and children is as important as resisting the coercion of pregnant women. There is a refusal among reproductive justice scholars to limit attention to "fetal value" or "choice." Instead, reproductive justice scholars forward consistent demands to foster structural change to improve the social conditions in which women and their children struggle.

A key feature of reproductive justice methodology is the inclusion of historical and social analysis. The right to have a child is asserted against a backdrop of forced sterilization campaigns and the criminalization of poverty and unwed parenting. The right to not have a child is asserted against a backdrop of pervasive gender-based violence, the highest levels of infant and maternal mortality in the developed world, and pervasive structural inequalities. The right to parent in safe and healthy conditions is asserted against a backdrop of racialized violence, redlining, voter suppression of communities of color, and disparities in access to equal educational opportunities, housing, health care access, health insurance coverage, and clean water.

There is significant resonance between a Catholic approach to social justice and the work of reproductive justice scholars and activists. Let's not forget that a significant amount of Jesus' preaching focused on social justice and the obligations his disciples have to live in right relationship with God, self, and others, including members of different social groups. The method of reproductive justice scholarship "places vulnerable people in the center,"[124] a method that aligns with the Catholic approach to preferential option for the vulnerable, and a Womanist commitment to take the "black woman's body as a starting point."[125] Catholic teachings on the common good resist an individualist way of thinking about a person's rights in the world and instead describe "the sum of those conditions of social life which allow social groups and their individual members relatively thorough and ready access to their own fulfillment."[126] This attention to the *social conditions for reproductive flourishing* means that we must train our eyes to see how interlocking systems of oppression can constrain the choices of pregnant women and restrict their full embodied freedom.

Feminist theorist Marilyn Frye compares an oppressed woman to a bird in a cage; she notes that a bird could easily move around a single wire barrier, but taking a macroscopic view, one sees not just one barrier but "a network of forces and barriers which are systematically related and which conspire to the immobilization, reduction and molding of women and the lives we live."[127] Paying attention to the everyday struggles of ordinary women is a key part of doing reproductive justice work. This allows one to see connections between different aspects of political and social life and their impact on reproductive decision-making. Ross explains that "policies that at first glance appear disconnected have implications for reproductive decision-making. Fighting police brutality, gun violence, or tainted water supplies so our children can survive is as equally urgent as fighting for bodily integrity and self-determination."[128] To use Frye's analogy, each of these injustices is in itself a wire of the cage, but taken together, represents a more systemic and confining network that thwarts women's integral flourishing.

A challenge of reproductive justice work is that it can feel unwieldy. Reproductive justice encapsulates so many areas of everyday life: the health of intimate relationships and especially freedom from sexual violence; access to food, shelter, education, and health care; fair wages and just policies in the workplace; and many more aspects of the good life. A reproductive justice framework requires that we see reproductive decisions in their wider context, and that we recognize how structural injustices shape that context. Audre Lorde's often-quoted line, "There is no such thing as a single-issue struggle because we do not live single-issue lives," is particularly meaningful today in a movement for reproductive justice.[129] Like the original founders of the movement in 1994, scholars push back against any attempt to see abortion as a social issue that can be easily separated from other social issues. "Social institutions, the environment, economics, and culture affect each woman's reproductive life," explain Ross and Solinger.[130] This framework is an important resource for Catholic feminist theologians who challenge the moral absolutism of Catholic magisterial teachings from a commitment to contextual analysis and justice-based work. It is to this issue that we turn next, as chapter 2 examines the moral absolutism of magisterial teachings on reproduction and their wide-ranging implications for women.

NOTES

1. United States Conference of Catholic Bishops, "Abortion Is Not Healthcare," (2021), https://www.usccb.org/resources/abortion-not-healthcare. In their November 2023 meeting, the US Bishops voted (225 in favor, 11 against, and 7 abstentions) to approve a new introductory note and materials supporting the document on the

political responsibility of Catholics, *Forming Consciences for Faithful Citizenship.* See USCCB Office of Public Affairs, "Recap of the US Bishops' Fall Plenary in Baltimore," (November 16, 2023): https://www.usccb.org/news/2023/recap-us-bishops-fall-plenary-baltimore. The approved materials explain that "the threat of abortion remains our pre-eminent priority because it directly attacks our most vulnerable and voiceless brothers and sisters and destroys more than a million lives per year in our country alone." See "Introductory Note to *Forming Consciences for Faithful Citizenship*" (November 15, 2023), 1, https://www.usccb.org/resources/2023-Nov-15%20FCFC%20action%20item%20text%20final.pdf.

2. "Society of Jesus in the United States Welcomes Overruling of *Roe v. Wade*" (June 24, 2022): https://www.jesuits.org/stories/society-of-jesus-in-the-united-states-welcomes-overruling-of-roe-v-wade/. See also Gerard V. Bradley, "Dobbs Decision: A Monumental Moment in the March for Equal Rights for Every Human Life" (June 24, 2022), *National Catholic Register,* https://www.ncregister.com/commentaries/dobbs-decision-a-monumental-moment-in-the-march-for-equal-rights-for-every-human-life; "USCCB Statement on U.S. Supreme Court Ruling in Dobbs v. Jackson" (June 24, 2022), https://www.usccb.org/news/2022/usccb-statement-us-supreme-court-ruling-dobbs-v-jackson.

3. An example of this news coverage, implementing the *AP Stylebook,* can be seen in Veronica Stracqualursi, "Anti-abortion Activists Attend First March for Life 'With Fresh Resolve' Post-Roe," CNN (January 20, 2023), https://www.cnn.com/2023/01/20/politics/march-for-life-2023-abortion/index.html.

4. Laura Echevarria, "The Associate Press's Latest Gift to the Abortion Lobby." *National Right to Life News,* February 2023, 6. This article pertains to the *AP Stylebook* 2023 update, which says that journalists should avoid the phrase "pregnancy help centers" and instead use one of the following "anti-abortion counseling centers," "crisis pregnancy centers that oppose abortion," or "anti-abortion centers."

5. For example, Mary Krane Derr explains that her pro-life feminism leads her to support a welfare approach, not criminalizing abortion through legal bans, and she sees her pro-life feminism in alignment with the reproductive justice movement even as she describes abortion as an act of violence. See Mary Krane Derr, "Cardy-Carrying Marchers and Sister Travelers: Pro-Life Feminists and the Reproductive Justice Movement," in Loretta J. Ross, Lynn Roberts, Erika Derkas, Whitney Peoples, and Pamela Bridgewater Toure, eds., *Radical Reproductive Justice: Foundations, Theory, Practice, Critique* (New York: Feminist Press, 2017), 86–110, at 91. In contrast, Mallory Quigley, communications director for the Susan B. Anthony List, resisted the inclusion of immigrant justice in the pro-life movement, saying "I think it is problematic to merge all of these issues together into one." See Christopher White, "Francis Says, 'Pro-Life Means Supporting Immigrants, Others Disagree,'" *Crux* (September 12, 2017), https://cruxnow.com/global-church/2017/09/francis-says-pro-life-means-supporting-immigrants-others-disagree.

6. The term "seamless garment" is meant to convey the unity of the Church's teachings (like the seamless garment of Christ). Some critics argue that the phrase obscures the inconsistency within Church teachings. See Christine E. Gudorf, "To Make a Seamless Garment, Use a Single Piece of Cloth," *Conscience* 17:3 (1996): 10–21.

7. Democrats for Life of America is an example of this approach. See "What does Whole Life Mean?" (October 20, 2020), https://www.democratsforlife.org/index.php/about-us/what-is-whole-life.

8. Joseph Cardinal Bernadin, "A Consistent Ethic of Life: An American-Catholic Dialogue," (December 6, 1983), published in Thomas Fuechtmann, ed., *Consistent Ethic of Life: Joseph Cardinal Bernadin* (New York: Sheed & Ward, 1988), 1–2. The address can be found here: https://www.hnp.org/publications/hnpfocus/BConsistentEthic1983.pdf.

9. Bernadin, "A Consistent Ethic of Life."

10. James Martin, SJ, "Why I Am Pro-Life," *America Magazine* (January 10, 2019), https://www.americamagazine.org/2019/01/07/martin-why-i-am-pro-life#.

11. Charles C. Camosy, "The Consistent Ethic of Life under Pope Francis," *Crux* (October 4, 2016): https://cruxnow.com/commentary/2016/10/04/consistent-ethic-life-pope-francis/; *Beyond the Abortion Wars: A Way Forward for a New Generation* (Grand Rapids: Eerdmans, 2015); and "Consistent-Life-Ethics Catholics Can And Should Treat Abortion as Today's Preeminent Priority," *America* (July 8, 2021), https://www.americamagazine.org/faith/2021/07/08/abortion-politics-us-bishops-eucharist-ethics-240991.

12. In his letter to President Biden on July 24, 2023, Governor Greg Abbott (R-TX) defended the floating barriers his government installed in the Rio Grande River even as he acknowledges the higher risk of drowning that migrants face in going around the barriers. https://gov.texas.gov/uploads/files/press/O-BidenJoseph_07.24.23.pdf. Operation Lone Star, Abbott's border initiative, has also bused thousands of migrants out of state and increased use of razor wire and other deterrents along the border, which lead to injuries among migrants, including pregnant women and children. See Camilo Montoya-Galvez, "Texas Gov. Greg Abbott Defies Biden Administration Threat to Sue Over Floating Border Barriers," CBS News (July 24, 2023), https://www.cbsnews.com/news/texas-border-barriers-rio-grande-greg-abbott-biden-lawsuit/.

13. Catholics for Choice, "Abortion" (2023), https://www.catholicsforchoice.org/issues/abortion/.

14. Rebecca Todd Peters does identify abortion as a moral good; see Rebecca Todd Peters, *Trust Women: A Progressive Christian Argument for Reproductive Justice* (Boston: Beacon, 2018), 203–6.

15. Marvin Ellison, "Is Pro-Choice What We Mean to Say?" in *Making Love Just: Sexual Ethics for Perplexing Times* (Minneapolis: Fortress Press, 2012), 105.

16. Tricia Bruce et al., *How Americans Understand Abortion* (McGrath Institute for Church Life, University of Notre Dame, 2020), https://news.nd.edu/assets/395804/how_americans_understand_abortion_final_7_15_20.pdf.

17. Sarah Kliff, "What Americans Think of Abortion," Vox (April 8, 2015), https://www.vox.com/2018/2/2/16965240/abortion-decision-statistics-opinions. In the PerryUndem Poll cited by Vox, 32 percent of respondents identified as pro-choice and 26 percent as pro-life, but a larger number refused to be categorized with either of these labels—the remaining 42 percent either identified as "both," "neither," or "refused to answer." Survey here: https://cdn2.vox-cdn.com/uploads/chorus_asset/

file/3570070/Vox_Poll_Toplines__2_.0.pdf. See also: "Pro-choice or pro-life? 39% of Americans don't pick a side" (April 8, 2015), Vox, https://www.youtube.com/watch?v=ssSIUVPjDns.

18. Some of the material in this chapter is drawn from a lecture I gave at the Aquinas Center, Emory University. "Beyond Pro-Life/Pro-Choice: Catholic Perspectives on Life Issues" (March 18, 2021), available online: https://youtu.be/EIAVfvmHn3g.

19. I elaborate upon this point in chapter 3.

20. Carol Mason, *Killing for Life: The Apocalyptic Narrative of Pro-Life Politics* (Ithaca, NY: Cornell University Press, 2002).

21. Dorothy Roberts, *Killing the Black Body: Race, Reproduction, and the Meaning of Liberty* (New York: Vintage, 1997, 2017), 58, quoting Angela Davis. See Angela Davis, "Racism, Birth Control, and Reproductive Rights," in Marlene Gerber Fried, ed., *From Abortion to Reproductive Freedom: Transforming a Movement* (Boston: South End Press, 1990), 15, 20.

22. On insensitivity about the value of fetal life, Frances Kissling writes: "The fetus is more visible than ever before, and the abortion-rights movement needs to accept its existence and its value. It may not have a right to life, and its value may not be equal to that of the pregnant woman, but ending the life of a fetus is not a morally insignificant event." Frances Kissling, "Abortion Rights Are Under Attack, and Pro-Choice Advocates Are Caught in a Time Warp," *Washington Post* (February 18, 2011), https://www.washingtonpost.com/wp-dyn/content/article/2011/02/18/AR2011021802434.html. On the right to parent, Loretta J. Ross and Rickie Solinger, *Reproductive Justice: An Introduction* (Oakland: University of California Press, 2017), 168–237.

23. See Andrea Smith, "Beyond Pro-Choice versus Pro-Life: Women of Color and Reproductive Justice," in *Radical Reproductive Justice*, 151–69, at 162; and Loretta J. Ross, "Conceptualizing Reproductive Justice Theory," in *Radical Reproductive Justice*, 170–232, at 178–79.

24. Barbara Gurr, *Reproductive Justice: The Politics of Health Care for Native American Women* (New Brunswick, NJ: Rutgers University Press, 2015), 5.

25. Thomas A. Shannon and Allan B. Wolter, O.F.M., "Reflections on the Moral Status of the Pre-Embryo," *Theological Studies* 51 (1990): 603–26.

26. Mark A. Hill, *Embryology & Fertilization* (October 1, 2021), University of New South Wales Medicine, https://embryology.med.unsw.edu.au/embryology/index.php/Fertilization.

27. Fertility cycle lengths vary from woman to woman and across a woman's life span; these clinical estimates can be inaccurate, but as a pregnancy progresses, fetal development is monitored and measured in other ways including weight gain and ultrasound measurements. "Fetal ultrasonographic dating is accurate within 8%, which translates to an accuracy of 4 to 5 days at 8 to 9 weeks of gestation but nearly 2 weeks at 24 weeks of gestation." P. W. Callen, "The obstetric ultrasound examination," in *Ultrasonography in Obstetrics and Gynecology*, fifth ed. (Philadelphia: Saunders Elsevier, 2008), 3–25.

28. Mark A. Hill, *Embryology & Embryonic Development* (October 1, 2021), University of New South Wales Medicine, https://embryology.med.unsw.edu.au/embryology/index.php/Embryonic_Development.

29. The cardiovascular system is still very immature in the embryonic stage. Jennifer Kerns of UCSF and San Francisco General Hospital says that it would be more precise to say that what one hears at six weeks is "a group of cells with electrical activity." To say that this is a "heartbeat" plays upon people's emotions, says Dr. Kerns. Adam Rogers, "Heartbeat Bills Get the Science of Fetal Heartbeats All Wrong," *Wired* (May 14, 2019), https://www.wired.com/story/heartbeat-bills-get-the-science-of-fetal-heartbeats-all-wrong/. It is important to recognize that the prenate's organs develop in stages.

30. Chapter 6 elaborates on the ethical implications of the prenate's dependence on the woman's organs for survival.

31. Mark A. Hill, *Embryology & Embryonic Development* (September 30, 2021), University of New South Wales Medicine, https://embryology.med.unsw.edu.au/embryology/index.php/Fetal_Development. Note that embryologists measure from the date of fertilization, which is different than measuring gestational age by date of last menstrual period (approximately two weeks earlier than fertilization). The fact that clinicians and embryologists date fetal development differently contributes to significant confusion in public policy debates when politicians cite data from different sources.

32. American College of Obstetricians and Gynecologists, "Facts Are Important: Understanding and Navigating Viability," (2023), https://www.acog.org/advocacy/facts-are-important/understanding-and-navigating-viability#:~:text=Later%20in%20pregnancy%2C%20a%20clinician,6%20days%20of%20a%20pregnancy.

33. James Cummings and Committee on Fetus and Newborn, "Antenatal Counseling Regarding Resuscitation and Intensive Care Before 25 Weeks of Gestation," *Pediatrics* (September 2015) 136:6, 588–95. Cummings explains that many factors other than gestational age can affect pregnancy outcome, including maternal age, health, nutrition, substance use, genetics, and complications during pregnancy, including chorioamnionitis, preeclampsia, intrauterine growth restriction, or placental abruption.

34. American College of Obstetricians and Gynecologists and Society for Maternal-Fetal Medicine, *Obstetric Care Consensus, Number 6* (June 2016, reaffirmed October 2017 and 2021), https://www.acog.org/clinical/clinical-guidance/obstetric-care-consensus/articles/2017/10/periviable-birth.

35. James Cummings and Committee on Fetus and Newborn, "Antenatal Counseling Regarding Resuscitation and Intensive Care Before 25 Weeks of Gestation," *Pediatrics* (September 2015) 136:6, 588–95.

36. Ujwal Kariholu et al., Northwest London Perinatal Network, "Perinatal Network Consensus Guidelines on the Resuscitation of Extremely Preterm Infants Born at <27 Weeks Gestation," *European Journal of Pediatrics*, (2012) 171: 6, 921–26; Ruth Guinsburg et al., Brazilian Network on Neonatal Research, "Proactive Management of Extreme Prematurity," *Journal of Perinatology* (2012) 32:12, 913–19.

37. Their recommendation is to "consider" resuscitation and "a decision to proceed with resuscitation always should be informed by individual circumstances, including specific clinical issues, family values and wishes, and ongoing evaluation of fetal or

neonatal condition." Further, "a decision not to undertake resuscitation of a liveborn infant should not be seen as a decision to provide no care, but rather a decision to redirect care to comfort measures." See American College of Obstetricians and Gynecologists, *Obstetric Care Consensus Number 6*: https://www.acog.org/clinical/clinical-guidance/obstetric-care-consensus/articles/2017/10/periviable-birth.

38. Evangelia Gkiougki et al., "Periviable Birth: A Review of Ethical Considerations," *Hippokratia* 25:1 (January–March 2021): 1–7. See also American Heart Association, "2020 AHA Guidelines for CPR and ECC, Part 5: Neonatal Resuscitation," https://professional.heart.org/en/science-news/~/link.aspx?_id=42A8BC412197484485E7920852A51B0A&_z=z. See also American Medical Association, *Code of Ethics*, https://code-medical-ethics.ama-assn.org/.

39. In the literature, the fertile window is defined as the day of ovulation and the five days preceding it, where the probability of intercourse leading to conception is highest. See Wilson et al., "Timing of Sexual Intercourse in Relation to Ovulation- Effects on the Probability of Conception, Survival of the Pregnancy, and Sex of the Baby," *New England Journal of Medicine* (1995) 333, 1517–21. For a how-to manual, see Toni Weschler, *Taking Charge of Your Fertility: The Definitive Guide to Natural Birth Control, Pregnancy Achievement, and Reproductive Health, 20th Anniversary Edition* (New York: William Morrows/Harper Collins, 2015).

40. Louis Faust et al., "Findings from a mobile application-based cohort are consistent with established knowledge of the menstrual cycle, fertile window, and conception," *Fertility and Sterility* (September 2019) 112:3, 450–57.

41. Cristina L. H. Traina, "Papal Ideals, Marital Realities: One View from the Ground," in Patricia Beattie Jung and Joseph A. Coray, eds., *Sexual Diversity and Catholicism* (Collegeville, MN: Liturgical Press, 2001), 269–88. Some women stop contraception because of concern about side effects. H. Savonius, P. Pakarinen, L. Sjöberg, P. Kajanoja, "Reasons for Pregnancy Termination: Negligence or Failure of Contraception?" *Acta Obstetricia et Gynecologica Scandinavica* vol. 74, no. 10 (November 1995): 818–21; E. Weisberg, "Practical Problems which Women Encounter with Available Contraception in Australia," *Australian and New England Journal of Obstetrics and Gynaecology* vol. 34, no. 3 (June 1994): 312–15.

42. Diana Greene Foster, *The Turnaway Study: Ten Years, a Thousand Women, and the Consequences of Having—Or Being Denied—An Abortion* (San Francisco: Scribner, 2021).

43. Rebecca Todd Peters, *Trust Women*, 5. See also Sandra Sullivan-Dunbar, "Catholic Abortion Discourse and the Erosion of Democracy," *Journal of the Society of Christian Ethics*, vol. 43, issue 1 (Spring/Summer 2023): 55–73, https://doi.org/10.5840/jsce202341776.

44. Margaret D. Kamitsuka, *Abortion and the Christian Tradition: A Pro-Choice Theological Ethic* (Louisville: Westminster John Knox, 2019), 10.

45. Jason T. Eberl, *The Nature of Human Persons* (Notre Dame: University of Notre Dame Press, 2020); John F. Kavanaugh, *Who Counts as Persons? Human Identity and the Ethics of Killing* (Washington, DC: Georgetown University Press, 2001); Nicholas M. Ramirez, "Teleology and the Problem of Bodily-Rights Arguments," *National Catholic Bioethics Quarterly* (Spring 2023): 83–97.

46. Mayo Clinic Staff, "Miscarriage," (October 16, 2021), https://www.mayoclinic.org/diseases-conditions/pregnancy-loss-miscarriage/symptoms-causes/syc-20354298.

47. Vincent J. Genovesi, *In Pursuit of Love: Catholic Morality and Human Sexuality*, second ed. (Collegeville: Liturgical Press, 1996), 351, n. 24.

48. Genovesi, *In Pursuit*, 351, n. 24.

49. Genovesi, *In Pursuit*, 352.

50. See various testimonies online via the community blog at Exhale Pro-Voice: https://exhaleprovoice.org/post/category/community/.

51. See the stories of Seneca and Joyelle Nicole Johnson in Amelia Bonow and Emily Nokes, ed, *#ShoutYourAbortion* (Oakland: PM Press, 2018), kindle location 1122, 1400, and 1422.

52. Willie Parker, *Life's Work: A Moral Argument for Choice* (New York: 37 Ink/Simon & Schuster, 2017), see especially chapter 6.

53. See Jeff Wilson, *Mourning the Unborn Dead: A Buddhist Ritual Comes to America* (New York: Oxford University Press, 2009); Maureen Walsh, "Emerging Trends in Pregnancy Loss Memorialization in American Catholicism," *Horizons* 44 (2017): 369–98.

54. Peters, *Trust Women*, 5.

55. Tara C. Carleton and Jill L. Snodgrass, *Moral Injury after Abortion: Exploring the Psychospiritual Impact on Catholic Women* (New York: Routledge, 2023), 49–60.

56. Kaiser Family Foundation, "The Availability and Use of Medication Abortion" (June 1, 2023), https://www.kff.org/womens-health-policy/fact-sheet/the-availability-and-use-of-medication-abortion/. The second drug, misoprostol, works to empty the uterus by causing cramping and bleeding, similar to an early miscarriage. Parker describes a medication abortion as a pharmaceutically induced miscarriage. Parker, *Life's Work*, 105–6.

57. Parker, *Life's Work*, 105–6.

58. Parker, *Life's Work*, 91.

59. Parker, *Life's Work*, 100–101. All of these procedures are also described by the National Abortion Federation here: https://prochoice.org/patients/abortion-what-to-expect/

60. Sarah Prager, "Transgender Pregnancy: Moving Past Misconceptions," Healthline, October 22, 2020. Native American Two-Spirit people refer to people whose identities do not conform to a male-female gender binary. Indian Health Service, "Two-Spirit Health," https://www.ihs.gov/lgbt/health/twospirit/.

61. The same groups who celebrate the overturning of *Roe v. Wade* are also engaged in state-level activism to erase trans rights and to undermine support for LGBTQ rights more broadly. The Human Rights Campaign notes that 30 percent of trans youth now live in states that have passed bans on gender-affirming medical care. See Human Rights Campaign, "Map: Attacks on Gender Affirming Care by State," (July 13, 2023), https://www.hrc.org/resources/attacks-on-gender-affirming-care-by-state-map.

62. Thomas Aquinas, *Summa Theologiae* I–II, q. 94, a. 2.

63. Some Catholics withhold their abortion stories out of appropriate self-care, and those who are employed by the Catholic Church or a Catholic institution may face loss of employment if they share their story publicly, so this self-censorship can be very prudent indeed.

64. Administrative Board of the United States Catholic Conference, *Political Responsibility: Reflections on an Election Year* (1976), https://s3.amazonaws.com/berkley-center/19760212USCCBpoliticalresponsibilitylaw.pdf.

65. Cathleen Kaveny, "Toward a Thomistic Perspective on Abortion and the Law in Contemporary America" *The Thomist* 55, no. 3 (1991): 343–96.

66. Texas State Legislature, Texas Senate Bill 8 (2021–2022), https://legiscan.com/TX/text/SB8/id/2395961.

67. Pro-Publica, "Personhood Movement Timeline," https://www.propublica.org/article/the-personhood-movement-timeline.

68. Catholic hospitals do not identify direct contraception and direct abortion as legitimate medical procedures to which women have rights as patients because these violate Catholic teachings. See chapter 2.

69. Ross and Solinger, *Reproductive Justice*, 10.

70. The World Health Organization reports that because of systemic neglect of women's health care around the world, 45 percent of all abortions are unsafe and that unsafe abortion is a leading but preventable cause of maternal death. World Health Organization, "Abortion" (November 25, 2021), https://www.who.int/news-room/fact-sheets/detail/abortion.

71. *Amici Curiae Brief of Social Science Experts Urging the U.S. Supreme Court to Reject the Mississippi Abortion Ban*, https://www.supremecourt.gov/DocketPDF/19/19-1392/192992/20210920145519814_19-1392_Amicus%20Brief.pdf.

72. Foster, *Turnaway Study*, 21.

73. Foster, *Turnaway Study*, 21.

74. Foster, *Turnaway Study*, 151.

75. Sophia Chae, "Reasons Why Women Have Induced Abortions: A Synthesis of Findings," *Contraception* (2017): 233–37.

76. "The Cost of Abortion in California," Her Smart Choice (February 10, 2024), https://hersmartchoice.com/blog/the-cost-of-abortion-in-california/.

77. Alexa L. Solazzo, "Different and Not Equal: The Uneven Association of Race, Poverty, and Abortion Laws on Abortion Timing," *Social Problems* 66 (2019): 519–22.

78. United Nations Population Fund (UNFPA), "Family Planning," https://www.unfpa.org/family-planning.

79. United Nations Population Fund, "Gender-based Violence" (2022), https://www.unfpa.org/gender-based-violence.

80. Foster, *Turnaway Study*, 313.

81. Roberts, *Killing the Black Body*, chapters 1–3. See also Harriet A. Washington, *Medical Apartheid: The Dark History of Medical Experimentation on Black Americans from Colonial Times to the Present* (New York: Anchor, 2006).

82. The Hyde Amendment prohibits federal funds from being expended for abortion or health coverage that includes coverage of abortion. Abortions are eligible

for federal funding only in cases of rape or incest, or where a physical condition endangers a woman's life unless an abortion is performed. Currently, federal funding of abortion and health coverage that includes abortion is prohibited, with the same exceptions. See Kaiser Family Foundation, "Hyde Amendment" (March 5, 2021), https://www.kff.org/womens-health-policy/issue-brief/the-hyde-amendment-and-coverage-for-abortion-services/. For impacts to Indigenous women, see Gurr, *Reproductive Justice*. See also *Systemic Racism and Reproductive Injustice in the United States: A Report for the UN Commission on the Elimination of Racial Discrimination* (July 15, 2022), https://reproductiverights.org/wp-content/uploads/2022/08/2022-CERD-Report_Systemic-Racism-and-Reproductive-Injustice.pdf.

83. Margaret A. Farley, *Just Love: A Framework for Christian Sexual Ethics* (New York: Continuum, 2006), 175–78, 208–14.

84. While biblical authors do not speak directly about abortion, and Jesus does not preach about abortion, Christians continue to draw upon the Bible as a privileged source of God's revelation about wide-ranging issues today. For a range of perspectives on the Bible and abortion, see Allen Verhey, *Reading the Bible in the Strange World of Medicine* (Grand Rapids, MI: Eerdmans, 2003), 35–41; Paul D. Simmons, "Biblical Authority and the Not-So-Strange Silence of Scripture about Abortion," *Christian Bioethics* vol. 2, no. 1 (1996): 66–82; and John Gillman, *What Does the Bible Say About Life and Death?* (Hyde Park, NY: New City Press, 2020).

85. Ross, "Conceptualizing Reproductive Justice Theory," 189.

86. United States Conference of Catholic Bishops, *Open Wide Our Hearts: The Enduring Calling to Love, A Pastoral Letter Against Racism* (Washington, DC: USCCB, 2018). https://www.usccb.org/resources/open-wide-our-hearts_0.pdf.

87. Christopher J. Kellerman, SJ, *All Oppression Shall Cease: A History of Slavery, Abolitionism, and the Catholic Church* (Maryknoll: Orbis, 2022); John Francis Maxwell, "Correction of Pope Leo XIII Concerning Slavery," in *Slavery and the Catholic Church* (London: Barry Rose, 1975); Diana Hayes, "Reflections on Slavery" in Maureen Fiedler and Linda Rabben, eds., *Rome Has Spoken* (New York: Crossroad, 1998); Diana L. Hayes and Cyprian Davis, eds., *Taking Down Our Harps: Black Catholics in the United States* (Maryknoll: Orbis, 1998); Cyprian Davis, *The History of Black Catholics in the United States* (New York: Crossroad, 1990).

88. *Louisiana's Code Noir* (1724), available via Black Past digital archives (2017–2023). https://www.blackpast.org/african-american-history/louisianas-code-noir-1724/.

89. *Louisiana's Code Noir*, IX.

90. Roberts, *Killing the Black Body*, 22–23.

91. Roberts, *Killing the Black Body*, 23.

92. Jennifer Morgan, *Laboring Women: Reproduction and Gender in New World Slavery* (University of Pennsylvania Press, 2004), 108. See also Sophie White, *Voices of the Enslaved: Love, Labor, and Longing in French Louisiana* (University of North Carolina Press).

93. Morgan, *Laboring Women*, 115.

94. Morgan, *Laboring Women*, 115.

95. Morgan, *Laboring Women*, 115.

96. Morgan, *Laboring Women*, 116.
97. Morgan, *Laboring Women*, 132.
98. Morgan, *Laboring Women*, 111, n.10.
99. Morgan, *Laboring Women*, 113.
100. Morgan, *Laboring Women*, 114. To be clear, I am not advocating that readers employ these methods of fertility control in order to bypass anti-abortion laws today.
101. Morgan, *Laboring Women*, 128.
102. Emily A. Owens, *Consent in the Presence of Force* (Chapel Hill: University of North Carolina Press, 2023).
103. M. Shawn Copeland, *Enfleshing Freedom: Body, Race, and Being* (Minneapolis: Fortress, 2010), 37.
104. Roberts, *Killing the Black Body*, 23.
105. Washington, *Medical Apartheid*.
106. Rickie Solinger, *Pregnancy and Power: A Short History of Reproductive Politics in America* (New York: New York University Press, 2008), 7.
107. David Stannard, *American Holocaust* (Oxford: Oxford University Press, 1992), 121. See also Andrea Smith, "Better Dead Than Pregnant," in *Policing the National Body*, ed. Jael Silliam and Anannya Bhattacharjee (Cambridge, MA: South End Press, 2022), 123–24; Andrea Smith, "Sexual Violence and American Indian Genocide," *Journal of Religion and Abuse* 1, no. 2 (1999): 35–37.
108. Nicola Beisel and Tamara Kay, "Abortion, Race, and Gender in Nineteenth Century America," *American Sociological Review* 69:4 (2004): 498–518.
109. Cultural theorist Salamishah Tillet describes a "moral panic, a fear of the end of whiteness." "The Melissa Harris-Perry Show for Sunday June 16, 2013," MSNBC. com, cited in Jennifer Leath, "Out of Places, Please! Demystifying Opposition to Procreative Choice in Afro-Diasporic Communities in the United States" *Journal of Feminist Studies in Religion* 30:1 (2014): 156–65, at 159.
110. Odette Yousef, "How Is the Great Replacement Theory Tied to the Buffalo Shooting Suspect?" National Public Radio (May 16, 2022), https://www.npr.org/2022/05/16/1099070428/how-is-the-great-replacement-theory-tied-to-the-buffalo-shooting-suspect.
111. Willie James Jennings, *After Whiteness: An Education in Belonging* (Grand Rapids, MI: Eerdmans, 2020), 82.
112. Jennings, *After Whiteness*, 88.
113. Jennings, *After Whiteness*, 99.
114. Bryan Massingale, "A Parallel that Limps: The Rhetoric of Slavery in the Pro-Life Discourse of U.S. Bishops," in *Voting and Holiness: Catholic Perspectives on Political Participation*, ed. Nicholas Cafardi (Mahwah, NJ: Paulist, 2012), 158–77.
115. Jennings, *After Whiteness*, 149.
116. Gillian Brockell, "Some White People Don't Want to Hear About Slavery," *Washington Post* (August 8, 2019). Brockell cites the following review by a tourist of a tour at a plantation home in Louisiana: "We didn't come to hear a lecture on how the white people treated slaves, we came to get this history of a southern plantation and get a tour of the house and grounds. . . . I am by far not a racist or against all Americans having equal rights but this was my vacation and now we are crossing

all plantation tours off our list, it was just not what we expected." https://www.washingtonpost.com/history/2019/08/08/some-white-people-dont-want-hear-about-slavery-plantations-built-by-slaves/.

117. USCCB, *Open Wide Our Hearts*.

118. On this point, see Hoon Choi, "The Case for Intersectional Theology: An Asian American Catholic Perspective," *Journal of Moral Theology* 12 (Special Issue 1, 2023): 62–81, https://doi.org/10.55476/001c.75194.

119. Jael Silliman, Marlene Gerber Fried, Loretta Ross, and Elena R. Gutiérrez, *Undivided Rights: Women of Color Organize for Reproductive Justice* (Cambridge, MA: South End Press, 2004), 32–43.

120. Ross, "Conceptualizing Reproductive Justice Theory," 172.

121. Ross, "Conceptualizing Reproductive Justice Theory," 173.

122. The websites of each organization provide more information about each organization. This is by no means an exhaustive list of reproductive justice organizations in the United States. SisterSong, https://www.sistersong.net/; New Voices, https://newvoicesrj.org/; COLOR (Colorado Organization for Latina Opportunity and Reproductive Rights), https://www.colorlatina.org/; Native Youth Sexual Health Network, https://www.nativeyouthsexualhealth.com/; SisterLove, https://www.sisterlove.org/; CARA (Communities Against Rape and Abuse), www.cara-seattle.org; the Afiya Center, https://www.theafiyacenter.org/; SisterReach, https://www.sisterreach-tn.org/; Indigenous Women Rising, https://www.iwrising.org/; Black Mamas Matter Alliance, https://blackmamasmatter.org/; Birthmark Doula Collective, https://www.birthmarkdoulas.com/; In Our Own Voice, https://blackrj.org/about-us/; and SACReD (Spiritual Alliance of Communities for Reproductive Dignity), https://www.sacreddignity.org/.

123. The collaborative nature of multi-organizational activism has its critics as well. In particular, Jade S. Sasser notes that the term "reproductive justice" can be easily co-opted by White elites because of the way that reproductive justice "operates as a shorthand signifying progressive politics" and this helps activists "navigate thorny racial politics without addressing them directly." Sasser is especially critical of the way that the Sierra Club use reproductive justice as a "buzzword." See Jade S. Sasser, *On Infertile Ground: Population Control and Women's Rights in the Era of Climate Change* (New York: New York University Press, 2018), 127.

124. Ross, "Conceptualizing Reproductive Justice Theory," 176.

125. Copeland, *Enfleshing Freedom*, 2.

126. Paul VI, *Gaudium et spes* (December 7, 1965), 26. https://www.vatican.va/archive/hist_councils/ii_vatican_council/documents/vat-ii_const_19651207_gaudium-et-spes_en.html.

127. Marilyn Frye, "Oppression," in Lorraine Code, ed., *Encyclopedia of Feminist Theories* (New York: Routledge, 2000), 370. See also Marilyn Frye, *The Politics of Reality: Essays in Feminist Theory* (Freedom, California: Crossing Press, 1983), 2–7.

128. Ross, "Conceptualizing Reproductive Justice Theory," 186.

129. Audre Lorde, "Learning from the 60s," (1982), Black Past Digital Archives: https://www.blackpast.org/african-american-history/1982-audre-lorde-learning-60s/.

130. Ross and Solinger, *Reproductive Justice*, 69.

Chapter 2

How Moral Absolutism Undermines Reproductive Justice

Between 1973 and 2022, pregnant women in the United States had a constitutional right to abortion before prenatal viability, and later in pregnancy when her health was endangered. After the 2022 Supreme Court decision in *Dobbs vs. Jackson Women's Health*, which overturned *Roe vs. Wade*, state-level abortion restrictions have led to new kinds of dilemmas for patients as well as for the doctors and nurses who care for them.[1] These dilemmas undermine reproductive flourishing for pregnant patients in the United States. In Louisiana, Dr. Valerie Williams reported that the standard of care previously available in the state (legal before *Dobbs*), and what her patient requested in a recent case, could no longer be offered when the patient experienced premature rupture of membranes. The person who made the decision was not the patient or the doctor but the hospital's lawyer.

> I saw a patient whose water broke at 16 weeks, which is far before viability. There was no way for the pregnancy to continue without putting the patient's health at risk, as the fetus was already starting to deliver. I originally offered to perform a medical procedure called a D&E (or dilation and evacuation) to quickly and safely end the pregnancy. A D&E would have lasted approximately 15 minutes. After our consultation, the patient expressed that this was her preferred option, since she was already traumatized from her experience and felt that an induction, which would require labor and delivery of the fetus, would be too much for her. Once I left the room, however, I heard from my hospital's lawyer that I could no longer perform the requested procedure because the trigger bans had gone into effect. Going back into the hospital room and telling the patient that she would have to be induced and push out the fetus was one of the hardest conversations I've ever had. The trigger bans have turned a hospital room and medical procedure into a legal consultation, all while patients' health and safety are at risk. As a result of the trigger bans being in effect for just a few hours, this particular patient was forced to go through a painful, hours-long labor to deliver a nonviable fetus, despite her wishes and best medical advice. She was

screaming—not from pain, but from the emotional trauma she was experiencing. Then after all of that, it was taking hours for the placenta to deliver, and she began hemorrhaging. She lost close to a liter of blood before I was able to stop the bleeding. There is absolutely no medical basis for my patient, or any other patient in this state, to experience anything like this. This was the first time in my 15-year career that I could not give a patient the care they needed. This is a travesty. As the above demonstrates, the trigger bans will make treating pregnant women who are already suffering from complications even harder.[2]

The confusing legal and ethical landscape for health care providers post-*Dobbs* is troubling, especially because legal provisions that encourage health care providers to safeguard prenatal life may incentivize a provider to wait as long as possible to initiate treatment of a woman facing complications from ectopic pregnancy, miscarriage, premature rupture of membranes, or other potentially dangerous conditions. For example, Tennessee's Human Life Protection Act incentivizes providers to wait as long as possible before inducing labor—a delay that can result in hemorrhage, sepsis, and even death—rather than perform a surgical abortion.[3] Doctors who fear legal prosecution and bankruptcy now have less incentive to prioritize the pregnant person's life and medical decisions. A physician in central Texas was instructed not to treat an ectopic pregnancy until a rupture had occurred, according to media reports.[4] Fifteen plaintiffs in a lawsuit in Texas have sought to clarify the meaning of medical exceptions in the state's anti-abortion statutes.[5] "The idea of having to wait until pregnant patients get sick is just counterintuitive to what we train to do as physicians," Nisha Verma, MD, an OB-GYN, told the Subcommittee on Oversight and Investigations of the Committee on Energy on July 19, 2022, less than a month after the *Dobbs* decision.[6] One physician explained: "I have to wait until my patient comes in with an emergency. Wait until the patient is bleeding profusely. Wait until there are signs of infection. Wait until the patient goes into labor, which for some may not ever happen."[7] Compounding these legitimate problems are the closure of rural hospitals[8] and the impacts of the Covid-19 pandemic on staffing in hospitals around the country.[9] When a pregnant woman is sent home for "expectant management" (meaning one waits to see how a situation progresses or deteriorates) because a hospital does not have a bed for her, it becomes the patient's job to interpret future signs of infection because she is no longer under the direct supervision of a hospital staff member. If she does need to return to the hospital for an emergent crisis, she may find herself waiting in an overcrowded and under-staffed emergency room, further delaying her care and unjustly compounding her suffering. How might the resources of the Catholic tradition speak to this situation of unjust suffering?

The United States Conference of Catholic Bishops (USCCB) is "an assembly of the hierarchy of bishops who jointly exercise pastoral functions on behalf of the Christian faithful of the United States and the US Virgin Islands."[10] In their collective action as a regional conference, Catholic bishops in the United States have advocated for legal protections for prenatal life and celebrated the *Dobbs* decision that overturned *Roe v. Wade*.[11] Procedures that were once banned only at Catholic hospitals are now forbidden across hospitals in states with abortion bans in place.[12] Pro-life leaders argue that these laws safeguard human life and foster a culture of life. If that is the case, how are we to understand the reporting by physicians and patients when they report unnecessary maternal distress because of these laws? When Catholic leaders present abortion teachings as abstract norms detached from relevant circumstances, they create costly confusion. Are their positions appropriate applications of the Catholic tradition broadly understood? Catholic hospitals cannot perform direct abortions. What is *direct* abortion? When can an abortion be considered justified, and who decides? These are ethical questions but they are also theological, legal, and political questions.

This chapter describes authoritative teachings of the Catholic Church on abortion and their implications in the lives of women. I describe how the moral absolutism of papal teachings on abortion departs from the ways that Catholic moralists within the tradition have approached the complexity of moral discernment when an agent faces a moral dilemma. I explain that moral absolutism undermines reproductive justice by advancing policies that limit the reproductive agency of women. Future chapters will elaborate on the claim that women are human persons who should be accompanied in complex discernments about reproduction instead of being dictated to by more powerful others.

AUTHORITATIVE TEACHINGS ON ABORTION

Pope John Paul II, whose papacy lasted from 1978 to 2005, significantly shaped contemporary abortion discourse, especially in the way that he described the need for a "culture of life" in opposition to a "culture of death." This either/or framing of the issues in the public square enabled the pope to speak prophetically but without appropriate nuance. He was canonized on April 27, 2014, in an unusually speedy process that did not allow for decades of research into the far-reaching effects of his decisions and greater knowledge of his shortcomings.[13]

Pope Benedict XVI, whose papacy lasted from 2005 to 2013, resigned and became "Pope Emeritus." Before his election as pope in 2005, he served as the prefect of the Congregation for the Doctrine of the Faith; as pope,

Benedict XVI continued to emphasize doctrinal purity and critiqued secularism and relativism. In addition to restating previous teachings on abortion, Benedict lauded women's sacrifices; for example, he said in 2008 that "even in the most difficult circumstances human freedom is capable of extraordinary acts of sacrifice and solidarity to welcome the life of a new human being."[14] Pope Emeritus Benedict XVI passed away on December 31, 2022.

Pope Francis became pope in 2013, and has maintained significant continuity with his predecessors regarding abortion norms even as he regularly emphasizes accompaniment, compassion, and the mercy of God. Francis has continued in interviews to refer to abortion as "murder," even though he has also encouraged bishops to act with pastoral sensitivity.[15] The overview that follows draws from magisterial teachings promulgated during the papacies of all three of these leaders and explains magisterial teachings on abortion.

Abortion as Killing of Innocent Human Life

Authoritative documents of the Catholic tradition describe abortion as *direct* killing of *innocent* human life. *Evangelium Vitae*, promulgated by Pope John Paul II in 1995, defines procured abortion as "the deliberate and direct killing, by whatever means it is carried out, of a human being in the initial phase of his or her existence, extending from conception to birth."[16] Importantly, this definition excludes *spontaneous* abortion (miscarriage).[17] One can find different definitions of "direct killing" in magisterial documents, leading to considerable confusion. In *Evangelium Vitae*, John Paul II interprets direct killing to mean "an abortion willed as an end or as a means."[18] Moral theologians do not speak with a unified voice about what constitutes "direct" abortion. Vincent Genovesi explains that a direct abortion is "one that is intentional or intended, and one's intention is revealed by looking at what is the sole and immediate object of the physical act or medical procedure that is performed."[19] M. Therese Lysaught faults definitions that rely on the physical structure of the act, noting that "in the Catholic tradition, the moral object of an act is not equivalent or reducible to its physical/material component."[20] Ongoing disagreement among theologians and clinical ethicists about how to determine an agent's "intent" is significant and has real consequences for women's health care decisions. Magisterial teachings claim that a pregnant woman cannot licitly intend to kill the prenate. There is considerable debate among moral theologians and medical ethicists about which abortions are properly described as direct, and which ones are indirect; for example, there is not agreement regarding whether a craniotomy to save a pregnant woman's life would be categorized as direct or indirect abortion.[21]

The innocence of prenatal life is used both to elicit sympathy for the contingent life—"no one more absolutely innocent could be imagined," according to John Paul II[22]—and to conjure horror at the thought of killing the prenate and disgust at anyone who would consider such an act morally legitimate. Even when the human life is unborn and even before viability (the date by which, if born, the baby is reasonably expected to survive outside the womb), the prenate is given moral consideration equivalent to the pregnant person. Pope Francis repeats the norm opposing direct abortion by emphasizing the innocence of prenatal life in *Amoris Laetitia*:

> So great is the value of a human life, and so inalienable the right to life of an innocent child growing in the mother's womb, that no alleged right to one's own body can justify a decision to terminate that life, which is an end in itself and which can never be considered the "property" of another human being.[23]

From Moment of Conception

The *Catechism of the Catholic Church* teaches that "human life must be respected and protected absolutely from the moment of conception. From the first moment of his [sic] existence, a human being must be recognized as having the rights of a person—among which is the inviolable right of every innocent being to life,"[24] a norm restated from the 1987 document from the Congregation for the Doctrine of the Faith (CDF), *Donum Vitae*.[25] Before she even knows that she is pregnant—before a pregnancy test would reliably confirm that she is pregnant—a pregnant woman is understood as having the "absolute" duty to "respect and protect" another being's life, a life that has value equivalent to hers.

Donum Vitae did not explicitly declare that emerging prenatal life "*is* a person," as the CDF demanded only that contingent life be "treated *as* a person." This claim enabled the CDF to sidestep the "personhood" debates, disregarding past precedents in Church teachings by which prenatal personhood was defined later in pregnancy, after "quickening."[26] But Church teaching on the personhood of the prenate did evolve somewhat after 1987. In 1995, in *Evangelium Vitae*, John Paul II described contingent life as "a human being, in whom the image of God is present,"[27] from the moment of conception, without any nuanced understanding of the stages of development explained in the first chapter of this book. Similarly, in *Dignitas Personae* in 2008, the CDF claimed that "the human embryo has, therefore, from the very beginning, the dignity proper to a person."[28] And further: "The dignity of a person must be recognized in every human being from conception to natural death."[29] They reason, thus, that just as the killing of an innocent person can never be allowed, so the killing of an embryo cannot be tolerated.

When authoritative documents from the Catholic tradition claim that human life begins at conception, few details or evidence are given.[30] Instead, theological warrants are offered, as in this passage from the Vatican II document *Gaudium et spes:* "For God, the Lord of Life, has conferred on men [*sic*] the surpassing ministry of safeguarding life in a manner which is worthy of man [*sic*]. Therefore from the moment of its conception life must be guarded with the greatest care while abortion and infanticide are unspeakable crimes."[31] And in the *Catechism*: "Human life is sacred because from its beginning it involves the creative action of God and it remains forever in a special relationship with the Creator, who is its sole end."[32] John Paul II explained that the human person is not the master of life but rather the "minister" of God's plan; theologically, the argument here is that God is the master of life, not the human person, and the appropriate response of the human person is to care for and treasure life even at great cost to oneself.[33]

Because magisterial teaching names human life as sacred from the moment of conception (even prior to implantation), prohibitions of pharmaceuticals marketed as contraception are presented as abortion by another name. For example, *Dignitas Personae* declares: "Anyone who seeks to prevent the implantation of an embryo which may possibly have been conceived and who therefore either requests or prescribes such a pharmaceutical, generally intends abortion."[34]

Always Grave Matter

The gravity of direct abortion is a central theme in papal and conciliar teachings. "Mortal" sins require three conditions: grave matter, full knowledge, and deliberate consent.[35] Considerable attention has been paid to sexual sins within the Catholic moral tradition; an example is the axiom *"Nulla parvitas materiae in Sexto,"* translated as "there is no paucity of matter in the Sixth Commandment,"[36] which prohibits adultery.[37] Whatever the stage of prenatal development, the moral vocabulary used in authoritative Church documents permits no claim of "light matter." Pope John Paul II taught that direct abortion is "murder," terminology repeated by Pope Francis in 2021.[38] Pope John Paul II further described abortion as "evil,"[39] "a grave moral disorder,"[40] and an "intrinsically illicit act."[41]

Sinful

Abortion is sometimes described as sinful without attention to circumstances or intentions, as we see in the phrase "sin of abortion."[42] This shorthand for describing abortion can make it seem that every abortion is sinful no matter the circumstances or intentions of the pregnant person. Emphasizing the moral gravity of every abortion comes with additional consequences for sin-talk. There are many ways to discuss sin in the Bible, including sin as "missing the mark" and sin as a failure to love.[43] The broader Catholic tradition does recognize that some sins are more serious than others. Mortal sins are the most serious sins. When abortion is described as grave matter, then the person who has procured a direct abortion with full knowledge and freedom is in a state of serious sin—that is, separation from God. *Dignitas Personae* adds that there are "serious penalties in canon law."[44] The term for the penalty in canon law is *latae sententiae* excommunication, which is imposed on one who knowingly and willfully commits a particular offense.[45] More recently, Francis issued permission for all confessors to absolve women of grave sin in confession, specifically via absolution to women who have procured abortion.[46] This permission continues to assume moral gravity and sinfulness as constitutive of every elective abortion. The ecclesial and theological model here is legalistic and juridical, presenting God as a divine law-giver and clerics as God's appointed judges on earth.

Intrinsically Evil

In *Veritatis Splendor*, John Paul II included abortion among its list of intrinsically evil acts. The terminology used in the tradition—*intrinsece malum in se*—is translated "intrinsically evil in itself." He described acts which "always and per se, in other words, on account of their very object, and quite apart from the ulterior intentions of the one acting and the circumstances," are "incapable of being ordered to God."[47] Drawing on *Gaudium et Spes* from the Second Vatican Council, *Veritatis Splendor* lists abortion among the acts deemed "whatever is hostile to life itself."[48]

DEVELOPMENT OF THESE TEACHINGS

Defenders of magisterial teachings regarding abortion have further developed this discourse in three ways: first, by emphasizing gender complementarity in theological anthropology; second, by describing motherhood as a sacred duty for women; and third, by claiming that the prenate has equal human rights.

Gender Complementarity

Gender complementarity plays an important role in arguments about finding "true joy" and "true happiness" through conformity to magisterial teachings.[49] Magisterial teachings assert that a gender binary is part of God's plan for creation, and that while men and women have equal dignity, they also have different and complementary roles in family and in society. According to the Congregation for Catholic Education, "sexual difference between male and female is constitutive of human identity" and "the physiological complementarity of male-female sexual difference assures the necessary conditions for procreation."[50] John Paul II taught that men and women are equal, and also different; in their differences, they complement one another as God intended.[51] Francis employs this language within *Amoris Laetitia* as well, explaining that men offer "protection and support" in family life while a woman's "specifically feminine abilities—*motherhood in particular*—also grant duties."[52] Catholic author Laura Garcia explains: "Taking human nature as the ontological basis for the equal dignity of all human beings provides a basis for male/female equality that is compatible with acknowledging differences between women and men."[53] Men and women have different roles in God's plan; conforming to God's design is a key feature of responsible discipleship.[54] A woman will find true empowerment only when she accepts that her feminine nature distinguishes her from men and calls her to a different task.[55] Garcia argues that the "true freedom" women should seek is not freedom to be autonomous agents, but rather the "freedom to love."[56] Often authors who draw on this language do so as part of a larger critique of progressive feminist movements. They see feminist movements as problematic because (in their view) feminists tell women and girls that they will only be free when they become like men, rejecting their true feminine nature.

Motherhood as Sacred Duty

Motherhood is held up in Catholic discourse as a defining feature of a woman's contribution to family life and to the social order. Defenders of Catholic orthodoxy such as Janet E. Smith emphasize procreative love as central to married life, and motherhood as central to a woman's identity (inclusive of spiritual motherhood for vowed religious).[57] Describing herself as a pro-life feminist, Catholic author Erika Bachiochi explains gestation as a mothering process, arguing that an authentically pro-life feminist argument must "embrace the unique reproductive capacity of women."[58] Motherhood begins prior to birth; she continues: "A woman becomes a mother not when she labors to bring her child out into the world, but also when God has labored to create another eternal soul in her very womb."[59] Maternal sacrifice is part of the vocation of being a woman, Bachiochi explains, for "we truly find ourselves when we give of ourselves to others in love."[60] She goes on: "The *sacred duty* of a mother to care for her child exists as soon as the child does."[61] This duty brings responsibility and authority unique to the gestating woman, who is called to "selflessly" embrace this responsibility and ask God for the grace needed to take on the maternal role.[62] Even a victim of sexual violence is expected to sacrifice for the good of the prenate; Bachiochi writes: "as a matter of principle, abortion, even in the case of rape, is terribly tragic and objectively wrong. Aborting an unborn child conceived through rape makes the child, rather than the rapist, ultimately responsible for the grievous violence perpetrated on the woman."[63] Authors defending the claim that motherhood is a sacred duty often reference the apostolic letter *Mulieris Dignitatem* by Pope John Paul II, which explained that "women are more capable than men of paying attention to another person, and motherhood develops this predisposition even more."[64] The Congregation for Catholic Education explained that "women have a unique understanding of reality" and they "possess a capacity to endure adversity."[65] Fatherhood is not given the same treatment in these teachings.

Catholic theologian Sidney Callahan expands on the moral duty of gestation through an expansive understanding of moral responsibility. She writes: "A woman, involuntarily pregnant, has a moral obligation to the now-existing dependent fetus whether she explicitly consented to its existence or not."[66] Nicholas M. Ramirez argues that "an unborn child has a right to his mother's uterus" because a woman's uterus "is teleologically ordered to gestate him [sic] and keep him [sic] alive."[67] To use Garcia's phrase, a woman is "truly free" when her body is used by others. According to these thinkers, a woman who procures an abortion rejects her God-given natural role as a mother; abortion is *unnatural* not only because of the disvalue of prenatal death but because abortion prevents the gestating person from becoming a mother as God intended. In this way of thinking, procured abortion rejects God's plan for the woman as well as for the prenate.

Equal Human Rights for the Prenate

Theologian Charles C. Camosy advocates for "equal justice under law" for "prenatal children."[68] In this framework, the prenate is a human being whose life has *equal value* to the gestating mother. Together with David McPherson, Camosy argues that it is appropriate for pro-life Catholics to see abortion as a preeminent priority because "prenatal human life is equally sacred to postnatal human life."[69] Equal justice for all human persons, they argue, requires continuation of the pregnancy, even if that requires coercion of the gestating person.[70]

The prenate's equal right to life is claimed as an absolute moral principle, without attention to the particularities of an individual pregnant person's life story or interests. In a Catholic ethics manual for medical practitioners, one expert summarizes the argument: "Even in rare situations where the life of both mother and child seem to be at stake, one may not directly take the life of the child to save the mother or take the life of the mother to save the child."[71] This equal rights framework functions to minimize conflicts between the gestating woman and contingent life; Sidney Callahan explains that sometimes there are "temporary conflicts of interest," but "pitting women against their own offspring is not only morally offensive, it is psychologically and politically destructive."[72]

Gender difference, motherhood, and equality are important themes worthy of further dialogue within the Church. My concern, however, is that the positions described here unfairly tolerate the coercion of women's bodies by establishing contingent life as equal to the life of the gestating women. In practice, I fear that Catholic teachings about natural maternal roles for all women prevent individual women from fully exploring and discerning their own particular vocations. Future chapters attend to these concerns in greater detail.

IMPLICATIONS OF MAGISTERIAL TEACHINGS ON ABORTION IN EVERYDAY LIFE

The prophetic mode of speech of John Paul II's advocacy for a "culture of life" has animated Catholic discourse on abortion in the past fifty years, but his presentation of the issue as one of moral clarity and moral gravity has actually functioned in counterproductive ways. The culture-war rhetoric adopted by clerical leaders does not erase the very real complexity of the issue of abortion; it masks it. Popes have used language that appears simple, when women in the pews know all too well that the issue is not at all simple. Here we will review some of the implications of the moral absolutism employed by some Catholic leaders in order to point out that the language used by popes and bishops does matter for everyday people in the pews.

Sacraments[73]

How do women encounter abortion discourse or seek healing in Church spaces after pregnancy loss? Eucharist and Reconciliation remain the two primary sacramental experiences to facilitate healing after pregnancy loss. Both can present obstacles for Catholic women's full flourishing because these sacraments provide spaces where priests can assert shame-based claims about abortion.

In some parishes, Mass has become part of the culture wars. The homily is when the priest or deacon offers a gospel reflection in order to help the scriptures come alive for people in the pews. Even though Jesus did not preach directly about abortion, sometimes the priest or deacon preaching makes the personal judgment to draw on abortion as a fitting example of the meaning of the lectionary readings that week. Other Catholic resources confirm this emphasis on abortion as worthy of special attention, as seen, for example, in the Respect Life materials suggested by the United States Conference of Catholic Bishops,[74] the newsletters of Walking with Moms in Need,[75] programming by Eternal Word Television Network,[76] programming on Catholic radio, and social media. Shaming language persists, even if a pastor is just "explaining what the Church teaches," since authoritative teachings describe abortion as killing, grave matter, and sinful. According to research conducted by the Pew Center, more than four in ten Catholics have recently heard a homily about abortion.[77]

But it is not just the homily. There is also the March for Life (January),[78] Lent's seasonal focus on sin and repentance (March/April), May Crowning and Mother's Day (May), Fortnight for Freedom (June),[79] Respect Life month (October),[80] and the liturgical focus on Mary's pregnancy during Advent and Christmas (December and January). Each of these provides thematic connections to the issue of abortion for prayers (related to life, sin, motherhood, religious freedom, pregnancy, and so on) that may surface in the liturgy experience. Prayers of the Faithful toolkits promoted by USCCB resources sometimes reinforce the moral absolutism and sin-talk that can lead to a sense of shame for people in the pews, even if God's mercy is the focus of the prayer. For example: "For those who have participated in an abortion and feel they have committed an unforgiveable sin: May they come to know the Lord's limitless mercy, and turn to Him for forgiveness and healing; We pray to the Lord."[81] Such a petition focuses on God's mercy, but does so by first using the language of "unforgiveable sin" to describe an act that many Catholic women in the pews will have experienced. Some petitions advance particular policy proposals: "For the legal protection of unborn children and for loving support for their mothers before and after their births; We pray to the Lord."[82]

One ongoing source of conflict in the US Catholic context is the question of who is deemed worthy to receive the Eucharist at Mass. Senator Dick Durbin (D-IL) confirmed in 2021 that for seventeen years he had been denied communion in Springfield, Illinois, where he grew up, and that it is "uncomfortable" when he goes to a Catholic parish he has never been to before because he does not know how local clergy will react.[83] Archbishop Salvatore Cordileone of San Francisco, California, declared on May 20, 2022 to then-House Speaker Nancy Pelosi (D-CA):

> You are not to present yourself for Holy Communion and, should you do so, you are not to be admitted to Holy Communion, until such time as you publicly repudiate your advocacy for the legitimacy of abortion and confess and receive absolution of this grave sin in the sacrament of Penance.[84]

Cordileone justifies this position on the basis of canon law,[85] the 2002 Doctrinal Note from the Congregation for the Doctrine of the Faith,[86] and a 2004 letter from Cardinal Joseph Ratzinger, Prefect, Congregation for the Doctrine of the Faith, to US bishops.[87] Notably, he does not cite Francis's *Fratelli Tutti*, which is a more recent teaching on the important work of politicians in securing the common good.[88]

It is hard to track how widespread the practice of denying Holy Communion to pro-choice Catholics has become, but it is not hard to see how the power dynamics of clericalism shape the discussion and reverberate in Catholic spaces. Cordileone does not make careful distinctions between procuring a direct abortion and working as a politician in a pluralist democracy in which a two-party system sets the context for political decisions, negotiations, and policy proposals. Cordileone placed himself as a gatekeeper of God's grace, determining for himself who is worthy and unworthy of the graces that flow from the Sacrament of the Eucharist. Pope Francis stated that he has "never denied Eucharist to anyone," and some US bishops reject attempts to politicize the Eucharist.[89] Cardinal Robert McElroy of San Diego argues that "the Eucharist must never be instrumentalized for a political end, no matter how important."[90] In fact, shortly after Cordileone denied communion to Pelosi, she traveled to Rome, where she attended Mass with Pope Francis and received communion there.[91]

Since Church teachings describe abortion as a sin, the remedy is sacramental confession. But the Sacrament of Reconciliation has three main limitations: the lack of trauma-informed pastoral care; the experiential and gender gap between priest and penitent when a woman confesses an abortion; and the limitations of framing abortion exclusively as a personal sin.

The sacrament of reconciliation is supposed to provide an opportunity for the sinner to name her sin, ask for forgiveness, receive a penance, and receive absolution from the priest. Some theorists of the sacrament defend the focus on God's peace and God's pardon, saying that the sacrament is not a time for counseling or crisis management.[92] But lack of knowledge about trauma triggers and emotional distress could lead to a confessor asking inappropriate questions or making harmful claims to a woman who confesses an abortion as sin.[93]

The experiential gap between priest and penitent can also create limitations in the confessor's knowledge. While certainly there are many priests who are compassionate and pastoral, there are also very real structural injustices in place. No matter how mature, respectful, and empathetic he is, a male priest can never fully understand what it feels like to be a woman who was sexually violated. A male priest may struggle to understand what it feels like to experience the world as an embodied woman, given the sexism that is pervasive in the Church and in the world. It is curious that the popes have focused so much on gender difference,[94] but failed to understand the impact of gender difference on actual women's experiences of an exclusively male priesthood caste who are empowered to dispense God's grace, and who withhold that same grace.[95] Rather than acknowledge the pain caused by this sacramental injustice, some authors engage in gaslighting by trying to minimize the pain women share.[96] One guide to confession, written by two priests, explains that the priest is "still a human being." "Sometimes human beings have bad days," it observes. "Sometimes human beings are not as gentle or as patient as we would like them to be. Sometimes, instead of having words of counsel for us, a priest had words of annoyance or condemnation, even in confession—because the priest is human." However, they go on: "Confession is an encounter with Jesus even in those cases when it does not feel that way."[97] But women who experience sexism within the sacrament may be less likely to return for a future "encounter with Jesus."

Thinking of sacramental confession as a way to resolve the moral problem of abortion reflects a flawed answer because abortion is a complex *social* phenomenon. This narrow approach aligns in some respects with the manualist tradition and its focus on rules, deontology, deductive logic, act-centered theology, and a world rife with moral pathology.[98] The manualist period in Catholic moral theology lasted from the nineteenth century to the Second Vatican Council, with a resurgence in some themes in the 1968 birth control encyclical *Humanae Vitae*.[99] One problem of the notion of sin in the manualist period is that "sin itself was essentially violating whatever Rome prohibited"; in other words, sin was collapsed with violation of Church law.[100] When abortion stories surface in a sacramental confession, the operative assumption is that the abortion is best categorized as a *personal* sin. This claim means that the individual who procures an abortion has engaged in a personal act that offends God and violates the moral law. Canon law[101] and papal teachings have asserted that abortion is a personal sin, "a grave sin," in the words of Pope Francis.[102]

To confess personal sin means to take personal responsibility for one's immoral actions in order to seek repair of one's relationship to God and the Church. But given the data we have already reviewed about the testimonies of women who procure abortions and the social factors that contribute to their decision-making, it is not self-evident that every abortion is best categorized as a *personal* sin even when we recognize a disvalue in the act itself and its consequences in the lives of affected persons.

Taking seriously the social and relationship constraints pregnant women face, legitimate concerns pregnant women navigate regarding their own health, and the absence of alternate choices pregnant women perceive, it is clear that we need a more expansive vocabulary to adequately name the disvalue experienced in abortion decisions while simultaneously rooting ourselves in a tradition that recognizes the importance of taking responsibility for actions that cause deliberate harm to one's self, another, and to one's relationship to God. Theologian Charles Curran is among those who have argued for a distinction between the subjective and the objective dimensions of the moral act. The manuals of moral theology should have recognized that they were "dealing only with the aspect of grave matter and not with mortal sin as such," he explains. "But often the moral theology textbooks themselves referred to the objective acts themselves as mortal sin," as Pope Francis has continued to do. In reality, "no confessor or other outside observer can ever know for sure the subjective reality of the person who did the act."[103]

A confusing aspect of Catholic discourse on abortion can be found in the fact that popes from John Paul II to Francis have treated abortion as a social problem that should be seen through the lens of social sin but they have not drawn out the implications of these claims for sacramental reform or political participation. In his 1995 encyclical *Evangelium Vitae*, Pope John Paul II named as complicit in the social evil of abortion many different community members who fail to respond in love and justice.[104] The pope did not simply blame women, as one might expect him to do given the papal emphases on personal sin and the need for the sacrament of confession; instead he expressed the concern that some women are victims of a "culture of death" because of the pervasiveness of social sin that influences their judgments and actions (and in some cases limits their culpability). Pope John Paul II explicitly stated, "Abortion goes beyond the responsibility of individuals and beyond the harm done to them, and takes on a distinctly social dimension."[105]

Scholars of reproductive justice point to the social dimensions of healthy decisions about gender, bodies, sexuality, reproduction, and families;[106] they also demonstrate that laws and policies can unfairly limit a person's reproductive choices. In the context of abortion, what is needed is a comprehensive social response that creates a culture in which women who face unplanned pregnancies feel that they have the power, resources, and hope to welcome new life. This approach must be part of a comprehensive effort to eliminate sexism, combat violence against women, provide affordable health care, and ensure that families can afford high-quality childcare—in short, create systems in which people have what they need to thrive, it is easier to make good choices, and new life is welcomed with joy. Seen from this perspective, the confessional is hardly the place to initiate such a social movement. The reconciliation required after abortion is not only between the woman and God, or the woman and the Church, but between all of the social actors who have failed her—and the human-made social systems that did not offer her the structural and spiritual supports she needed when she discovered she was pregnant. The sacrament of reconciliation does not heal the deeper wounds that led to this action in the first place, nor will it bring true healing without a transparent communal apology and amends to actually repair the harm that has been done. Serious reform of sacramental practice will be necessary, but it is not enough by itself. Reproductive justice requires striving for social repair while simultaneously supporting women in their own discernments based on their own concrete circumstances.

Political Action and Lobbying

Religious voices have always shaped and will continue to shape politics in the US context; the question is what kind of voice is most appropriate.[107] For the past fifty years, it has been difficult for any religious leader who wishes to influence US politics to avoid participation in the "culture wars" that have dominated political speech.[108] For some time, abortion has been at the center of those debates. While in the next chapter I will give significant attention to the vices of the pro-life movement, here the focus is on how some Catholic leaders have shaped their position on abortion such that it is not simply a position "for Catholics," but rather framed as a universal moral claim that should be adopted by a pluralist democracy's laws. Catholic magisterial teachings, then, have consequences not only for women in the pews, but women who never plan to sit in the pews—indeed, for women of other faiths and of no faith tradition at all.

One of the fundamental claims of Catholic social ethics is that Church teachings are rooted in the natural law, and thus do not depend exclusively on justifications that are sectarian in nature (that is, from Divine Revelation known through the specifically Christian sources of authority). Catholic magisterial documents claim that the Church is "an expert in humanity."[109] Addressed to "all people of good will," documents from the Church's tradition of social teachings claim that reasonable people can reflect on God's natural laws as revealed in nature and human experience, in order to arrive at moral norms that are universal, even for nonbelievers. Theologians who study the natural law have taken great care to point out the contextual and revisable nature of natural law claims as they have developed over time,[110] but some Catholic prelates employ natural law arguments in deductive and absolutist ways.[111] For example, the US bishops in 2002 urged "all people of good will" to "speak out on behalf of the sanctity of each and every human life wherever it is threatened, from conception to natural death." They claim that nonbelievers and believers alike can review the "scientific evidence" that human life begins at conception. They quote John Paul II's *Evangelium Vitae*: "it is impossible to further the common good without acknowledging and defending the right to life, upon which all the other inalienable rights of individuals are founded and from which they develop."[112] Here and elsewhere, abortion is framed as a human rights issue, but the only person whose rights are threatened is the prenate. The bishops do not acknowledge any legitimate conflict over different theological, conceptual, or pragmatic understandings of human rights. They do not position their stance as one voice among other religious voices in the public square. They do not admit that Catholics themselves remain divided on these issues. They do not admit that they have anything to learn from listening to others. Instead, they assert their position as a moral claim that should be adopted by others because (presumably) they believe it is the most reasonable and persuasive possible argument.

Catholic teachings considered holistically provide a challenge to both Democratic and Republican platforms and legislative agendas; neither political party maps neatly onto Catholic teachings. But when abortion is prioritized above all other life issues—as regularly happens in Catholic publications and ministries—this prioritization tips the scales toward Republican agendas.[113] The alliances forged between the pro-life movement and the Republican Party seem to have the blessing of many Catholic pastors and bishops, especially those who have become more partisan in their own rhetoric.[114] Voter guides distributed by some Catholic groups demonstrate that abortion is often used as a political tool to push a particular candidate or agenda.[115]

A key question is whether Church teachings justify coercive actions by sectarian leaders such as Catholic bishops. What justifies religious leaders in asserting that their understanding is the only morally acceptable legal option? The bishops cite the Second Vatican Council when they claim a right to teach the faith and pass moral judgment in the public square:

> The political community and the Church are autonomous and independent of each other in their own fields. Nevertheless, both are devoted to the personal vocation of man, though under different titles. . . . [Yet] at all times and in all places, the Church should have the true freedom to teach the faith, to proclaim its teaching about society, to carry out its task among men without hindrance, *and to pass moral judgment even in matters relating to politics, whenever the fundamental rights of man or the salvation of souls requires it.*[116]

Both the US Constitution and Catholic teaching protect the rights of Catholic leaders to talk about Catholic teachings from the pulpit and even in the public square. Regarding abortion, their public witness is clear: "Direct abortion is *never* a morally tolerable option. It is *always* a grave act of violence against a woman and her unborn child. This is so even when a woman does not see the truth because of the pressures she may be subjected to, often by the child's father, her parents or friends."[117] If bishops only attempted to *persuade* their fellow citizens of these moral claims, their roles as teachers, shepherds, and ministers would be self-evident. But collectively, Catholic bishops have done more than "pass moral judgment." They have actively campaigned for particular policies, including laws and policies that align with their vision of what justice for prenatal life means. The bishops justify their approach on the basis of religious liberty claims, even as they fail to recognize that observant religious adherents in the United States have different (and contradictory) positions on abortion.[118]

The Catholic bishops' focus on abortion as a preeminent moral issue since 1973 has been divisive.[119] In 1973 the National Conference of Catholic Bishops explicitly called for civil disobedience to resist laws legalizing abortion.[120] In 1975, they crafted their Pastoral Plan for Pro-Life Activities,[121] which outlined a grassroots mobilization effort against abortion and initiated a strategy of endorsing a "single issue" approach to election politics, focusing on abortion policy in their analysis of candidates for office. The plan specifically encouraged Catholics to oppose each and every political candidate who supported the legalization of abortion. When they updated their action plan over forty years later, the bishops restated the need to give "urgent attention and *priority*" to abortion as a life issue.[122] Even Cardinal Robert McElroy and Cardinal Blaise Cupich, both known for their advocacy of the Francis agenda and known to be more moderate than other US bishops, advocate explicitly for legal protections for unborn children.[123]

There is not consensus among Catholics about this approach.[124] One would think that a lack of consensus would indicate a need for greater dialogue and communal discernment, but Catholic bishops have not sought dialogue; instead they operate by asserting their authority. A recent example unfolded on the evening of January 21, 2022, when Catholics for Choice projected light on the exterior of the Basilica of the National Shrine of the Immaculate Conception in Washington, DC, with informational messages and pro-choice messages, including "Pro-Choice Catholics: You Are Not Alone." Cardinal Wilton Gregory responded with a statement:

> The true voice of the Church was only to be found within the Basilica of the National Shrine of the Immaculate Conception last night. There, people prayed and offered the Eucharist asking God to restore a true reverence for all human life. Those whose antics projected words on the outside of the church building demonstrated by those pranks that they really are external to the Church and they did so at night—John 13:30.[125]

By citing that Bible verse, Cardinal Gregory seems to be saying here that Catholics for Choice represents Judas, the disciple who betrayed Jesus. But it is just as accurate to say that many Catholic women in the pews feel betrayed by their own leaders—leaders who refuse to engage in a serious discernment about the patriarchy of the Church's ecclesiology and the reluctance of bishops to listen to women's stories of reproductive loss. One of the messages projected on the Shrine said, "1 in 4 Abortion Patients is Catholic." Cardinal Gregory's response lacked pastoral sensitivity in his claim that only those inside the Basilica that night represented the "true voice of the Church." He overlooks the experiences of women in the Church whose lived experiences include abortion.

Steven P. Millies argues that after *Roe*, the USCCB "embarked on the path that significantly altered their public posture from spiritual leaders to lobbyists."[126] The USCCB engages in lobbying efforts via their Office for Government Relations, which "coordinates and directs the legislative activities of the USCCB staff and other church personnel to influence the actions of the Congress."[127] In practice, the USCCB's principled approach to lobbying leads to obstructionist tactics that can be described as sectarian. Top priorities in their lobbying efforts "seek to eliminate legalized abortion"; "support policies encouraging childbirth over abortion and assistance to children and pregnant women"; "oppose domestic and foreign abortion funding as well as efforts to force states and health plans to fund abortion and other services to which many have moral and religious objections"; and "support the legal protection of conscience for individuals and faith-based organizations so that they are not forced or pressured to abandon their religious principles."[128] In support of these goals, Catholic bishops opposed the Patient Protection and Affordable Care Act; advocated for restrictions on contraception access within employer health care plans for working women;[129] opposed the Women's Health Protection Act;[130] advocated in favor of the Conscience Protection Act;[131] advocated for the Helms Amendment and the Hyde Amendment;[132] opposed the Violence Against Women Act; wrote in opposition to the Equal Rights Amendment;[133] and opposed the Equality Act.[134] In other words, Catholic bishops in the United States have explicitly argued in opposition to specific laws and policies that would have advanced reproductive justice. The Church's position on abortion was a central aspect of the moral reasoning for the bishops who opposed the Affordable Care Act, and they invoked moral absolutism in their argumentation. "We will never conclude that we must accept what is intrinsically evil so that some good may be achieved," wrote Cardinal Daniel DiNardo, Bishop William Murphy, and Bishop John Wester.[135] And further: "Whatever might be the positive aspects of the Senate bill, we had no choice but to oppose the Senate version as a matter of principle. As bishops we must faithfully proclaim the truth. We must defend the rights of the unborn and the weakest and most vulnerable among us."[136] Those familiar with the outcome will know that the Affordable Care Act passed, despite the opposition of leading Catholic bishops.[137]

The USCCB lobbying is not limited to the legislative branch. The bishops have sought to influence the executive branch through direct outreach and public shaming of presidents.[138] They have also sought to use their influence in the judicial branch. They do so by cultivating networks of legal scholars who will endorse Church teachings,[139] advancing law school curricula that align with Catholic teachings,[140] and advocating for judicial appointments who support Catholic teachings. The bishops have submitted *amici curiae* (friend of the court briefs) in order to advocate in particular cases, including in support of the State of Mississippi in the *Dobbs v. Jackson Women's Health* case.[141] The brief, signed by an all-male team of lawyers, positions itself as the authoritative voice of the Catholic Church on the case before the Court. The brief adopts the moral absolutism we've seen already in this chapter; for example, they write that "abortion involves the purposeful taking of an innocent human life and, like the homicide of a born person, it is a proper subject of prohibition by the state."[142] They cite John Paul II's *Evangelium Vitae*: "Among all the crimes which can be committed against life, procured abortion has characteristics making it particularly serious and deplorable."[143] They do not acknowledge any medical cases in which there may be unresolvable conflict between the health and life of the gestating mother and the life of the contingent prenate. Their efforts are not focused on support for pregnant people but legal protections of contingent life. They argue that the issue of abortion should "return to the states."[144]

It is important to point out that this legal argument—that laws should be determined based on the state in which one lives—is not found in the Bible or in Church teaching. It is not an argument advanced by theologians with support from the history and tradition of the Church. It does not reflect the data emerging from parish listening sessions in light of the ongoing synod.[145] It is an argument made by a team of lawyers paid by Catholic bishops to advance their judicial agenda, which includes pragmatic attempts to limit access to legal abortion and an overarching goal of creating legal protections for unborn life. While the USCCB's amicus brief was not cited in the final opinion, the arguments were adopted by Justice Alito. The bishops were, thus, part of a group of religious leaders who advocated for a change to the law, with implications not only for Catholic women but for all women, especially women in states positioned to implement new anti-abortion restrictions.[146] When bishops claim to speak on behalf of the Catholic Church by calling women criminals and murderers and by paying their lawyers to craft a legal strategy that aims to restrict the choices pregnant women have, they damage not only their own credibility to speak on behalf of the whole Church (inclusive of women!) but also any good will among people who do not find their legislative strategy to be in alignment with the gospel.

Steven Millies suggests that reflecting on the turmoil of the past decades can help Catholics to discern a more productive way forward. He writes:

Catholic political action is necessary, and the Catholic faith teaches us that it is an important duty. Defending the dignity of each and every human person depends on it. Yet, politics is a realm of prudence. . . . [S]ome greater thought and some better checks are needed in how Catholics generally, and Catholic bishops specifically, approach politics. The answers of moral theology and Christian ethics are not always appropriate to problems in politics and law.[147]

What constitutes appropriate Catholic political action? Catholic theologians are not in universal agreement that abortion bans are in alignment with the common good. I take the position that the role of the faith leader in the political realm is to raise awareness about key values at stake when moral questions arise, but not to foreclose an individual's discernment in conscience. Catholic leaders should be free to explain authoritative teachings in public, but should never be in a position to force other citizens to comply with those teachings when there is not a moral consensus on the question. Catholic leaders should never overstate or distort Catholic teachings when they advocate in the public square; unfortunately, such overreach has become commonplace. We should be willing to call this overreach what it is: an abuse of power.

Catholic Health Care

A third significant arena in which magisterial teachings on abortion lead to serious consequences for everyday people can be seen in the delivery of health care in Catholic hospitals and in health insurance provided by Catholic employers. The bishops draw upon Church teachings regarding the sanctity of life and religious freedom to justify the policies in place, but patients and employees are beginning to raise more questions about whether it is appropriate for religious leaders to wield their power in this way, by constraining the medical choices for patients in Catholic facilities and for employees of Catholic institutions.

In the United States, Catholic health systems control 16.6 percent (one in six) of the hospital beds in the country, and in some states more than 20 percent of the hospital beds.[148] Catholic hospitals must conform to the *Ethical and Religious Directives for Catholic Health Care Services* promulgated by the USCCB.[149] In alignment with authoritative magisterial teachings, these directives forbid direct contraception, direct sterilization, direct abortion, and some infertility treatments including in vitro fertilization. They can also limit the treatment options patients have to prevent pregnancy that results from sexual assault. In one case from 2013, a pregnant patient was discharged from a Catholic hospital in Detroit after a diagnosis of preterm premature rupture of membrane, which can pose significant risks to the mother.[150] According to reporting by Judy Stone, patients have been turned away from treatment while actively miscarrying.[151] In Phoenix, Arizona, in 2009, a Catholic hospital was stripped of its Catholic status and Sister Margaret McBride, a hospital administrator, was excommunicated because physicians carried out a procedure on a pregnant patient to save her life, knowing they could not save the prenate.[152] This case was also analyzed by the National Catholic Bioethics Center.[153] Bishop Thomas J. Olmsted expressed discomfort about the death of the prenate, who could not be saved, and claimed that the medical team had acted against Church teachings when they took measures to save the mother's life. She was a twenty-seven-year-old Catholic woman with four other children.

The *Ethical and Religious Directives for Catholic Health Care Services* is in its sixth edition and governs the delivery of care in institutionally based Catholic health care services.[154] It begins with a description of the importance of the healing ministries in Jesus's own life and in the lives of his followers, including religious congregations through the years who have seen care for the sick and dying as a central part of their Christian discipleship.[155] But read on, and one soon finds evidence of concern not just for the well-being of patients, but reassertion of a hierarchical structure of authority that seems to isolate and consolidate power and decision-making in a way that elevates the local ordinary (bishop).[156] Catholic bishops do not train in medical school on their path to the priesthood and the episcopacy. One of the curious aspects of the *Directives* is the way that they assume that bishops have competency to adjudicate difficult medical cases.

The *Directives* assert that "when the health care professional and the patient use institutional Catholic health care, they also accept its public commitment to the Church's understanding of and witness to the dignity of the human person."[157] The *Directives* assume that all patients voluntarily choose to seek care in the Catholic system, and that medical providers voluntarily choose to work in the Catholic system. It is worth probing if such an assumption holds up to further scrutiny. After all, patients regularly enter the emergency rooms of Catholic hospitals while unconscious or in severe distress; emergency medical technicians may also be routed to a particular hospital via their ambulance dispatch because of other needs that have nothing to do with the patient requests.[158] But not all cases are extreme. More often the constraints are subtle. It may be that the Catholic hospital is the only one in town,[159] or the only one accessible via public transportation, or the only one that accepts the patient's employer-provided health insurance. Patients on Medicaid or other governmental assistance programs are likely to experience compounding constraints. Similarly, physicians and nurses are like other skilled workers who must find a position of employment that suits their unique skill set and training.[160] Some medical workers may have the luxury of a job search that spans the country, where the mission of the institution can be a determining factor of whether or not to accept a job, but most have other real-life constraints that must be considered when they seek employment, including proximity to family members, quality of local schools for their dependent children, compensation for the work performed, expected patient case load, first impression of the quality of life at the workplace, resources of the institution in comparison to peer institutions, and other considerations. For those fortunate enough to have more than one job offer at the end of a long process, it is hard to imagine that the mission of the hospital would be the determining factor for a physician or a nurse when making the final decision.

Patients and providers at Catholic health care facilities need not share the Catholic faith, but they must comply with the policies in place as set forth in the *Directives* and interpreted by the local ordinary (bishop).[161] This requirement may not seem to be a difficult imposition upon first glance, given that one may interpret the support of human dignity and social justice as a kind of "We love everybody" approach to health care. But in practice, conflicts do arise, and the USCCB document proscribes some treatments and interventions. Since Catholic magisterial teachings ascribe personhood to prenatal life, conflicts arise in care of pregnant persons in fairly obvious ways.

"Part Four: Issues in Care for the Beginning of Life" is where we find the Catholic bishops affirming their "concern for the sanctity of human life from its very beginning."[162] The document is consistent with the moral norms within authoritative documents as described in the opening section of this chapter, teachings that I have characterized as moral absolutism because they are cited with the assumption that they propose rules that are clear, unambiguous, easily interpreted and applied, and admit of no legitimate exceptions. The assumption is that these principles are not simply guides for the reflection of the medical team and patient, but rather that they *direct* patient care—they delineate clear limits based on what authoritative teachers have concluded are moral or immoral acts. When a pregnant person seeks care in a Catholic hospital, then, there are two patient lives at stake: the pregnant person and the unborn life, held sacred "from the moment of conception." The bishops write: "The Church's defense of life encompasses the unborn and the care of women and their children during and after pregnancy."[163] Directive 44 goes on: "A Catholic health care institution should provide prenatal, obstetric, and postnatal services for mothers and their children in a manner consonant with its mission."[164] This last phrase, "consonant with its mission," carries a heavy load of meaning, given that the "mission" of the institution is bound up in its Catholicity, and thereby in its application of Church teachings to the policies of the hospital or treatment center. Other directives relevant to reproductive injustice are worth citing in their entirety:

Directive 45: Abortion (that is, the directly intended termination of pregnancy before viability or the directly intended destruction of a viable fetus) is never permitted. Every procedure whose sole immediate effect is the termination of pregnancy before viability is an abortion, which, in its moral context, includes the interval between conception and implantation of the embryo. Catholic health care institutions are not to provide abortion services, even based upon the principle of material cooperation. In this context, Catholic health care institutions need to be concerned about the danger of scandal in any association with abortion providers.[165]

Directive 47: Operations, treatments, and medications that have as their direct purpose the cure of a proportionately serious pathological condition of a pregnant woman are permitted when they cannot be safely postponed until the unborn child is viable, even if they will result in the death of the unborn child.[166]

Directive 48: In case of extrauterine pregnancy, no intervention is morally licit which constitutes a direct abortion.[167]

Directive 49: For a proportionate reason, labor may be induced after the fetus is viable.[168]

Directive 70: Catholic health care organizations are not permitted to engage in immediate material cooperation in actions that are intrinsically immoral, such as abortion, euthanasia, assisted suicide, and sterilization.[169]

Within these cited directives, specific moral terminology is employed (direct intent, immediate effect, material cooperation, scandal, proportionate reason, intrinsically evil acts) without sufficient elaboration regarding the development of these terms or an argument explaining the rationale for why a particular principle is invoked to address the "act" in question. An unacknowledged fact is that the principles that underlie the moral analysis in this document from the Catholic bishops have developed over centuries in the Catholic moral tradition and continue to evolve in the work of medical ethicists, clinicians, and theologians. The *Directives* present these principles as static norms and ahistorical tools that can be applied easily to situations, but that is not the way that moral reasoning works, nor is it a fair characterization of the way that these principles developed in the tradition.

PRINCIPLES AND MORAL REASONING

Catholic theologian and Jesuit James Bretzke explains that "often moral principles seem to overlap and even conflict with one another, and in these sorts of cases the discipline of casuistry is helpful in determining which particular moral principle applies or has precedent in this or that particular case."[170] Coming to a morally correct decision in a particular case is not as straightforward as it may seem, since one has to determine how to describe the act, what information is relevant in that determination, then which principle best applies to that act, and how it applies to render a judgment. The principles do not function alone; the moralist is also engaging in moral reasoning any time they describe the human act and the values at stake in a discernment. Disagreement can emerge among moralists over how to describe a human act, even before the more complex evaluation of the relevant norms, laws, or principles that might apply to that situation.[171]

Moral theology in the Catholic Church has developed over time. Specific moralists in specific contexts developed the hagiography and moral theology of the patristic period in the first to fifth centuries, the penitentials of the sixth to ninth centuries, the scholastic texts of the twelfth to thirteenth centuries, the casuistry of the sixteenth and seventeenth centuries, and the moral manualism of the nineteenth and twentieth centuries.[172] And we should not assume that story is inevitably one of linear progression toward more perfect knowledge; sometimes the most innovative moral thinking involves the work of creative retrieval.[173] In the history of casuistry, hard cases helped moralists to understand and appreciate the values at stake in a case, and how our perception of these can develop over time. In some cases, new principles developed when previous norms were deemed inadequate to resolve the case at hand. Moralists in the tradition have wrestled with complexity as they made precise distinctions and with variability as they recognized the uniqueness of circumstances that can shape the evaluation of a particular case. For example, in their analysis of the period of high casuistry, Stephen Toulmin and Albert Jonsen show how moralists compared cases to show congruency and to make careful distinctions in order to express new moral knowledge. For example, in order to address new situations of religious conflict, questions arose such as "Could a Roman Catholic priest lie about his identity to Queen Elizabeth's soldiers?" A paradigm case invoked by moralists was the case of the Risen Christ who acted as if he did not know what had happened in Jerusalem when speaking to the disciples on the road to Emmaus (Lk 24:19) and as if he intended to go further in his journey that day (Lk 24:28). The two cases established the principle that lying is forbidden, but pretense is sometimes permitted.[174]

Some mischaracterize casuistry as just a clever way to look for loopholes, but that is not a fair description of the moral reasoning embedded in this moral method. In fact, an approach to the moral life that recognizes complexity at the level of the particular moral situation is very traditional. For the scholastic theologian St. Thomas Aquinas, there are some universal moral norms that hold in all times, places, and situations; in his treatise on natural law, he explains that the first principle of practical reason is that "good is to be done and pursued, and evil is to be avoided."[175] Some norms of the natural law, however, are not universal and may change over time or due to circumstances. Aquinas writes: "Although there is necessity in the general principles, the more we descend to matters of detail, the more frequently we encounter defects."[176] Aquinas understood that principles are valuable in moral reasoning, but that principles are not articulated in such a way as to clearly address every possible circumstance and detail. Thus, practical wisdom is required when one deliberates about how a particular principle applies to specific "matters of detail."

Pope Francis recognizes that persons sometimes find themselves in true moral dilemmas in his apostolic exhortation *Amoris Laetitia*. There, he writes that a person may be in a "concrete situation, which does not allow him or her to act differently and decide otherwise without further sin."[177] Theologian Gerald Bednar explains: "some people become locked in dilemmas which offer no way out that is both virtuous and practicable."[178] How are Christians to navigate such morally complex situations? The principles employed by the *Directives* have been very helpful for guiding discernment in the Church's tradition. But we mistake their use if we begin to see them as abstract rules that easily apply in specific cases. The principles of double effect, cooperation, and toleration developed over time, and the history of that unfolding by various thinkers in the tradition is complex. These principles have been invoked in various situations of moral conflict, including war, policing, prevention of disease, withholding of truth, and other situations. And those who developed them did so with the caution of Aquinas in mind: namely, an understanding of the limits of general principles when faced with diverse contexts and circumstances.

Toleration of the Lesser Evil (Minus Malum)

The medieval theologian Thomas à Kempis explained that "in matters concerning two evils, the lesser is always to be chosen."[179] If we cannot avoid evil entirely, we should try to minimize it. Bednar puts it this way: "God does not will only the intrinsically good; sometimes God wills the lesser of two evils when only evil alternatives exist. When good alternatives do not exist in a given situation, God wills the least evil alternative that does exist."[180] But can this principle ever apply to killing? Augustine of Hippo, who is sometimes called the "father of the just war theory," was a fourth-century North African bishop who wrote extensively about theology, sacraments, and ethics. Augustine's treatment of the sin of killing and his simultaneous justification of the use of force represents an early example of the principle that came to be known as the principle of "toleration of the lesser evil." Sometimes, Augustine reasoned, Christians have to use violence (which is sinful) in order to prevent a greater evil.[181]

The principle of toleration has been invoked in a variety of contexts: from a physician explaining to a patient the lesser evil of condom use in comparison to the greater evil of spreading disease from unprotected sexual activity;[182] to clean syringe programs as a method of tolerating the lesser evil of substance use while limiting the greater harm of the spread of hepatitis and HIV through substance use;[183] to the lesser evil of taking the life of a fetus while limiting the greater harm of allowing both mother and fetus to die;[184] to the lesser evil of tolerating a second "irregular" marriage in comparison to the greater evil of dissolving the second marriage.[185] Bednar explains that when we are talking about moral dilemmas, "whatever [the people involved] do is wrong. Dilemmas have no solutions. They can only be managed, not solved."[186] The way out of a dilemma is to choose the lesser of two evils; "the merciful application of the law can tolerate what the law does not permit."[187]

Cooperation (Cooperatio in malum)

The principle of cooperation developed in the Catholic moral tradition as a way to minimize the harm of the evil actions of another or distance oneself from that evil. To cooperate with evil means to assist in the sin of another; in some cases, this is tolerated to prevent a greater evil. Theologian James Bretzke explains that "in many circumstances, one lacks sufficient power to rectify the evil or ignorant intention of the person(s) or institutions engaged in the violations of the moral order."[188] A person engages in *formal cooperation* when they share in the sinful intent of the principal agent of the immoral act; formal cooperation is always illicit. *Material cooperation* is the objective aid that is given or allowed to enable the immoral act, and can be licit. Bretzke further explains that "the closer or more essential the cooperation rendered is to the evil act, the greater the responsibility."[189] *Mediate material cooperation* is when the person's cooperation is closely connected to the evil act, whereas *remote material cooperation* is further away from the evil act. Theologian Julie Hanlon Rubio summarizes: "We have a duty not to contribute to the harm of others that cannot be lightly excused."[190] Still, in the manualist tradition, sometimes material cooperation was considered justifiable given the situational dilemma.

Double Effect

The principle of double effect was developed for situations of moral constraint in which the agent did not perceive a perfect course of action. When thinking about alternatives, this principle gives some parameters for what actions should be permitted and which should be forbidden. An unintended bad effect can be tolerated for serious proportionate reasons when the agent's direct intent is the good effect of the action. Thomas Aquinas invoked the principle of double effect when establishing the right of personal self-defense:

> Nothing hinders a single act from having two effects, only one of which is intended, while the other is beside the intention. Now moral acts get their character in accordance with what is intended, but not from what is beside the intention since the latter is incidental. . . . Accordingly, the act of self-defense may have a double effect: the saving of one's life, on the one hand, and the slaying of the attacker, on the other. Since saving one's life is what is intended, such an act is not therefore illicit, seeing that it is natural to everything to keep itself in existence as far as possible.[191]

As moralists began to employ the tradition in a variety of contexts, greater specificity emerged. Theologian Mark Allman summarizes the four required conditions of the principle of double effect as it is commonly rendered by Catholic moral theologians in medical ethics and just war theory today:

1. The action cannot be intrinsically evil.
2. The evil effect cannot be intended, even if it is foreseeable.
3. The good effect cannot be a direct result of the bad effect.
4. There has to be a very good or proportionate reason for pursuing this action that has both good and bad effects.[192]

In order to satisfy these criteria, a medical procedure must be good in itself (or at least neutral); only the good effect is intended and not the bad effect; the good and bad effects must occur simultaneously; and there should be a sufficiently serious reason for allowing the bad effect to occur. The *Directives* apply the principle of double effect in order to affirm that indirect abortion and indirect sterilization are licit; direct abortion and direct sterilization are illicit. Spontaneous abortion (miscarriage) is not a *moral* act, since it does not result from the freedom of the agent, and therefore carries no weight of sin or blame. The distinction between "direct" and "indirect" concerns the relationship of the agent's intention to the choice and execution of the action or moral object of the action. In Catholic hospitals, the directly intended termination of pregnancy before viability or the directly intended destruction of a viable fetus is never permitted.[193] However, "operations, treatments, and medications that have as their direct purpose the cure of a proportionately serious pathological condition of a pregnant woman are permitted when they cannot be safely postponed until the unborn child is viable, even if they will result in the death of the unborn child."[194] This assertion means that a medical procedure to cure a pathological condition experienced during pregnancy (for example, administering chemotherapy to treat a pregnant mother's cancer) can sometimes be permitted, even though it has the unintended effect of prenatal death. When politicians and clerical leaders discuss "abortion" in the abstract, these important distinctions (between direct and indirect abortion) can be lost.

A complicating factor is that the *Directives* do not offer a list of medical procedures or example cases, and practices vary across hospitals based on factors that are usually not transparent to potential patients. The interpretation of the *Directives* by the local bishop, hospital board of directors, ethics board, legal team, and health care provider(s) may not align with each other, and may not align with the patient's own decisions for medical treatment. The most recent version of the *Directives* gives final authority to the local bishop for their "interpretation and applications."[195]

An "indirect abortion," which is also called a "therapeutic abortion" by some authors in the tradition, developed as a moral term historically when theologians sought to preserve the moral norm that abortion was wrong while also upholding the value of a pregnant woman's life. For example, Antoninus of Florence (1389–1459) endorsed a position held by John of Naples regarding a therapeutic abortion of an unformed fetus; a debate among moralists ensued regarding what constituted the grounds and means of a therapeutic abortion.[196] For many decades, the exemplar cases taught in seminaries were the licit removal of a fallopian tube to treat ectopic pregnancy, and the licit removal of a cancerous uterus of a pregnant woman, to treat cancer. In both cases, prenatal demise is unintended but foreseen; proportionate reasons justify the action taken in order to save the pregnant woman's life. John Noonan's historical analysis shows that there was strong support for weighing the life of the mother over prenatal life in cases between 1450 and 1895, but that a growing absolutism emerged over time. Noonan is clear that "in Catholic moral theology, as it developed, life even of the innocent was not taken as absolute." But he documents a move toward moral absolutism in the twentieth century.[197] Thomas Slater, SJ, an influential moralist, declared in his manual in 1898 that directly procuring an abortion was an intrinsic evil but noted that a pregnant woman may appropriate life-saving means even if the means were indirectly to cause the fetus's death. But he argued against the direct killing of a fetus to save the mother's life "even if otherwise both child and mother were certain to die."[198] The *Directives* uphold Slater's norm, even though theologians and clinical ethicists have defended the position that in a case in which the fetus is expected to die, the moral course of action should be to save the only life that can be saved, the mother's.[199]

The application of these various principles from the tradition raises practical questions for health care providers today. Is it sufficient simply to invoke the principle of toleration, or must one satisfy all conditions of the principle of double effect? Who determines which principle is applicable in a particular case? Church teachings since John Paul II have emphasized that it is not enough to simply assert one's intent to save a pregnant woman's life because other conditions must be met.

Medicine has advanced considerably since Slater's manual was published in 1898. New methods of treating ectopic pregnancy and cancer have required moral theologians to develop the way they invoke the principle of double effect. In the case of ectopic pregnancy, removal of the fallopian tube will have lasting consequences for the woman's fertility, so salpingectomy is no longer seen by many providers as a preferred choice, even as some ethicists defend the practice. Two other methods, salpingostomy and administration of methotrexate, continue to be debated among ethicists, since some argue that these methods constitute direct attack on the embryo, while others describe these procedures as indirect abortion.[200] Given this good faith disagreement between clinical ethicists and among bishops, informing potential patients about hospital policies should be a moral requirement. But too often, the determination about what kind of care is possible in a particular Catholic hospital is not transparent to patients in advance of care.

In defending the *Directives* against their critics, health care ethicist Ron Hamel does not express a desire for immediate reform of practice. "In cases of obstetrical complications, Catholic hospitals will attempt to save both lives [mother an unborn] when that is possible. In the vast majority of cases, this is exactly what the mother/parents want."[201] Regarding reported cases of maternal distress and threats to maternal health, Hamel speculates:

> The situations that these and other authors describe are rarely the result of the *Ethical and Religious Directives* themselves, though these tragic events have been attributed precisely to observance of the *Directives*. In some instances, there may have been a lack of knowledge about what specific *Directives* actually say, or a misunderstanding or misapplication of the certain *Directives*. But this is not the fault of those *Directives* that are relevant to early pregnancy complications. In other instances, the *Directives* simply made and make an easy target. The cause of these situations, assuming they occurred as described, may have had nothing to do with the *Directives* or with the hospital's being Catholic.[202]

Hamel faults the medical professionals who misinterpreted the *Directives*, not the *Directives* themselves. But he does not acknowledge that the *Directives* are crafted not to inform the discernment for physicians but to "direct" their decision-making. If the pedagogical function of the document is unclear, or the principles confusing for people practicing medicine in a Catholic hospital, this should be a significant cause for concern for those who care about patient consent and patient well-being.

The *Directives* are an example of *reproductive injustice* because they remove decision-making from the pregnant patient, leaving her health care decisions to be made by more powerful others (ultimately, the local bishop). In this framework, many defenders of the Church's position will emphasize that pregnancy is one of the possible consequences of sexual activity, and because of this biological reality, they say that a pregnant person "consented" to the possible pregnancy when she had sex.[203] The passivity to the naturally unfolding process of gestation expected of the woman—to provide life support to contingent life without considering her own desires, values, or needs—derives from a physicalist natural law understanding of sexuality whereby intervention in any "natural" process is interpreted as opposition to God's divine law, known by reflection on the natural processes of the human body and the natural world.[204] Add to these the papal teachings on what it means to be "feminine" (pure, self-sacrificial love, always directed to the "other" and not to oneself)[205] and we see a construction of gender norms that leave women little room for real agency. Such a claim can make a pregnant woman feel as if she has no "choice" in Catholic teachings; once conception occurs, women are told that they only have one moral option in front of them.[206] Critics have argued that when a pregnant woman's life is endangered by pregnancy, the principles of the just war tradition should offer some tools of moral reasoning to guide her in an argument of self-defense, which was justified in scholastic theology, as we've seen before. But the moral manual authored by Thomas Slater before Vatican II explained his counter-position in this way:

> In no sense can it be allowed that the child is an unjust assailant of a mother's life; it is where nature placed it, through no fault of its own, and it has a right to be there and to be born. If either is an unjust assailant of the other's life, it is the mother, who voluntarily undertook the obligations of motherhood.[207]

Slater's analysis of fetal innocence has had damaging consequences in the Catholic tradition, consequences that we continue to see today in the *Directives* employed in Catholic hospitals. Slater references the just war tradition here, but argues that principles from that tradition that lead moralists to permit killing for proportionate reasons cannot be applied in the case of abortion. The unborn child is "innocent" and is endangered by the pregnant woman "through no fault of its own." It has the "right to be there and to be born." John Paul II adopts this analysis of prenatal innocence in *Evangelium Vitae*. But it is worth exploring whether it would ever make sense to argue that "the child is an unjust assailant of a mother's life." Does the papal claim of prenatal innocence hold absolutely? What would justify such a claim?

Christian ethicist Lloyd Steffen has analyzed the argument, unpacking how "innocence" functions in the just war theory, which is a moral framework that always seeks a just and peaceful resolution of conflict but recognizes that sometimes force is justified for limited and specific purposes.[208] In just war theory, directly intending to harm noncombatants is wrong.[209] But Steffen explains that while innocent bystanders are moral agents and members of the community who have a right not to be harmed, the just war tradition does not absolutize their claim to a right to life.[210] He applies this reasoning to prenatal life as well, noting that a prenate can pose a material threat to a pregnant woman.[211] In such a case, appeals to a right to life do not resolve the moral conflict. Steffen argues that life is not an absolute value that trumps other values.[212] Papal teachings since John Paul II have absolutized the prenate in this way, which elevates a prenate to a position *above* the moral category of person.[213]

Steffen's argument gets to the heart of the problem of Catholic teachings on abortion: moral absolutes are never invoked in favor of the pregnant woman but only in favor of prenatal life. In this framework, a women's value is not intrinsic but transactional and instrumental. Women are there as helpers to men, as bodies to provide life support to others, and as breeders for society.[214] For them to have dreams and ambitions of their own, or to advocate for their own lives in self-defense, is contrary to the pope's understanding of a woman's rightful place.[215]

We have lost our way—the *Directives* do not help moralists and clinicians to resolve *all* of the values at stake, inclusive of women's dignity and moral agency. Restating principles as if their application is straightforward is damaging patient care in Catholic hospitals. In the Catholic tradition, as theologian Richard McBrien has explained, "no teaching of the Church can hope to account for every moral situation and circumstance." He continues: "Every teaching still has to be applied in particular cases. One is not necessarily repudiating the values affirmed in the teaching if one decides that the teaching does not bind or apply in a particular instance."[216] We need to open the process so that clinicians can apply this understanding of moral complexity in hard cases—seeking to affirm the values of life, dignity, and justice even though the principles as currently stated in the *Directives* do not apply in every instance. We need a new approach that privileges the patient's discernment, the patient's conscience, the medical team's role in accompaniment, and proportionate reason as a valuable tool to weigh values and disvalues in a complex discernment. I am particularly concerned that the moral vocabulary used to describe abortion (murder, crime, mortal sin) unnecessarily shames women who reasoned they had no viable alternatives (no real choices given their situations of constraint) and delays or obstructs their spiritual healing after abortion. In other words, our moral language has become a barrier to people's reconciliation with God, undermining human flourishing.

It is also important to note that moral teachings on abortion from a particular religious community do not easily translate to appropriate laws for a pluralist democracy. While it is appropriate for Catholic bishops to explain Catholic teachings in the public square, working to build consensus on topics that are morally fraught is far more difficult. What would bring greater legitimacy to Catholic teachings in the public square is a moral method that is attentive to plurality and ambiguity. We need leaders who are comfortable with the qualifiers *"in most cases*, X is wrong" and "our Church teaches the inherent value of the human person, which is why *we continue to debate this complicated issue* and respect the consciences of people who approach this moral question from very different positions." Pastors who can lead people through a principled discernment and encourage moral growth over time would be doing a great service for the people of God and for the public good. "The key," according to Cristina Traina, "is to walk between tentativeness and absolutism: to develop descriptions credible and detailed enough to yield morally normative, prophetic claims yet flexible enough to accommodate a degree of cultural pluralism and historical change."[217]

CONCLUSION

In John 8:1–11, a group of men bring a woman to Jesus, saying, "Teacher, this woman was caught in the very act of committing adultery. Now in the law Moses commanded us to stone such women. Now what do you say?" (Jn 8:4–5 NRSV-CE). While this case is not about abortion, it does show us a situation in which Jesus responds when a woman's life is threatened. Does she have a right to self-defense? Jesus is critical of patriarchal oppression here and throughout the four gospels. In this scene, he is critical of the death-dealing rules enforced on women by men. "Let anyone among you who is without sin be the first to throw a stone at her" (Jn 8:8 NRSV-CE). Jesus asks the men to reevaluate their own roles in violence; he uses creative means to liberate the woman accused of adultery and in so doing affirms her life even after allegedly wrong behavior. "Neither do I condemn you. Go on your way, and from now on do not sin again" (Jn 8:11 NRSV-CE). Jesus does not condemn but enables her journey to continue. Just as Jesus was sensitive to the social conditions in which he preached, healed, and ministered, so too moralists today must advance justice with regard to the social conditions of sexual and reproductive health.

Magisterial teachings on abortion in the past fifty years do not reflect this way of thinking about the ministry of Jesus and his care for women. Magisterial teachings have instead rendered women as less than persons by privileging prenatal life over pregnant women's lives. Catholic leaders have advanced policies that limit the reproductive agency of women and elevate the moral status of contingent prenatal life. Magisterial teachings have overstated key claims and fostered shame for women in the pews. Magisterial teachings use prophetic speech that oversimplifies complex realities and masks the traumatic choices many women face. Magisterial teachings use language that undermines the healing of women who have procured abortion, further alienating women who may seek comfort in their religious community at a difficult time in their lives. Popes and bishops have made the "culture of life" an idol, sacrificing moral clarity and compassion in the process.

Moral absolutism is not a traditional method of doing moral theology. It is a *distortion* of the tradition that has gained traction in the past fifty years. Seminary professor Gerald J. Bednar has wisely cautioned that "the application of abstract principles regardless of circumstances tends to cruelty."[218] The Catholic moral tradition contains immense resources for contemporary believers who seek to expand our understanding of moral discernment, including the principles of toleration, cooperation, and double effect described above. We need a new way forward on discourse about sexual and reproductive health in the Catholic Church, a way forward that moves away from moral absolutism but that remains true to the Catholic tradition broadly understood, a tradition ever mindful of the way that Jesus responded creatively and compassionately when presented with moral dilemmas.

NOTES

1. Guttmacher Institute, "Interactive Map: US Abortion Policies and Access After Roe"(July 25, 2023), https://states.guttmacher.org/policies/?gclid=Cj0KCQjwjIKYBhC6ARIsAGEds-LPK2Tl_JUaGUfpIim3TDpYywH9bEXExPt2T_GHH1r01kaomSVeDtUaArN-EALw_wcB.

2. Testimony of Dr. Valerie Williams, within court filings as part of a challenge to the Louisiana trigger law. Sam Karlin, "With Abortion Access on the Line in Louisiana, Lawyers Debate in Court if Ban is Ambiguous," *The Advocate* (July 18, 2022), https://www.theadvocate.com/baton_rouge/news/article_e6ab3b78-06bf-11ed-82b2-1ff4e4f596d6.html.

3. Jessica Winter, "The Dobbs Decision Has Unleashed Legal Chaos for Doctors and Patients," *The New Yorker*, July 2, 2022: https://www.newyorker.com/news/news-desk/the-dobbs-decision-has-unleashed-legal-chaos-for-doctors-and-patients.

4. Reese Oxner and Maria Mednez, "Texas Hospitals Are Putting Pregnant Patients at Risk," *Texas Tribune* (July 15, 2022), https://www.texastribune.org/2022/07/15/texas-hospitals-abortion-laws/.

5. Sarah McCammon, "More Women Sue Texas Saying the State's Anti-Abortion Laws Harmed Them," All Things Considered, NPR News (May 22, 2023), https://www.npr.org/2023/05/22/1177425651/texas-women-sue-abortion.

6. Dave Muoio, "Dobbs Decision Opened the Door for Complete and Utter Chaos," July 20, 2022. *Fierce Healthcare*: https://www.fiercehealthcare.com/providers/dobbs-decision-opened-door-complete-and-utter-chaos-physicians-and-legal-experts-tell.

7. Dr. CeCe Cheng, a maternal fetal medicine specialist in San Antonio, quoted in Sneha Dey and Karen Brooks Harper, "Abortion Restrictions Threaten Care," *Texas Tribune* (May 24, 2022), https://www.texastribune.org/2022/05/24/texas-abortion-law-pregnancy-care/. See also the story of Elizabeth and James Weller in Carrie Feibel, "Because of Texas Abortion Law, Her Wanted Pregnancy Became a Medical Nightmare," National Public Radio (July 26, 2022), https://www.npr.org/sections/health-shots/2022/07/26/1111280165/because-of-texas-abortion-law-her-wanted-pregnancy-became-a-medical-nightmare.

8. More than 150 rural hospitals closed between 2005 and 2019, and another nineteen shut down in 2020. See Dennis Thompson, "Hundreds of Hospitals Across America Close," *US News and World Report* (January 16, 2023), https://www.usnews.com/news/health-news/articles/2023-01-16/hundreds-of-hospitals-could-close-across-rural-america#:~:text=More%20than%20150%20rural%20hospitals,received%20while%20the%20pandemic%20raged. More than 600 rural hospitals—nearly 30 percent of rural hospitals nationwide—are at risk of closing in the near future, according to the Center for Healthcare Quality and Payment Reform. See Marcus Robertson, "631 Hospitals At Risk of Closure, State by State," Becker's Healthcare Report (January 3, 2023), https://www.beckershospitalreview.com/finance/631-hospitals-at-risk-of-closure-state-by-state.html?utm_medium=email&utm_content=newsletter.

9. Hailey Mensik, "Staffing Overtakes Financial Challenges as Top Concern," Health Care Dive (February 7, 2022), https://www.healthcaredive.com/news/staffing-shortages-top-concern-for-hospital-CEOs-COVID/618402/.

10. United States Conference of Catholic Bishops, "About Us," https://www.usccb.org/about.

11. USCCB, "USCCB Statement on U.S. Supreme Court Ruling in Dobbs v. Jackson" (June 24, 2022), https://www.usccb.org/news/2022/usccb-statement-us-supreme-court-ruling-dobbs-v-jackson. Their December 2021 statement asked Catholics to pray and said, "We pray that the Court will do the right thing and allow states to once again limit or prohibit abortion, and in doing so protect millions of unborn children and their mothers from this painful, life-destroying act. We invite all people of good will to uphold the dignity of human life by joining us in prayer and fasting for this important case." USCCB, "U.S. Bishops' Pro-Life Chairman on Supreme Court's Dobbs Case" (December 1, 2021), https://www.usccb.org/news/2021/us-bishops-pro-life-chairman-supreme-courts-dobbs-case. Their March statement in anticipation of

the ruling was called "Standing with Moms in Need" and can be found here: https://www.usccb.org/resources/statement-standing-with-moms-031522.pdf.

12. Selene Simmons-Duffin, "Her Miscarriage Left Her Bleeding Profusely. An Ohio ER Sent Her Home to Wait," National Public Radio (November 15, 2022), https://www.npr.org/sections/health-shots/2022/11/15/1135882310/miscarriage-hemorrhage-abortion-law-ohio.

13. More information continues to emerge about clerical sexual abuse during John Paul II's papacy, the lack of due process accorded to theologians and women religious who were investigated by the Curia, and other aspects of his leadership. See Ekke Overbeek, *Maxima Culpa* (Wydawnictwo Agora: 2024), https://kulturalnysklep.pl/product-pol-99723-Maxima-Culpa-Jan-Pawel-II-wiedzial.html. See also Agnieszka Pikulicka-Wilczewska, "New Book on Pope John Paul II Stirs Up Heated Debate in Polish Politics," Reuters (March 9, 2023), https://kulturalnysklep.pl/product-pol-99723-Maxima-Culpa-Jan-Pawel-II-wiedzial.html. Regarding women religious, see Christine Schenk, CSJ, *To Speak the Truth in Love: A Biography of Theresa Kane, RSM* (Maryknoll: Orbis, 2019).

14. Benedict XVI, from Speech to Participants at the International Congress, "Oil in the Wounds: A Response to the Aftermath of Abortion and Divorce," organized by the Pontifical John Paul II Institute for Studies on Marriage and the Family and the Knights of Columbus (April 5, 2008). http://www.vatican.va/holy_father/benedict_xvi/speeches/2008/april/documents/hf_ben-xvi_spe_20080405_istituto-gpii_it.html. Catholic feminist theologian Tina Beattie notes that in his 2009 encyclical *Caritas in Veritate*, Benedict XVI made reference to abortion without showing concern for high rates of maternal mortality or discussing access to reproductive health care for women. See Tina Beattie, "Catholicism, Choice, and Consciousness: A Feminist Theological Perspective on Abortion," *International Journal of Public Theology* 4 (2010): 51–75, at 52, referencing Benedict, XVI, *Caritas in Veritate* (2009), https://www.vatican.va/content/benedict-xvi/en/encyclicals/documents/hf_ben-xvi_enc_20090629_caritas-in-veritate.html.

15. Philip Pullella, "Pope Says Abortion Is 'Murder' but the US Bishops Should Not Be Political," Reuters (September 15, 2019), https://www.reuters.com/world/europe/pope-says-abortion-is-murder-us-bishops-should-not-be-political-2021-09-15/.

16. John Paul II, *Evangelium Vitae* (On the Inviolability of Human Life), 1995, par. 58. Available online: https://www.vatican.va/content/john-paul-ii/en/encyclicals/documents/hf_jp-ii_enc_25031995_evangelium-vitae.html#%24II.

17. The medications and surgical procedures that are sometimes required to prevent infection and protect the life of the mother who experiences pregnancy loss through spontaneous abortion can be identical to the medications and surgical procedures that women who terminate their pregnancies elect: for example, Mifepristone and Misoprostol for medicated abortions and suction dilation and curettage (D&C) for surgical abortions. Sometimes women facing pregnancy loss due to spontaneous abortion have unnecessary limitations on their care or delays on their treatment plans because of state regulations mandating waiting periods, verified ultrasounds, and other requirements to complete care. There is no basis for this in official Church teachings. In

countries in which abortion is illegal, women who have experienced miscarriage can be "reported" by medical staff to the police and are at risk of incarceration if they cannot "prove" that their pregnancy loss was due to spontaneous abortion. See Jennifer Wright, "Women Who Miscarry Could Be Criminally Investigated Under Georgia's New Abortion Law," *Harper's Bazaar* (May 15, 2019), https://www.harpersbazaar.com/culture/politics/a27454956/what-does-georgias-abortion-law-mean-women-who-miscarry/.

18. John Paul II, *Evangelium vitae*, 62.

19. Vincent Genovesi, *In Pursuit of Love: Catholic Morality and Human Sexuality*, second ed. (Collegeville: Liturgical, 1996), 369.

20. M. Therese Lysaught, "Moral Analysis of Procedure at a Phoenix Hospital," *Origins* 40, no. 33 (2011): 537–52, 542.

21. John Haldane and Patrick Lee, "Aquinas on Human Ensoulment, Abortion, and the Value of Life," *Philosophy* 78:2 (2003): 278. Genovesi summarizes the traditional position as "better two deaths than one murder" (in other words, better for the pregnant woman to die with the prenate than directly attack prenatal life to save the pregnant woman). Genovesi, *In Pursuit*, 383. An example can be seen in the 1971 and 1975 *Ethical and Religious Directives*: "Regarding the treatment of hemorrhage during pregnancy and before the fetus is viable: Procedures that are designed to empty the uterus of a living fetus still effectively attached to the mother are not permitted; procedures designed to stop hemorrhage (as distinguished from those designed precisely to expel the living and attached fetus) are permitted insofar as necessary, even if fetal death is inevitably a side effect." United States Catholic Conference, *Ethical and Religious Directives* (1971), cited in Genovesi, *In Pursuit*, 383–84. John Haas invokes similar reasoning in describing abortion in the case of cardiomyopathy as "direct abortion." See John M. Haas, "Moral Theological Analysis of Direct versus Indirect Abortion," *Linacre Quarterly* 84:3 (2017): 248–60, at 250–51. In the same article, Haas explains the moral reasoning of Catholic moralists who identify craniotomy as indirect abortion (for example, Martin Rhonheimer), though Haas's own position is that craniotomy should be described as a direct abortion. Margaret Kamitsuka explains that even Tertullian described an embryotomy procedure as "a cruel necessity," noting that he is an example of early church leaders who conceded that some abortions may be necessary. Margaret D. Kamitsuka, *Abortion and the Christian Tradition: A Pro-Choice Theological Ethic* (Louisville: Westminster John Knox, 2019), 43, 45.

22. John Paul II, *Evangelium vitae*, 58. See also Pius XI, *Casti Connubii* (1930), nos. 63–64: https://www.vatican.va/content/pius-xi/en/encyclicals/documents/hf_p-xi_enc_19301231_casti-connubii.html.

23. Francis, *Amoris Laetitia* (2016), 83, https://www.vatican.va/content/dam/francesco/pdf/apost_exhortations/documents/papa-francesco_esortazione-ap_20160319_amoris-laetitia_en.pdf. Pope Francis reaffirms that every life is sacred and an end in itself, so no human person should be treated as property.

24. *Catechism of the Catholic Church* (1993), no. 2270. https://www.vatican.va/archive/ENG0015/_INDEX.HTM.

25. Congregation for the Doctrine of the Faith (CDF), *Donum Vitae* (1987), I.,1. https://www.vatican.va/roman_curia/congregations/cfaith/documents/rc_con_cfaith_doc_19870222_respect-for-human-life_en.html. The person who has the "right" to life in this framing is the unborn life.

26. Cathleen Kaveny, "Toward a Thomistic Perspective on Abortion and the Law in Contemporary America," *The Thomist* 55, no. 3 (1991): 343–96.

27. John Paul II, *Evangelium vitae*, 55.

28. CDF, Instruction *Dignitas Personae*: On Certain Bioethical Questions (2008), 5: https://www.vatican.va/roman_curia/congregations/cfaith/documents/rc_con_cfaith_doc_20081208_dignitas-personae_en.html.

29. CDF, *Dignitas Personae*, 1.

30. *Donum Vitae* acknowledges that fertilization can take place outside the woman's body, as happens in the case of in vitro fertilization procedures, but these are described as illicit since they separate reproduction from the marital act (also described as the conjugal act, or intercourse). CDF, *Donum vitae*, 5–8.

31. Second Vatican Ecumenical Council, Pastoral Constitution on the Church in the Modern World *Gaudium et Spes* (December 7, 1965), 51, "Abortus necnon infanticidium nefanda sunt crimina." https://www.vatican.va/archive/hist_councils/ii_vatican_council/documents/vat-ii_const_19651207_gaudium-et-spes_en.html.

32. *Catechism*, no. 2258, citing *Donum Vitae*, 5.

33. John Paul II, *Evangelium vitae*, 52–53, 55.

34. CDF, *Dignitas Personae*, 23. The CDF distinguishes between *interceptive* medications that interfere with the embryo before implantation and *contragestative* medications that cause the elimination of the embryo once implanted. Both are said to "fall within the sin of abortion and are gravely immoral" with serious penalties in canon law.

35. *Catechism*, 1857.

36. Translation by James T. Bretzke, SJ, in *Handbook of Roman Catholic Moral Terms* (Washington, DC: Georgetown University Press, 2013), 172. See also Patrick J. Boyle, *Parvitas Materiae in Sexto in Contemporary Catholic Thought* (Lanham, MD: University Press of America, 1987).

37. An example of catechetical materials employing this analysis can be found in Archdiocese of St. Paul & Minneapolis, "What Is the Sixth Commandment?" (2006), https://www.archspm.org/faith-and-discipleship/catholic-faith/what-is-the-sixth-commandment-what-does-it-mean-for-my-life-how-does-the-virtue-of-chastity-apply/.

38. John Paul II, *Evangelium vitae*, 58. Francis, as quoted in Junno Arocho Esteves, "Pope Francis Speaks about Abortion and Communion," *America* (September 15, 2021), https://www.americamagazine.org/politics-society/2021/09/15/pope-francis-joe-biden-bishops-communion-241424

39. John Paul II, *Evangelium vitae*, 58.

40. John Paul II, *Evangelium vitae*, 62.

41. John Paul II, *Evangelium vitae*, 62.

42. CDF, *Dignitas Personae*, 23.

43. Richard M. Gula, *Reason Informed by Faith: Foundations of Catholic Morality* (New York: Paulist, 1989), chapters 7–8.

44. CDF, *Dignitas Personae*, 23.

45. *Code of Canon Law*, no. 1398.

46. Harry Bruinius, "In Change on Abortion, Pope Francis Sends Big Message," *Christian Science Monitor* (November 21, 2016), https://www.csmonitor.com/USA/Society/2016/1121/In-change-on-abortion-Pope-Francis-sends-big-message.

47. John Paul II, *Veritatis Splendor* (1993), 80. https://www.vatican.va/content/john-paul-ii/en/encyclicals/documents/hf_jp-ii_enc_06081993_veritatis-splendor.html.

48. John Paul II, *Veritatis Splendor*, 80, quoting *Gaudium et spes*, 27. Nenad Polgar and Joseph A. Selling, eds., *The Concept of Intrinsic Evil and Catholic Theological Ethics* (Lanham: Lexington, 2019).

49. Christopher West, *Good News about Sex and Marriage: Answers to Your Honest Questions about Catholic Teaching*, Rev. ed. (Cincinnati: Servant Books, 2004), 17.

50. Congregation for Catholic Education, *Male and Female He Created Them: Towards a Path of Dialogue on the Question of Gender Theory in Education* (Vatican, 2019), https://www.vatican.va/roman_curia/congregations/ccatheduc/documents/rc_con_ccatheduc_doc_20190202_maschio-e-femmina_en.pdf.

51. John Paul II, *Mulieris Dignitatem* (15 August 1988), 14: https://www.vatican.va/content/john-paul-ii/en/apost_letters/1988/documents/hf_jp-ii_apl_19880815_mulieris-dignitatem.html. Emily Reimer-Barry, "*Mulieris Dignitatem* and *Redemptoris Custos*," in *Catholic Family Teachings*, ed. Jacob Kolhaas and Mary Doyle Roche (Washington, DC: Georgetown University Press, 2023), forthcoming.

52. Francis, *Amoris Laetitia*, 55, 173.

53. Laura L. Garcia, "Authentic Freedom and Equality in Difference," in *Women, Sex, and the Church: A Case for Catholic Teaching*, ed. Erika Bachiochi (Boston: Pauline, 2010), 15–33, at 21.

54. Janet E. Smith and Christopher Kaczor, *Life Issues, Medical Choice: Questions and Answers for Catholics* (Cincinnati: Servant Media, 2016). Chapter 2 focuses on abortion, but a physicalist approach to the natural law and God's design for sexuality and bioethics can be found throughout. See also Christopher Kaczor, *The Ethics of Abortion: Women's Rights, Human Life, and the Question of Justice* (New York: Routledge, 2014).

55. Erika Bachiochi, "The Uniqueness of Woman: Church Teaching on Abortion," in Erika Bachiochi, ed., *Women, Sex, and the Church: A Case for Catholic Teaching* (Boston: Pauline, 2010), 37–55, at 43.

56. Garcia, "Authentic Freedom," 27.

57. Janet E. Smith, *Why Humanae Vitae Is Still Right* (San Francisco: Ignatius Press, 2018).

58. Bachiochi, "The Uniqueness," 40.

59. Bachiochi, "The Uniqueness," 54.

60. Bachiochi, "The Uniqueness," 55.

61. Bachiochi, "The Uniqueness," 54.

62. Bachiochi, "The Uniqueness," 54.

63. Bachiochi, "The Uniqueness," 50.
64. John Paul II, *Mulieris Dignitatem*, 18.
65. Congregation for Catholic Education, *Male and Female He Created Them*, 18.
66. Sidney Callahan, "Abortion and the Sexual Agenda: A Case for Pro-Life Feminism," *Readings in Moral Theology, No. 9: Feminist Ethics and the Catholic Moral Tradition*, eds. Charles E. Curran, Margaret A. Farley, and Richard A. McCormick, SJ (New York: Paulist, 1996), 422–39, at 430.
67. Nicholas M. Ramirez, "Teleology and the Problem of Bodily-Rights Arguments," *National Catholic Bioethics Quarterly* (Spring 2023): 83–97, at 84.
68. Charles Camosy, *Resisting Throwaway Culture: How a Consistent Life Ethic Can Unite a Fractured People* (New York: New City Press, 2019). Chapter 4 focuses on abortion, and the first chapter explain a consistent ethic of life. See also "Fighting the Language Battle for Prenatal Justice," *Catholic Review* (January 12, 2023), https://catholicreview.org/fighting-the-language-battle-for-prenatal-justice/.
69. Charles C. Camosy and David McPherson, "Consistent-Life-Ethic Catholics Can (and Should) Treat Abortion as Today's Preeminent Priority," *America* (July 8, 2021), https://www.americamagazine.org/faith/2021/07/08/abortion-politics-us-bishops-eucharist-ethics-240991. It is worth noting that when Francis uses the phrase "Equally Sacred" in *Gaudete et Exultate* (101), he does so in order to name issues other than abortion that should receive equal attention, including poverty, human trafficking, and more. See Francis, *Gaudete et Exultate* (2018), https://www.vatican.va/content/francesco/en/apost_exhortations/documents/papa-francesco_esortazione-ap_20180319_gaudete-et-exsultate.html.
70. Charles C. Camosy, *Beyond the Abortion Wars: A Way Forward for a New Generation* (Grand Rapids: Eerdmans, 2015), 90.
71. Albert S. Moraczewski, OP and Richard M. Doerflinger, "The Fetal and Embryonic Human Being," in Edward J. Furton, ed., *Catholic Health Care Ethics*, third ed. (Philadelphia: The National Catholic Bioethics Center, 2020), 9.1–9.13, at 9.3.
72. Callahan, "Abortion," 432.
73. There are seven sacraments in the Roman Catholic tradition: Baptism, Reconciliation, Eucharist, Confirmation, Marriage, Holy Orders, and Anointing of the Sick. In the church's theology, the sacraments provide special opportunities for graced encounters with God. During the renewal of Vatican II, *Sacrosanctum Concilium* reaffirmed this sacramental theology even as some rites were revised: "the purpose of the sacraments is to sanctify men [sic], to build up the body of Christ, and, finally, to give worship to God; because they are signs they also instruct." Paul VI, *Sacrosanctum Concilium* (December 4, 1963), 59. https://www.vatican.va/archive/hist_councils/ii_vatican_council/documents/vat-ii_const_19631204_sacrosanctum-concilium_en.html.
74. USCCB Secretariat of Pro-Life Activities (2023), https://www.respectlife.org/.
75. USCCB, Walking with Moms in Need (2021), https://www.walkingwithmoms.com/newsletters.
76. Eternal Word Television Network, "Pro-Life Weekly," https://www.ewtn.com/tv/shows/ewtn-pro-life-weekly.

77. Dalia Fahmy, "8 Key Findings about Catholics and Abortion," Pew Research Center (October 20, 2020), https://www.pewresearch.org/fact-tank/2020/10/20/8-key-findings-about-catholics-and-abortion/.

78. March for Life Education and Defense Fund (2023), https://marchforlife.org/.

79. USCCB, Religious Liberty (2023), https://www.usccb.org/committees/religious-liberty.

80. USCCB Secretariat of Pro-Life Activities, "Respect Life Month Resources" (2023), https://www.respectlife.org/respect-life-month.

81. USCCB, "Word of Life: Special Edition Dobbs Parish Leader Kit" (2022), https://www.usccb.org/resources/dobbs-parish-leader-kit-wol-special-edition.pdf. According to the toolkit, these intentions "are appropriate for inclusion in the Prayer of the Faithful at Sunday Mass. They can also be printed in the weekly bulletin, included in parish Holy Hours or Rosaries, featured in email newsletters, shared on social media platforms, or prayed during personal or family prayer."

82. USCCB, "Word of Life: Special Edition Dobbs Parish Leader Kit" (2022), https://www.usccb.org/resources/dobbs-parish-leader-kit-wol-special-edition.pdf.

83. Jim McDermott, "Senator Dick Durbin on Being Denied Communion Over Abortion Stance: 'I am careful when I go to a church.'" *America* (November 8, 2021), https://www.americamagazine.org/politics-society/2021/11/08/dick-durbin-denied-communion-abortion-241795. Durbin is able to receive communion in the Archdiocese of Chicago, given that policies vary by bishop.

84. Archbishop Cordileone to Nancy Pelosi, "Notification" (May 19, 2022), published in full by Catholic News Agency Staff (May 20, 2022), https://www.catholicnewsagency.com/news/251315/read-the-letter-from-pelosi-s-archbishop-barring-her-from-communion. He elaborates on the "medicine of excommunication" in his pastoral document. See Cordileone, "Before I Formed You in the Womb I Knew You" (2021), https://sfarchdiocese.org/wp-content/uploads/2021/09/Pastoral_Letter_LetterSize_0501.1.pdf.

85. Cordileone cites *Code of Canon Law*, canon 915, claiming that one who is committing grave sin is not to be admitted to Holy Communion; and canon 383, stating his own responsibility to be "concerned for all the Christian faithful entrusted to his care." Vatican, *Code of Canon Law*: https://www.vatican.va/archive/cod-iuris-canonici/cic_index_en.html.

86. CDF, *Doctrinal Note on Some Questions Regarding the Participation of Catholics in Political Life* (2002), https://www.vatican.va/roman_curia/congregations/cfaith/documents/rc_con_cfaith_doc_20021124_politica_en.html.

87. The letter was later published under the title "Worthiness to Receive Holy Communion: General Principles." Ratzinger, "Worthiness to Receive Holy Communion: General Principles," made public July 2004, published by Eternal Word Television Network: https://www.ewtn.com/catholicism/library/worthiness-to-receive-holy-communion-general-principles-2153. The original context for the letter was the US presidential election of 2004 when Catholic Democrat John Kerry was a candidate, and Ratzinger advances the position that Kerry should not be admitted to Holy Communion. The US bishops took the position in their annual meeting that year that each individual bishop would have the discretion to decide whether or not to

give communion to pro-abortion Catholic politicians. Their document, "Catholics in Political Life," passed with 183 votes in favor and 6 against. See USCCB, "Catholics in Political Life" (2004), https://www.usccb.org/issues-and-action/faithful-citizenship/church-teaching/catholics-in-political-life.

88. Francis, *Fratelli Tutti* (October 3, 2020), 108, 193–97. https://www.vatican.va/content/francesco/en/encyclicals/documents/papa-francesco_20201003_enciclica-fratelli-tutti.html.

89. Christopher White, "Pope Francis Says He Has Never Denied Communion," National Catholic Reporter, September 15, 2021: https://www.ncronline.org/news/vatican/pope-francis-says-he-has-never-denied-communion-warns-against-politicizing-eucharist. It is also noteworthy that Ratzinger's "Worthiness" references the case of divorced and remarried Catholics presenting themselves for communion, a topic that received attention in the Synod on the Family and the subsequent document *Amoris Laetitia* (2016), which opened up new possibilities for inclusion of divorced and remarried persons.

90. Mark Pattison, "Bishop McElroy: Don't Weaponize the Eucharist for Political Ends," *National Catholic Reporter* (May 6, 2021), https://www.ncronline.org/news/bishop-mcelroy-dont-weaponize-eucharist-political-ends.

91. Christopher White, "Despite Row at Home, Speaker Pelosi Receives Communion at Papal Mass," *National Catholic Reporter* (June 29, 2022), https://www.ncronline.org/news/vatican/despite-row-home-speaker-pelosi-receives-communion-papal-mass-headlines-vatican-events.

92. Kurt Stasiak, OSB, *A Confessor's Handbook: Revised and Expanded* (New York: Paulist, 2010), 95. Particularly troubling in this section of the text is the author's description of how limited he perceives his options if a penitent confesses to ongoing incest and abuse of his twelve-year old daughter. See Stasiak, 96–97.

93. Some priests are trained to ask invasive questions in order to determine the species of sin. Without a trauma-informed approach this is can be very problematic. One of the dictates of the Council of Trent was that penitents needed to give a complete account of their sins so that the priest could administer the proper penance. Charles Curran explains: "The penitent is a true culprit who accuses himself before the priest. The priest or minister is a true judge who authoritatively declares the sentence of granting or refusing absolution. The forgiveness itself is a judicial act that is authoritatively given according to the governing norms. The same session of Trent insisted on the integral confession of sins as necessary for the priest to carry out his role as judge. It condemned those who (like Luther) said that such a confession of all of one's sins is impossible. The Council maintained that by divine law, it is necessary to confess all and every mortal sin, even occult sins and those against the last two precepts of the Decalogue, and the circumstances that change the species of sin insofar as one can recall these with due and diligent examination." Charles Curran, *The Development of Moral Theology: Five Strands* (Washington, DC: Georgetown University Press, 2013), 18.

94. Francis, *Amoris Laetitia,* 52, 56, 80, 172–73, 250, 292; Congregation for Catholic Education, *Male and Female He Created Them,* 2; John Paul II, "Letter to Women"

(1995), https://www.vatican.va/content/john-paul-ii/en/letters/1995/documents/hf_jp-ii_let_29061995_women.html.

95. Confessors have to judge whether the sinner demonstrates "repentance" and "the desire to strive to abstain from sinning again." Pontifical Council for the Family, *Vademecum* for Confessors Concerning Some Aspects of the Morality of Conjugal Life (1997), https://www.vatican.va/roman_curia/pontifical_councils/family/documents/rc_pc_family_doc_12021997_vademecum_en.html. That document reads: "19. Regarding absolution for the sin of abortion, the obligation always exists to have regard for the canonical norms. If repentance is sincere and it is difficult to send the penitent to the competent authority to whom the absolution of the censure is reserved, every confessor can absolve according to can. 1357, suggesting an adequate penitential act, and indicating the necessity to have recourse, possibly offering to draft and forward it himself" (*Vademecum*, 19). The relevant note reads: "It is to be kept in mind that the faculty to absolve in the internal forum in this matter belongs '*ipso iure*,' as for all censures not reserved to the Holy See and not declared, to any bishop, even if only titular, and to the diocesan or collegiate Penitentiary (can. 508), as well as to chaplains of hospitals, of prisons and of voyagers (can. 566 § 2). Confessors belonging to a mendicant Order or to certain modern religious Congregations enjoy, by privilege, the faculty to absolve only for the censure regarding abortion" (*Vademecum*, n. 53).

96. Gaslighting means to manipulate someone into questioning their own sanity. If a woman expresses outrage that she was treated poorly in the confessional, but that harm is not acknowledged and instead she is told that she really did experience Jesus in the sacrament, even if it did not feel that way at all, this is gaslighting. It is a tactic of avoidance of responsibility by those in power.

97. Josh Johnson and Mike Schmitz, *Pocket Guide to the Sacrament of Reconciliation* (West Chester, PA: 2021), 140–41.

98. James F. Keenan, SJ, *A History of Catholic Theological Ethics* (New York: Paulist, 2022), chapter 7. Keenan cites the moral manual by Thomas Slater, SJ, which claimed: "The manuals of moral theology are technical works intended to help the confessor and the parish priest in the discharge of their duties. They are as technical as the text-books of the lawyer and the doctor. They are not intended for edification; nor do they hold up a high ideal of Christian perfection for the imitation of the faithful. They deal with what is of obligation under the pain of sin, they are books of moral pathology." Keenan, *A History*, 255.

99. Charles E. Curran, *Catholic Moral Theology in the United States: A History* (Washington, DC: Georgetown University Press, 2008), 2–6, 35–49.

100. Keenan, *A History*, 261.

101. The 1917 *Code of Canon Law* punished abortion with excommunication. Canon 2350, § 1. cited by John Paul II in *Evangelium Vitae,* 62. The 1983 *Code of Canon Law* was revised to state that "a person who procures a completed abortion incurs a *latae sententiae* excommunication." *Code of Canon Law*, canon 1398; cf. *Code of Canons of the Eastern Churches*, canon 1450, § 2. The canon immediately following 1398 is described as a general norm: "In addition to the cases established here or in other laws, the external violation of a divine or canonical law can be punished by a

just penalty only when the special gravity of the violation demands punishment and there is an urgent need to prevent or repair scandals." Canon 1399. Vatican, *Code of Canon Law*. https://www.vatican.va/archive/cod-iuris-canonici/eng/documents/cic_lib6-cann1364-1399_en.html. I am grateful for the reviewer who pointed out, after reading an earlier version of this text, that *latae sententiae* excommunication is often misleadingly translated as "automatic excommunication." A simple google search of "abortion and excommunication" will prove this reader's point. James T. Bretzke, SJ, explains that "canon law lists a number of situations that either mitigate or even block the imposition of penalties." See canons 1323 and 1324. See also "Canonical penalties" in Bretzke, *Handbook*, 26–27. See also John Huels, *The Pastoral Companion: A Canon Law Handbook for Catholic Ministry*, fourth ed. (Montreal: Wilson & LaFleur, 2009).

102. In *Misericordia et Misera*, Francis reflected on how Jesus responded to the woman accused of adultery in John 8:1–11, with an emphasis on listening and compassion. Francis went on to say: "Given this need, lest any obstacle arise between the request for reconciliation and God's forgiveness, I henceforth grant to all priests, in virtue of their ministry, the faculty to absolve those who have committed the sin of procured abortion. The provision I had made in this regard, limited to the duration of the Extraordinary Holy Year, is hereby extended, notwithstanding anything to the contrary. I wish to restate as firmly as I can that abortion is a grave sin, since it puts an end to an innocent life. In the same way, however, I can and must state that there is no sin that God's mercy cannot reach and wipe away when it finds a repentant heart seeking to be reconciled with the Father. May every priest, therefore, be a guide, support and comfort to penitents on this journey of special reconciliation." Francis, *Misericordia et misera* (November 20, 2016), 12. https://www.vatican.va/content/francesco/en/apost_letters/documents/papa-francesco-lettera-ap_20161120_misericordia-et-misera.html.

103. Charles Curran, *The Development of Moral Theology*, 25. He goes on: "If we see mortal sin as the breaking of our fourfold relationships with God, neighbor, world, and self, then it is evident that one can never judge or determine the existence of mortal sin simply on the basis of the objective or external act itself. This also furnishes a very significant reason why the Catholic understanding of penance today should no longer emphasize as much the judicial nature of confession." Curran, *The Development of Moral Theology*, 25.

104. John Paul II, *Evangelium Vitae*, 59.

105. John Paul II, *Evangelium Vitae*, 12. Francis said "It is also true that we have done little to adequately accompany women in very difficult situations, where abortion appears as a quick solution to their profound anguish, especially when the life developing within them is the result of rape or a situation of extreme poverty. Who can remain unmoved before such painful situations?" Francis, *Evangelii Gaudium* (2013), 214: https://www.vatican.va/content/francesco/en/apost_exhortations/documents/papa-francesco_esortazione-ap_20131124_evangelii-gaudium.html.

106. Jessica González-Rojas and Kierra Johnson, as quoted in "Sexual and Reproductive Justice," in Joanne L. Bagshaw, *The Feminist Handbook* (Oakland: New Harbinger, 2019), 117.

107. Clark E. Cochran, in *Wall of Separation? Debating the Public Role of Religion*, eds. Mary C. Segers and Ted G. Jelen (Lanham, MD: Rowman & Littlefield, 1998), x.

108. James Davison Hunter, *Culture Wars: The Struggle to Define America* (New York: Basic Books, 1991).

109. Pontifical Council for Justice and Peace, *Compendium of the Social Doctrine of the Church* (Vatican, 2004), 61: https://www.vatican.va/roman_curia/pontifical_councils/justpeace/documents/rc_pc_justpeace_doc_20060526_compendio-dott-soc_en.html. Paul VI, *Populorum Progressio* (1967), 13. https://www.vatican.va/content/paul-vi/en/encyclicals/documents/hf_p-vi_enc_26031967_populorum.html.

110. Jean Porter, *Natural and Divine Law: Reclaiming the Tradition for Christian Ethics* (Grand Rapids: Eerdmans, 1999); Cristina L. H. Traina, *Feminist Ethics and Natural Law: The End of the Anathemas* (Washington, DC: Georgetown University Press, 1999); Gula, *Reason Informed by Faith*.

111. A recent example can be found in the essay by Bishop Thomas Paprocki imagining "heretical" cardinals who approve of giving Holy Communion to grave sinners including homosexuals; Paprocki does not name, but is responding to, Bishop Robert McElroy's article in *America Magazine*. See Bishop Thomas Paprocki, "Imagining a Heretical Cardinal," in *First Things* (February 28, 2023). https://www.firstthings.com/web-exclusives/2023/02/imagining-a-heretical-cardinal. See also Bishop Robert W. McElroy, "Cardinal McElroy on 'Radical Inclusion' for LGBT People, Women and Others in the Catholic Church," *America* (January 24, 2023), https://www.americamagazine.org/faith/2023/01/24/mcelroy-synodality-inclusion-244587?gclid=Cj0KCQiA6fafBhC1ARIsAIJjL8kstNOHcGK6eZYjjaHURYcTDNy8IOGNHB0d5lD80bj0RkYgInlZ1LIaAjQqEALw_wcB.

112. USCCB, "A Matter of the Heart: On the 30th Anniversary of Roe v. Wade" (November 12, 2002). https://www.usccb.org/issues-and-action/human-life-and-dignity/abortion/a-matter-of-the-heart-on-the-30th-anniversary-of-roe-vs-wade. The bishops cite John Paul II, *Evangelium Vitae*, no. 101, but neglect the preceding sentence, which reads: "To be actively pro-life is to contribute to the renewal of society through the promotion of the common good."

113. Emily Reimer-Barry, "Another Pro-Life Movement is Possible," Catholic Theological Society of America *Proceedings* 74: 1 (2019): 21–41, at 28.

114. See the discussion of the writings of Charles Chaput, Raymond Burke, Joseph Naumann, and Robert Finn, in Cathleen Kaveny, *Law's Virtues: Fostering Autonomy and Solidarity in American Society* (Washington, DC: Georgetown University Press, 2012), 252–56.

115. The EWTN party platform comparisons, for example, employs the language of "non-negotiable" issues (including abortion) and "negotiable" issues (including war and peace). Church teachings do not make distinctions between "non-negotiable" and "negotiable" moral issues. The voter guide distorts church teachings in order to justify the author's own political narrative. EWTN "2020 General Election of the United States Major Party Platforms in Comparison with Catholic Teaching on the Non-Negotiable Moral Issues and the Negotiable Policy Issues" (2020), https://www.ewtn.com/img/catholicism/downloads/voting/2020-platforms.pdf.

116. USCCB, "Living the Gospel of Life: A Challenge to American Catholics" (1998), 18. https://www.usccb.org/issues-and-action/human-life-and-dignity/abortion/living-the-gospel-of-life.

117. USCCB, "Living the Gospel of Life," 20.

118. Rebecca Todd Peters and Margaret D. Kamitsuka, eds., *T&T Clark Reader in Abortion and Religion: Jewish, Christian, and Muslim Perspectives* (London: T&T Clark, 2023); Andrew L. Seidel, *American Crusade: How the Supreme Court Is Weaponizing Religious Freedom* (New York: Union Square, 2022).

119. Steven P. Millies, *Good Intentions: A History of Catholic Voters' Road from Roe to Trump* (Minneapolis: Liturgical, 2018), 195–99.

120. Eva R. Rubin, *Abortion, Politics, and the Courts:* Roe v. Wade *and Its Aftermath* (Westport: Greenwood Press, 1982), 87–100, at 88. Note that the bishops have not issued similar calls of civil disobedience to border patrol agents, military officers, or other Catholics engaged in occupations on contested "life" issues. And in their explicit responses to racial injustice, the bishops often remind Catholics to respect law enforcement and obey civil laws as good citizens. See United States Conference of Catholic Bishops, *Open Wide Our Hearts* (2018), 5: http://www.usccb.org/_cs_upload/issues-and-action/human-life-and-dignity/racism/271721_3.pdf. The contrast in their approach to "the law" across "life" issues is stark.

121. USCC, *Pastoral Plan for Pro-Life Activities* (Washington, DC: United States Catholic Conference, 1975). The plan was reaffirmed ten years later. USCC, *Pastoral Plan for Pro-Life Activities* (Washington, DC: United States Catholic Conference, 1985). The most recent version is available on the USCCB website. USCCB, *Pastoral Plan for Pro-Life Activities*: https://www.usccb.org/prolife/pastoral-plan-pro-life-activities.

122. USCCB, *Pastoral Plan for Pro-Life Activities*: https://www.usccb.org/prolife/pastoral-plan-pro-life-activities.

123. Robert W. McElroy, "Cardinal-designate Issues Statement about Abortion Ruling by the U.S. Supreme Court" (June 24, 2022), https://sdcatholic.org/bishop/cardinal-designate-mcelroy-issues-statement-about-abortion-ruling-by-the-u-s-supreme-court/. See also "Statement of Cardinal Blase J. Cupich, Archbishop of Chicago, on the Supreme Court's Decision in *Dobbs v. Jackson Women's Health*" (June 24, 2022), https://www.archchicago.org/en/statement/-/article/2022/06/24/statement-of-cardinal-blase-j-cupich-archbishop-of-chicago-on-the-supreme-court-s-decision-in-dobbs-v-jackson-women-s-health-organization.

124. Pew Research Center, "Religious Landscape Survey: Views About Abortion Among Catholics," https://www.pewforum.org/religious-landscape-study/religious-tradition/catholic/views-about-abortion/.

125. Cardinal Wilton Gregory, "Statement from Cardinal Wilton Gregory on Light Show Protest Outside the Basilica of the National Shrine of the Immaculate Conception" (January 21, 2022), https://twitter.com/WashArchdiocese/status/1484535970976317443/photo/1. John 13:30 refers to the story of Judas departing from the last supper after Jesus announced that he would be betrayed. "And it was night." The Cardinal seems to be saying that Catholics for Choice has betrayed the Church. Tablet Staff, "Cardinal Gregory Responds to Pro-Abortion Light Show

Projected on National Basilica" (January 21, 2022), https://thetablet.org/cardinal-gregory-pro-abortion-light-show-national-basilica/.

126. Millies, *Good Intentions*, 196.

127. USCCB, Office of Government Relations, https://www.usccb.org/offices/government-relations. See also U.S. Catholic, "Sorting out the bishops' lobbying budget" (December 5, 2011), https://uscatholic.org/blog/sorting-out-the-bishops-lobbying-budget/.

128. USCCB, Office of Government Relations, https://www.usccb.org/offices/government-relations.

129. USCCB Office of General Counsel, "Legal Analysis of the Provisions of the Patient Protection and Affordable Care Act and Executive Order" (March 25, 2020), https://www.usccb.org/resources/legal-analysis-provisions-patient-protection-and-affordable-care-act-and-executive-order; Bishop Frank J. Dewane, Chairman, Committee on Domestic Justice and Human Development, "Letter to Congress on Affordable Care Act" (January 18, 2017), https://www.usccb.org/resources/letter-congress-bishop-dewane-affordable-care-act-january-18-2017-0; Cardinal Daniel DiNardo, Bishop William Murphy, and Bishop John Wester, "Setting the Record Straight" (May 10, 2010), https://www.usccb.org/resources/statement-healthcare-may-21-2010. See also Mary Jo McConahay, *Playing God: American Catholic Bishops and the Far Right* (Brooklyn: Melville House, 2022).

130. USCCB, "Letter of Opposition to H.R.8296, the Women's Health Protection Act" (July 14, 2022), https://www.usccb.org/resources/WHPA%20opposition%20letter%20House%20and%20fact%20sheet%20July%202022%20clean.pdf.

131. USCCB Committee on Pro-Life Activities and USCCB Committee for Religious Liberty, "Letter in Support of H.R. 6060, Conscience Protection Act" (December 6, 2021), https://www.usccb.org/resources/CPA%20House%20Letter%202021%20final.pdf.

132. Cardinal Timothy Dolan, Archbishop Joseph F. Naumann, and Bishop David J. Malloy, "Joint Statement on H.R.4373" (July 30, 2021), https://www.usccb.org/news/2021/us-bishops-chairmen-respond-house-vote-force-taxpayers-fund-abortion-overseas; USCCB Committee on Pro-Life Activities, "Backgrounder: Hyde Amendment and Related Policies" (2021), https://www.usccb.org/resources/backgrounder-hyde-amendment-and-related-policies.

133. USCCB, "Letter to Members of Congress on the Equal Rights Amendment" (March 12, 2021), https://www.usccb.org/resources/2021.ERA%20Letter%20to%20Congress%20final.pdf.

134. Bishop Michael C. Barber, Archbishop Paul S. Coakley, Cardinal Timothy Dolan, Bishop David A. Konderla, and Archbishop Joseph F. Naumann, "Letter to Congress opposing the reintroduction of the Equality Act" (February 23, 2021), https://www.usccb.org/resources/Letter_to_Congress_on_Equality_Act_Feb_23_2021.

135. DiNardo, Murphy, and Wester, "Setting the Record Straight."

136. DiNardo, Murphy, and Wester, "Setting the Record Straight."

137. Fifty-five percent of Americans hold a favorable opinion of the ACA while 42 percent hold a negative opinion of the law. Ashley Kirzinger, Alex Montero, Liz Hamel, and Mollyann Brodie, "Five Charts about Public Opinion on the Affordable

Care Act" (April 14, 2022), https://www.kff.org/health-reform/poll-finding/5-charts-about-public-opinion-on-the-affordable-care-act-and-the-supreme-court/.

138. Most Reverend José H. Gomez, "Statement on the Inauguration of Joseph R. Biden, Jr., as 46th President of the United States of America" (January 20, 2021), https://www.usccb.org/news/2021/usccb-presidents-statement-inauguration-joseph-r-biden-jr-46th-president-united-states.

139. For example, Notre Dame Law School, "U.S. Supreme Court Justice Samuel Alito Delivers Keynote Address at 2022 Notre Dame Religious Liberty Summit in Rome" (July 28, 2022), https://law.nd.edu/news-events/news/2022-religious-liberty-summit-rome-justice-samuel-alito-keynote/.

140. Christopher Wolfe, "The Ideal of a (Catholic) Law School" *Marquette Law Review* 78:2 (Winter 1995), article 18: 487–505. https://scholarship.law.marquette.edu/cgi/viewcontent.cgi?article=1585&context=mulr.

141. Anthony R. Picarello Jr., General Counsel, United States Conference of Catholic Bishops, *Brief Amici Curiae of USCCB and Other Religious Organizations in Support of Petitioners*," No. 19–1392, *Dobbs v. Jackson Women's Health* (July 28, 2021), https://www.supremecourt.gov/DocketPDF/19/19-1392/185030/20210727130348783_13-1932.Dobbs.final.pdf.

142. USCCB, Amicus Brief, 18.

143. USCCB, Amicus Brief, 18, citing John Paul II, *Evangelium Vitae*, 58.

144. USCCB, Amicus Brief, 31.

145. USCCB, Synod on Synodality: https://www.usccb.org/synod; Vatican, Synod on Synodality 2021–2024: https://www.synod.va/en.html.

146. Trigger laws have gone into effect in fourteen states. See Guttmacher, "Interactive Map" (2023).

147. Millies, *Good Intentions*, 187–88.

148. Hayley Penan and Amy Chen, "The Ethical & Religious Directives: What the 2018 Update Means for Catholic Hospital Mergers," *National Health Law Program* (January 2, 2019), 2.

149. USCCB, *Ethical and Religious Directives for Catholic Health Care Services*, sixth ed. (Washington, DC: USCCB, 2018), https://www.usccb.org/resources/ethical-religious-directives-catholic-health-service-sixth-edition-2016-06_0.pdf.

150. See Nelson's analysis of *Means vs. USCCB*, a case argued by the ACLU, in Lawrence J. Nelson, "Disputes over Previability Pregnancy Termination" in David E. DeCosse and Thomas A. Nairn, OFM, eds., *Conscience & Catholic Health Care: From Clinical Contexts to Government Mandates* (Maryknoll: Orbis, 2017), 131.

151. Judy Stone, "Healthcare Denied at 550 Hospitals Because of Catholic Doctrine," *Forbes* (May 7, 2016). See also Michael Hiltsiz, "Here's Another Case of a Catholic Hospital Interfering with Patient Care," *Los Angeles Times* (January 11, 2016); Claudia Buck and Sammy Caiola, "Transgender Patient Sues Dignity Health for Discrimination over Hysterectomy Denial," *Sacramento Bee* (April 20, 2017).

152. Lysaught, "Moral Analysis," 537–49; Bishop Thomas J. Olmsted determined that the procedure constituted a direct abortion. McBride's excommunication was later lifted and she was reinstated in her position. Giacomo Galeazzi,

"Excommunication Lifted on Nun who Approved an Abortion" (December 16, 2011), https://www.ucanews.com/news/excommunication-lifted-on-nun-who-approved-an-abortion/38039#.

153. National Catholic Bioethics Center, "Commentary on the Phoenix Hospital Situation," *Origins* 40, no. 33 (January 27, 2011), 549–51.

154. USCCB, *Ethical and Religious Directives*, 4.

155. USCCB, *Ethical and Religious Directives*, 6–8. For a wider view, see the stories about Sisters of Mercy and their advocacy for patients' needs in Christine Schenk, CSJ, *To Speak the Truth in Love,* as well as Anne E. Patrick, SNJM, "Framework for Love: Toward a Renewed Understanding of Christian Vocation," in Maura A. Ryan, Brian F. Linnane, SJ, eds., *A Just & True Love: Feminism at the Frontiers of Theological Ethics: Essays in Honor of Margaret A. Farl*ey (Notre Dame: University of Notre Dame Press, 2007), 303–37; and Margaret A. Farley, "The Church in the Public Forum: Scandal of Prophetic Witness?" *Proceedings of the Catholic Theological Society of America* 55 (2000): 89–101.

156. USCCB, *Ethical and Religious Directives*, 8–9, 25. "The ultimate responsibility for interpreting and applying the *Directives* rests with the diocesan bishop." *Directives*, 25.

157. USCCB, *Ethical and Religious Directives*, 13.

158. Rod Brouhard, "How Paramedics Choose Where to Take You" (April 16, 2020), Well Health, https://www.verywellhealth.com/how-do-paramedics-choose-a-hospital-1298357.

159. Anna Maria Barry-Jester and Amelia Thomson-DeVeaux, "How Catholic Bishops Are Shaping Health Care in Rural America," *FiveThirtyEight*, July 25, 2018: https://fivethirtyeight.com/features/how-catholic-bishops-are-shaping-health-care-in-rural-america/.

160. Information can be found at the website of the American Medical Association: https://www.ama-assn.org/.

161. USCCB, *Ethical and Religious Directives*, 23.

162. USCCB, *Ethical and Religious Directives*, 16.

163. USCCB, *Ethical and Religious Directives*, 16. The document cites Pope John Paul II, "Address of October 29, 1983, to the 35th General Assembly of the World Medical Association," *Acta Apostolicae Sedis* 76 (1984): 390.

164. USCCB, *Ethical and Religious Directives*, Directives no. 44, 18.

165. USCCB, *Ethical and Religious Directives*, Directive 45, 18–19.

166. USCCB, *Ethical and Religious Directives*, Directive 47, 19.

167. USCCB, *Ethical and Religious Directives*, Directive 48, 19. Cf. directive 45.

168. USCCB, *Ethical and Religious Directives*, Directive 49, 19.

169. USCCB, *Ethical and Religious Directives*, 25. N. 48: "While there are many acts of varying moral gravity that can be identified as intrinsically evil, in the context of contemporary health care the most pressing concerns are currently abortion, euthanasia, assisted suicide, and direct sterilization." See Pope John Paul II's *Ad Limina* Address to the bishops of Texas, Oklahoma, and Arkansas (Region X), in *Origins* 28 (1998): 283. See also "Reply of the Sacred Congregation for the Doctrine of the Faith on Sterilization in Catholic Hospitals" (*Quaecumque Sterilizatio*), March 13, 1975,

Origins 6 (1976): 33–35: "Any cooperation institutionally approved or tolerated in actions which are themselves, that is, by their nature and condition, directed to a contraceptive end . . . is absolutely forbidden. For the official approbation of direct sterilization and, a fortiori, its management and execution in accord with hospital regulations, is a matter which, in the objective order, is by its very nature (or intrinsically) evil." This directive supersedes the "Commentary on the Reply of the Sacred Congregation for the Doctrine of the Faith on Sterilization in Catholic Hospital" published by the National Conference of Catholic Bishops on September 15, 1977, in *Origins* 7 (1977): 399–400.

170. Bretzke, SJ, *Handbook*, 153.

171. An example is the description of multiple evaluations of a single case outlined by M. Therese Lysaught regarding the medical procedure in a Phoenix hospital. Cf. n. 20.

172. Many superb texts explore this history in further detail. See James F. Keenan, SJ, *A History of Catholic Theological Ethics* (New York: Paulist, 2002); John Mahoney, *The Making of Moral Theology: A Study of the Roman Catholic Tradition* (Oxford: Clarendon, 1987); Charles E. Curran, *The Development of Moral Theology: Five Strands* (Washington, DC: Georgetown University Press, 2013); Servais Pinckaers, *Sources of Christian Ethics*, trans. Mary Thomas Noble (Washington, DC: Catholic University Press, 1995); Eric Marcelo Genilo, *John Cuthbert Ford, SJ: Moral Theology at the End of the Manualist Era* (Washington, DC: Georgetown University Press, 2007); Paulinus Ikechukwu Odozor, *Moral Theology in an Age of Renewal* (Notre Dame: University of Notre Dame Press, 2003); Charles E. Curran and Richard A. McCormick, Eds., *The Historical Development of Fundamental Moral Theology in the United States* (New York: Paulist, 1999).

173. Keenan, *A History*, 289. Resourcement and retrieval were themes of the renewal of Vatican II but they are also methodologically significant for feminist scholarship and hermeneutics as women mine the tradition for the lost stories of women.

174. Keenan, *A History*, 174–77. Keenan relies heavily on Albert Jonsen and Stephen Toulmin, *The Abuse of Casuistry: A History of Moral Reasoning* (Berkeley: University of California Press, 1988).

175. Thomas Aquinas, *Summa Theologiae* I–II, Q. 94, a. 2.

176. Thomas Aquinas, *Summa Theologiae*, I–II, Q.94, a.4.

177. Francis, *Amoris Laetitia*, 301.

178. Gerald J. Bednar, *Mercy and the Rule of Law: A Theological Interpretation of Amoris Laetitia* (Collegeville: Liturgical, 2021), 15.

179. Cited by Bretzke, *Handbook*, 137.

180. Bednar, *Mercy and the Rule of Law*, 15. See also Eleonore Stump, *Wandering in Darkness: Narrative and the Problem of Suffering* (Oxford: Clarendon Press, 2010), 428.

181. See Mark Allman, *Who Would Jesus Kill?* (Winona, MN: St. Mary's, 2008), 167.

182. USCC, *Many Faces of AIDS: A Gospel Response* (November 14, 1987), https://www.usccb.org/resources/statement-many-faces-aids-november-14-1987. See Emily

Reimer-Barry, *Catholic Theology of Marriage in the Era of HIV and AIDS: Marriage for Life* (Lanham, MD: Lexington, 2015), 109.

183. Bretzke, *Handbook*, 138. See Daniel P. Sulmasy, "Catholic Participation in Needle-and-Syringe-Exchange Programs for Injection-Drug Users: An Ethical-Analysis," *Theological Studies* 73 (June 2012): 422–41.

184. Richard A. McCormick, SJ, "Abortion: A Changing Morality and Policy?" *Catholic Mind* 77 (October 1979): 42–59, at 48.

185. Bednar, *Mercy and the Rule of Law*, 44–49.

186. Bednar, *Mercy and the Rule of Law*, 71.

187. Bednar, *Mercy and the Rule of Law*, 48.

188. Bretzke, *Handbook*, 39.

189. Bretzke, *Handbook*, 40.

190. Julie Hanlon Rubio, *Hope For Common Ground: Mediating the Personal and the Political in a Divided Church* (Washington, DC: Georgetown University Press, 2016), 31.

191. Allman, *Who Would Jesus Kill?* 175, citing Aquinas, *Summa Theologiae* II–II, Q 64, A 7.

192. Allman, *Who Would Jesus Kill?* 177.

193. USCCB, *Ethical & Religious Directives*, Directive 45.

194. USCCB, *Ethical & Religious Directives*, Directive 47.

195. USCCB, *Ethical & Religious Directives*, Directive 25. Todd Salzman and Michael Lawler point out that the *Directives* do not give the bishop this authority because of his competence but because of the office he holds, noting that this "hierarchical" approach to ecclesiology is different from a "synodal" approach advocated by Pope Francs. See Todd A. Salzman and Michael G. Lawler, *Pope Francis and the Transformation of Health Care Ethics* (Washington, DC: Georgetown University Press, 2021), 192–93.

196. John R. Connery, *Abortion: The Development of the Roman Catholic Perspective* (Chicago: Loyola University Press, 1977), 116–67, 309–13. John T. Noonan, Jr., "Abortion and the Catholic Church: A Summary History," *The American Journal of Jurisprudence* 12, no. 1 (1967): 85–131; Keenan, *A History*, 205.

197. John T. Noonan Jr., "An Almost Absolute Value in History," in *Vice and Virtue in Everyday Life*, seventh ed. Christina Sommers and Fred Sommers, eds. (Belmont, CA: Wadsworth, 2006), 391.

198. Thomas Slater, SJ, *A Manual of Moral Theology*, 314–15, public domain, available via Los Angeles: Create Space, 2018.

199. Richard McCormick, "Abortion: A Changing Morality and Policy?" *Catholic Mind* 77 (October 1979): 42–59, at 48; Bernard Häring, *Medical Ethics* (Notre Dame, Fides, 1973), 108; Catholic Bishops of Belgium, "Declaration des Eveques Belges Sur L'Avortement," *Documentation Catholique* 70 (1973): 423–38, at 434. See also Lisa A. Fullam, "Abortion in the Catholic Conscience: The Truth about Catholic Teaching," *Conscience* 44:1 (2023): 12–17. On probabilism, see Julia Fleming, *Defending Probabilism: The Moral Theology of Juan Caramuel* (Washington, DC: Georgetown University Press, 2006), 143–51.

200. Stephen Doran, "4 Persistent Abortion and Pregnancy Myths Debunked," *Church Life Journal* (August 11, 2022); Ron Hamel, "Early Pregnancy Complications and the ERDs [Ethical Religious Directives]" *Health Care Ethics USA* (St. Louis: Catholic Health Association: February 10, 2014).

201. Hamel, "Early Pregnancy Complications."

202. Hamel, "Early Pregnancy Complications."

203. See *Gaudium et spes*, 51, on the "virtue of conjugal chastity" in harmony with "the responsible transmission of life."

204. Gula, "The Natural Law in Tradition" and "The Natural Law Today," in *Reason Informed by Faith*, 220–30, 231–49. See also Sandra Sullivan-Dunbar, "Catholic Abortion Discourse and the Erosion of Democracy," *Journal of the Society of Christian Ethics* 43:1 (2023): 55–73. https://doi.org/10.5840/jsce202341776.

205. John Paul II, *Mulieris Dignitatem* and "Letter to Women."

206. When moral theologian Christine Pohl conducted a literature review of women's abortion narratives, one of her major takeaways from the study was that "Christians with pro-life commitments ought to recognize the compelling power of appeals to control, choice, and autonomy." Christine Pohl, "Abortion: Responsibility and Moral Betrayal," *Bioethics and the Future of Medicine* (Grand Rapids, MI: Eerdmans, 1995), 212–23, at 219.

207. Slater, *Manual of Moral Theology*, 314–15, cited in Keenan, *A History*, 260.

208. Lloyd Steffen, *Ethics and Experience: Moral Theory from Just War to Abortion* (Lanham, MD: Rowman & Littlefield, 2012), 177.

209. Steffen, *Ethics and Experience*, 177–78.

210. Steffen, *Ethics and Experience*, 178. See also David L. Clough and Brian Stiltner, *Faith and Force: A Christian Debate about War* (Washington, DC: Georgetown University Press, 2007), 55–56.

211. Steffen, *Ethics and Experience*, 181.

212. Steffen, *Ethics and Experience*, 182.

213. Steffen, *Ethics and Experience*, 187.

214. Ramirez, "Teleology and the Problem of Bodily-Rights Arguments," 84.

215. For an important essay on bodily life support within the Catholic tradition, and internal inconsistencies within the tradition when bodily life support is optional in the case of organ donation but required in the case of pregnancy, see Patricia Beattie Jung, "Abortion and Organ Donation: Christian Reflections on Bodily Life Support," in *Readings in Moral Theology, No. 9: Feminist Ethics and the Catholic Moral Tradition*, eds. Charles E. Curran, Margaret A. Farley, and Richard A. McCormick, SJ (New York: Paulist, 1996), 440–80.

216. Richard P. McBrien, *Catholicism* (New York: Harper One, 1994), 973–74.

217. Traina, *Feminist Ethics and the Natural Law*, 43.

218. Bednar, *Mercy and the Rule of Law*, 41.

Chapter 3

The Shadow Side of the Pro-Life Movement

1973–2022

"Save Babies, Empower Women, Abolish Abortion." Such is the slogan of Students for Life of America.[1] It is powerful because it reflects key values, but the slogan also distorts the real policy debates at issue, policy debates that are anything but simple. How do we save babies while also empowering women? Would a woman seeking an abortion find it empowering if the law governing her medical care excluded the very procedure she requests in conscience? Can politicians who vote to abolish abortion claim to be pro-life, even if they do not advance legislation that actually empowers women? Why is the feminist movement—which includes decades of scholarship about what it would mean to empower women—sidelined in pro-life politics? These questions reflect some of the challenges of evaluating the achievements of the pro-life movement in US politics.

The Catholic hierarchy in the United States has never shied away from political activities. US bishops have rightly argued that the Catholic faith is not merely private, but that faith has implications for public life. But the way that bishops have engaged in discourse about faith in the public square has changed over time. The US bishops used to be known for political action focused on immigrant rights, robust labor laws, support for workers' unions, and their criticism of the stockpiling of nuclear weapons. But their priorities have since changed, reflecting both the changing landscape of Catholicism and of the bishops' own self-identity in the political landscape.

This chapter builds on the previous chapters by more closely examining the history and aims of the pro-life movement and the important role of the Catholic hierarchy in shaping that movement. In the first chapter I described Cardinal Bernadin's consistent ethic of life and the heroic social ethic for which Bernadin advocated in his Catholic approach to public policy. Here

I explore the pro-life movement's political successes as well as its shadow side, including the way that the pro-life movement has fostered both sexist and racist agendas in US politics. While the second chapter exposed the moral absolutism of official Catholic teachings on abortion during the papacies of John Paul II, Benedict XVI, and Francis, this chapter demonstrates the political consequences of that abortion discourse in the Catholic Church.

Since 1973, Catholic political action has gradually become more partisan and has concentrated on overturning *Roe v. Wade* more than other "life" issues. In celebrating the overturning of *Roe* in 2022, the official United States Conference of Catholic Bishops (USCCB) statement issued by Archbishop José H. Gomez and Archbishop William E. Lori included the following:

> Now is the time to begin the work of building a post-*Roe* America. It is a time for healing wounds and repairing social divisions; it is a time for reasoned reflection and civil dialogue, and for coming together to build a society and economy that supports marriages and families, and where every woman has the support and resources she needs to bring her child into this world in love.[2]

Their claim was echoed by other activists on the ground. Pro-life mom and activist Serena Sigillito from Pennsylvania explained: "Now is when the real work begins, right? Like, this was the thing that had to happen before we could really build a pro-life culture and support women and make it so that no one ever feels like they have to have an abortion."[3]

We must interrogate the assumption that the first goal of the pro-life movement should have been overturning *Roe v. Wade*, and only after that should priorities include building a society that supports pregnant women. As a result of the fifty-year pro-life campaign to overturn *Roe*, the *Dobbs* decision can look like a victory worth celebrating. But it has come with a cost. Today's partisan divides are deep, exacerbated by the pro-life and pro-choice movements, and these partisan divides have real implications for pregnant women because they undermine bipartisan support for social welfare reform aligned with Bernadin's heroic social ethic. But beyond that, the "*Roe* must go first" assumption forwards the false narrative that the pro-life movement's goals have focused primarily on protection of the unborn, when in reality there have been other social issues at work motivating both leaders and grassroots activists. The interconnected nature of pro-life politics' support for unborn life and simultaneous conservative backlash against minority rights and the feminist movement require further examination.

Focusing "sanctity of life" lobbying on the single issue of abortion was not the only option available to leaders of the pro-life movement and Catholic bishops. But a focus on abortion laws and policies did become a key feature of the pro-life movement over time. Catholic bishops rejected opportunities to seek common ground with feminist movements that were increasingly focusing on justice-based concerns (equal pay, nondiscrimination, universal health care, paid family leave, violence against women, and so forth), to instead focus on policies that eroded women's rights and undermined the progress of the feminist movement. Pro-choice politicians seek to stabilize abortion rights in states where they remain legal, and require their own kind of litmus test in order to seek funding and support in the Democratic caucus. On both sides, the moral absolutism of pro-life and pro-choice commitments have neglected common ground initiatives. Pope Francis explains that the goal of politics is not to win elections, but rather to serve the common good.[4] Unfortunately, this noble aim has too often been compromised, and when that happens, those already marginalized by race, class, and gender suffer most. A reproductive justice framework that centers women of color and advances reproductive agency and the social conditions for families to flourish would be more authentically pro-life than the laws currently advanced by the pro-life movement.

STREAMS AND STRATEGIES OF THE PRO-LIFE MOVEMENT

The pro-life movement is a collection of groups, organizations, and actors who have formed working relationships in order to further their own social goals, most notably, to end the practice of abortion in the United States.[5] They are organized around the central belief that abortion is the killing of innocent human life and is therefore wrong.[6] But as sociologist Ziad Munson explains, "there is no consensus, even within the pro-life movement, on how to understand the abortion issue," or on how to respond to it.[7] Munson's own extensive field research with pro-life activists in Oklahoma City, Minneapolis/St.Paul, Charleston, and Boston, yielded more than four thousand pages of transcripts from interviews in activists' homes.[8] From those conversations, Munson came to understand that while the pro-life movement is "a long-standing, mature social movement,"[9] "the moral concern about abortion has been constructed in bits and pieces over the course of American history by different sets of people and organizations."[10] Munson's research shows that there are different social movement *streams* within the pro-life movement. Streams are "subsets of individuals and organizations that approach social movement action in a way that is distinct from others that are part of the movement."[11] There are four such streams in the pro-life movement: politics, direct action, individual outreach, and public outreach.[12] This way of understanding the pro-life movement allows us to see the variation in the goals and organizations within the movement. The fact that there are extremists and ideological activists within each stream makes it complicated for Catholic activists to discern how to best live out their faith in the midst of a situation of inevitable moral compromise.

The *politics stream* of the pro-life movement focuses on legislative and legal arenas. Activists in this stream see abortion as "a political problem that requires a political solution."[13] They work on political campaigns, lobbying, and litigation. Goals of pro-life activists interviewed by Munson in the political stream of the pro-life movement included support for pro-life candidates for office at the local, state, and federal levels; passage of a human life amendment to the US Constitution; overturning *Roe v. Wade*; and passage of laws that would restrict abortion rights at the state level. These state laws would include restrictions on federal funding for abortion, restrictions on particular kinds of abortion procedures, new regulations for abortion clinics and providers, parental notification laws, waiting periods, and other rules that make abortion more difficult to access even when it is legal.[14] Without a clear majority of pro-life voters among the US electorate, and lacking a true consensus for pro-life legislation, the movement needed to take an approach that would compensate for its minority status. For decades, the pro-life movement invested in a legal strategy focusing on challenges to *Roe v. Wade*, with the intention of shifting the makeup of the Supreme Court and continuing to bring new litigation from a variety of states. In addition, pro-life organizations wrote model legislation that lobbyists sought to pass in state legislatures across the country by partnering with pro-life politicians, who themselves were offered funding and strategic assistance by the pro-life organizations who sought to work with them while they were in office, and to assist in their reelection campaigns if they maintained a pro-life voting record. Publishing score cards of pro-life politicians then became a tool for publicity and campaigning on pro-life and family values platforms. Activists in the political stream of the pro-life movement were not opposed to using coercive tactics of minority rule when it suited their goals instead of gradually persuading voters toward a common ground consensus.

The *direct-action stream* of the pro-life movement focuses on staging clinic protests in order to attempt to intervene as patients seek care in an abortion facility. Through prayer chains, sidewalk counseling, protests, picketing, demonstrations, vigils, civil disobedience, and sometimes direct violence, activists in the direct-action stream attempt to convert medical providers, staff, security, patients, and those who accompany them to their movement's understanding of the harm of procured abortion.[15]

The *individual outreach stream* of the pro-life movement focuses on helping individual pregnant women so that they can forgo abortion.[16] Most of their work is carried out in what is called "crisis pregnancy centers" or "pregnancy help centers." These centers outnumbered abortion clinics nationwide even before the *Dobbs v. Jackson* decision overturning *Roe vs. Wade*. While some programs focus on nonjudgmental support, others offer help and support together with misinformation and shaming rhetoric.[17] Munson includes post-abortion counseling and retreat programs in this stream, including the Catholic programs called Project Rachel.[18] The largest national networks of pregnancy centers are called Birthright, National Institute of Family and Life Advocates, and Care-Net.

The fourth stream of the pro-life movement is called the *public outreach stream*. This stream seeks to educate the public through advertising and special education programs.[19] Advertising venues include billboards, bus banners, print media ads, radio and television commercials, films, speakers' bureaus, and school and Church curricula. This group of activists diagnose the problem as one of ignorance and misinformation, the solution to which is education. They create materials tailored to their audiences, and their goal is to "change hearts and minds" so that social acceptance of abortion diminishes over time.[20] Increasingly, social media ads, emails, and posts by media influencers are more effective than traditional print advertisements.

Munson's research showed that the four streams of the pro-life movement were highly differentiated and heterogenous, and that the activism of most people in the pro-life movement was confined to a single stream.[21] Moreover, the professionalization of activism has led to a reduction in the impact of exclusively grassroots movements in the past decades.[22] Most provocatively, Munson argues that it is not the case that activists get involved because of the importance of the issue of abortion to them.[23] Rather, pro-life activists are mobilized when they become part of a community of people through an organization that offers them a sense of meaning and purpose. Munson describes this as "action before belief."[24] That organization, in turn, shapes the activist's worldview and nurtures new and existing grievances as the activist remains engaged and mobilized to continue to work on the issue at stake, in whatever stream of the movement they work.[25]

BEFORE *ROE*: CATHOLICS AND POLITICS BEFORE 1973

Catholic political life was not always focused on abortion. Indeed, in the first decades of the twentieth century, the most influential public theologian of the Catholic Church was Monsignor John A. Ryan, a priest and professor who sought to apply the principles of social justice and welfare espoused by papal teaching since Leo XIII's *Rerum Novarum* (1893) to the American context. Catholic theologian Christine Firer Hinze explains that Ryan's "energies centered on the plight of working-class families in the industrialized cities where Catholic populations were largest," and reflected the interests of (largely

White) Catholic immigrant communities in a context of waves of nativist discourse and industrialization.[26]

Ryan advocated for President Franklin D. Roosevelt's New Deal, a series of government spending programs intended to rebuild the US economy after the Great Depression. The New Deal included new restrictions on the banking sector as well as publicly funded infrastructure, welfare, and arts programs. While Catholic support for the New Deal was not universal (with New York's John Cardinal O'Connor a vocal critic), Firer Hinze explains that in large cities, White Catholic voters became New Deal supporters and remained "reliable Democratic voters" not only between 1936–1940 but for decades afterward.[27] However, the benefits of New Deal policies were not extended equally to all Americans. Agricultural and domestic workers were excluded from coverage under the Social Security Act and from wage protections of the Fair Labor Standards Act. While strengthening support for labor unions was a key component of the economic stability experienced by White workers, labor unions themselves engaged in racial discrimination.[28] New Deal policies stabilized the US economy but the benefits were not distributed equally; nevertheless, support for New Deal policies led to a Democratic coalition that brought together labor unions, blue-collar workers, intellectuals, racial and religious minorities, and White working-class Southerners.

Historian Daniel K. Williams argues that the origins of the pro-life movement were not rooted in political conservativism but rather New Deal liberalism.[29] In the 1930s, the Catholic campaign against legal abortion was "inseparable" from the Catholic Church's fight against contraception, says Williams. In the 1940s pro-life activists began to argue that the law should protect the lives of all human beings, born and unborn.[30] Catholic clerics of the 1930s and 1940s paired their opposition to contraception, sterilization, and abortion with a "call for government social programs, aid to the impoverished, and a living wage for workers."[31] Clericalism dominated the Catholic experience at this time; bishops thought they could deliver the Catholic vote through their advocacy of certain issues from the pulpit and within the media. Clerics expected Catholics in the pews to react with docility to authoritative teachers.

Protection of prenatal life was connected to other social issues. Catholic pro-life leaders in this period were suspicious of emerging feminist claims about sexual freedom and reproductive rights and instead advanced the claim that American society would be strengthened by family values that included promotion of heterosexual marriage ordered toward the welcoming of children. Pro-life authors such as law professor Charles E. Rice claimed that one of the lessons of the Second World War was that the ideology of eugenics leads to the ideology of genocide; to be pro-life means to stand for human rights and against Nazism.[32] Framing the "enemy" of life in this way, Williams explains that pro-life leaders became increasingly unwilling to compromise with their opponents or to seek common ground or incremental justice. "In their view, any removal of legal protection for the fetus was a step toward the eugenic and genocidal policies of the Nazis. They would fight each attempt to liberalize an abortion law as though the future of civilization depended on it."[33] Historian James Mohr documents the complaint of a woman from Iowa who felt frustrated because "the Catholic Church has the money and the muscle to impose its will on the rest of society."[34]

When John F. Kennedy sought election as president in 1960, Catholics who supported Kennedy sought to justify the place of a Catholic lay leader in US politics, distancing Kennedy's work from the authoritative structures of ecclesial life. Kennedy's coalition included segregationist politicians in the Deep South, Democrats who sought to uphold White supremacy and who denied the civil rights of Black citizens. As the turbulent decade of the 1960s unfolded, contraception and civil rights were social issues that were increasingly gaining greater attention in the media. But neither issue became a central focus for Catholic political action and coalition-building. On the issue of contraception, Catholic clerical leaders sided with political conservatives; they were critical of the 1965 *Griswold v. Connecticut* decision that made contraception legal for married couples.[35] But forming a coalition with other Christian leaders was not possible, as other Christian churches did not share the Catholic opposition to artificial birth control.[36] Even among Catholics, the 1968 birth control encyclical *Humanae Vitae* (which described artificial birth control as immoral) was not well-received.[37] On civil rights, the bishops published pastoral statements and calls for action rooted in charity, but chose not to make racial justice a focal point of their social justice preaching or pastoral implementation in a national, structured way. Catholic bishops condemned racial segregation and discrimination at their annual meeting in 1958, but they also called for gradual change, warned against "rash impetuosity," and did not address segregation in Catholic institutions.[38] In *On Racial Harmony*, published August 23, 1963, the National Catholic Welfare Conference explained that all people should be treated with dignity and charity.[39] The document confirmed Catholic opposition to racial discrimination and segregation, but it also encouraged minority groups to "respect the lawful rights of others."[40] Even in the midst of obviously unjust laws, including Jim Crow laws, the bishops emphasized the importance of maintaining peace, and of law and order. In 1966, eleven years after the Montgomery bus boycott and five years after the Freedom Rides, the bishops issued their *Pastoral Statement on Race Relations and Poverty*, and in 1968, their *Statement on the National Race Crisis*. This was followed by their release of *Brothers and Sisters to Us* in 1979. Despite these publications, Catholic bishops did not take up the invitation to build a racial justice grassroots movement.[41] To be sure, there were Catholic leaders engaged in organizing on behalf of racial justice, voting rights, and expanding ministries for Black Catholics, but their organizing was not centered and funded through the bishops' conference itself, which was influenced by the dominant culture of Whiteness among the US episcopacy.[42] At a time when men and women of color were cast as "agents of social destruction," and blamed for "urban decay, crime, and pollution," the US bishops avoided public confrontations on race and did not make racial justice a key part of their pro-life agenda.[43]

US bishops were outspoken critics of the liberalization of abortion laws at the state level well before the *Roe* decision in 1973.[44] *Human Life in Our Day* was promulgated in 1969, *Statement on Abortion and Declaration on Abortion* in 1970, and *Population and the American Future: A Response* in 1972.[45] When Catholic bishops first began their work of anti-abortion advocacy, they did not engage in single-issue politics. Instead, in 1972, their *Respect Life Program* invited the Catholic community to focus on the "sanctity of human life and the many threats to human life in the modern world, including war, violence, hunger, and poverty."[46] This multi-prong approach was sidelined after *Roe* in 1973, in order to both explain the "foundational right to life of the unborn" and to build coalitions with conservative Christian leaders opposed to legal abortion.

Kennedy's election in 1960 certainly raised the profile of Catholics in politics, but the emergence of a "Catholic vote" influenced by moral absolutism on abortion took decades to accomplish. The labor priests who followed in the footsteps of Monsignor Ryan were gradually sidelined as immigrant communities of the 1920s and 1930s assimilated in US society; as their children and grandchildren moved to the suburbs, their political activism was shaped by new interests. The White affluent culture warriors in the suburbs shaped policies that were different from the social justice policies of their grandparents.[47] Catholics too experienced the racial divide. Richard Nixon's first term as president, beginning in 1968, mobilized the grievances of White voters after the passage of the 1964 Civil Rights Act.[48] The Republican party's courting of White Southern voters had an impact.[49] Margaret Sammon Parsons explains that the reelection of Nixon in 1972 "increased his margin of Catholic voters by 33 percent from the 1968 election," and "signaled the loss of a major electoral group for the Democratic Party and the end of the New Deal Coalition."[50] These changes, together with the 1973 *Roe* decision, catapulted the US Catholic bishops to center stage in national politics.

A SHIFTING LANDSCAPE: 1973–1988

While the pro-life movement preceded *Roe*, the outrage against the Supreme Court decision in 1973 inspired a new wave of ecclesial activism. After *Roe v. Wade*, Catholic bishops advanced the claim that disobeying civil laws was justified—a claim they had refused to make in the context of civil rights advocacy. On January 24, 1973, the Committee for Pro-Life Affairs of the National Conference of Catholic Bishops (precursor to the USCC) explained:

> Although as a result of the Court decision abortion may be legally permissible, it is still morally wrong, and no Court opinion can change the law of God prohibiting the taking of innocent human life. Therefore, as religious leaders, we cannot accept the Court's judgment and we urge people not to follow its reasoning or conclusions.[51]

The bishops then set out to create an infrastructure of communications and ministries that would reflect their priorities. Msgr. James Thomas McHugh led early work in the National Conference of Catholic Bishops as administrator of the Family Life Bureau and guide of the bishops' National Right to Life Committee.[52] Some at the time credited the Catholic Church with the creation of the right-to-life movement, as Connie Paige did in 1973: "Without the church, the movement would not exist as such today."[53] Historian Robert Karrer explains that at the time, the US Catholic bishops began to see the benefit of a post–Vatican II political strategy that appealed to a broader population and sought social change through partnerships and affiliations with non-Catholics. In 1973, pro-life leaders, with McHugh and his executive assistant Michael Taylor taking the lead, decided to shift the organizational structure of the bishops' pro-life organization so that the National Right to Life Committee would be separate from the work of the National Conference of Catholic Bishops. When the newly independent National Right to Life Committee (NRLC) was formed in 1973, Marjory Mecklenburg, a Methodist, was its first leader. In its first decade of operations it became more ecumenical, but was still mostly made up of Catholics.[54] The NRLC went on to sponsor independent state affiliates in every state in the country in its first two years.[55] Other organizations were formed at this time, including national pro-life organizations like American Citizens Concerned for Life and the March for Life.[56]

In 1975, the bishops created their *Pastoral Plan for Pro-Life Activities*,[57] which guided their anti-abortion activism.[58] It consisted of four specific areas: education, pastoral care, public policy, and prayer. Although it referenced the consistent ethic of life, the plan prioritized abortion and euthanasia. They identified a need to educate lay people in government "so that legislation will always reflect those principles and moral values which are in conformity with a sound anthropology and advance the common good." The bishops explained that their own priorities in this matter were passage of a constitutional amendment protecting unborn children's right to life; state laws restricting abortion rights; overturning *Roe v. Wade*; and legislation to prevent euthanasia and end the death penalty. The bishops advocated for partnerships with other religious and secular groups in order to achieve these goals. The *Pastoral Plan for Pro-Life Activities* also advocated for the inclusion of abortion in preaching, petitions for the unborn at every Mass, prayer vigils, and other ways of fostering a "culture of life" at the grassroots level. The *Pastoral Plan* was not simply aspirational but for the first time in the Catholic bishops' history outlined implementation, including state-level committees, diocesan structures of implementation, and a central organizing framework from the Secretariat for Pro-Life Activities. The *Pastoral Plan* was updated in 1985 and again in 2001.[59] The idea that every parish would have a dedicated minister engaging in grassroots pro-life activism, coordinating with other parish through a paid Diocesan staff member, meant that Catholic anti-abortion advocacy was built into the employment and structural mechanisms of the Church in a way that was unlike any other Catholic social action campaigns.

The Catholic moral tradition emphasizes political participation focused on the common good,[60] and encourages people to work together to build consensus across partisan divides. In the 1980s, three examples of this strategy on the part of the National Conference of Catholic Bishops included the pastoral letters on peace, on poverty, and on AIDS. The NCCB issued its pastoral letter on war and peace on May 3, 1983, just ten years after *Roe v. Wade*. *The Challenge of Peace: God's Promise and Our Response* examines and evaluates the crisis of nuclear weaponry. The document begins by urging mutual respect, recognizing that "on some complex social questions, the Church expects a certain diversity of views even though all hold the same universal moral principles."[61] The bishops upheld both the just war tradition and pacifism as authentically Catholic and complementary perspectives, because both seek a just peace and the common good, albeit with different methods.[62] They reject nuclear escalation and advocate for public policies that respect conscientious objection and prioritize the needs of the poor and vulnerable as more important than military spending.[63] Only three years later, the United States Catholic Bishops promulgated *Economic Justice for All: A Pastoral Letter on Catholic Social Teaching and the U.S. Economy*.[64] The bishops address urgent challenges related to economic injustices including unemployment, poverty, food insecurity, and sweeping changes in farming and agriculture. They call for "sustained reflection on the values that guide economic choices and are embodied in economic institutions."[65] In 1987, the administrative board of the NCCB issued *The Many Faces of AIDS*, followed in 1989 by *Called to*

Compassion and Responsibility. These documents on the AIDS crisis drew explicit connections between personal responsibility for disease prevention and social responsibility for compassionate care for those most marginalized and structural supports for those facing discrimination, poverty, and barriers to health care access.[66] In 1987, the bishops wrote: "We have a responsibility to stand in solidarity with and reach out with compassion and understanding to those exposed to or experiencing this disease."[67] In these important pastoral letters, the bishops of the United States crafted arguments for policy priorities that were rooted in interpretations of the Bible and of the Christian tradition, but intelligible to nonbelievers. The bishops wrote with both urgency and openness, describing the values of human dignity, solidarity, and the common good. The bishops adopted a non-partisan approach to these important social justice issues (of war, of the economy, and of the need for compassionate care of people living with HIV and AIDS), advancing an approach that would build bridges between political parties. Their method of argumentation was invitational; the documents were the fruit of robust consultation with experts in the fields of military ethics, public policy, economics, medicine, and public health.

The bishops' anti-abortion efforts took a somewhat different approach, one characterized less by an invitational tone and more by a politics of coercion. While the bishops were vocal in their opposition to legal abortion, they also supported other strategies to limit access to legal abortion. Congressman Henry Hyde (R-IL), a Catholic, worked alongside other conservative politicians including Congressman Chris Smith (R-NJ) and Senator Jesse Helms (R-NC) to achieve pro-life ends.[68] An early strategic goal of the pro-life movement was attaching a "Human Life Amendment" to the U.S. Constitution.[69] This strategy, led by Jesse Helms in 1975, was not successful, and there was not unity within the pro-life movement about the best way to achieve its ends. The first major legislative achievement of the pro-life movement was the Hyde Amendment (1976), which prohibited federal funding of elective abortions. As opposition to abortion became a priority for US bishops and their lobbying efforts, they sought to collaborate with like-minded religious leaders. Rick Perlstein explains that an unintended consequence of the Tax Reform Act of 1976 was that it allowed organizations that were mainly "educational" to use 20 percent of their budget for direct lobbying without losing their tax-exempt status.[70] The tax loophole enabled pro-life groups to purchase new mailing lists and to use direct mailing to nurture grievances among pro-life voters.[71]

Abortion became increasingly partisan over time; it was not so in the early days of the pro-life movement. The nation's first abortion liberalization bill was signed into law in Colorado by a Republican governor in 1967.[72] As

Republican governor of California, Ronald Reagan had signed that state's abortion reform into law.[73] Historian Daniel K. Williams documents how before *Roe*, party affiliations were not part of the abortion conversation. Democrats Jesse Jackson and Ted Kennedy were staunchly pro-life, while Republican Reagan became more pro-life as he saw the appeal among voters during his bid for the presidency.[74] Democrat Jimmy Carter personally opposed abortion but was committed to upholding the Supreme Court decision in *Roe*.[75] During the Carter administration (1977–1981), the partisan lines were drawn more distinctly in abortion politics, with emerging pro-life leaders organizing for the passage of the Hyde Amendment and Republican leaders shifting to a posture more open to collaboration with pro-life organizations who felt their Democratic president, while being a man of Christian faith, did not take abortion seriously enough.

Leaders of the Catholic Church have not been as successful in addressing the issue of abortion in a non-partisan way (as they had previously in their documents on the economy, nuclear war, and AIDS). Instead, principled objections to legal abortion have become an obstacle to the non-partisan mindset that sees moral action in the messy middle of common ground and compromise. From 1973 on, the bishops have rejected compromise on abortion politics, framing the issue instead as a call to moral absolutism. Bishops' writings on abortion do not take up the same invitational approach to recognize the complexity of the issue of abortion and seek common ground among conflicting positions as they had in their documents on war, the economy, and the AIDS crisis. As leaders of the Catholic Church aligned themselves with partisan actors in order to advance the Church's pro-life position against legal abortion, many in the hierarchy of the Church elevated abortion to a new and higher status, giving abortion more weight in deliberations about lobbying and political strategies. In their *Pastoral Plan for Pro-Life Activities*, Catholic bishops initiated, funded, and amplified the message of a grassroots pro-life strategy that focused on shaping public opinion and advocating for legal protections for the unborn; they did not prioritize social support for vulnerable pregnant persons, but merely encouraged volunteers at the parish level to get involved in this work. By describing abortion as murder, advocating for legal protections for unborn life, and describing the need for traditional family values, the bishops placed themselves firmly within partisan narratives in alignment with Republican operatives and against Democratic leaders.[76] At the conclusion of the 1976 Democratic Convention, Rev. Edward O'Connell's impression was that based on the party's opposition to a human life amendment, "The Democratic Party doesn't want Catholics."[77]

Elevating abortion as a preeminent moral issue, and framing abortion as a personal moral choice akin to murder, departed from the thoughtful analysis provided by Catholic theologians at the time.[78] While scholars wrote with nuance about the difference between a person's right to life and a person's right to use the body of another human being,[79] distinctions between morality and public policy and between morality and pastoral care,[80] analysis of delayed hominization,[81] the principle of double effect as it applied to hard cases,[82] and the role of probabilism in moral arguments about abortion,[83] these debates seemed to proceed on a parallel track entirely separate from the political lobbying of the National Conference of Catholic Bishops. Official pronouncements by the bishops did not result from deep engagement and collaboration with theologians.[84] There was an increasing divide between the bishops (arguing they are the authentic teachers of the faith) and theologians (who practice the vocation of teaching within their classrooms, but are sidelined in ecclesial discernments).

The Religious Right developed as a coalition of conservative religious voices who sought to influence politics in their coordinated efforts. Robert Balmer, author of *Bad Faith: Race and the Rise of the Religious Right*, explains that the Religious Right combined concern for protection of unborn life with protection of religious liberty, family values, and resistance to civil rights legislation (in particular resistance to school desegregation laws). Paul Weyrich, a conservative Catholic whose work was instrumental in forming the Religious Right, did not hide the fact that solidifying power among White conservatives was part of the overall strategy, telling the *New York Times* in 1980: "This is not a minority movement."[85] Balmer calls this the "abortion myth"—the myth that groups came together under the banner of helping vulnerable children.

Balmer argues that a case can instead be made that pro-life activism for the Religious Right was motivated by a desire to protect White political power, first by securing the right to discriminate at White schools and churches. Balmer explains that in 1967, when the Commonwealth of Virginia mandated the desegregation of the state's public schools, Jerry Falwell formed his own segregated school, Lynchburg Christian Academy, which was for Whites only.[86] In 1967, Senator Strom Thurmond praised "independent, non-governmental schools" for sustaining both "prayers to God in schools" and "regional ideals and values."[87] Perlstein explains that "segregation academies, as much as violent state terror, were part and parcel of the South's desperate, last-ditch efforts to preserve White supremacy."[88] White flight from public schools to Catholic parochial schools followed a similar pattern across the country, and is well documented.[89] One of the ways that White Catholics concentrated power was through institutions such as Catholic schools. Balmer argues that it was the Religious Right that brought White Protestants and White Catholics together. It was not only opposition to *Roe v. Wade*, but opposition to *Engel v. Vitale*, which outlawed state-sponsored prayer in schools in 1962, and *Alexander v. Holmes County Board of Education*, the 1969 Supreme Court decision that ordered municipalities to "fashion steps which promise realistically to convert promptly to a system without a 'white' school and a 'Negro' school, but just schools."[90] When the Internal Revenue Service announced a review of tax-exempt private schools during the Carter administration, Christian conservatives claimed that their values were being attacked.

Republican politicians including Nixon and Reagan sought to appeal to White voters by denigrating Black culture, describing Black neighborhoods as dangerous, and complaining that women on public aid wasted taxpayer money (what came to be known as the stereotype of the welfare queen).[91] In conservative politics, "giving birth while poor" was described as irresponsible and a drain on the national economy, thereby vilifying the decisions of poor mothers of color.[92] Conservative evangelical women mobilized against both the Equal Rights Amendment and gay rights, calling both feminism and homosexuality threats to the traditional family. Among the most vocal were Anita Bryant, Beverly LaHaye, and Phyllis Schlafly.[93]

While abortion was not the only issue that animated conservative Christian voters, the 1978 election signaled the growing influence of abortion-centric messaging. Republican candidates began to successfully draw Catholic voters away from Democratic candidates by appealing to abortion. The on-the-ground-activism of the National Right to Life Committee, paired with direct mailing tactics used by Catholic political activist Richard Viguerie, shifted the role of abortion in framing party platforms and candidate priorities. CBS's Roger Mudd, covering Iowa politics in 1978, said "abortion could be the most volatile single political issue in the country today, and the right-to-lifers the most powerful single-issue block."[94]

It was the conservative religious coalition that came together to defeat Jimmy Carter and get Ronald Reagan elected in 1980 that solidified the political strategy of leaders of the pro-life movement, who sought to align themselves with the party of "family values" and not the party of "feminism." Framing the women's movement as an enemy to Christian families was one of the early strategies of pro-life political operatives, and abortion was easily exploited as a wedge issue in that logic. By 1984, the partisan alignment had been cemented, with very few cases of common ground crossover in the intervening decades. Catholic Democratic leaders defended their political priorities and sought to push back against the issues-based activism of the US bishops. For example, Governor Mario Cuomo (D-NY), in a speech at the University of Notre Dame, explained that he accepted the Church's teaching on abortion, but that his role as governor was not to impose Catholic teachings on nonbelievers. Arguing that "public morality depends on a consensus view of right and wrong," Cuomo argued that no such consensus existed yet on abortion. Cuomo further argued that the application of Church teachings to the political realm requires prudential judgments.⁹⁵ New York's Archbishop John J. O'Connor did not find Cuomo's argument convincing.⁹⁶

A comparison of the 1984 political platforms of the Republican Party and the Democratic Party can serve as a useful examination of this trend by which Catholic clerics seemed to emphasize issues-based voting toward partisan ends. In 1984, the Republican candidates for president and vice president were Ronald Reagan and George H. W. Bush, respectively, first elected in 1980. The Democratic candidates were Walter Mondale and Geraldine Ferraro. The Republican platform emphasized tax cuts, limited government, pro-business policies, increased military spending, and family values. The Democratic platform supported a nuclear freeze, support for the Equal Rights Amendment, and robust social programs to meet the needs of the poor. All of these issues—on both sides of the aisle—are issues with significant moral implications for society. The Democratic platform discussed family values differently than the Republican platform; while Republicans focused on protecting the nuclear family, Democrats focused on changes to family life including the special needs of single parents, the threat of violence, and the impact of poverty on family life. As the Democratic party began to appeal to women in the feminist movement, the Republican party emphasized family values and a man's rightful place as the head of the household. Republican strategists sought to emphasize Catholic teachings on the family, sexuality, and gender roles as conservative values that were part of their platform, in contrast to what they painted as the secularism of their opponents. As the Democratic party championed programs for the working poor and immigrants, the Republican party emphasized nativist resentments. The issues raised by the Democratic platform—the wellbeing of children, stable employment, health and human rights—are also issues of concern in Catholic teachings.⁹⁷ Authoritative Church teachings of the time reflected these same values, with specific attention to systemic injustices; the Synod of Bishops in 1971 described "great numbers of 'marginal' persons, ill-fed, inhumanly housed, illiterate, and deprived of political power as well as of the suitable means of acquiring responsibility and moral dignity."⁹⁸ In 1981, John Paul II had emphasized "the principle of the priority of labor over capital" in the social encyclical *Laborem Exercens*, which also advocated for the rights of workers to unionize, demanded a fair wage and safe working conditions, and explained that the obligation to provide unemployment benefits is a "duty springing form the fundamental principle of the moral order in this sphere, namely the principle of the common use of goods."⁹⁹ Given the intersecting issues, one could make a case that both platforms aligned with some Catholic values and that neither reflected the fullness of an approach to politics and social justice as proclaimed by the Catholic Church. But that did not prevent the bishops from urging a focus on abortion to lend support to the Republican candidates. During the election of 1984, John O'Connor, archbishop of New York, and Bernard Law, archbishop of Boston, urged an abortion-centered approach to public policy. The New England bishops explained: "While nuclear holocaust is a future possibility, the holocaust of abortion is a present reality. Indeed, we believe that the enormity of the evil makes abortion the critical issue of the moment."[100] Archbishop O'Connor regularly criticized Ferraro, a Catholic, for her pro-choice position.[101] Despite the fact that Catholic teachings do not align neatly with either political party, a prominent archbishop of the Church regularly weighed in against the Democratic ticket, giving the impression that the Republican ticket was morally superior. Reagan won a landslide victory.[102] But it was a victory built on the rhetoric of racial grievances, a rejection of the feminist movement, and a narrative about maintaining the status quo of racial and gender hierarchies in society. Many White working-class voters who had previously voted for the Democratic ticket supported Reagan, and political scientists began to refer to this voting pattern as the "Reagan Democrat."[103] Catholics who became loyal Republican voters began to emphasize how Catholic social teachings were out of touch with the realities of a capitalist economy, and reflected an idealism that was not practical given their own understanding of political realism.

The trend continued as Republican (pro-life) and Democrat (pro-choice) operatives realized the success of the strategy of using abortion as a wedge issue in American politics. Many in the pro-life movement became disenchanted by the lack of forward progress during the Reagan administration.[104] Reagan employed pro-life rhetoric but the justices he nominated to the Supreme Court—Sandra Day O'Connor and Anthony Kennedy—failed to overturn *Roe v. Wade* in the *Planned Parenthood v. Casey* case. Then, in 1987, President Reagan promised his supporters: "I will not rest until a human life amendment becomes a part of our Constitution. At the same time, we must continue to search for practical steps that we can take now, even before the battle for the human life amendment is won."[105] The Human Life Amendment never passed because it did not have popular support since the electorate was still deeply divided on abortion rights. But both partisan "sides" motivated the voters in their respective bases by talking about it. In time, the Democratic party began to solidify coalitions rooted in a pro-choice perspective, with key alliances between Democratic candidates and the National Organization for Women, Planned Parenthood Federation of America, and National Association for the Repeal of Abortion Laws.

But exploiting abortion as a single issue for religious voters is not the only strategy that made this era of US political history divisive. Gerrymandering is the manipulation of election districts for partisan gain.[106] Partisan gerrymandering, which was employed by both political parties during this period and became even more extreme in the early 2000s, further undermined common ground initiatives on abortion. Partisan gerrymandering furthers tactics of minority rule and leads to more extremist politicians on both sides given that voting districts are set up as uncontested partisan districts.[107] This partisan strategy reduces the need for centrist politicians who seek common ground and compromise with members of the other party on legislation.

The impact on Catholic politicians because of the bishops' privileging of abortion has been challenging for some Catholic Democrats. Joseph Biden decided as a senator that he would remain in the Democratic party and describe his position as personally opposed to abortion while politically pro-choice. Pro-life Democrats have had a harder time navigating the middle position they tried to carve out; in 1992 Governor Robert Casey (D-PA) lost his reelection bid, and in 2020 Congressman Dan Lipinski (D-IL) lost his reelection bid, in part because of his failure to support abortion rights as a Democratic lawmaker.[108]

The Catholic bishops' alignment with the Republican party had significant drawbacks. The decision led to moral sacrifices on important ethical issues that were not priorities for the Republican party. In order to advance their anti-abortion policy, the Catholic bishops made moral sacrifices for political gain. Given the breadth of Catholic teachings on human dignity, respect for the immigrant and marginalized, and emerging teaching on labor justice at the time, it was not inevitable that the Church would develop a pro-life campaign focusing on abortion. *Gaudium et Spes* advances a broader political agenda for the Church in terms of seeing its place advocating for the human dignity of all in the modern world. As we've seen, Cardinal Joseph Bernardin explicitly advocated for a "consistent ethic of life" that linked anti-war, anti-poverty, and anti-abortion principles in a coherent framework.[109] Bernardin's opposition to abortion was a key part of his consistent ethic of life position, but Bernardin's vision of the pro-life movement saw abortion as one part of a larger movement to affirm the human dignity of all. Bernardin was not able to persuade other powerful Catholic clerics about the importance of this consistent approach; in particular, Cardinal Bernard Law of Boston and Cardinal John O'Connor of New York (both elevated to cardinal in 1985 by John Paul II) jettisoned the consistent ethic framework in favor of an issues-based approach that described abortion as the preeminent political issue and respect for unborn human life as the foundation of just politics. Strategically, some Catholic leaders, including those responsible for lobbying and public relations in the USCCB Washington, DC, office, saw an advantage in aligning with Republican leaders, implicitly and explicitly, in order to forward an anti-abortion agenda on multiple levels.

PREEMINENT MORAL ISSUES AND
RELIGIOUS CONSERVATIVISM: 1988–2023

The shadow side of the pro-life movement became more apparent in the 1990s and 2000s as partisanship, political violence, racist stereotypes, communion wars, and dark money influenced pro-life strategies. In 1995, John Paul II promulgated *Evangelium Vitae*, and in 1998 the US bishops issued *Living the Gospel of Life*[110] in order to encourage Americans to take up the multi-prong challenges of the pope's challenge. *Living the Gospel of Life* acknowledges wide-ranging life issues such as abortion, euthanasia, military force, capital punishment, fetal tissue experimentation, and more. The document named a holistic heroic social ethic as Bernadin had suggested, but managed to privilege abortion at the same time. This framing has led to the distorted understanding that there are some "non-negotiable" social issues and other "negotiable" social issues." The document argues:

> Opposition to abortion and euthanasia does not excuse indifference to those who suffer from poverty, violence and injustice. Any politics of human life must work to resist the violence of war and the scandal of capital punishment. Any politics of human dignity must seriously address issues of racism, poverty, hunger, employment, education, housing, and health care. Therefore, Catholics should eagerly involve themselves as advocates for the weak and marginalized in all these areas. Catholic public officials are obliged to address each of these issues as they seek to build consistent policies which promote respect for the human person at all stages of life.

In this holistic framing, abortion is described alongside other important social/moral issues. but the document continues:

> *But being "right" in such matters can never excuse a wrong choice regarding direct attacks on innocent human life.* Indeed, the failure to protect and defend life in its most vulnerable stages renders suspect any claims to the "rightness" of positions in other matters affecting the poorest and least powerful of the human community. If we understand the human person as the "temple of the Holy Spirit"—the living house of God—then these latter issues fall logically into place as the crossbeams and walls of that house. *All direct attacks on innocent human life, such as abortion and euthanasia, strike at the house's foundation.* These directly and immediately violate the human person's most fundamental right—the right to life.[111]

Here we see the privileging of abortion and euthanasia via a moral absolutism that fails to situate abortion decisions within the wider contexts of a pregnant woman's actual discernment, impacted by structural injustices.

The inherent contradiction of a consistent ethic of life combined with a single-issue approach can be seen in this document, which names a broad range of issues but then prioritizes anti-abortion politics. In this framing, Catholic Republicans could make the case that they were more "pro-life" than Democrats because they voted for abortion restrictions even if they did not seriously address "issues of racism, poverty, hunger, employment, education, housing, and health care." After all, those do not, according to the bishops, constitute a "direct attack on innocent human life." Moral absolutism has significant political consequences.

One of the challenges pro-life activists faced during the 1990s was how to activate conservative voters to turn out in elections while distancing themselves from violent extremists in the pro-life movement. Carol Mason, author of *Killing for Life*, exposed the relationships between militant anti-abortion extremists and White nationalist groups in the 1990s.[112] In 1985, the Ku Klux Klan began creating WANTED posters listing the personal information of abortion providers. This tactic was adopted by pro-life leaders such as Randall Terry, founder of Operation Rescue, and John Burt, regional director of Rescue America. Dr. David Gunn, whose information appeared on a WANTED poster created by Randall Terry, was assassinated in Pensacola, Florida, in 1993, by Michael Griffin.[113] Dr. John Britton, exposed by a Rescue America poster, was assassinated in Pensacola in 1994 by Paul Hill. After Paul Hill killed Dr. John Britton and his escort, the editors of the conservative religious journal *First Things* convened a symposium titled "Killing Abortionists," in which Christian leaders debated the merits of killing doctors as part of a pro-life strategy.[114] The editors found Hill's moral claim to be "persuasive," since "the moral status of the unborn is the same as that of the born," and asked respondents to address whether the use of "lethal force against those who perform abortions" is justified in the pro-life movement. While some were opposed to the assassination in principle, others were opposed on the basis of strategy, and others took the opportunity to remind readers that doctors who perform abortions "deserve no special sympathy and certainly no admiration."[115] Hadley Arkes explained that the difference between Paul Hill and a doctor who performed abortions was that Paul Hill "did not engage in killing as his office work," and therefore that "these two acts of killing cannot stand on the same moral plane."[116] In other words, some members of the pro-life movement began to assert theological and ethical justifications for killing doctors who provided abortions, even as they continued to identify as pro-life. Christian ethicist Lloyd Steffen characterizes Arkes's position as the rhetoric of holy war.[117] An obvious impact to abortion care included reasonable fear among both patients and staff.[118] As the pro-life movement evolved over time, harassment of pregnant people seeking abortions became commonplace, and Catholic parishes, including youth groups and parish-based diocesan pro-life groups, included direct-action protests at clinics as part of their regular work.[119] It became socially acceptable in Catholic parish life to shame pregnant women seeking abortion without providing concrete assistance to her. In many parishes, this is still the case.

The Democratic party solidified its support for feminism and pro-choice legislation, but its approach to the feminist movement was dominated by White women with privilege instead of a broader coalitional framework.[120] Black women who came together to discuss their community's exclusion from health care reform noted that the Clinton administration's priorities did not reflect their community's holistic needs.[121] Critics of the Democratic party during this period argue that Democratic candidates were taking Black voters for granted, seeking their support while advancing legislation that failed to meet their needs, including the 1994 crime bill and 1996 welfare reform.[122] In the 1990's, the Republican party's platforms combined anti-abortion activism with pro-business legislation, deregulation, support for gun-owner's rights, increased military spending, and rejection of same-sex marriage initiatives. In 1996, a group of pro-life authors published "The America We Seek: A Statement of Pro-Life Principles and Concerns" in *First Things*, describing the collapse of American society because of a "virtue deficit" and saying that the "abortion license has poisoned relationships between women and men."[123] Rickie Solinger faults the statement for blaming women for society's ills:

> [The authors] agreed that the source of the country's problems was not employers who paid women nonliving wages inadequate for supporting a child; nor was it men who preyed sexually on teenage girls or men who behaved violently toward women, or school systems that disallowed birth control education, or politicians who cut allocations for child care, ignoring the needs of working mothers. The problem was women themselves. The problem was women having children under the wrong conditions and women having abortions.[124]

Even when collaborating on a statement of pro-life values, Solinger explains, leaders of the pro-life movement sought to blame and shame women of color instead of seeking opportunities to forge a nonpartisan consensus that would result in actual support for pregnant women marginalized by the compounding oppressions of race and class.

The partisan divides, on abortion and on other social issues, prevented activists on both sides from coming together. The differentiated positions of the two dominant political parties continued through the 2000 and 2004 elections, in a closely divided country with very close elections and an appeal by both parties for swing voters.

During this period, Catholic bishops initiated the communion wars to shame Catholic Democratic candidates. We can see in this development the concrete effects of moral absolutism on abortion. In 2004, Republican candidate George W. Bush sought reelection and the Democratic nominee was John Kerry. President George W. Bush appealed to pro-life voters by explaining his position that "the ideal world is one in which every child is protected in law and welcomed in life."[125] Cardinal Raymond Burke declared that he would deny communion to Catholic John Kerry on the basis of Kerry's pro-choice position. The pro-life movement supported George W. Bush as a pro-life candidate because of Bush's stated opposition to abortion, even though Bush strongly supported the death penalty. When Bush was governor of the state of Texas, his state had the highest number of capital executions in the country.[126] During his presidency, Bush took the country to war in Iraq, a clear violation of Catholic just war teachings, and despite the 2003 Ash Wednesday diplomatic visit by Vatican envoy Cardinal Pio Laghi, who attempted to persuade Bush not to go to war with Iraq. When Bush tried to end the diplomatic visit on shared ground by pointing out his opposition to abortion, Laghi reportedly replied that those issues were not the purpose of his mission.[127] The Vatican envoy could see that there were other pressing "life" issues at stake besides abortion, even when US bishops and the Republican party could not. Republican strategists also employed tactics designed to appeal to their voting base, including religious conservatives, such as opposition to same sex marriage initiatives that began at the state level.

Use of dark money has also become a key strategy of the pro-life movement. In the wake of the Supreme Court's 2010 ruling in *Citizens United v. Federal Election Commission*, which reversed campaign finance restrictions, corporations and other outside groups can spend unlimited funds on elections if they are not formally coordinating with a candidate or political party. The ruling gives special interest groups more influence in elections, and has led to the creation of super-PACS (political action committees) and nonprofits who do not disclose their donors (known as "dark money"). "Dark money" donations made in secret by super-rich elites have changed the rules of pro-life politics.[128] Barre Seid's $1.6 billion donation to create Marble Freedom Trust in support of the Federalist Society is but one example of the huge sums of money that are now influencing judicial appointments, political campaigns, elections, lobbying, and litigation.[129] Other dark money pro-life groups include the Alliance Defending Freedom, the American Center for Law and Justice, the Family Research Council, and Heartbeat International. Texas Right to Life, a 501(c)(4) "social welfare" organization, has spent millions of dollars to influence elections through lobbying, a state political action campaign (PAC), and online advertising.[130] Leaders of the Catholic Church have spent millions of dollars on their lobbying efforts and political advertising related to abortion. Recent examples include over $2.5 million in spending to fight a constitutional amendment in Kansas,[131] and the California Catholic Conference's spending in the "No on Prop 1" campaign during the 2022 midterm elections.[132]

The conservative Catholic media ecosystem of the past twenty years actively participated in absolutist anti-abortion messaging, amplifying the voices of the USCCB on "life" issues in a way that focused on abortion. The USCCB's own communications team crafted abortion-first messaging,[133] and the moral absolutism employed in Catholic teachings found emphasis in diocesan newspapers across the country.[134] But other institutions officially separate from the USCCB also gained influence during this time. Examples include the Eternal Word Television Network, Guadalupe Radio, Life Site News, Catholic Answers, *First Things*, *National Catholic Register*, and Church Militant. As Rush Limbaugh was developing a radio talk show audience in the secular media focused on conservative values and White male grievances, Catholic television and radio personalities developed similar strategies that demonized feminist thinkers as anti-family and weaponized Church teaching so that the *Catechism* could be used reductively in apologetics arguments.

Republican opposition to social welfare programs—from Reagan's tax cuts in 1981 to the Tea Party of 2010 to the 2023 standoff over raising the debt ceiling—have become an expected part of the party's platform. But opposition to social welfare programs is not an obvious pro-life position for a party to take. After all, social welfare programs provide direct assistance to the poor, vulnerable, and marginalized members of society—through nutrition assistance programs, Medicaid, and other effective means of creating a safety net. These are exactly the programs that the USCCB explicitly supports in their own pro-life documents, including both the *Pastoral Plan for Pro-Life Activities* and *Living the Gospel of Life*. But the bishops characterize the Democratic party as anti-life on the basis of abortion politics, without attention to the platform's positions on taxation, anti-poverty programs, social welfare programs, and so forth. Unfortunately, those most vulnerable members of society have been sacrificed by the pro-life movement in an effort to make gains in other ways, including legislative and judicial gains.

Many credit Catholic voters in swing states with electing Donald Trump in 2016,[135] in part because of his promises to "Make America Great Again" by nominating pro-life judges, defunding Planned Parenthood, and by reinstating and expanding the Mexico City Policy.[136] When he spoke at the 2020 March for Life, President Donald Trump described himself and his administration as pro-life and explained that he believed in the sanctity of every human life.[137] Despite what one journalist described as Trump's "morally and practically disastrous" first term, Republican voters in his base continue to support him.[138]

VICIOUS POLITICAL CHOICES

Fifty years after *Roe*, the culture wars rage on. *Dobbs* will not end them, but will send them into a new phase at the state level. While gun violence, climate change, political corruption, and other destabilizing issues are not going away, Catholic bishops continue to advocate for an approach to political life that sees abortion as the preeminent moral issue.[139] Christian ethicist Sandra Sullivan-Dunbar explains how pro-life politicians have even endangered democracy itself.[140] Catholic bishops have contributed to this political climate in a way that increases polarization and demonizes people in the public square with whom they disagree. Even in the face of growing evidence about moral problems in the pro-life movement[141] and growing polarization in the United States electorate,[142] leaders of the Catholic Church have not backed away from their explicit support of the pro-life movement.

While the *rhetoric* of the pro-life movement is certainly focused on talk about protecting unborn life, the movement itself has encompassed much more than an attempt to make abortion illegal. Pro-life activists sought support for segregation academies, fought marriage equality, rejected the Equal Rights Amendment, endorsed political violence, employed dark money to influence politics through nondemocratic means, and rejected expansion of social welfare programs, all in the name of "protecting life." Often, though, these other aims are unacknowledged publicly, or purposefully hidden. Uncovering the distortions, lies, and unholy alliances that have become commonplace for people who call themselves pro-life is thus an important part of telling a broader story in this book about why the Catholic Church should reject the pro-life movement and instead support a movement for reproductive justice.

Our response to the complexity of abortion should not be a single-axis or oversimplified approach, but rather one that supports women, contributes to healing for people who have experienced pregnancy loss, and reaffirms the importance of self-determination and conscience in cases of moral dilemma. This is the wisdom of reproductive justice. Catholics need a new approach— one that rejects the partisan approach thus far undertaken by US bishops and instead focuses on the social teachings of the Church and the kinds of structural and spiritual supports that women say would actually empower them. Such an approach requires a willingness to enter into messy dialogues and reject simplistic answers. It means creating a culture and a Church in which women have full equality. It will require rebuilding trust across partisan lines and working together to foster pragmatic solidarity in both Church life and in public life. Criminalizing abortion without addressing structural change furthers racist and sexist agendas in US culture. Addressing the underlying causes that compel women to seek abortions would be a more helpful and more just approach to the moral problems we face. The next chapter takes up the question of what structural change is needed in order to empower pregnant women to choose to continue pregnancy.

NOTES

1. Students for Life of America, 2023, https://studentsforlife.org/.
2. Archbishop José H. Gomez and Archbishop William E. Lori, "USCCB Statement on U.S. Supreme Court Ruling in *Dobbs v. Jackson*," June 24, 2022. https://www.usccb.org/news/2022/usccb-statement-us-supreme-court-ruling-dobbs-v-jackson.
3. John Yang, "The Shifting Battle Over Abortion Rights 50 Years After Roe," PBS News Weekend (January 22, 2023), https://www.pbs.org/newshour/show/the-shifting-battle-over-abortion-rights-50-years-after-roe.
4. Francis, *Fratelli Tutti* (2020), 154–214. https://www.vatican.va/content/francesco/en/encyclicals/documents/papa-francesco_20201003_enciclica-fratelli-tutti.html.
5. Ziad W. Munson, *The Making of Pro-Life Activists: How Social Movement Mobilization Works* (Chicago: University of Chicago Press, 2008), 99. "The movement is completely united in its pursuit of a single, ultimate goal: an end to all abortions in the United States. There is universal consensus regarding this goal among pro-life organizations and activists, even if they disagree on everything else about the abortion debate." Munson, 99.
6. Munson, *The Making of Pro-Life Activists*, 134–36.
7. Munson, *The Making of Pro-Life Activists*, 149.
8. Munson, *The Making of Pro-Life Activists*, 199. Munson's study covers the period from 1973 to 2008.
9. Munson, *The Making of Pro-Life Activists*, 94.
10. Munson, *The Making of Pro-Life Activists*, 95.
11. Munson, *The Making of Pro-Life Activists*, 102.
12. Munson, *The Making of Pro-Life Activists*, 102.
13. Munson, *The Making of Pro-Life Activists*, 105.
14. Munson, *The Making of Pro-Life Activists*, 103–4.
15. Munson, *The Making of Pro-Life Activists*, 106–7.
16. Munson, *The Making of Pro-Life Activists*, 113–15.
17. For example, pro-life activist Abby Johnson explained the marketing strategies of crisis pregnancy centers: "Women seeking abortions, women that are pregnant, that are vulnerable, they are going into Google, and they are typing 'pregnancy symptoms.' There's a way in Google where you can basically set that search to your website. We want to look professional, business-like. And yeah, we do kind of want to look medical. The best client you ever get is one that thinks they're walking into

an abortion clinic." See DeShawn Taylor, *Undue Burden* (Charleston: Advantage, 2023), 133.

18. Munson, *The Making of Pro-Life Activists*, 115.

19. Munson, *The Making of Pro-Life Activists*, 117–20.

20. Munson, *The Making of Pro-Life Activists*, 116–20.

21. Munson, *The Making of Pro-Life Activists*, 127, 123.

22. Munson, *The Making of Pro-Life Activists*, 188.

23. Munson, *The Making of Pro-Life Activists*, 195.

24. Munson, *The Making of Pro-Life Activists*, 32.

25. Munson, *The Making of Pro-Life Activists*, 95.

26. Christine Firer Hinze, *Radical Sufficiency: Work, Livelihood, and a US Catholic Economic Ethic* (Washington, DC: Georgetown University Press, 2021), 19.

27. Firer Hinze, *Radical Sufficiency*, 186.

28. Firer Hinze, *Radical Sufficiency*, 137.

29. Daniel K. Williams, *Defenders of the Unborn: The Pro-Life Movement Before Roe v. Wade* (New York: Oxford University Press, 2016), 4.

30. Williams, *Defenders*, 4–5.

31. Williams, *Defenders*, 19, citing John T. McGreevy, *Catholicism and American Freedom: A History* (New York: W. W. Norton, 2003), 150–54.

32. Charles E. Rice, *The Vanishing Right to Life: An Appeal for a Renewed Reverence for Life* (Garden City, NJ: Doubleday, 1969).

33. Williams, *Defenders*, 38.

34. James Mohr, "Iowa's Abortion Battles of the Late 1960s and Early 1970s: Long-Term Perspectives and Short-Term Analysis," *Annals of Iowa* 50 (1989): 82, cited by Rickie Solinger in *Pregnancy and Power: A Short History of Reproductive Politics in America* (New York: New York University Press, 2005), 183.

35. Leslie Woodcock Tentler, *Catholics and Contraception: An American History* (Ithaca, NY: Cornell University Press, 2004).

36. Before the promulgation of *Humanae Vitae* in 1968, the Lambeth Conference had declared that contraceptive use by married couples could be licit, and many Catholics hoped that the pontifical commission on birth control initiated by Pope John XXIII would come to similar conclusions. See Emily Reimer-Barry, "On Women's Health and Women's Power: A Feminist Appraisal of *Humanae Vitae*," *Theological Studies* 79:4 (2018): 818–40.

37. Many Catholics thought after the Second Vatican Council that the lived experiences of lay Catholic couples would have a greater impact on ecclesial discernment about marital sexuality and were disappointed when Paul VI rejected the majority report of his own papal birth control commission in order to promulgate the encyclical against artificial means of birth control in 1968. See Mark S. Massa, SJ, *The Structure of Theological Revolutions: How the Fight Over Birth Control Transformed American Catholicism* (New York: Oxford, 2018).

38. Mark Newman, "The Catholic Diocese of Mobile-Birmingham and Parochial School Desegregation, 1962–1969," *The Alabama Review* 74:1 (January 2021), 24–61, at 33.

39. The National Catholic Welfare Conference was the authoritative teaching body of the US bishops at the time. See USCCB, "A Brief History of the USCCB" (2023), https://www.usccb.org/about/a-brief-history-of-usccb.

40. National Catholic Welfare Conference, *On Racial Harmony* (August 23, 1963), no. 6. https://www.usccb.org/issues-and-action/cultural-diversity/african-american/resources/upload/On-Racial-Harmony-Aug-23-1963.pdf.

41. Bryan Massingale, *Racial Justice and the Catholic Church* (Maryknoll: Orbis, 2010); Michael Warner, *Changing Witness: Catholic Bishops and Public Policy 1917–1994* (Grand Rapids: Eerdmans, 1995).

42. Shannen Dee Williams, *Subversive Habits: Black Catholic Nuns in the Long African American Freedom Struggle* (Durham, NC: Duke University Press, 2022); Cyprian Davis, *The History of Black Catholics in the United States* (New York: Herder & Herder, 1990).

43. Solinger, *Pregnancy and Power*, 182–83.

44. Protestants did not have an active campaign to protest abortion rights, though they did speak out against feminism and secularism during this time. Daniel K. Williams, *God's Own Party: The Making of the Christian Right* (New York: Oxford, 2010), 105–20.

45. United States Catholic Conference, *Human Life in Our Day* (1968), https://www.usccb.org/issues-and-action/human-life-and-dignity/abortion/excerpts-from-human-life-in-our-day.

46. National Conference of Catholic Bishops, "Respect Life Resolution," April 13, 1972.

47. Steven P. Millies, *Good Intentions: A History of Catholic Voters' Road from Roe to Trump* (Collegeville: Liturgical, 2018), 144–46.

48. Daniel K. Williams explains that Sunbelt voters in the 1968 election "disliked the overt racism and economic populism of southern Democrats such as Wallace, but they supported Republicans such as Nixon and Reagan who knew how to denounce crime, drugs, and welfare without mentioning race." Williams, *God's Own Party*, 93.

49. Rick Perlstein, *Nixonland* (New York: Scribner, 2008), 340–43, 463–67.

50. Margaret Sammon Parsons, "Abortion and Religion: The Politics of the American Catholic Bishops," PhD diss. Catholic University of America, 2011, 33.

51. *Documentation on the Right to Life and Abortion* (Washington, DC: United States Catholic Conference, 1974), 59.

52. Robert N. Karrer, "The National Right to Life Committee: Its Founding, Its History, and the Emergence of the Pro-Life Movement Prior to *Roe v. Wade*," *Catholic Historical Review* 97, no. 3 (2011): 527–57. DOI: 10.1353/cat.2011.0098.

53. Van Gelder, *New York Times*, 1973, 51.

54. A 1980 study of National Right to Life Committee membership found that 70 percent of the members were Catholic. Donald Granberg, "The Abortion Activists," *Family Planning Perspectives* 12, no. 5 (July–August 1981): 157–63.

55. Munson, *The Making of Pro-Life Activists*, 86.

56. March for Life was founded by Nellie Gray, a Democrat who had previously worked at the US Department of Labor before founding the annual protest of legal abortion. Gray's positions on abortion admitted of no exceptions, not even

to save a woman's life. In the early days she advocated for a constitutional amendment that would make abortion illegal nationwide. See Mary Ziegler, *Dollars for Life: The Anti-Abortion Movement and the Fall of the Republican Establishment* (New Haven: Yale University Press, 2022), 23. See also Mary Ziegler, *Abortion and the Law in America: Roe v. Wade to the Present* (Cambridge: Cambridge University Press, 2020); Mary Jo McConahay, *Playing God: American Catholic Bishops and the Far Right* (New York: Melville House, 2022); Michele Goodwin, *Policing the Womb: Invisible Women and the Criminalization of Motherhood* (Cambridge: Cambridge University Press, 2020).

57. *The Pastoral Plan for Pro-Life Activities* (1975), in *Documentation on Abortion and the Right to Life II* (Washington, DC: United States Catholic Conference), 46.

58. Emily Reimer-Barry, "Another Pro-Life Movement is Possible," Catholic Theological Society of America *Proceedings* 74 (2019): 21–41. For an early critique, see Frances Kissling, "Religion and Abortion: Roman Catholicism Lost in the Pelvic Zone," *Women's Health Issues* 3, no. 3 (Fall 1993): 132–37. DOI: 10.1016/s1049-3867(05)80246-4.

59. The 2001 update is available on the website of the USCCB: *Pastoral Plan for Pro-Life Activities* (2001), https://www.usccb.org/prolife/pastoral-plan-pro-life-activities.

60. Paul VI, *Gaudium et spes* (1965), 75.

61. National Conference of Catholic Bishops, *The Challenge of Peace* (1983), https://www.usccb.org/upload/challenge-peace-gods-promise-our-response-1983.pdf, 12.

62. *Challenge of Peace*, 73–74.

63. *Challenge of Peace*, 127, 83, 91, 128.

64. National Conference of Catholic Bishops, *Economic Justice for All: A Pastoral Letter on Catholic Social Teaching and the U.S. Economy* (1986), https://www.usccb.org/upload/economic_justice_for_all.pdf.

65. *Economic Justice for All*, 21.

66. Administrative Board of the National Conference of Catholic Bishops, *The Many Faces of AIDS* (1987), https://www.usccb.org/resources/statement-many-faces-aids-november-14-1987; National Conference of Catholic Bishops, *Called to Compassion and Responsibility* (1989), https://www.usccb.org/resources/called-compassion-and-responsibility-0.

67. https://www.usccb.org/resources/statement-many-faces-aids-november-14-1987.

68. Jack Willke, "For Better or Worse," in Teresa R. Wagner, *Back to the Drawing Board: The Future of the Pro-Life Movement* (South Bend, IN: St. Augustine's Press, 2003), 125.

69. K. Cassidy, "The Right to Life Movement: Sources, Development, and Strategies," *Journal of Policy History* 7, no. 1 (1995): 128–59. DOI: 10.1017/s0898030600004176

70. Rick Perlstein, *Reaganland* (New York: Simon & Schuster, 2020), 172.

71. Perlstein, *Reaganland*, 172. Perlstein argues that groups on the right nurtured discontents that reinforced one another, noting that conservative Christian voices were

not only present in anti-abortion campaigns (such as resistance to the Equal Rights Amendment) but also pro-gun lobbying and the "Stop the Panama Canal Giveaway."

72. Williams, *God's Own Party*, 113.

73. Mary Ziegler, *Dollars for Life*, 18–19; *Abortion and the Law in America*, 42.

74. On Reagan's appeal to the pro-life movement, see Williams, *Defenders of the Unborn*, 239–41.

75. Williams, *God's Own Party*, 154.

76. This Catholic strategy is not adopted by orthodox Christians, who also oppose abortion in their teachings but have a more pastoral approach to abortion in politics. Thank you to Steven Millies for sharing wisdom here.

77. Williams, *God's Own Party*, 130.

78. Two notable voices who urged caution and careful distinctions in their work are Richard McCormick, SJ and Lisa Sowle Cahill. See for example: Richard McCormick, SJ, "Rules for Abortion Debate," *America* (July 22, 1978); Lisa Sowle Cahill, "Abortion, Autonomy, and Community" from Daniel and Sidney Callahan, eds., *Abortion: Understanding Difference* (New York: Plenum Press, 1984).

79. Celeste Michelle Condit, *Decoding Abortion Rhetoric: Communicating Social Change* (Urbana: University of Illinois Press, 1990); Patricia Beattie Jung, "Abortion and Organ Donation," "Abortion and Organ Donation: Christian Reflections on Bodily Life Support," in *Readings in Moral Theology, No. 9: Feminist Ethics and the Catholic Moral Tradition*, eds. Charles E. Curran, Margaret A. Farley, and Richard A. McCormick, SJ (New York: Paulist, 1996), 440–80.

80. McCormick, "Rules."

81. Joseph F. Donceel, SJ, "Immediate Animation and Delayed Hominization," *Theological Studies* 31:1 (1970): 76–105. https://doi.org/10.1177/004056397003100103.

82. Daniel Callahan, *Abortion: Law, Choice, and Morality* (New York, Simon & Schuster, 1970).

83. Daniel C. Maguire, "Abortion: A Question of Catholic Honesty," *The Christian Century* (September 14–21, 1983).

84. During this time period, there was a growing divide between Catholic bishops and Catholic academic theologians; as women began to join the ranks of theologians and feminist theology flourished, the bishops distanced themselves from the work of theologians.

85. Randall Balmer, *Bad Faith: Race and the Rise of the Religious Right* (Grand Rapids, MI: Eerdmans, 2021), chapter 9.

86. Balmer, *Bad Faith*, chapter 9.

87. Perlstein, *Reaganland*, 347. Perlstein cites Joseph Crespino, *Strom Thurmond's America* (New York: Hill & Wang, 2012), 268.

88. Perlstein, *Reaganland*, 347.

89. James T. Hannon, "The Influence of Catholic Schools on the Desegregation of Public School Systems: A Case Study of White Flight in Boston," *Population Research and Policy Review* no. 3 (1984): 219–37. See also Katie Walker Grimes, *Divided Christ: Anti-blackness as Corporate Vice* (Fortress, 2017).

90. *Alexander v. Holmes County Board of Education* 396 U.S. 19 (1969), https://www.loc.gov/item/usrep396019/. See also Stephanie R. Rolph, *Resisting*

Equality: The Citizen's Council, 1954–1989 (Baton Rouge: Louisiana State University Press, 2008).

91. The "dog whistle" politics employed by Nixon and Reagan meant that they sought to signal to racist voters that they agreed with them. Perlstein, *Reaganland*, 673. Trump took this further by making explicitly racist comments. On the original "welfare queen," see Josh Levin, "Linda Taylor, Welfare Queen," *Slate* (December 19, 2013), https://www.slate.com/articles/news_and_politics/history/2013/12/linda_taylor_welfare_queen_ronald_reagan_made_her_a_notorious_american_villain.html. On the stereotype of the welfare queen, see Dorothy Roberts, *Killing the Black Body: Race, Reproduction, and the Meaning of Liberty*, twentieth anniversary edition (New York: Vintage, 2017), 8, 17–19, 111, 207–208.

92. Solinger, *Pregnancy and Power*, 189–90.

93. Williams, *God's Own Party*, 102–10, 146–47.

94. Perlstein, *Reaganland*, 395, citing Robert O. Self, *All in the Family: The Realignment of American Democracy since the 1960s* (New York: Hill & Wang, 2012), 370. See also William C. Inboden III, "Divine Elections: Abortion, Evangelicalism, and the New Right in American Politics, 1973–1980: The Politicization of Morality," Stanford University Department of History, Honors Thesis.

95. Mario Cuomo, "Religious Belief and Public Morality: A Catholic Governor's Perspective," *The Notre Dame Journal of Law, Ethics, and Public Policy* 1:1 (1984), reprinted in *Abortion: A Reader*, ed. Lloyd Steffen (Cleveland: Pilgrim Press, 1996), 373–88.

96. Robert N. Karrer, "Abortion Politics: The Context of the Cuomo-O'Connor Debate, 1980–1984," *U.S. Catholic Historian* 34:1 (Winter 2016): 103–24.

97. Democratic Party Platforms, 1984 Democratic Party Platform Online by Gerhard Peters and John T. Woolley, *The American Presidency Project*, https://www.presidency.ucsb.edu/node/273258.

98. Synod of Bishops, *Justice in the World* (1971), 10. https://www.cctwincities.org/wp-content/uploads/2015/10/Justicia-in-Mundo.pdf.

99. John Paul II, *Laborem Exercens* (1981), 12, 16–18. https://www.vatican.va/content/john-paul-ii/en/encyclicals/documents/hf_jp-ii_enc_14091981_laborem-exercens.html.

100. Parsons, *Abortion and Religion*, 140. See also Timothy Byres, *Catholic Bishops in American Politics* (Princeton, NJ: Princeton University Press, 1991).

101. Robert D. McFadden, "Archbishop Calls Ferraro Mistaken on Abortion Rule," *New York Times* (September 10, 1984), https://www.nytimes.com/1984/09/10/nyregion/archbishop-calls-ferraro-mistaken-on-abortion-rule.html. On October 7, 1984, the Catholic Committee on Pluralism and Abortion took out a full-page advertisement in the *New York Times* to share their Catholic statement on pluralism and abortion. The statement claims that a diversity of opinions regarding abortion exists among committed Catholics and calls for "candid and respectful discussion on this diversity of opinion within the Church." Ecclesial sanctions and reprimands were swift, and in some cases fierce. See "A Diversity of Opinions Regarding Abortion Exists Among Committed Catholics," *New York Times* (October 7, 1984), E7; Kate M. Ott, "From Politics to Theology: Responding to Roman Catholic Ecclesial Control

of Reproductive Ethics," *Journal of Feminist Studies in Religion* 30:1, 138–47; Mary E. Hunt and Frances Kissling, "New York Times Ad: A Case Study in Religious Feminism," *Journal of Feminist Studies in Religion* 3, no. 1 (Spring 1987): 115–27; Barbara Ferraro, Patricia Hussey, and Jane O'Reilly, *No Turning Back: Two Nuns' Battle with the Vatican over Women's Right to Choose* (New York: Poseiden, 1990).

102. Williams, *God's Own Party*, 187–211.

103. Julio Borquez, "Partisan Appraisals of Party Defectors: Looking Back at the Reagan Democrats," *American Review of Politics* 26 (2005): 323–46.

104. Mary Ziegler, *Abortion and the Law in America*, 77.

105. President Ronald Reagan, "Remarks at a White House Briefing," July 30, 1987. Ronald Reagan Presidential Library, Master Tapes, 543–44. https://www.youtube.com/watch?v=5mIJy5kLQmA.

106. Nick Seabrook, *One Person, One Vote: A Surprising History of Gerrymandering in America* (New York: Knopf, 2022).

107. Anthony J. McGann, Charles Anthony Smith, Michael Latner, and Alex Keena, *Gerrymandering in America: The House of Representatives, the Supreme Court, and the Future of Popular Sovereignty* (New York: Cambridge University Press, 2016). https://doi.org/10.1017/CBO9781316534342.

108. John Murdock, "The Future of the Pro-Life Democrat," *National Affairs* (Winter 2020), https://www.nationalaffairs.com/publications/detail/the-future-of-the-pro-life-democrat; Alexandra Desanctis, "Farewell to the Pro-Life Democrats," *National Review* (March 18, 2020), https://www.nationalreview.com/2020/03/farewell-to-the-pro-life-democrats/.

109. Joseph Bernardin, *Consistent Ethic of Life* (Kansas City: Sheed & Ward, 1988). See also Thomas Nairn, ed., *The Consistent Ethic of Life: Assessing Its Reception and Relevance* (Maryknoll: Orbis, 2008).

110. United States Conference of Catholic Bishops, *Living the Gospel of Life* (1998), https://www.usccb.org/issues-and-action/human-life-and-dignity/abortion/living-the-gospel-of-life.

111. USCCB, *Living the Gospel of Life*, 23.

112. Carol Mason, *Killing for Life: The Apocalyptic Narrative of Pro-Life Politics* (Cornell University Press).

113. Jim Little, "Pensacola Was Once the Anti-Abortion Battleground," *Pensacola News Journal* (June 24, 2022), https://www.pnj.com/story/news/2022/06/24/abortion-pensacola-has-long-complex-role-roe-vs-wade-debate/9648854002/.

114. Various, "Killing Abortionists: A Symposium," *First Things* (December 1994), https://www.firstthings.com/article/1994/12/killing-abortionists-a-symposium.

115. Francis Canavan, "Killing Abortionists," *First Things* (December 1994), https://www.firstthings.com/article/1994/12/killing-abortionists-a-symposium.

116. Hadley Arkes, "Killing Abortionists," *First Things* (December 1994), https://www.firstthings.com/article/1994/12/killing-abortionists-a-symposium.

117. Lloyd H. Steffen, *Ethics and Experience: Moral Theory from Just War to Abortion* (Lanham, MD: Rowman & Littlefield, 2012), 192. Steffen refers in his notes to the killing of Dr. John Bayard Britton and Lt. Col. James Herman Barrett, outside the Ladies Center in Pensacola, Florida, on July 29, 1994, by Paul Hill.

118. Two novels capture this well. See Jennifer Haigh, *Mercy Street* (New York: Harper, 2022) and Jodi Picoult, *A Spark of Light* (New York: Random House, 2018).

119. For example, "Pro-Life Action League," https://prolifeaction.org/action/prayatclinic/; George Goss, "Bishop, Pro-Life Advocates Pray Outside Abortion Clinic," *The Arlington Catholic Herald* (April 6, 2019), https://www.catholicherald.com/article/local/bishop-pro-life-advocates-pray-outside-abortion-clinic/; Forty Days for Life (2023), https://www.40daysforlife.com/en/.

120. Marlene Gerber Fried, "Reproductive Rights Activism after Roe," in *Radical Reproductive Justice: Foundations, Theory, Practice, Critique*, eds. Loretta J. Ross et al. (New York: Feminist Press, 2017), 139–50; Rickie Solinger, *Pregnancy and Power*, 209–54.

121. Loretta J. Ross, "Conceptualizing Reproductive Justice Theory: A Manifesto for Activism," in *Radical Reproductive Justice: Foundations, Theory, Practice, Critique*, eds. Loretta J. Ross et al. (New York: Feminist Press, 2017), 170–232.

122. For example, critics argue that the 1994 crime bill led to mass incarceration of people of color. See Michelle Alexander, *The New Jim Crow: Mass Incarceration in the Age of Colorblindness* (New York: New Press, 2010).

123. "The America We Seek: A Statement of Pro-Life Principles and Concerns" (1996), https://www.firstthings.com/article/1996/05/the-america-we-seek-a-statement-of-pro-life-principle-and-concern. Signatories included Ralph Reed, Frank Pavone, Richard John Neuhaus, Beverly LaHaye, Michael Novak, George Weigel, Jim Wallis, Jack C. Wilke, and more.

124. Rickie Solinger, *Pregnancy and Power*, 222.

125. "Transcript of Debate between Bush and Kerry," *New York Times*, October 13, 2004. https://www.nytimes.com/2004/10/13/politics/campaign/transcript-of-debate-between-bush-and-kerry-with-domestic.html.

126. David Hancock, "Kerry's Communion Controversy," CBS News (April 6, 2004), https://www.cbsnews.com/news/kerrys-communion-controversy/.

127. Paul Moses, "Vatican Diplomacy and the Iraq War," *Commonweal* (January 13, 2020), https://www.commonwealmagazine.org/vatican-diplomacy-iraq-war.

128. Tim Lau, "Citizens United Explained," Brennan Center for Public Policy (December 12, 2019), https://www.brennancenter.org/our-work/research-reports/citizens-united-explained.

129. Andrew Perez, Andy Kroll, and Justin Elliott, "How a Secretive Billionaire Handed His Fortune to the Architect of the Right-Wing Takeover of the Courts," *ProPublica* (August 22, 2022), https://www.propublica.org/article/dark-money-leonard-leo-barre-seid. See also Andy Kroll, Andrea Bernstein, Ilya Marritz, and Nate Sweitzer, "We Don't Talk About Leonard: The Man Behind the Right's Supreme Court Supermajority," ProPublica (October 11, 2023), https://www.propublica.org/article/we-dont-talk-about-leonard-leo-supreme-court-supermajority.

130. Isaiah Poritz, "Texas' Largest Anti-Abortion Group Spent Millions on Public Information Campaign, Lobbying" (September 9, 2021), https://www.opensecrets.org/news/2021/09/texas-largest-anti-abortion-group-spent-millions-on-public-campaign-lobbying-in-past-decade/.

131. Michael Sean Winters, "What Can the Church Learn from Kansas' Vote to Protect Abortion Rights," *National Catholic Reporter* (August 5, 2022), https://www.ncronline.org/news/opinion/what-church-can-learn-kansas-vote-protect-abortion-rights.

132. California Catholic Conference, "No on Prop 1" (2020), https://cacatholic.org/prop1.

133. For example, opportunities to "Take Action!" on the USCCB website include "Tell the House to pass No Taxpayer Funding for Abortion!" https://www.votervoice.net/USCCB/Campaigns/100286/Respond.

134. For example, through the syndicated columns of George Weigel, Catholic neoconservative writer.

135. Michael J. O'Loughlin, "Catholic Voters Helped Give Trump His Unexpected Victory," *America Magazine*. November 9, 2016. https://www.americamagazine.org/politics-society/2016/11/09/catholic-voters-helped-give-trump-his-unexpected-victory.

136. See Mary Ziegler, "Trump's Triumph," in *Abortion and the Law in America*, 201–206. The Mexico City Policy was reinstated and expanded by President Trump; it requires foreign nongovernmental organizations to certify that they will not perform or actively promote abortion as a method of family planning if they want to receive US government global family planning assistance. See Kaiser Family Foundation, "Mexico City Policy Explainer," https://www.kff.org/global-health-policy/fact-sheet/mexico-city-policy-explainer/. But the Mexico City policy is ineffective in reducing abortions globally. See Yana Rodgers' data that abortion rates go up when the global gag orders are in effect, https://www.pri.org/stories/2019-03-04/abortions-rise-worldwide-when-us-cuts-funding-women-s-health-clinics-study-finds.

137. President Donald Trump said during his 2020 March for Life speech: "All of us here understand an eternal truth: Every child is a precious and sacred gift from God. Together, we must protect, cherish, and defend the dignity and the sanctity of every human life." "Trump Tells Anti-Abortion Marchers Unborn Children Have Never Had Stronger Defender in the White House," *New York Times* (January 24, 2020), https://www.nytimes.com/2020/01/24/us/politics/trump-abortion-march-life.html. Emily Reimer-Barry, "Conscience at the Polls: Abortion and the Election," Catholic Moral Theology blog, October 26, 2020, https://catholicmoraltheology.com/conscience-at-the-polls-abortion-and-the-election/. Trump's vices are well documented and include marital infidelity, lying, idolatry of wealth, racist, sexist, and anti-immigrant rants, threats to journalists, bullying tactics, failure to pay his bills, and political corruption. It is hard to imagine a president who is less pro-life. Citizens for Responsibility and Ethics in Washington, "President Trump's Legacy of Corruption" (January 15, 2021), https://www.citizensforethics.org/reports-investigations/crew-reports/president-trump-legacy-corruption-3700-conflicts-interest/.

138. David A. Graham, "They Still Love Him," *The Atlantic* (June 1, 2023), https://www.theatlantic.com/ideas/archive/2023/06/why-trump-supporters-still-love-him/674248/.

139. Archbishop José Gomez, "Statement on the Inauguration of Joseph R. Biden, Jr., as 46th President of the United States of America from Most Reverend José

H. Gomez, President, United States Conference of Catholic Bishops," https://www.usccb.org/news/2021/usccb-presidents-statement-inauguration-joseph-r-biden-jr-46th-president-united-states.

140. Sandra Sullivan-Dunbar, "Catholic Abortion Discourse and the Erosion of Democracy," *Journal of the Society of Christian Ethics* 43:1 (Spring/Summer 2023), 55–74. On America's democratic decline, see Rachel Kleinfeld, *Five Strategies to Support U.S. Democracy* (Carnegie Endowment for International Peace, September 2022), 4–14.

141. For example, sexual harassment allegations of defrocked priest Frank Pavone (formerly of Priests for Life), and Abby Johnson's support for Donald Trump at the January 6, 2020, political rally-turned-insurrection, and Raymond Arroyo's commentary on ETWN. See Heidi Schlumpf, "EWTN: Connected to Conservative Catholic Money, Anti-Francis Elements," National Catholic Reporter (July 17, 2019), https://www.ncronline.org/culture/ewtn-connected-conservative-catholic-money-anti-francis-elements. Associated Press, "Vatican Defrocks an Anti-Abortion Priest Who Once Placed an Aborted Fetus on an Altar," *National Public Radio* (December 18, 2022), https://www.npr.org/2022/12/18/1143935979/vatican-defrocks-an-anti-abortion-priest-who-once-placed-an-aborted-fetus-on-an-. Nate Blakeslee, "Sorting Fact from Fiction in the Story of Pro-Life Celebrity Abby Johnson," *Texas Monthly* (April 16, 2019), https://www.texasmonthly.com/news-politics/fact-fiction-pro-life-celebrity-abby-johnson-unplanned/.

142. Drew Desilver, "The Polarization in Today's Congress Has Roots that Go Back Decades," Pew Research Center (March 10, 2022), https://www.pewresearch.org/short-reads/2022/03/10/the-polarization-in-todays-congress-has-roots-that-go-back-decades/.

Chapter 4

Structural Change for Reproductive Justice

Pregnant women today have reasonable concerns about what is expected of them if they continue a pregnancy. Caring for children means experiencing interruptions, prioritizing the needs of a vulnerable other, and struggling to balance other responsibilities. Caring for children with special needs, while often joyful and personally rewarding, can also bring additional challenges for caregivers. Class, race, and gender complicate the ways that parents experience and navigate these responsibilities. While Catholic teachings affirm the care of children as a social responsibility, practically speaking it is parents who shoulder most of the responsibility of caring for children. But parents make decisions based on the practical realities and social conditions in which they find themselves. The Catholic moral tradition has rightly emphasized the interdependence of human persons and the importance of fostering the social conditions for families to thrive. Reproductive justice scholarship does the same. As Deshawn Taylor explains, the method of reproductive justice "shifts the conversation from abstract rights to everyday justice. The reproductive justice framework engages people in their everyday lives and centers the people who need help the most."[1] In what follows, we examine different dimensions of everyday life that must be reformed so that pregnant women have the structural supports they need. Such an approach could create the possibilities for more pregnant women to reasonably see a way forward that safeguards both their well-being and the well-being of their dependent children.

STRUCTURAL CHANGE NEEDED

One striking aspect of the Catholic conversation about abortion in the US context is the reluctance among American Catholics to probe the ways in which the US economy disincentivizes pregnancy for women. Instead of seeing pregnancy as a social good and a reminder of our relationality, interdependence, and vulnerability, we see pregnancy described as a burden to employers,[2] a cost to the health care system,[3] and a marker of class status.[4] Pro-choice feminists bemoan the implication that the "choice" to carry a pregnancy to term leads to the personal responsibility to parent, often without sufficient assistance and resources from the social community.[5]

Pregnant women in the United States today face choices in a context where the dominant model of economic orthodoxy is that of *neoliberalism*, defined by economist Anthony M. Annett as "the premise that free markets and free flows of goods and capital, unrestrained by government interventions, represent the best route to rising prosperity."[6] While the US economy does have regulatory frameworks in place, reproductive justice scholars have called for renewed attention to the ways that government programs should benefit all citizens, not further enhance the power of the elite. They question, for example, the decision of federal regulators to backstop the investors of Silicon Valley Bank in 2023[7] while the temporary Child Tax Credit expired at the end of 2021.[8] The Catholic tradition has rich resources for making normative claims about what structural supports facilitate the flourishing of families and society. But these resources are all too often marginalized in discourse in the United States that focuses on the market economy as the framework by which the goods of the earth should be distributed.

In the Church's body of social teachings, popes of the past century have reminded Catholics that the central litmus test of a good economy is how it treats the vulnerable. This is in contrast with neoliberal capitalism which prioritizes profits and economic growth above all. The place of child welfare and work-family balance is not the same in Catholic teachings about social justice and in neoliberal capitalism. Care work in particular is exhausting and poorly (if even) compensated, even as we know that care work makes possible all other economic activity necessary to meet human needs.[9] These issues were compounded during the COVID-19 pandemic, especially during the first months of national lockdown when schools and childcare centers closed in order to protect public health. Catholic theologian Kristin Heyer has examined how the pandemic "exacerbated the gendered nature of the work of social production for women across classes and cultures," further exploiting women in the commodified care economy.[10] Drawing on the work of Catholic theologian Christine Firer Hinze, Heyer notes that economic policies are part of the problem. "Emphasis on free markets and personal responsibility in the United States has obstructed coherent work-family policies to support caregiving, such as universal healthcare, childcare, basic income, paid parental or illness leave."[11] If pregnant women could depend on practical supports such as good jobs, fair wages, safe housing, opportunities for home ownership, adequate nutrition, affordable health care, affordable child care, quality public education, increased supports for caring for children with special needs, and freedom from sexual and relationship violence, this would radically reshape the discernments pregnant women face. Women still face the finitude that comes with being human,[12] but removing the social constraints that are currently barriers to continuing pregnancies would be a huge and important shift. Such structural supports are possible, but require significant social change and radical solidarity to achieve. All of the following constitute essential—though not comprehensive—aspects of what families need to flourish today.

Good Jobs and Fair Wages

Good jobs—jobs that pay sufficient wages to support a family with benefits and flexible scheduling—are hard to come by in today's economy. While employers may tout the benefits of the "gig" economy, workers suffer when they lack job security, and when they have to work multiple jobs just to pay bills. Households need income; many parents today see a good, stable job as necessary for good parenting (in some households there is only one working adult, but many today have two working adults). The federal minimum wage, $7.25/hour, has not changed since 2009.[13] When a pregnant woman is considering whether she will have the resources in the future to provide for a child—a commitment lasting decades of her life—one part of her analysis is the income she and/or her partner can expect to earn, and the standard of living they can expect as parents.

Workers today are understandably anxious about future earnings. In the first quarter of 2023, median weekly earnings were 6.1 percent higher than a year earlier, but those gains were offset by the 5.8 percent increase in the Consumer Price Index over the same period.[14] Previous generations of US workers saw rises in productivity and corresponding purchasing power in their lifetimes, but today's workers do not see these benefits.[15] Between 1980 and 2018, income growth was stagnant for all non-elite workers and families.[16] Economist Anthony Annett explains that salary is not the only factor that leads to job satisfaction; numerous other factors, including working conditions, autonomy, engagement, and the social capital built from workplace relationships also matter.[17] But a just wage is essential to thriving in the modern economy. In practice, it can be difficult to determine what counts as a just wage.[18] But it is clearly unjust if a company's profits are not shared with the workers whose labors generated the productivity in the first place. The Economic Policy Institute estimates that CEO compensation has grown 1,460 percent since 1978, while typical worker compensation has risen just 18 percent. In 2022, CEOs of the top 350 firms in the United States made an average of $27.8 million each, which is an 11.1 percent increase from 2020, and represents 399 times more than their workers. The EPI report explains that "exorbitant CEO pay is a contributor to rising inequality that we could restrain without doing any damage to the wider economy."[19] Most pregnant women are not, it turns out, CEOs.

The effects of systemic racism on US workers are complex, and they shape the particular experiences of Black, Indigenous, and Latina pregnant women in the workforce and in many cases other members of their household as well. Racial bias impacts recruitment and hiring decisions,[20] worker satisfaction, and productivity.[21] Racism also has long term impacts on generational wealth. Thomas Shapiro exposes the disadvantages experienced by communities of color because of the persistence of the racial wealth gap.[22] Focusing on inherited wealth and the advantages that inherited wealth yields, Shapiro shows that when people who are already privileged by race and class have greater access to educational resources and better-paying jobs, this perpetuates racial inequality. Racism is also a factor in unemployment and underemployment trends in the United States. The unemployment rate for Black Americans fell below 5 percent in the United States for the first time ever in April 2023, after peaking at 16.8 percent in May 2020.[23] But still, the Black-White unemployment gap persists.[24] Anthony Annett explains that "prolonged unemployment is corrosive to human flourishing; not only does it lead to a loss of lifetime earnings, but it also worsens health, impedes the educational achievement of children, and depletes trust and social capital."[25] Jennifer Hochschild's research points out that predominantly White communities in the United States do not suffer the same levels of high and persistent unemployment, erosion of public trust and civic engagement, and family dissolution as Black communities.[26] She argues that both class and race matter when analyzing impacts of joblessness on communities. Declining opportunities in American urban centers for manufacturing jobs is one part of the picture. Raj Chetty's analysis of tax records from 40 million families from 1996 to 2012 demonstrated that "upward income mobility is significantly lower in areas with larger African-American populations" and that "more racially segregated areas have less upward mobility."[27] Anti-racist practices in the workplace will continue to be necessary to implement reproductive flourishing.

A good job—that is, a job in which one is treated with dignity and paid a fair wage—should not be a 24/7 commitment. Further, pregnant and nursing workers often have specific bodily needs that require accommodation (restroom breaks, space and time for pumping breastmilk, time off for doctor appointments, workspace that accommodates a growing belly). These too constitute essential aspects of reproductive flourishing long supported by the Catholic Church and yet rarely part of the conversation about what it means to advance pro-life policies.

Working for the Catholic Church is also a challenge for employees for very practical reasons. Low wages, incomplete benefits,[28] overwork, and discriminatory hiring and firing practices are only part of the story of what it means to work as a diocesan employee today.[29] While this could be an opportunity for bishops to "walk the talk" about building a culture of life for working families today, it has not been a focus of their assemblies or of any published documents.[30] Catholic universities deserve scrutiny in this regard as well, since the labor of contingent faculty, graduate students, and staff is not always fairly compensated.[31]

In part because of the precarity of work in the United States today, some advocate for a universal basic income in order to advance justice. Catholic theologian Kate Ward explains that universal basic income provides cash income to every adult in a society, regardless of income and without means testing.[32] Such a program would avoid the problematic costs associated with means-tested programs that end up funding bureaucracy; further, it would establish a "society-wide basic needs 'floor' below which no one can fall, no matter what," and in doing so, would challenge pervasive messages "that the poor are less worthy of human dignity."[33] Annett explains that one of the key benefits for workers is that "the recipient would have the freedom to walk away from demeaning work, which should bid up wages and the attractiveness of jobs."[34] Such an approach is worthy of sustained attention by Catholics, especially since experts note that every basic income experiment has led to increased well-being without diminished impact to work hours.[35]

Safe Housing and Equal Opportunities for Home Ownership

Safe and affordable housing should not be considered a privilege that only the wealthiest can afford. But in the United States today, affording a place to live in dignity remains elusive for far too many families. According to the National Alliance to End Homelessness, approximately 421,392 people were homeless in the United States last year.[36] According to a report issued by the US Department of Housing and Urban Development, 582,462 people were experiencing homelessness across America.[37] In San Diego County, where I live, the homeless count rose to 10,264 in 2022, a 22 percent increase from the previous year.[38] The real numbers of people facing housing insecurity are even larger; the "point in time" homelessness counts are based on a single night in January and do not account for the fluidity of the population who experiences housing insecurity and who may go uncounted because they are couch-surfing or temporarily sheltered. The National Law Center on Homelessness and Poverty estimates that each year 2.5–3.5 million Americans sleep in shelters, transitional housing, and public places not meant for human habitation; more than 7 million have lost their homes and are sheltered with family or friends due to economic necessity.[39] The root causes of homelessness include lack of affordable housing, poverty, unemployment, domestic violence, homophobia, and transphobia.[40] Known breakdowns within the social safety net include failures to address the needs of veterans, minors transitioning out of foster care, previously incarcerated offenders transitioning from confinement, and the needs of people who face substance abuse and mental illness and lack adequate treatment.[41] Without a stable address, it can be difficult for someone to find stable employment; "housing first" programs aim to get people into safe shelter first before addressing other important needs including substance abuse or unemployment.[42]

Low wages and high housing costs create impossible scenarios for working Americans. According to the National Low Income Housing Coalition, in 2022, a person working full-time, year-round at minimum wage could not afford the monthly Fair Market Rent (FMR) for a two-bedroom rental unit in any state or the District of Columbia.[43] Consider the following, from the State of America's Children 2023 report:

> To afford FMR for a two-bedroom rental nationally, a single person working full-time must make almost $26 an hour, more than 3.5 times the federal minimum wage of $7.25 an hour. And while 30 states and the District of Columbia now have minimum wages higher than the federal minimum wage, the average minimum-wage worker must still work 96 hours per week—nearly 2.5 full-time jobs—to afford a two-bedroom rental. Even in states with the most affordable housing, Arkansas, Missouri, and New Mexico, a family still must have at least 1.5 full-time jobs at minimum wage to afford a two-bedroom rental. In the least affordable states, New Hampshire and Hawaii, it takes 3.6 and 4 full-time jobs at minimum wage, respectively, to afford housing.[44]

These impossible scenarios are commonplace all over the country. The complexity and interrelated nature of the US housing crisis and of persistent low wages requires us to think about structural responses. Interpersonal aid, local charities, and crisis pregnancy centers can offer some assistance to women and children in need, but they do not solve the underlying root causes. In addition, the high cost of housing is not a problem that is easily isolated from issues of racial discrimination, income inequality, education, or neighborhood segregation.

The rental market is not the only aspect of the housing crisis worthy of sustained reflection; home ownership is a critical way for families to invest and can lead to long-term financial security. But here too we see evidence of the influence of systemic racism. While the US homeownership rate increased to 65.5 percent in 2021, the Black-White homeownership gap remains significant. Racial disparities in homeownership persist; the homeownership rate for White Americans is 72.7 percent, followed by Asian Americans at 62.8 percent, followed by Hispanic Americans at 50.6 percent, and Black Americans at 44 percent.[45] Black homeowners spend more of their income to own their homes than other racial groups, with 30 percent being cost-burdened because they spend more than 30 percent of their income on housing. Beyond affordability, other factors that contribute to racial differences include discriminatory practices within the lending and refinancing process and realtors steering buyers toward or away from particular neighborhoods.[46] The history of housing discrimination in the United States includes redlining policies of the Federal Housing Administration after the New Deal, policies that refused to insure mortgages in and near African American neighborhoods even as the same program was investing in White-dominant suburban developments.[47]

Other factors that demonstrate housing inequities in the United States today include lack of access to parks and over-policing in communities of color. People of color are three times more likely to live in nature-deprived neighborhoods, where they have diminished access to parks, walking paths, and green spaces in comparison to White families.[48] Just policing remains an important aspect of building a culture of life in the United States today.[49] Policing today is under scrutiny for failing to address discriminatory practices.[50] The right to raise a family in safe and healthy environments is a key focus of reproductive justice activism precisely because these racialized realities (unsafe and unhealthy neighborhoods) intersect with the health care and family planning decisions that pregnant women face.

Affordable Nutrition

It is a cruel irony that the year following the *Dobbs* ruling was also a year for high food prices. While food prices generally increase about 2 percent, they increased 11 percent in 2022 and 6.7 percent in 2023. Some cities saw higher costs than others. For example, in Philadelphia food prices increased 13.63 percent; in Detroit, 14.49 percent.[51] There are complex reasons for these increases. Inflation is part of the picture, but the US Government Accountability Office also explains that there were unique challenges in 2022. Those included an outbreak of avian flu which increased the prices of eggs; the war in Ukraine which disrupted the global supply of agricultural commodities such as wheat, corn, sunflower oil, and fertilizer; and drought in some growing regions, which influenced supply and therefore prices.[52] The United States is one of the wealthiest countries in the world, and yet millions suffer from hunger and malnutrition. According to the United States Department of Agriculture, household food insecurity affected 12.5 percent of households with children in 2021 and 17.3 percent of households with children in 2022.[53] Food insecurity means that a person has limited or uncertain availability of nutritionally adequate and safe foods, or limited ability to acquire acceptable foods in socially acceptable ways (for example, without resorting to scavenging or stealing).[54] In 2021, 33.8 million people lived in food-insecure households. In 2022, 44.2 million people lived in food insecure households.[55] Rates of food insecurity were higher than the national average for households with children headed by a single woman, as well as households with incomes below 185 percent of the poverty line. Food insecurity is related to larger patterns of income inequality, unemployment or underemployment, the costs of housing and transportation, the gender wage gap, environmental racism, and other factors. For example, there are over 6,500 food deserts in the United States. A food desert is a geographic area where residents have few to no convenient options for securing affordable and healthy foods, especially fresh produce. According to research by Kelly M. Bower, food deserts disproportionately impact communities of color, especially Black Americans.[56]

Not only do pregnant women need affordable healthy foods, but so do their children. If a family is already struggling to meet the nutritional needs of members of the household, welcoming another child can seem not only unwise but unjust for the already born malnourished children for whom one is obliged to care. Addressing hunger and food insecurity must be part of our approach to reproductive flourishing. As with other complex social issues, addressing food insecurity requires a multi-layered approach inclusive of federal, state, local, and parish-based levels. Catholic organizations such as Catholic Charities are often already involved in food distribution and food justice issues, and expanding these critical programs remains an integral part of building a culture of support for families.

Affordable and Accessible Health Care

According to research by the Kaiser Family Foundation, health costs associated with pregnancy, childbirth, and postpartum care average a total of $18,865 and the average out-of-pocket payments total $2,854 for women enrolled in large group insurance plans.[57] Many factors influence the costs of maternity care. For example, vaginal delivery is less expensive than delivery by caesarean section. A medicated birth or induction can also increase costs. Mothers and infants who require intensive care or prolonged hospitalization will incur larger hospital bills. Insurance plans vary, as do the costs of "in network" versus "out of network" costs. Some families qualify for Medicaid or state-level Children's Health Insurance Program (CHIP) coverage.[58]

But the problem is not only about affordability; it is also about accessibility. Finding a provider who will accept Medicaid and/or CHIP can be difficult.[59] Compounding these problems are the closures of hospital maternity wards, especially in rural communities. Hospital administrators say the closures are driven by low Medicaid reimbursement rates, staffing shortages, and declining birth rates.[60] From 2004 to 2014, 9 percent of rural counties lost their obstetrics services, with an additional 45 percent of rural counties having no obstetrics services.[61] The loss of hospital obstetrics services impacts more than 18 million women of reproductive age who live in rural counties; nearly half a million women give birth each year in rural hospitals.[62]

Even though Catholic teachings describe access to health care as a human right, the US bishops lobbied against the Affordable Care Act and seem poised to further restrict health care for patients in Catholic hospitals as they revise the *Ethical and Religious Directives*.[63]

Affordable Childcare

Parents with minor children at home make up one-third of the workforce, and finding affordable childcare is essential both to child welfare and to parental employment.[64] But too often in the United States context, such issues are framed as personal dilemmas instead of structural problems.

Navigating the workplace leave policies and childcare availability and affordability requires suspension of the laws of mathematics. Consider, for example, that a full-time worker today earning minimum wage in California ($15.50)[65] would be expected to pay half of their pre-tax earnings on one child's full-time day-care expenses ($1,412/month).[66] The Family and Medical Leave Act enables eligible employees to take up to twelve weeks of job-protected unpaid leave for certain family and medical reasons.[67] But only 56 percent of US employees are eligible for FMLA.[68] Further, taking an *unpaid* leave is out of reach for many families who depend on the regular salary of working parents. Navigating existing childcare financial assistance programs, which vary by state and require an application process, can be challenging.[69] Even when children mature to school age, finding affordable after-school and summertime programs is a struggle. A US Census Bureau survey found that more than 365,000 adults reported losing a job because they needed to take time to care for children under the age of five in the four weeks preceding the survey.[70]

One of the structural issues that parents face is that there are not enough childcare centers. A 2020 report found that there were only enough licensed child care slots to provide care for 23 percent of infants and toddlers.[71] The term "child care desert" refers to an area in which licensed child care supply is far short of the population of children and reflected the status of 80 percent of the counties studied.[72] But even when families find a childcare center, day care costs an average of $11,000 and is more than the price of public college in thirty-three states.[73] Low pay for childcare center employees, long commutes for parents, daunting waitlists, high costs, and severe staffing shortages contribute to the complexity of the problem.[74]

Just Adoption and Foster Care Programs

From approximately 1940 to 1970, an estimated four million mothers in the United States surrendered newborn babies to adoption.[75] For many mothers who placed their children for adoption, the process was a result of the stigma and shame they were made to experience for having a child "out of wedlock." Catholic priests sometimes contributed to this shame and the resulting emotional distress.[76] Unfortunately, some women continue to report being "pushed" into adoption instead of having "the space to make my decision."[77] Post-*Dobbs*, some women in states with abortion bans may feel that their options are reduced to parenting or placing their child for adoption. One of the challenges that states with abortion bans in place must take up is assuring that women who place children for adoption post-*Dobbs* are doing so out of freedom and genuine choice and not because the state is coercing their pregnancy and adoption.

Adoption can be a beautiful opportunity for the just care of infants and children, but is not without its challenges and is certainly not an easy answer to the complex social problem of abortion. For pregnant women who are willing and able to continue a pregnancy and birth but unwilling or unable to parent, placing a child with adoptive parents can serve the needs of all parties.[78] Many birth parents report high satisfaction with their placement decisions, even as these are accompanied by grief and mixed emotions.[79] But there can also be numerous challenges in this process, and those are complicated by financial costs, identity of children and parents, legal barriers, and the problematic ways in which the "adoption industry" fosters a transactional and consumerist approach to child welfare. In fact, adoption placement is a rare choice for people who become pregnant; infant adoptions in the United States constitute approximately 0.5 percent of live births.[80] Scholars note that among women motivated to avoid parenthood, adoption is considered infrequently. Reasons vary, and include the emotional difficulty of letting go and placing a child for adoption after birth and fear that their child would find them and confront them later.[81] Scholars conclude that "political promotion of adoption as an alternative to abortion is likely not grounded in the reality of women's decision making."[82]

Further, child welfare programs in the United States are failing to meet the needs of vulnerable children. In 2019, there were approximately 424,000 children in foster care.[83] In some cases, the neglect children experience in the home is rooted in poverty, but the foster care system removes children from their home instead of addressing the social supports that would enable caregivers to provide a more stable home life for the children.[84] Youth in foster care experience disruptions in care, and in some cases, abuse by foster parents. One in nine Black children and one in seven Native American children spend part of their childhood in foster care. In South Dakota, Peter Lengkeek, a Crow Creek Tribal Council member, describes these patterns as "kidnapping."[85]

Advocates say that the foster care system is failing. Foster America reports that 70 percent of youth in the juvenile justice system have been involved with the child welfare system; 50 percent of foster youth will not graduate from high school on time; 48 percent of girls in foster care become pregnant by age nineteen; 60 percent of child trafficking victims have been in foster care; 33 percent of homeless young adults have been in foster care; and kids in foster care are four times more likely than other children to attempt suicide.[86] These patterns of suffering are related to other kinds of systemic social problems, including structural racism and the broken social safety net. Some researchers predict that the overturning of *Roe v. Wade* will be harmful for teens, particularly for populations at higher risk of unintended pregnancy including foster youth.[87]

The complicity of the Catholic Church in forced adoptions and the abuse of children in Catholic orphanages and schools is slowly coming to light and requires additional reflection and analysis.[88] Catholic policies are also related to heterosexism in the US Catholic Church; in order to avoid placing children with same-sex couples, Catholic adoption agencies closed. Representatives of the US Conference of Catholic Bishops complain that forcing Catholic agency to place children with same-sex adoptive parents is a violation of religious liberty and should be described as discrimination against Catholic adoption services.[89] Evidence suggests, however, that same-sex couples and heterosexual couples experience similar parenting outcomes, and same-sex couples experience even better outcomes in "child psychological adjustment and child-parent relationships."[90] Bishops undermine social justice when they put doctrinal purity ahead of child welfare.

Reproductive flourishing after *Dobbs* requires new attention to adoption programs in accordance with justice, which must include nonjudgmental support as pregnant women discern how best to proceed.

Quality Public Education

While an education experience that integrates Catholic religious and spiritual formation can be a wonderful experience (whether through a Catholic grammar or high school or through homeschooling), these can be cost-prohibitive for families. Catholic schools can also contribute to racial segregation in education.[91] Access to quality public education is a social good that should receive Catholic support. But support for educational excellence, freedom from gun violence, and racial equity in schools are now controversial in US society, while opposition to critical race theory and anti-racist pedagogies and support for gun ownership have become talking points for politicians who claim to be pro-life.[92]

Educational inequality in the United States begins at the age of three; in a 2019 study, among three- and four-year-olds, only 1 percent of Latino children and 4 percent of Black children were enrolled in a high-quality preschool program.[93] Racial inequities persist through the high school experience. More than 50 million students were enrolled in public elementary and secondary schools in fall 2017. The percentage of White students has been decreasing in the past twenty-five years.[94] The National Association of Secondary School Principals reports that in many urban areas, a majority of students of color attend public schools where at least 75 percent of students are from low-income families. Segregation and redlining in US history have led to lower property values in neighborhoods with concentrated populations of students of color. This results in fewer financial resources for their schools. Districts serving the largest populations of students of color receive, on average, about $1,800 less per student—or $23 billion total—in federal, state, and local funding than school districts that predominantly serve White students.[95]

These disparities lead to what educators call the "opportunity gap," whereby students of color have fewer educational opportunities than White students. As a result, average reading and math scores have been lower for students of color than their White peers since 1992.[96] The COVID-19 pandemic exacerbated existing inequalities in education. 2023 math and reading scores for American thirteen-year-olds dropped to their lowest level in decades, reflecting losses caused by COVID and school closures.[97] The "digital divide" exacerbated learning barriers. During the pandemic, many students lacked access to the technology that enabled remote learning, including computers and internet connectivity; Black and Hispanic households with school-aged children were 1.3 to 1.4 times more likely as White ones to face limited access to computers and the internet.[98]

Compounding these known injustices are parents' and students' reasonable fears about gun violence on school campuses. There were 650 mass shootings in 2022 and 328 in the first six months of 2023.[99] Guns are the leading cause of death among American children and teens, surpassing motor vehicle deaths and those caused by other injuries.[100] Four in ten Americans think schools in their communities are not safe from gun violence, according to a 2023 poll.[101] But the outsized influence of the gun lobby, led by the National Rifle Association, means that national conversations about sensible gun legislation are often met by distortions and obstructions.[102] When pregnant women are discerning whether they can reasonably accept the responsibilities of parenthood, access to safe, quality education is part of a broader discernment process.

Increased Supports for Raising Children with Special Needs

Improved prenatal diagnostic testing procedures have resulted in increased detection rates of fetal anomalies during pregnancy, with the resultant discernment for pregnant patients as they determine the best course of action in their situation.[103] Many in the pro-life community have expressed concerns about the rationale women give for terminating pregnancies due to fetal anomaly, which assumes that the quality of life for someone living with a disabling condition is so compromised that death is perceived as a better outcome.[104] This idea is prevalent among many physicians, as testimonies of pregnant women who were advised to abort indicates.[105] Ethicists caution that a eugenic mindset is at work in such evaluations of the quality of life that a person with a disabling condition will experience.[106] Even experts who affirm a woman's right to abortion in such contexts recognize that it is an "emotionally traumatic experience" and that women who face the question of whether to continue a pregnancy after diagnosis of fetal anomaly deserve "compassionate and person-centered care, good information and communication, and a thoughtful and integrated care pathway."[107] Perinatal hospice is an often underutilized opportunity for palliative care plans when families continue their pregnancies but expect that newborns' lives will be brief.[108]

Approximately 3 percent of babies are born with some type of birth defect, and they can be very mild or life-threatening.[109] The most common birth defects are heart defects, cleft lip/palate, Down syndrome, and spina bifida. Here I want to address the structural needs that pregnant women facing diagnosis of fetal anomaly experience. Giving women an opportunity to name and reflect upon their reasons for continuing or terminating a pregnancy can illuminate some of the structural barriers that have an impact on women's decision-making.[110] But even describing some of those barriers can be offensive to readers who care for and love persons with disabilities. For example, each year six thousand babies are born with Down syndrome.[111] They are our neighbors, our siblings,[112] our fellow Mass-goers. It is also the case that our social world is not set up to provide optimal support to people with Down syndrome and their families. The Centers for Disease Control and Prevention reports that over 40 percent of families of children with Down syndrome had a family member who stopped working because of the child's condition, and 40 percent reported that the child's condition caused financial problems for the family.[113]

Catholic ethicists should rightly resist the ways that neocapitalism constrains the moral imagination, especially when it does so in ways that seem to propose that members of our families are burdens to the family or to society. Scholars of theology and disability have continued to probe experiences of vulnerability, impairment, and interdependency as theological motifs—even finding in Christian understandings of the Trinity resources for thinking of God as disabled.[114] Catholic theologian Mary Jo Iozzio explains that in medical literature and political discourse, we too often describe a dignified life as a life that is free of dependency. "When the hegemonic norms of independence are held as sacrosanct," Iozzio explains, "it is no wonder that many would begin to think that any condition resembling dependence ought to be shunned or that death (or abortion for the fetus diagnosed with genetic anomaly) ought to be preferred."[115] Instead, Iozzio calls our attention to the data that many persons living with disability report that they are happy and that except for the stigma associated with disabilities, their lives are satisfying.[116]

But it is also the case that the systems in place today (health care, education, low wages, and so forth) put too many parents in an impossible situation, and in some cases raise doubts for pregnant women about whether and how they can afford to raise a child with special needs. The questions families face will depend on the diagnosis and on their situational context. Will our insurance plan cover the surgeries our doctors say will be necessary? How will we pay to renovate our home to make it wheelchair accessible? Does our school district offer inclusive education that will meet our child's needs? Will I be able to return to work? I think it is important not to censor such questions or describe them as selfish on the part of the pregnant woman discerning how best to proceed given her finite resources and the many unknowns she faces. Such reflection indicates the *social failures* of US society. If we want to create incentives for pregnant women to continue pregnancy after diagnosis of fetal anomaly, there are specific resources that those women need to see in place. Those resources are connected to other social conditions such as safe and affordable housing, inclusive education, affordable health care, welcoming Catholic liturgies and religious education curricula, reduced stigma, and greater social support.

Freedom from Sexual and Relationship Violence

Home is not always safe for women and children. On a typical day, domestic violence hotlines in the United States receive over 19,000 calls.[117] Thirteen percent of ever-partnered women and girls, aged fifteen to forty-nine years, have been subjected to intimate partner violence in the past twelve months.[118] Globally, one in three women have been subjected to physical and/or sexual intimate partner violence, or both, at least once in their lifetime.[119] Globally, 47,000 women in 2020 died at the hands of an intimate partner or a family member, which equals to a woman or girl being killed every eleven minutes in their home.[120] Women are more likely than men to be sexually harassed and stalked online.[121] Fewer than 40 percent of women who experience violence in the home seek help of any sort.[122] Some women report that they believe violence against them is justifiable if they refuse to have sex with their partner.[123] Across justice systems, there are low rates of reporting sexual violence, low rates of prosecution of perpetrators, and insufficient penalties even when victims take on the life-altering burden of pressing charges against their rapists.[124]

Sometimes, it is the pregnancy itself that triggers abuse from a controlling partner, who is jealous that a pregnant woman's attention is focused on meeting her own needs. The American College of Obstetricians and Gynecologists reports that one in six abused women were first abused during pregnancy. Physical abuse during pregnancy can lead to miscarriage, premature birth, and/or injuries to the prenate.[125]

Sometimes the pregnancy discernment is as much about the quality of the sexual relationship as anything else. Women ask questions such as, "Does my partner put me down and make me feel bad about myself? Does my partner threaten me or the baby? Does my partner blame me for his own actions? Would co-parenting with this person be possible? Is this someone that I want to be in relationship with for the next two decades?"[126]

In order to truly make the world safe for women and children, faith communities must understand their role in shaping toxic masculinity.[127] Men's violence against women is rarely addressed in Catholic spaces, even though the US bishops have clearly taught that "violence against women, inside or outside the home, is never justified."[128] But too often in Catholic communities, commands to forgive others for their wrongs in combination with teachings about the indissolubility of marriage can make women in abusive relationships feel trapped. An abusive partner can also engage in reproductive coercion, attempting to control the pregnant woman's decisions about the pregnancy. According to the American College of Obstetricians and Gynecologists, the most common forms of reproductive coercion are sabotage of contraceptive methods, pregnancy coercion, and pregnancy pressure.[129]

A population of survivors who receive too little attention include the survivors of reproductive abuse by Catholic clergy, whose trauma is compounded by clericalism and mechanisms of silencing and control, even when clergy abusers coerced their victims into obtaining abortions.[130] Archival records indicate that most clerical perpetrators whose female victims became pregnant sought to persuade them to have an abortion. Many paid for the procedure and brought their victims to the clinic. The primary rationale for the abortion was to maintain the priest's reputation. For example, when one of Nicholas

Cudemo's victims named "Ruth" testified before the Philadelphia Grand Jury, she recalled that Cudemo took her for an abortion after she conceived from his abuse, and that "he was mad because he was very pro-life."[131] It is hard to imagine what the term "pro-life" means in such a context.

Sexual violence is also an ordinary aspect of confinement; women in jails, detention centers, and prisons in the United States experience dehumanizing and violent conditions that undermine their reproductive flourishing. In 2023, the California Department of Corrections and Rehabilitation logged more than 800 complaints of staff sexual abuse, but most advocates believe this to be a significant undercount.[132] In addition to rape and other forms of sexual abuse, human rights abuses within the carceral state also include family separation policies, coerced sterilization of immigrant women, the shackling of pregnant and laboring women, and the withholding of sanitary napkins from menstruating women.[133]

Trauma-informed approaches to working with survivors of sexual assault emphasize the importance of securing safety for the victim first, and prioritizing the victim's control over any reporting process. Victim advocate groups argue that reporting of rape and incest can be retraumatizing, especially when trying to advocate for oneself in a medical context.[134] Many advocate groups oppose the way that rape and incest exceptions in abortion bans require a pregnant woman to report to multiple parties in order to receive health care.[135] Such requirements do not align with trauma-informed approaches to care for survivors of sexual assault.

THE ROAD AHEAD

At this point, many readers are likely to lose heart. Even if you find this argument compelling, the road ahead is anything but easy. I have argued that in order to foster reproductive flourishing in the United States today, all of the following are needed:

- Good jobs and fair wages
- Safe housing and opportunities for home ownership
- Affordable nutrition
- Affordable and accessible health care
- Affordable childcare
- Just adoption programs
- Quality public education
- Increased support for raising children with special needs
- Freedom from sexual and relationship violence

Such a list can be overwhelming, and it remains an incomplete sketch of a flourishing life. Naming the complexity of our current situation is the first honest step we can take together. Pro-life and pro-choice slogans and bumper stickers both fail to address these complex social realities. But there are no magic potions or easy answers to the dilemmas facing our communities.

Faith communities have an important role in addressing structural harms as well as in addressing local needs. Womanist ethicist Emilie M. Townes asks: "What kinds of social structures do we need to help form people to achieve the society we want?"[136] It is this approach to structural change that forms the basis of shared commitments between a Catholic social ethic and the work of reproductive justice advocates. The ecclesial witness of US Catholicism could focus on these structural supports and on continued advocacy—on the federal, state, and local levels—for policies and programs that would serve the goals of reproductive flourishing and the common good. To achieve justice requires communal action within messy structures, be they political, ecclesial, or familial.

To see abortion as a *personal* choice without giving sustained attention to the *structural* factors that impact a pregnant woman's decision-making represents a failure of theological and social analysis. Since *Dobbs*, little progress has been made in achieving structural justice; in some cases, vulnerable populations are in a *more* precarious situation now. But reproductive flourishing requires social supports. Decisions about fertility and reproduction are made within this fundamentally unjust society—in which race, class, and sex determine options and fundamental freedoms are not equal for all. Because of the lack of social supports, many women report that abortion seems like the best option for them. I have identified specific structural supports that would promote reproductive flourishing in the United States today, and I believe these are nonpartisan issues that could promote common ground among activists who seek the full flourishing of women and children in US society. In the Catholic Church in particular, Church teachings already provide robust critique of neoliberal capitalism and strong supports for child welfare, fair wages, and an end to violence against women and children. The fact that social change is difficult should not deter us.

Catholic teachings offer a robust critique of capitalism and of the market economy in general. A perennial challenge is how to move from theory to practice. In his 1991 social encyclical, *Centesimus Annus*, John Paul II explained how economics was changing, and cautioned that the exploitation of workers was exacerbating problematic trends in economics that prioritized profits over people.[137] "The fact is," wrote the pope, "that many people, perhaps the majority today, do not have the means which would enable them to take their place in an effective and humanly dignified way within a productive system in which work is truly central."[138] John Paul II's approach acknowledged the reality of market economies but also explained the importance of meaningful regulation. For example, he writes: "It would appear that, on the level of individual nations and of international relations, the free market is the most efficient instrument for utilizing resources and effectively responding to needs. But this is true only for those needs which are 'solvent,' insofar as they are endowed with purchasing power, and for those resources which are 'marketable,' insofar as they are capable of obtaining a satisfactory price. But there are many human needs which find no place on the market."[139]

John Paul II affirmed "the legitimate role of profit," but cautioned that "profitability is not the only indicator of a firm's condition."[140] Contrary to the central claims of neoliberal market capitalism, twenty-first-century popes have repeated the demand "that the market be appropriately controlled by the forces of society and by the State, so as to guarantee that the basic needs of the whole of society are satisfied."[141] John Paul II argued for a just family wage that would enable working parents to provide a dignified life for their families. Benedict XVI expounded on this vision by explaining that we will not solve all social problems through "commercial logic," but rather that economic justice must be tethered to a robust understanding of both the common good and of the practices of solidarity.[142] Benedict explained that it is proper for the Catholic Church to have a "public role" in fostering integral human development, inclusive of specific goals such as addressing hunger and food insecurity.[143]

Francis expounds on the advocacy for economic justice that his predecessors highlighted as central to the mission of the Church. In *Evangelii Gaudium* Francis describes the malicious effects of "an evil embedded in the structures of society," explaining that this "evil [is] crystalized in unjust social structures."[144] Francis describes neoliberal capitalism as an "economy of exclusion."[145] While the superrich manipulate markets to their advantage, Francis sees the ways in which the poor are marginalized and even discarded as outcasts in a throwaway culture.[146] Later in the same document, Francis proposes economic reforms that would eliminate the structural causes of poverty, address inequality, and emphasis social solidarity.[147] In alignment with the activism of scholars of reproductive justice, Francis writes that we need "more politicians who are genuinely disturbed by the state of society, the people, the lives of the poor!" He goes on to say that "government leaders and financial leaders" should "work to ensure that all citizens have dignified work, education, and healthcare."[148] Francis is explicitly critical of Church communities who engage in "empty talk" without "creative concern and effective cooperation in helping the poor to live with dignity."[149]

Creating the social conditions for reproductive flourishing is a complex undertaking and will not be accomplished overnight. By naming specific structural supports that pregnant women need, I have suggested a new approach that could bring together advocates from across the political spectrum. One sign of hope on the horizon in the United States today is the bicameral Momnibus Act to End America's Maternal Health Crisis, which is made up of thirteen bills, including legislation that would make critical investments to address social determinants of health, extend WIC (food assistance) eligibility in the postpartum and breastfeeding periods, provide funding for community-based organizations that promote equity, expand access to maternal mental health care, improve programs for mothers who are incarcerated, and more.[150] Such an approach would be an important first step toward a more just future. If Catholic social teachings are to be meaningful in the midst of the complex social injustices that women face today, we should support structural reforms such as the Momnibus Act. Reducing the number of abortions will require significant social investment in programs that would give women more confidence to bring their pregnancies to term. Addressing the root causes of social injustice is a key aspect of reproductive justice feminism and could lead to long-lasting positive impacts for pregnant women and vulnerable children.

NOTES

1. Deshawn Taylor, MD, *Undue Burden: A Black, Woman Physician on Being Christian and Pro-Abortion in the Reproductive Justice Movement* (Charleston, SC: Advantage, 2023), 105.

2. With his typical inflammatory rhetoric, Fox News host Tucker Carlson proclaimed in summer 2022 that corporations were paying for abortions because maternity leave was a financial burden. See Nicole Silverio, "A Lot Cheaper to Get Rid of Them" (June 29, 2022), https://dailycaller.com/2022/06/29/tucker-carlson-corporations-telling-people-cant-have-children-abortion/.

3. Gabriela Dieguez, Bruce S. Pyenson, Amy W. Law, Richard Lynen, and James Trussell, "The Cost of Unintended Pregnancies for Employer-Sponsored Health Insurance Plans," *American Health Drug Benefits*, vol. 8, no. 2 (April 2015): 83–92. Danielle H. Sandler and Nichole Szembrot, "New Mothers Experience Temporary Drop in Earnings" (US Census Bureau: June 16, 2020), https://www.census.gov/library/stories/2020/06/cost-of-motherhood-on-womens-employment-and-earnings.html.

4. Tina Fey, "Confessions of a Juggler," *The New Yorker* (February 6, 2011), https://www.newyorker.com/magazine/2011/02/14/confessions-of-a-juggler-tina-fey. Saman Shad, "The Ultimate Status Symbol? Why Wealthy Families Are Opting for More Kids," *The Sydney Morning Herald* (September 22, 2017), https://www.smh.com.au/money/planning-and-budgeting/the-ultimate-status-symbol-why-wealthy-families-are-opting-for-more-kids-20170922-gyn4a7.html.

5. Andrea Smith, "Beyond Pro-Choice Versus Pro-Life: Women of Color and Reproductive Justice" *National Women's Studies Association Journal*, vol. 17, no. 1 (2005): 119–40.

6. Anthony M. Annett, *Cathonomics: How Catholic Tradition Can Create a More Just Economy* (Washington, DC: Georgetown University Press, 2022), xiv.

7. Lizette Chapman and Jason Leopold, "The FDIC Has Accidentally Released a List of Companies it Bailed Out for Billions in the Silicon Valley Bank Collapse," *Fortune* (June 23, 2023), https://fortune.com/2023/06/23/fdic-accidentally-released-list-of-companies-it-bailed-out-silicon-valley-bank-collapse/.

8. Kris Cox, Chuck Marr, Sarah Calame, and Stephanie Hingtgen, "Top Tax Priority," Center on Budget and Policy Priorities (June 12, 2023), https://www.cbpp.org/research/federal-tax/top-tax-priority-expanding-the-child-tax-credit-in-upcoming-economic.

9. Sullivan-Dunbar, "Valuing Family Care," in Jason King and Julie Hanlon Rubio, eds., *Sex, Love, and Families: Catholic Perspectives* (Minneapolis: Liturgical, 2020), 151–62, 151–53.

10. Kristin E. Heyer, "Enfleshing the Work of Social Production: Gender, Race, and Agency," *Journal of Moral Theology*, vol. 12, special issue 1 (2023), 81–107, at 81.

11. Heyer, "Enfleshing," 86; Christine Firer Hinze, *Glass Ceilings and Dirt Floors: Women, Work, and the Global Economy* (Mahwah, NJ: Paulist, 2015), 5–7, 76–77.

12. Cristina L. H. Traina, "Feminism, Finitude, and Flourishing: On 'Being Mortal, Like Everyone Else' (Wis 7:1)." Madeleva Lecture, St. Mary's College, South Bend, Indiana, April 13, 2023; "Between a Rock and a Hard Place: Unwanted Pregnancy, Mercy, and Solidarity," *Journal of Religious Ethics* 46:4 (2018): 658–81.

13. US Department of Labor, "History of Changes to the Minimum Wage Law," https://www.dol.gov/agencies/whd/minimum-wage/history.

14. Bureau of Labor Statistics, "Usual Weekly Earnings of Wage and Salary Workers" (April 18, 2023), https://www.bls.gov/news.release/pdf/wkyeng.pdf.

15. Robert J. Gordon, *The Rise and Fall of American Growth: The U.S. Standard of Living since the Civil War* (Princeton, NJ: Princeton University Press, 2016). See also Thomas Piketty, *Capital in the Twenty-First Century* (Cambridge, MA: Belknap Press, 2014).

16. Tamara Draut, *Understanding the Working Class* (New York: Demos, 2018); Nancy Folbre, *Who Pays for the Kids? Gender and the Structures of Constraint* (New York: Routledge, 1994).

17. Annett, *Cathonomics*, 162. Annett references Jan-Emmanuel De Neve and George Ward, "Happiness and Work" in *World Happiness Report* (New York: UN Sustainable Development Solutions Network, 2017), 144–77.

18. Annett, *Cathonomics*, 164.

19. Josh Bivens and Jori Kandra, "CEO Pay Has Skyrocketed 1,460 percent Since 1978," Economic Policy Institute report (October 4, 2022), https://www.epi.org/publication/ceo-pay-in-2021/.

20. Patrick M. Kline, Evan K. Rose, and Christopher R. Walters, "Systemic Discrimination Among Large U.S. Employers," National Bureau of Economic Research working paper (July 2021), https://www.nber.org/papers/w29053. In their timely study, the researchers found that "distinctively Black names reduce the probability of employer contact by 2.2 percent relative to distinctively White names."

21. Society for Human Resource Management, *The Cost of Racial Injustice: Absenteeism, Productivity Loss, and Turnover* (2022), https://shrm.org/ResourcesAndTools/tools-and-samples/toolkits/Documents/TFAW21_CostOfInjustice.pdf?_ga=2.99483613.2138800626.1687390208-2068108372.1687390208.

22. Thomas Shapiro, *The Hidden Cost of Being African American: How Wealth Perpetuates Inequality* (New York: Oxford University Press, 2004), with Melvin Oliver, *Black Wealth/White Wealth*, second ed. (New York: Routledge, 2006), *Toxic Inequality* (New York: Basic Books, 2017).

23. Felix Salmon, "An Unemployment Rate Milestone," Axios Economy & Business (May 5, 2023), https://www.axios.com/2023/05/05/unemployment-rate-milestone-black-americans.

24. The April 2023 reporting saw this gap decrease to 1.6 percent, down from 5.4 percent in August 2020; despite moving in the right direction, the gap persists. For analysis of 2020 data, see Olugbenga Ajilore, "One the Persistence of the Black-White Unemployment Gap," Center for American Progress (February 24, 2020), https://www.americanprogress.org/article/persistence-black-white-unemployment-gap/.

25. Annett, *Cathonomics*, 162. Annett references Mai Dao and Prakash Loungani, "The Human Cost of Recessions: Assessing It, Reducing It," *International Monetary Fund Staff Position Notes*, no. 17, 1 (2010), https://doi.org/10.5089/9781462308163.004.

26. Jennifer L. Hochschild, "Race, Class, Politics, and the Disappearance of Work," *Ethnic and Racial Studies*, vol. 40, no. 9 (2017): 1492–501, at 1493. Hochschild's article is a commentary on William Julius Wilson's landmark essay, "When Work Disappears: New Implications for Race and Urban Poverty in the Global Economy," *Ethnic and Racial Studies*, vol. 22, no. 3 (1999).

27. Raj Chetty, Nathaniel Hendron, Patrick Kline, and Emmanuel Saez, "Where Is the Land of Opportunity? The Geography of Intergenerational Mobility in the U.S." (2014), https://scholar.harvard.edu/files/hendren/files/geo_slides.pdf?m=1438802042.

28. Isabella Volmert, Kelly Sankowski, and Renée Roden, "What's the State of Maternity Leave in the US Catholic Church," *FemCatholic* (March 25, 2022), https://www.femcatholic.com/post/paid-leave-report.

29. Emily Reimer-Barry, "How to Be Fired from Your Job at a Catholic Institution: It Is Easier Than You Think!" *Catholic Moral Theology* blog (June 18, 2013), https://catholicmoraltheology.com/how-to-be-fired-from-your-job-at-a-catholic-institution-it-is-easier-than-you-think/; "Another Pro-Life Movement Is Possible," Catholic Theological Society of America *Proceedings*, vol. 74 (2019): 21–41; Matthew Junker, "Ending LGBTQ Employment Discrimination by Catholic Institutions," *Berkeley Journal of Employment and Labor Law*, vol 40 no. 2 (2019): 403–42.

30. United States Conference of Catholic Bishops, https://www.usccb.org/. On the one year anniversary of the *Dobbs* decision, the bishops issued a statement calling for "radical solidarity" with women facing an unexpected or challenging pregnancy. But there have not been announcements of budgetary investments or revised lobbying priorities to reflect this call. See Most Reverend Michael F. Burbidge, "Chairman's Statement on *Dobbs* Anniversary" (June 24, 2023), https://www.usccb.org/resources/23-chairman-statement-dobbs-anniversary%20rev%20clean%20BB.pdf.

31. James F. Keenan, *University Ethics: How Colleges Can Build and Benefit from a Culture of Ethics* (Lanham, MD: Rowman & Littlefield, 2015).

32. Kate Ward, *Wealth, Virtue, and Moral Luck: Christian Ethics in an Age of Inequality* (Washington, DC: Georgetown University Press, 2022), 217, citing Philippe Van Parijs, "Universal Basic Income," *Politics & Society* vol. 41, no. 2 (2013): 171–82.

33. Ward, *Wealth, Virtue, and Moral Luck*, 217. Anthony Annett criticizes means testing in *Cathonomics*, 115.

34. Annett, *Cathonomics*, 211. Ultimately, Annett does not strongly support the universal basic income, arguing instead for support of policies and institutions that allow workers to share fairly in the creation of wealth and that also provide universal benefits such as healthcare, education, and child support. See Annett, *Cathonomics*, 212.

35. Rachel Treisman, "California Program Giving $500 No-Strings-Attached Stipends Pays Off, Study Finds," National Public Radio (March 4, 2021), https://www.npr.org/2021/03/04/973653719/california-program-giving-500-no-strings-attached-stipends-pays-off-study-finds; Megan Greenwell, "Universal Basic Income Has Been Tested Repeatedly. It Works. Will America Ever Embrace It?" *Washington Post Magazine* (October 24, 2022), https://www.washingtonpost.com/magazine/2022/10/24/universal-basic-income/.

36. National Alliance to End Homelessness, "Key Facts" 2023, https://endhomelessness.org/homelessness-in-america/homelessness-statistics/state-of-homelessness/.

37. Office of Policy, Development, and Research, *Estimates of Homelessness in the US* (December 2022), https://www.huduser.gov/portal/datasets/ahar/2022-ahar-part-1-pit-estimates-of-homelessness-in-the-us.html.

38. Gary Warth, "Homelessness in San Diego County Rose 22% Last Year," San Diego Union Tribune (June 8, 2023), https://www.sandiegouniontribune.com/news/homelessness/story/2023-06-08/homelessness-in-san-diego-county-rose-22-percent-last-year-more-of-them-are-women-seniors-and-veterans.

39. National Law Center on Homelessness and Poverty, "Homelessness in America: Overview of Data and Causes" (2018), https://homelesslaw.org/wp-content/uploads/2018/10/Homeless_Stats_Fact_Sheet.pdf.

40. LGBTQ youth and young adults experience disproportionate rates of exclusion from family life and suicide than their heterosexual peers. Twenty-eight percent of LGBTQ youth report experiencing homelessness or housing instability at some point in their lives. See the Trevor Project, "Homelessness and Housing Instability among

LGBTQ Youth," https://www.thetrevorproject.org/research-briefs/homelessness-and-housing-instability-among-lgbtq-youth-feb-2022/.

41. See United States Conference of Mayors, "A Comprehensive Approach to Homelessness" (2020), https://www.usmayors.org/2020-vision/make-housing-more-affordable-and-address-homelessness/#:~:text=The%20United%20States%20Conference%20of,the%20leading%20cause%20of%20homelessness.

42. National Alliance to End Homelessness, "Housing First," March 20, 2022, https://endhomelessness.org/resource/housing-first/.

43. National Low Income Housing Coalition, *Out of Reach: 2022*, https://nlihc.org/sites/default/files/oor/2022/OOR_2022_Mini-Book.pdf. Cited in Children's Defense Fund, *State of America's Children, 2023*, table 8, https://www.childrensdefense.org/wp-content/uploads/2023/05/SOAC-2023-Tables.pdf.

44. Children's Defense Fund, *The State of America's Children 2023* (https://www.childrensdefense.org/the-state-of-americas-children/soac-2023-housing/).

45. National Association of Realtors, "More Americans Own Their Own Homes, but Black-White Homeownership Rate Gap Is Biggest In a Decade" (March 2, 2023), https://www.nar.realtor/newsroom/more-americans-own-their-homes-but-black-white-homeownership-rate-gap-is-biggest-in-a-decade-nar.

46. National Association of Realtors, "More Americans Own Their Own Homes, but Black-White Homeownership Rate Gap Is Biggest In a Decade" (March 2, 2023), https://www.nar.realtor/newsroom/more-americans-own-their-homes-but-black-white-homeownership-rate-gap-is-biggest-in-a-decade-nar.

47. Richard Rothstein, *The Color of Law: A Forgotten History of How Our Government Segregated America* (New York: Norton, 2018).

48. Alejandra Borunda, "How 'Nature Deprived' Neighborhoods Impact the Health of People of Color," *National Geographic* (July 29, 2020), https://www.nationalgeographic.com/science/article/how-nature-deprived-neighborhoods-impact-health-people-of-color.

49. Tobias Winright, *Serve and Protect: Selected Essays on Just Policing* (Eugene, OR: Cascade Books, 2020).

50. Daanika Gordon, *Policing the Racial Divide: Urban Growth Politics and the Remaking of Segregation* (New York University Press, 2022).

51. "Average Annual Increase in Food Prices in Selected Metro Areas, 2021–2022," Government Accountability Office analysis of data from the United States Department of Agriculture and the Bureau of Labor Statistics. GAO 23–105846. https://www.gao.gov/blog/sticker-shock-grocery-store-inflation-wasnt-only-reason-food-prices-increased.

52. US Government Accountability Office, "Food Prices: Information on Trends, Factors, and Federal Roles" (March 28, 2023), GAO-23–105846, https://www.gao.gov/products/gao-23-105846.

53. United States Department of Agriculture (USDA) Key Statistics and Graphics (2021), https://www.ers.usda.gov/topics/food-nutrition-assistance/food-security-in-the-u-s/key-statistics-graphics/. See also United States Department of Agriculture, "Food Insecurity by Household Characteristics" (2023), https://www.ers.usda.gov/topics/food-nutrition-assistance/food-security-in-the-u-s/key-statistics-graphics/

#householdtype. Data regarding food insecurity in 2023 will be published in October 2024.

54. Life Sciences Research Office, S. A. Andersen, ed., "Core Indicators of Nutritional State for Difficult to Sample Populations," *The Journal of Nutrition* 120:1557S-1600S, 1990.

55. Matthew P. Rabbitt, Laura J. Hales, Madeline Reed-Jones, and Alisha Coleman-Jensen, *Household Food Security in the United States in 2022* (Washington, DC: United States Department of Agriculture, 2023), https://www.ers.usda.gov/topics/food-nutrition-assistance/food-security-in-the-u-s/key-statistics-graphics/.

56. Kelly M. Bower et al., "The Intersection of Neighborhood Racial Segregation, Poverty, and Urbanicity and its Impact on Food Store Availability in the United States," *Preventive Medicine* vol. 58, (January 2014): 33–39, https://www.ncbi.nlm.nih.gov/pmc/articles/PMC3970577/.

57. Matthew Rae, Cynthia Cox, and Hanna Dingel, "Health Costs Associated with Pregnancy, Childbirth, and Postpartum Care" (July 13, 2022), Kaiser Family Foundation, https://www.healthsystemtracker.org/brief/health-costs-associated-with-pregnancy-childbirth-and-postpartum-care/.

58. "Medicaid and CHIP," https://www.healthcare.gov/medicaid-chip/childrens-health-insurance-program/.

59. Medicaid and CHIP Payment and Access Commission (MACPAC), "Physician Acceptance of New Medicaid Patients" (June 2021), https://www.macpac.gov/wp-content/uploads/2021/06/Physician-Acceptance-of-New-Medicaid-Patients-Findings-from-the-National-Electronic-Health-Records-Survey.pdf.

60. Arielle Dreher, "Hospital Obstetrics on Chopping Block as Facilities Pare Costs," *Axios Health Reporting* (January 17, 2023), https://www.axios.com/2023/01/17/hospital-obstetrics-chopping-block.

61. Peiyin Jung, Carrie E. Henning-Smith, Michelle M. Casey, and Katy B. Kozhimannil, "Access to Obstetric Services in Rural Counties Still Declining," *Health Affairs* vol. 36, no. 9 (2017), https://doi.org/10.1377/hlthaff.2017.0338.

62. Jung et al., "Access to Obstetric Services."

63. Michael J. O'Loughlin, "The Controversial History of the U.S. Bishops' Catholic Health Care Guidelines," *America* (June 22, 2023), https://www.americamagazine.org/politics-society/2023/06/22/ethical-religious-directives-revision-catholic-health-care-245541.

64. Nicole Bateman, "Working Parents Are Key to Covid-19 Recovery," Brookings Institution (July 8, 2020), https://www.brookings.edu/articles/working-parents-are-key-to-covid-19-recovery/.

65. State of California Department of Industrial Relations, "Minimum Wage," https://www.dir.ca.gov/dlse/faq_minimumwage.htm.

66. Paulina Richter, "San Diego Daycare & Child Care Costs" (2023), https://tootris.com/edu/blog/parents/san-diego-daycare-child-care-costs-999-per-month-in-2021-heres-how-that-fee-breaks-down/.

67. US Department of Labor, "Family and Medical Leave" https://www.dol.gov/general/topic/benefits-leave/fmla#:~:text=FMLA%20is%20designed%20to%20help,opportunity%20for%20men%20and%20women.

68. Twenty-one percent are ineligible due only to having worked too few hours or for an insufficient period of time for their employer; 15 percent are ineligible due only to their worksite being too small; 7 percent are ineligible due to both tenure/hours requirements and worksite size. See Scott Brown, Jane Herr, Radha Roy, and Jacob Alex Kleman, "Who Is Eligible?: Employee and Worksite Perspectives of the FMLA" (July 2020), https://www.dol.gov/sites/dolgov/files/OASP/evaluation/pdf/WHD_FMLA2018PB1WhoIsEligible_StudyBrief_Aug2020.pdf.

69. Administration for Children and Families, "Child Care Financial Assistance Options," https://childcare.gov/consumer-education/get-help-paying-for-child-care.

70. US Census Bureau, "Household Pulse Survey" (August 17, 2022), https://www.census.gov/data/tables/2022/demo/hhp/hhp48.html.

71. Steven Jessen-Howard, Rasheed Malik, and MK Falgout, "Costly and Unavailable: America Lacks Sufficient Child Care Supply for Infants and Toddlers," Center for American Progress (August 4, 2020), https://www.americanprogress.org/article/costly-unavailable-america-lacks-sufficient-child-care-supply-infants-toddlers/.

72. Steven Jessen-Howard, Rasheed Malik, and MK Falgout, "Costly and Unavailable: America Lacks Sufficient Child Care Supply for Infants and Toddlers," Center for American Progress (August 4, 2020), https://www.americanprogress.org/article/costly-unavailable-america-lacks-sufficient-child-care-supply-infants-toddlers/.

73. Child Care Aware of America, *2018 Annual Report* (Arlington, VA, 2019), https://www.childcareaware.org/wp-content/uploads/2019/09/2018-annual-report-final-interactive-pdf.pdf.

74. Jackie Mader, "Finding Child Care Is Still Impossible for Many Parents," *The Hechinger Report* (October 28, 2022) https://hechingerreport.org/finding-child-care-is-still-impossible-for-many-parents/.

75. Rickie Solinger, *Wake Up Little Susie: Single Pregnancy and Race Before* Roe v. Wade (New York: Routledge, 2000). See also Ann Fessler, *The Girls Who Went Away: The Hidden History of Women Who Surrendered Children for Adoption in the Decades before* Roe v. Wade (New York: Penguin, 2007).

76. Emily Davies, "I Want to See My Baby," *Washington Post* (August 20, 2019), https://www.washingtonpost.com/nation/2019/08/20/catholic-priest-baby-forced-adoption-lawsuit/.

77. Testimony of Leslie, who gave birth at eighteen years old and reflected years later on her experience of placing her child for adoption. See Lauren Kirkpatrick, Lauren Bell, Crystal P. Tyler, Elizabeth Harrison, Margaret Russell, Tahniat Syed, Nicholas Szoko, and Traci M. Kazmerski, "Health Care and Adoption Service Experiences of People Who Placed Children for Adoption During Adolescence: A Qualitative Study," *Journal of Pediatric and Adolescent Gynecology*, vol. 36, issue 1 (February 2023): 58–64. https://doi-org.sandiego.idm.oclc.org/10.1016/j.jpag.2022.08.006.

78. Holly Taylor Coolman, "Adoption and the Goods of Birth," *Journal of Moral Theology*, vol. 1, no. 2 (2012): 96–114. See also Lisa Sowle Cahill, "Adoption: A Roman Catholic Perspective," in *The Morality of Adoption: Social-Psychological, Theological, and Legal Perspectives*, ed. Timothy P. Jackson (Eerdmans, 2005).

79. Lauren Kirkpatrick, Lauren Bell, Crystal P. Tyler, Elizabeth Harrison, Margaret Russell, Tahniat Syed, Nicholas Szoko, and Traci M. Kazmerski, "Health Care and Adoption Service Experiences of People Who Placed Children for Adoption During Adolescence: A Qualitative Study," *Journal of Pediatric and Adolescent Gynecology*, vol. 36, issue 1 (February 2023): 58–64. https://doi-org.sandiego.idm.oclc.org/10.1016/j.jpag.2022.08.006.

80. Kirkpatrick, "Health Care and Adoption Service," citing Gretchen Sisson, "Estimating the Annual Domestic Adoption Rate and Lifetime Incidence Rate of Infant Relinquishment in the United States," *Contraception*, 105 (2022): 14–18. In 2002 fewer than 2 percent of live births resulted in adoption. See Olga Khazan, "Why So Many Women Choose Abortion Over Adoption," *The Atlantic* (May 20, 2019), https://www.theatlantic.com/health/archive/2019/05/why-more-women-dont-choose-adoption/589759/. Note that the studies in this reporting predate the *Dobbs* decision in 2022. But a noticeable trend among women with unplanned pregnancies is that they tend to think of the decision more as a choice between whether to seek abortion or to parent.

81. For example, Sue, who was part of a research study, explained that "There is just no way that I can go through the whole thing, see the baby, and be able to give it up." See Foster, *Turnaway Study*, 209, 304–305.

82. Gretchen Sisson, Lauren Ralph, Heather Gould, and Diana Greene Foster, "Adoption Decision Making among Women Seeking Abortion," *Women's Health Issues*, vol. 27, no. 2 (2017): 136–44, at 136.

83. US Department of Health and Human Services, *Child Welfare Outcomes* (2019), https://www.acf.hhs.gov/cb/resource/cwo-2019.

84. Office of the Administration for Children & Families, "Child Welfare Practice to Address Racial Disproportionality and Disparity" (April 2021), https://www.childwelfare.gov/pubpdfs/racial_disproportionality.pdf.

85. Laura Sullivan and Amy Walters, "Native Foster Care: Lost Children, Shattered Families" National Public Radio (October 25, 2011), https://www.npr.org/2011/10/25/141672992/native-foster-care-lost-children-shattered-families.

86. "The Problem," Foster America (2023), https://www.foster-america.org/the-problem.

87. Hannah Lantos, Emma Pliskin, Elizabeth Wildsmith, and Jennifer Manlove, "State-level Abortion Restrictions Will Negatively Impact Teens and Children," *Child Trends* (October 19, 2022), https://www.childtrends.org/blog/state-level-abortion-restrictions-will-negatively-impact-teens-and-children.

88. Jeremy M. Bergen, "Papal Apologies for Residential Schools and the Stories They Tell," *Journal of Moral Theology* 12:1 (2023): 48–62.

89. USCCB, "Discrimination Against Catholic Adoption Services" (2018), https://www.usccb.org/issues-and-action/religious-liberty/upload/Discrimination-against-Catholic-adoption-services.pdf.

90. Yun Zhang, Haimei Huang, and Min Wang, "Family Outcome Disparities between Sexual Minority and Heterosexual Families: A Systematic Review and Meta-Analysis," *BMJ Global Health* 8 (2023), https://gh.bmj.com/content/8/3/e010556.

91. "Study Finds Church Schools Racially Segregated," *New York Times* (June 27, 2002), https://www.nytimes.com/2002/06/27/us/study-finds-church-schools-racially-segregated.html.

92. An example is Governor Ron DeSantis (Florida), who claims that critical race theory aims to "treat kids differently based on the color of their skin," and who has used his executive powers in the state of Florida to block colleges from having diversity, equity, and inclusion programs. DeSantis, who is Catholic and claims to be pro-life, focuses exclusively on abortion politics when discussing what it means to be pro-life, disregarding the climate of exclusion in Florida public schools as a life issue. The "Stop W.O.K.E. Act" claims to protect students from indoctrination and protect employees from a hostile work environment due to critical race theory training. See https://www.flgov.com/wp-content/uploads/2021/12/Stop-Woke-Handout.pdf and the governor's website, https://www.flgov.com/.

93. Carrie Gillispie, "Young Learners, Missed Opportunities," The Education Trust (2019), https://s3-us-east-2.amazonaws.com/edtrustmain/wp-content/uploads/2014/09/05162154/Young-Learners-Missed-Opportunities.pdf.

94. According to a report by the National Association of Secondary School Principals, in fall 2017, 24.1 million were White, 7.7 million were Black, 13.6 million were Hispanic, 2.8 million were Asian/Pacific Islander, half a million were American Indian/Alaska Native, and 2 million were two or more races. The percentage of students who were White decreased from 61 to 48 percent between fall 2000 and fall 2017, and is projected to continue decreasing to 44 percent by fall 2029. See NASSP, *Racial Justice and Educational Equity* (January 2021), https://www.nassp.org/top-issues-in-education/position-statements/racial-justice-and-educational-equity/.

95. See NASSP, *Racial Justice and Educational Equity* (January 2021), https://www.nassp.org/top-issues-in-education/position-statements/racial-justice-and-educational-equity/.

96. See NASSP, *Racial Justice and Educational Equity* (January 2021), https://www.nassp.org/top-issues-in-education/position-statements/racial-justice-and-educational-equity/.

97. Sequoia Carrillo, "U.S. Reading and Math Scores Drop to Lowest Level in Decades," National Public Radio (June 21, 2023), https://www.npr.org/2023/06/21/1183445544/u-s-reading-and-math-scores-drop-to-lowest-level-in-decades#:~:text=The%20average%20scores%2C%20from%20tests,but%20dropped%20across%20all%20percentiles.

98. Paul M. Ong, UCLA Center for Neighborhood Knowledge, *COVID-19 and the Digital Divide in Virtual Learning* (Fall 2020), https://knowledge.luskin.ucla.edu/wp-content/uploads/2020/12/Digital-Divide-Phase2_brief_release_v01.pdf, 13.

99. Gun Violence Archive (Washington, DC: 2023), https://www.gunviolencearchive.org/.

100. Jason E. Goldsick, Rebecca M. Cunningham, and Patrick M. Carter, "Current Causes of Death in Children and Adolescents in the United States," *New England Journal of Medicine* (May 19, 2022), DOI: 10.1056/NEJMc2201761.

101. "Gun Violence in the United States," NPR/PBS News Hour/Marist National Poll (May 24, 2023), https://maristpoll.marist.edu/polls/gun-violence-in-the-united-states/.

102. Allison Jordan, "Debunking Myths the Gun Lobby Perpetuates Following Mass Shootings," Center for American Progress (September 8, 2022), https://www.americanprogress.org/article/debunking-myths-the-gun-lobby-perpetuates-following-mass-shootings/.

103. Alison Piepmeier, "The Inadequacy of 'Choice': Disability and What's Wrong with Feminist Framings of Reproduction," *Feminist Studies* 39:1 (2013): 159–86; Ruth Hubbard, "Abortion and Disability: Who Should and Should Not Inhabit the World?" in *The Disability Studies Reader*, ed. Lennard J. Davis (New York: Routledge, 2013), 74–86; Marsha Saxton, "Disability Rights and Selective Abortion," in *The Disability Studies Reader*, 87–99.

104. Charles C. Camosy, *Beyond the Abortion Wars: A Way Forward for a New Generation* (Grand Rapids: Eerdmans, 2015), 144.

105. Mary Jo Iozzio, "Justice Is a Virtue Both in and out of Healthcare," *Irish Theological Quarterly* vol. 63, issue 2 (1998): 151–66. Adrienne Asch, "Prenatal Diagnosis and Selective Abortion: A Challenge to Practice and Policy," *American Journal of Public Health* vol. 89 (1999): 1649–57.

106. Mary Jo Iozzio, *Disability Ethics and Preferential Justice: A Catholic Perspective* (Washington, DC: Georgetown University Press, 2023), 16.

107. Suzanne Heaney, Mark Tomlinson, Aine Aventin, "Termination of Pregnancy for Fetal Anomaly: A Systematic Review of the Healthcare Experiences and Needs of Patients," *BMC Pregnancy Childbirth* vol. 22, (2022): doi: 10.1186/s12884-022-04770-4.

108. Testimonies and resources for parents can be found here, https://www.perinatalhospice.org/resources-for-parents.

109. Centers for Disease Control and Prevention, "Data and Statistics on Birth Defects" (December 21, 2022), https://www.cdc.gov/ncbddd/birthdefects/data.html.

110. Rebecca Todd Peters, "Listening to Women: Examining the Moral Wisdom of Women Who End Pregnancies," *Journal of Religious Ethics* 49:2 (2021): 290–313, at 309.

111. "Data and Statistics on Down Syndrome," Centers for Disease Control and Prevention (December 16, 2022), https://www.cdc.gov/ncbddd/birthdefects/downsyndrome/data.html.

112. See the beautiful reflection by Christian ethicist Lorraine Cuddeback-Gedeon on the loss of her brother in Iozzio, *Disability Ethics*, 50.

113. "Data and Statistics on Down Syndrome," Centers for Disease Control and Prevention (December 16, 2022), https://www.cdc.gov/ncbddd/birthdefects/downsyndrome/data.html.

114. Lisa Powell, *The Disabled God Revisited: Trinity, Christology, and Liberation* (London: T&T Clark, 2023); Deborah Beth Creamer, *Disability and Christian Theology: Embodied Limits and Constructive Possibilities* (New York: Oxford, 2008).

115. Iozzio, *Disability Ethics*, 19. See also Erik Parens and Adrienne Asch, *Prenatal and Disability Rights* (Washington, DC: Georgetown University Press, 2000).

116. Tom Shakespeare, "A Life Worth Living," in *Disability: The Basics* (New York: Routledge, 2018), 45–67.

117. National Coalition Against Domestic Violence, "Domestic Violence Fact Sheet," https://assets.speakcdn.com/assets/2497/domestic_violence-2020080709350855.pdf?1596828650457.

118. United Nations, 2022, cited in UNFPA, State of the World Population Report 2022—*Seeing the Unseen: The Case for Action in the Neglected Crisis of Unintended Pregnancy* (New York: UNFPA, 2022), 113. https://www.unfpa.org/swp2022.

119. This figure does not include sexual harassment. UN Women: Facts and Figures, https://www.unwomen.org/en/what-we-do/ending-violence-against-women/facts-and-figures.

120. UN Women: Facts and Figures, https://www.unwomen.org/en/what-we-do/ending-violence-against-women/facts-and-figures.

121. Young women, aged eighteen to twenty-four, experience certain severe types of harassment at disproportionately high levels, including online stalking and online sexual harassment (name-calling, embarrassment, physical threats, even rape threats). Maeve Duggan, "Online Harassment" (October 22, 2014), Pew Research Center Report. https://www.pewresearch.org/internet/2014/10/22/online-harassment/.

122. UN Women: Facts and Figures, https://www.unwomen.org/en/what-we-do/ending-violence-against-women/facts-and-figures.

123. UNFPA, *Seeing the Unseen*, 113.

124. UNFPA, *Seeing the Unseen*, 113. See also Chanel Miller, *Know My Name: A Memoir*. Recently published data from 95 countries found that 63 percent of them lacked rape laws based on the principle of consent and half continue to restrict women from working in certain jobs or industries. Nearly a quarter of countries fail to grant women equal rights with men to enter into marriage or initiate divorce, according to the United Nations (2021), cited in UNFPA, 113.

125. March of Dimes, "Abuse During Pregnancy," https://www.marchofdimes.org/find-support/topics/pregnancy/abuse-during-pregnancy.

126. March of Dimes, "Abuse During Pregnancy," https://www.marchofdimes.org/find-support/topics/pregnancy/abuse-during-pregnancy.

127. Elisabeth T. Vasko, *Beyond Apathy: A Theology for Bystanders* (Minneapolis: Fortress, 2015), 29–68.

128. USCCB, *When I Call for Help* (2002), https://www.usccb.org/topics/marriage-and-family-life-ministries/when-i-call-help-pastoral-response-domestic-violence.

129. American College of Obstetricians and Gynecologists, "Reproductive and Sexual Coercion" (2022), https://www.acog.org/clinical/clinical-guidance/committee-opinion/articles/2013/02/reproductive-and-sexual-coercion#:~:text=Reproductive%20coercion%20is%20related%20to,pregnancy%20coercion%2C%20and%20pregnancy%20pressure.

130. Doris Reisinger, "Reproductive Abuse in the Context of Clergy Sexual Abuse in the Catholic Church," *Religions* 13: 198 (2022): 1–21. https://www.mdpi.com/2077-1444/13/3/198.

131. Reisinger, "Reproductive Abuse," 5.

132. Sam Levin, "The Women Trapped in Prison with Abusive Guards," *The Guardian* (October 29, 2023), https://www.theguardian.com/us-news/2023/oct/29/womens-prison-guards-sexual-abuse#:~:text=The%20California%20department%20of%20corrections,but%20has%20largely%20gone%20unacknowledged.%E2%80%9D. See also Bryan Stevenson, *Just Mercy: A Story of Justice and Redemption* (New York: OneWorld, 2015).

133. Over four thousand children were separated from their parents during the Trump Administration. See Caitlin Dickerson, "We Need to Take Away Children," *The Atlantic* (August 7, 2022), https://www.theatlantic.com/magazine/archive/2022/09/trump-administration-family-separation-policy-immigration/670604/; Institute for the Elimination of Poverty and Genocide, Testimony of Whistleblower Dawn Wooten, (September 14, 2020), https://projectsouth.org/wp-content/uploads/2020/09/OIG-ICDC-Complaint-1.pdf; Equal Justice Initiative, "Shackling of Pregnant Women in Jails and Prisons Continues" (January 29, 2020), https://eji.org/news/shackling-of-pregnant-women-in-jails-and-prisons-continues/; Gabrielle A. Perry, "In Prison, Having Your Period Can Put Your Life In Danger," *The Washington Post* (March 25, 2022), https://www.washingtonpost.com/opinions/2022/03/25/prison-period-danger-health-risks-sexual-abuse/.

134. Ashley Lopez, "How the Texas Ban on Most Abortions Is Harming Survivors of Rape and Incest," *National Public Radio* (November 15, 2021), https://www.npr.org/sections/health-shots/2021/11/15/1054710917/texas-abortion-law-harm-sexual-assault-survivors.

135. Stephanie Colombini, "Proof Is Required for Rape Exceptions in Florida's Proposed Abortion Law," WFSU Public Media (March 13, 2023), https://news.wfsu.org/state-news/2023-03-13/proof-is-required-for-rape-exceptions-in-floridas-proposed-abortion-law.

136. Emilie M. Townes, *Womanist Ethics and the Cultural Production of Evil* (New York: Palgrave Macmillan, 2006), 128.

137. John Paul II (1991), *Centesimus Annus*, 33. https://www.vatican.va/content/john-paul-ii/en/encyclicals/documents/hf_jp-ii_enc_01051991_centesimus-annus.html.

138. John Paul II, *Centesimus Annus*, 33.

139. John Paul II, *Centesimus Annus*, 34.

140. John Paul II, *Centesimus Annus*, 35.

141. John Paul II, *Centesimus Annus*, 35.

142. Benedict XVI, *Caritas in Veritate* (2009), 36, 71. https://www.vatican.va/content/benedict-xvi/en/encyclicals/documents/hf_ben-xvi_enc_20090629_caritas-in-veritate.html.

143. Benedict XVI, *Caritas in Veritate*, 11, 27.

144. Francis, *Evangelii Gaudium*, 59.

145. Francis, *Evangelii Gaudium*, see 52–60 but especially 53.

146. Francis, *Evangelii Gaudium*, 53.

147. Francis, *Evangelii Gaudium*, 186–216, especially 188, 192, 202, 189.

148. Francis, *Evangelii Gaudium*, 205.

149. Francis, *Evangelii Gaudium*, 207

150. United States House of Representatives, Black Maternal Health Caucus, "Black Maternal Health Momnibus" (May 2023), https://blackmaternalhealthcaucus-underwood.house.gov/Momnibus.

Chapter 5

Complexity and Ambiguity in Women's Experiences of Pregnancy and Pregnancy Loss

The method of Catholic feminism that informs this study requires fidelity to the Catholic moral tradition *and* fidelity to women's lived experiences. Listening to women who have experienced pregnancy loss is a vital task for ethicists. But such a task is not easy. Women's experiences vary considerably, and some women are justifiably nervous about sharing their experiences of pregnancy loss given the stigma that persists. Feminist and womanist theologians question whether theological discourse crafted by men can ever attend sufficiently to the embodied experiences of women. This raises particular challenges in the Catholic moral tradition, which privileges ordained men in the construction of magisterial teachings, even teachings about pregnancy and pregnancy loss. Creating spaces for women to tell their stories is a central feature of feminist and womanist theological methods.[1] As women tell their stories, we are able to see similarities and differences. Womanist theologian Yolanda Pierce explains: "I cannot divorce my faith from the realities of living in the body of a Black woman, born in a country whose original sin is racism."[2] Pierce advocates attention to the particularities of one's lived experience, inclusive of race, class, gender, and sexuality. Creating space for women to share their stories of pregnancy and pregnancy loss remains an important feature of reproductive justice work, so that we can move away from viewing women as *objects* of reproductive control to instead consider women as *subjects* who are fully human moral agents.[3] Women are not just breeders who exist to serve men's interests. Women have dignity and unique vocations. This chapter centers women's lived experiences of pregnancy, miscarriage, stillbirth, and abortion in order to consider an approach to pregnancy loss that leads to authentic healing for women in Catholic parish communities and to a more adequate formulation of Catholic teachings on pregnancy loss.

While pregnancy loss is common in women's experiences, the stigma of abortion in particular can lead to self-censoring among women. Often what is missing in politically divisive conversations about abortion is an opportunity for women to share the reasons why they felt they had to make that difficult decision. Women from all social groups, classes, and religious affiliations have abortions. The Guttmacher Institute reports that 18 percent of pregnancies (excluding miscarriages) in 2017 ended in abortion.[4] Abortions increased by 8 percent from 2017 to 2020, and early estimates indicated that the total number of abortions in 2023 would be higher than the 2020 numbers. The Guttmacher Institute explains that the actual increase in abortions is likely even larger since official reporting does not capture the number of abortions that occur outside of the formal health care system.[5] Twenty-four percent of abortion patients in 2014 identified as Catholic; more Catholics have abortions than mainline Protestants or evangelical Protestants.[6] The 2020 data showed that 86 percent of women who procured an abortion that year were unmarried, while 14 percent were married. Both the Guttmacher Institute and Centers for Disease Control and Prevention report that before the *Dobbs* decision, abortion rates had generally decreased since the 1980s.[7] The 2020 increases reverse thirty years of a declining abortion rate.[8]

Every pregnant person's context is unique and her life experience is shaped by her individual perceptions of what is possible for her to do. At the same time, reliable research studies have yielded data that can help us to identify some patterns in pregnant women's stories. Diana Greene Foster, lead investigator of the *Turnaway Study*, explains that there is usually more than one reason that a woman seeks an abortion. The study asked participants the open-ended question, "What are some of the reasons you decided to have an abortion?" Of the 954 participants, answers were grouped into twelve categories (see table 5.1).[9]

A different study reported that the three most common reasons—each cited by three-fourths of patients—were concern for or responsibility to other individuals; the inability to afford raising a child; and the belief that having a baby would interfere with work, school, or the ability to care for dependents. Half said they did not want to be a single parent or were having problems with their husband or partner.[10]

Attention to narratives of pregnancy loss can be challenging. Some women struggle to put words to their experiences. Some continue to process their past experiences as they age, and may change their interpretation of the past in light of the present. Protestant theologian Serene Jones writes that "reproductive loss is a topic that enables serious reflection on the traumas embedded in the everyday lives of those around us."[11] Given the stigma that many women still perceive in Church spaces, I thought it important to bring particular women's stories into this book in order to highlight both the complexity and

Table 5.1

Not financially prepared	40%
Not the right time for a baby	36%
Partner-related reasons	31%
Needs to focus on other children	29%
Interferes with future opportunities	20%
Not emotionally or mentally prepared	19%
Health-related reasons	12%
Wants a better life for the baby than she can provide	12%
Not independent or mature enough for a baby	7%
Influences from family or friends	5%
Doesn't want a baby or to place baby for adoption	4%
Other	1%

Source: Diane Greene Foster, *The Turnaway Study: Ten Years, A Thousand Women, and the Consequences of Having—or Being Denied—an Abortion* (New York: Scribner, 2020), 35.

ambiguity inherent in any experience of pregnancy loss. It would be impossible to claim that these vignettes capture all women's experiences. I have curated these from previously published accounts to represent a wide array of testimonies; but each woman speaks only for herself.

TESTIMONIES OF MISCARRIAGE

Elise

Elise Erikson Barrett is a United Methodist pastor who has experienced multiple early miscarriages. She describes her first:

> I knew that something was terribly, terribly, wrong, but I didn't know exactly what. I vividly remember staring at the black words and musical notation on the thin pages of the hymnal, unable to concentrate enough to understand what they meant. After what seemed like an eternity, worship was over and Chris and I pushed open the door of the parsonage. I went to the bathroom and saw blood. I changed clothes and went to my tired husband and said, "I think I'm having a miscarriage."
>
> He looked up at me, sitting on the side of the bed, one shoe off and one shoe on, in his shirtsleeves, and he was silent for a moment. Then he put his shoe back on, got up, put his hand on my shoulder, and said, "Well, let's go to the hospital." He paused. "Is that what we do?"
>
> I nodded, and we got into the car.[12]

Elise and Chris did not receive comforting news from the ultrasound technician or the emergency room physician. Elise was told, "It's probably that you've lost the pregnancy," but that she needed to see her OB-GYN doctor the following day.[13] She left the emergency room with paperwork diagnosing her situation as "spontaneous abortion," and the next day found herself in the waiting room of the OB-GYN office surrounded by pregnant women and publications such as *Baby Today* and *Parenting*, which was understandably upsetting given her own diagnosis.[14] When she was called back to see the doctor, he examined her and she completed bloodwork. Her doctor told her, "You were right, and I'm sorry. You have lost the pregnancy."[15] Crying, Elise asked for painkillers as she was cramping, and the doctor told her that it was normal to grieve an early miscarriage.

> This was absurdly comforting. In the halls of science and empirically verified truths, I received the news that science had given me permission to feel this wrenching hurt and emptiness and bewilderment with some sort of strange satisfaction. I left the office and trudged to the car, numb, adjusting to a new life I wasn't sure I liked very well.[16]

Elise found it profoundly unhelpful when friends and family members told her that there must be a reason for her miscarriage; even people who loved her very much seemed ill-equipped to support her in the way she needed support during her grief. Elise describes feeling betrayed by her body,[17] guilt for whatever she must have done to cause the miscarriage,[18] guilt for her inability to pull herself together and get past her loss,[19] and abandoned by God.[20] As a graduate student in divinity school Elise found that her miscarriage shook her faith.

> I wanted to pray, wanted to feel connected to the steadfast God I had loved and known and tried to follow, but I felt about God as I'd imagine feeling about my spouse if he were to have an affair—our whole history of relationship, our whole journey together, the collected life of brilliant moments of intimacy and plodding months of growth was called into question. *Who are you, anyway?* I wanted to shout, *I don't even know you anymore!*[21]

During her first experience of worship with her divinity school community after her miscarriage, Elise wanted to see if God had anything to say to her.

> The worship that day was an exuberant praise service. Had I been in a sunny mood, it would have been a delight. But everything sounded sarcastic to me. "The Lord delivers the righteous!" *Oh, great*, I thought, *so I'm unrighteous? That's why you killed my baby?* "Shout to the Lord!" *Shout what? "I hate you?"* "God has counted the hairs on your head!" That was the point at which I could

take no more. I waited as long as I could, but when the choir burst into clapping and song, and everyone around me was clapping and singing and smiling, tears erupted from my eyes and I roughly shoved my way down the row of chairs and escaped through the library door. I fled to the Women's Center, a small room off the hallway outside the student lounge. It was set up to allow breastfeeding, but there was a small altar and a bookshelf full of worship resources, and I collapsed there and cried until I was empty.[22]

"Empty," "angry," "numb," "confused," "emotional"—Elise found that she experienced a wide range of unsettling feelings and confusing thoughts in her journey of healing after her miscarriage. Elise learned, through her own experience and by talking about it with others in her path toward healing, that "there is no 'right' way to feel, no 'right' way for you to respond to your miscarriage."[23]

Jessica

Jessica Zucker describes herself as a psychologist and mother who was raised culturally Jewish and is aware of her privilege as a white person.[24] When she was sixteen weeks pregnant during her second pregnancy, she "went to the bathroom in my dermatologist's office on what should have been a standard Tuesday morning, wiped, and found cherry-red blood on the toilet paper."[25] She tried to remain optimistic as her OB-GYN confirmed a fetal heartbeat via ultrasound. But the next day, she began to have cramps.

> I was up most of the night, roiling in thought-stopping physical torment. For ten-plus hours, I was trying to ward off—or somehow make peace with—the ebb and flow of the pain. Some moments were so intense, though, I felt like the wind was knocked straight out of me. Unable to speak, unable to catch my breath. The spotting, at this point, was an unconvincing shade of dull red, which seemed like a positive development, but still, I was unsure of how anxious I should be.[26]

Jessica's husband went to work, and her son to school. She was alone in her home when, later that afternoon, she was overcome with feelings of panic and immediately went to her bathroom.[27]

> When I started to urinate, something I to this day have trouble even recalling occurred. Something that would change me in ways both diminutive and profound. Something that, unlike the "pop" that may or may not have occurred, I cannot force my mind to question. My baby slid out. I saw her there, dead, dangling from me mere inches from the toilet-bowl water. There was some movement—maybe just from falling? I don't know and will never know—and just

like that, I was overcome with physical relief, after having labored for hours. A relief that anyone who's experienced childbirth will understand: the quick kind that's instantly replaced with an overwhelming gravity. My window-clad house should have shattered from the pitch of my prolonged primordial scream. It didn't. I did.[28]

Jessica texted her husband: "The baby fell out. I need you. Please come home."[29] She contacted her doctor, who told her to use scissors to cut the umbilical cord.

I crouched over the toilet and cut the umbilical cord, then immediately began to bleed in an obviously emergent way. She was in my hands ever so briefly. She. But as the medical emergency I knew I was experiencing grew more dire, I placed her on a nearby hand towel. No longer part of a symbiotic union, dizzy with despair and confusion over this separation, I somehow found a way to stay the course on the practical matters of caring for myself: attempting to get dressed, stuffing towels into my underwear because the hemorrhaging wouldn't stop until the placenta was delivered. My doctor talked me through what to do, stressing the need to get to her office, and quickly, with my baby in a bag to send to the lab for testing.[30]

Jessica texted close friends and family: "I HAD A MISCARRIAGE."[31] Her husband came home from work, helped her to the car, drove her to the hospital, and dropped Jessica off so that he could find parking.

I was bleeding incessantly, and I couldn't fathom how I'd take my pants off when I arrived at the doctor's office. But when she ushered me in, I heeded her orders to do so, and a blood clot the size of a boulder splattered across the floor. A nurse muttered that it looked like a "murder scene." She wasn't wrong—a death had occurred, and it had felt violent and cruel. The only way to make the bleeding stop was to extract the placenta, and that meant proceeding with a dilation and curettage (D&C), a procedure to remove it and any remaining tissue inside my uterus.[32]

In her journey toward healing, Jessica started by repressing her emotions and trying to survive her trauma by staying busy: "I wanted order, predictability, and peace—the antithesis of the psychological chaos my miscarriage yielded."[33] Jessica found that what she really needed was "the space to fall apart," but she also found it terribly upsetting to acknowledge the grief she was experiencing.[34]

In the initial days and weeks that followed my miscarriage, I think it was primarily adrenaline that powered me through. *Must survive. Must continue. Must do.*

But then, when I finally grasped just how eviscerated I really was, I couldn't dodge the eventual downfall. This was only the beginning.[35]

Jessica documented her journey so that others can know that they are not alone, and to offer clear affirmations for women who have experienced miscarriage. "This is what we all deserve," she writes. "To be heard. To be validated. To be nurtured. To be safe. To be steady."[36]

Soniah

Soniah Kamal, who is Pakistani-American, describes herself as a "miscarriage veteran," with four miscarriages and two live births in her medical history.[37]

> The first time I miscarried I was a twenty-four-year-old newlywed, and because of a mix up in scheduling a D&C (a procedure to scape clean the uterine lining), I'd had to keep the dead baby inside of me for two days. While I mourned the loss, I found it macabre and scary to literally be carrying death.[38]

Soniah elaborates on her experience of a miscarriage ten years later in which she felt belittled by hospital staff. Soniah explains that as a woman of color, it was painful to have her OB-GYN glare at her and yell at her about how much she was costing the insurance companies by coming back for repeated check-ups when she experienced bleeding during pregnancy.[39] That same physician "fell silent" when she could not detect a fetal heartbeat when Soniah's pregnancy was sixteen weeks along. Soniah's fears were confirmed; the baby had died in the womb. The doctor told Soniah that a D&C would be scheduled in a few days. But before the D&C, Soniah began to deliver (unexpectedly and with frightening loss of blood) at home. Soniah describes:

> At exactly 7:02 p.m., I started to cramp. I sat up, experiencing the worst period pain ever, and it was only seconds later that I realized I was in the first stages of labor. The next few minutes were as if someone was turning a kaleidoscope at warp speed. While my husband called the ER—I might be in labor. Should I come in? Take a painkiller?—I was calling my next-door neighbor and friend Aruna to brief her. Could she stay with the kids until my husband and I returned from the ER? During the few minutes it took Aruna to cross her garden into mine and walk up our steps and inside my house, even as my husband ran to the garage and began backing out the car, a wave of intense pain hit me, and I rushed into the bathroom and lowered my pants and sat down.
>
> I wish the OB-GYN had mentioned the possibility. I wish she'd warned me that if I sat on the toilet seat, catching expelled blood clots in toilet tissue, I could

very well deliver my baby's face into my hands. The reason I was even sitting on the potty catching what came out of me was because my doctor mother, who lived overseas, had instructed me to catch everything I expelled in order to be able to give the D&C doctor a report.

Otherwise everything that came out of me would have simply been flushed away.

As I held his head in my palms, I could hear my husband and Aruna outside calming my scared kids, telling them that I was going to be okay.

His face was no bigger than a kitchen cabinet knob. It was opaque because cartilage is opaque. The outlines of his eyes, ears, nose, and mouth were clear. He looked like an alien out of *The X-Files* TV show. His outline resembled my older son. I can only describe the attendant wave coursing through me as aging. In those few moments, I'd accumulated decades of grief, and I felt old, forever divided between "before seeing his face" and "after seeing his face."

Should I kiss his face?

Finally, I held him to my heart and then came outside. I called the ER to update them, and then I put him in a ziploc sandwich bag so he could be sent for an autopsy. Aruna had taken my kids to their bedroom. My husband and I were silent as he drove us to the ER. The whole time I held the ziploc bag in my lap.[40]

Soniah was overcome with grief as she recovered in the emergency room. "According to science, it was an unviable fetus; according to my heart, it was my baby," she explained, to communicate her deep sense of loss. Friends and family members tried to cheer her up in the weeks and months afterward, saying, "Stop being so sad!" But Soniah explains that "their words left me upset, alone, and angry at having conditions put on grief and attachment."[41] Their local mosque could not provide burial for the remains, but a nurse from the hospital's perinatal loss clinic helped Soniah to arrange for her son's burial in a collective cremation and burial plot at Stone Mountain Cemetery.[42] There, Soniah and her family could visit the place where "the collected ashes of all miscarried babies were buried," which was shaded at one side by an oak tree, with a marble bench for resting.[43] This place of collective grief brought Soniah comfort when she visited with her husband and two children. "I recited a prayer for my baby," she writes. "I recited a prayer for all the babies."[44]

Susan

Susan Reynolds also describes feeling numb after her first miscarriage.

> I suffered my first miscarriage, and the two that followed it, when I was a young graduate student in theology. That morning, four days after I started to bleed, I dragged myself out of my small apartment and into the icy chill of early March in Boston, numbly heeding my dad's advice to somehow business-as-usual my way back to life. Seeking consolation, I drifted into weekday Mass in the school's chapel.[45]

Susan's experience of Catholic liturgy in the midst of her ongoing miscarriage was not consoling, however. The lectionary readings felt "cruelly ironic," and Susan felt that her process of grief was not recognized as legitimate. People wanted her to get over it or pretend that she was not hurting.

> In the realm of women's experience, the mandate to forget is magisterial. Pregnant women are typically cautioned to wait until their second trimester, after the risk of miscarriage has declined, to tell others that they are expecting. Implicitly contained within this well-meaning advice is the expectation of forgetting. If you have a miscarriage, the age-old wisdom seems to convey, the right thing to do is never to tell anyone about the child you carried and lost. Instead, you should go on with life as though nothing has happened and never speak of it again. In any other circumstance, we would find such advice monstrous. As it is, women's bodily experiences of loss are shuffled off to the attic of daily life, hidden firmly from sight like the senile spinster aunt in a Victorian novel.[46]

Susan longed for a way to express her loss in a healing ritual. Since one did not exist in an obvious form, she and her husband created one within their Catholic parish.

> We welcomed all families who had ever lost a child in the womb or who wanted to pray for someone who had. When the evening of the liturgy arrived, we were astounded to find that the gathering overflowed our small parish's chapel. Women came who had lost babies years and even decades before.[47]

Susan found consolation and community in this ritual. She and her husband "named our children in the presence of God and one another, in unity with the entire communion of saints."[48] Lighting candles in honor of each pregnancy loss, the mourners present experienced validation from the community, and solidarity among the families present. Now they knew that they were not alone in their loss.

TESTIMONIES OF STILLBIRTH

Janet

Janet Lee Ortiz's stillbirth story unfolded over five emotionally wrenching days. On day one, when she was almost eight months along in an otherwise healthy pregnancy, Janet made time in a busy work schedule for a check-up appointment. During the ultrasound, the physician did not detect a heartbeat, and asked Janet whether the baby had been moving recently.

> I scan my memory and think hard . . . *OH MY GOSH I don't remember it moving last night.* I feel like a horrible mother to not remember, nor did I keep kick counts. *It moved in the morning . . . but . . . OH NO. No, no no . . .*[49]

The physician called for a second opinion, and the two doctors concluded that Janet needed to go to the labor and delivery ward immediately. Another doctor joined the diagnostic team, and after an additional ultrasound, all three concluded that the baby had died in the womb, and that the next step would be to induce labor so that Janet could birth the baby.

> THIS IS REAL. THIS IS HAPPENING. I cover my face and lose it. Everything was going just fine. I was so close to the end, just shy of eight months. *Baby was strong and healthy. I have to start all over again? I miscarried last year! This is a cruel, sick joke. Why did this happen?*[50]

Janet reviewed her options with the doctors, and chose to delay the induction so that she could prepare herself physically and emotionally. She expressed gratitude for her husband's support and sadness because it was difficult to explain to her son what was happening. "It felt like I was preparing for my own death. In a way I was, because I was going to lose a part of me forever."[51]

Janet contacted friends, doulas, and family members, sharing news of the baby's death and her birth plans, saying that "they really came through for me in full force."[52] Janet and her husband Alex took their son, Essi, to SeaWorld, which was a high point of joy and family bonding in the midst of their evolving grief. The low point of the day was when the cashier at the grocery store asked Janet about her due date. Janet fumbled through a response, telling her the baby was no longer alive, and cursed herself for not having a better answer. On the third day, Janet found herself in a state of fear, and a conversation with a doula helped very much, as the doula told her she was preparing for birth. "This *was* a birth. I don't know why I didn't see it this way at first (in retrospect, probably because I associated birth with a live baby)."[53]

After their visit to SeaWorld, Janet and her family walked along the beach to enjoy the scenic beauty. Janet's body felt different after a bowel movement, and she wondered if her water would break soon. On the fourth day, Janet checked in to the hospital, accompanied by her friend and birth coach, Meisha. Alex and Essi left after dinner, and the induction process began slowly. Janet slept for a few hours that night. On the fifth day, contractions were becoming stronger and closer together.

> When a contraction comes, I lean over onto something and try my best to remember to breathe through it. They are painful, more than I ever remember the pain to be. I'm also not afforded the time in between to catch a breather in order to prepare for the next contraction. They have picked up. I ask out loud to no one why they are so close together, and why they hurt so much.[54]

The doctor rushed in, and confirmed that Janet's cervix was dilated to ten centimeters, and that it was time to push. "Then I'm hit hard with the worst contraction yet. I am on my side and writhing in pain. Through my clenched jaw I groan that I can't do this, it hurts too much."[55]

Delivery was underway. Janet could feel the baby's head crowning, and pushed out the head, and then the body. She cut the cord, and asked that the baby be placed on her chest.

> "Please rearrange his limbs so they don't look all twisted . . ." I needed him not to look like a dead body. I needed him to look like a sleeping baby. I can't stop crying. I finally hold him. He looks so frail, so peaceful, so innocent. I couldn't protect him. I keep hearing myself repeat, "This is all so sad. I can't believe this is my story." I repeatedly tell baby that I'm so sorry.[56]

After Janet birthed the placenta, her husband Alex and son Essi arrived. The family spent time together, taking pictures, crying, and taking turns holding the baby. Hours passed, and then Janet knew that it was time to let him go. They name him Kamali, which means spirit guide and protector. "We will always remember him. He will never be a passing memory. We will speak his name, we will share stories about him, we will celebrate his birthday and honor his life, he will forever be our son. Mama will always love you and remember you, Kamali."[57]

Taiyon

Taiyon J. Coleman was twenty weeks along in a pregnancy that was considered high risk because of her tilted uterus and uterine fibroids. She experienced severe cramping, but was encouraged by a doctor to just take Tylenol for the pain. Then her water broke unexpectedly while she and her boyfriend, Emmanuel, were on a road trip. They went to the nearest hospital, and doctors confirmed that her water had broken, but labor had not progressed. She was sent home, and they drove home, ending the road trip early. Taiyon was admitted to the hospital in her hometown when they returned from their trip, and was in the hospital for seven days. She delivered her baby girl.[58]

> She was so tiny and beautiful. I just kept smelling her because she smelled so good and so different. I had never smelled anything like it. She smelled like something from another world, and it smelled so good. My baby did not stink, and I couldn't believe that she came out of me and that I smelled that good on the inside. Even in that moment I wondered why my sixth-grade teacher had taught us that black girls stink. I knew then that she was a liar.[59]

> We called the priest to give last rites, and when he entered the room, we showed him our baby, who to us was the most beautiful girl in the world. The white Catholic priest physically recoiled as if he had seen something repulsive. I thought, "I'm Catholic, and Emmanuel is Catholic, named after Jesus. Why wouldn't he want to baptize our baby girl and give her last rites?"[60]

Taiyon and Emmanuel took pictures of their daughter's remains and then arranged for a cremation so that they could keep her remains in a special place in their home.[61] Taiyon now describes herself as a "recovering Catholic." She and Emmanuel are married and later joyfully welcomed a healthy nine-pound daughter, whom they named for Taiyon's mother.[62]

TESTIMONIES OF ABORTION

Viva

Viva Ruiz grew up Catholic, and says that "the story of Jesus and unconditional love provided a safe place for me when I desperately needed one."[63] Viva explains that as a child she was exposed to the crack cocaine epidemic in her neighborhood, and that her home was a difficult space to navigate as well. In Catholic grade school, Viva was shown anti-abortion films. She thought about those anti-abortion films when she had her first abortion.

> I was mostly surprised that the abortion was not the trauma [that] Catholic school promised. I did not suffer, inside or out. I wouldn't do it for fun, but I don't have teeth taken out for fun either (no shade to anybody who does). I was very much in love with the person who got me pregnant.[64]

When Viva discovered she was unexpectedly pregnant two years later, she was in a different relationship, one she describes as "a mess of abuse that mirrored the machismo of my upbringing."[65]

I sincerely understand how abortion can feel heart-breaking, emotional, or traumatic. But it also needs to be said that a lot of us are not upset about our abortions, then, now, or ever. Because of this, there needs to be more space and permission for people to have all sorts of different experiences with abortions, especially since the topic is so thoroughly drenched with Christian and patriarchal propaganda that wants us to feel guilt, secrecy, and shame. I am completely unbothered by the health care I chose, and I wouldn't do anything differently. Abortion is normal. Autonomy is *joyful*.[66]

Viva created a "sacred signage" T-shirt design with the phrase "Thank God for Abortion," and began to wear it to see how the message could "be a tool that causes people on both sides to reveal themselves, like a special tool used in hotel rooms to detect blood."[67] Viva finds that wearing the T-shirt is a conversation starter, and that sometimes strangers come up to her and hug her and want to tell Viva about their own abortion experience. "I love and receive them and I can say I get it, I really get it, and I listen."[68] Viva continues to identify as a person of faith, and asks, "If God is for us, who can be against us? I walk joyfully, arm in arm with the rest of you, pushing in all the different ways you can push, toward our collective liberation."[69]

Anna

Anna Wood was thirty-four years old, thought of herself as pro-choice and Catholic, but never thought she would have an abortion herself.[70] That changed when she found out that she was unexpectedly pregnant and in an unhealthy relationship that she had just tried to end. To carry on with the pregnancy would mean staying in some kind of co-parenting relationship with this man.[71]

> I was pregnant. I re-read the instructions just to be safe—did two lines really mean pregnant? Or was it one?[72]

> I was pregnant. Shock kept my mind from moving any further. I stared at my houseplants taking in the morning sun on the north wall of my living room. It was utterly silent in the room. The rise and fall of the emotion from the initial test result left me reeling, the inside of my mind quiet like the room around me. My life was forever changed, and yet when I looked around the room, everything remained the same. How is that possible?[73]

Anna found that the most reasonable approach to her situation required an honest assessment of the quality of her intimate relationship with her boyfriend, whom she calls "the broker," as well as her personal goals for her life.

> I don't envy any woman faced with electing to have an abortion, but I wish it had been that black and white for me. In the days and weeks after I found out I was pregnant, my thoughts were all over the place: initially I wanted to keep it, then as things became more complicated I was ambivalent, swinging wildly back and forth between keeping the baby and terminating the pregnancy. I don't like emotional messiness. I find scattered, competing thoughts uncomfortable and grasping. I read somewhere that a woman wants an abortion like an animal in a trap wants to chew its own leg off. I couldn't imagine a better metaphor for how I felt. Opting for an abortion is a miserable choice. But bringing a child into this toxic relationship and being bound to the broker for life seemed the greater of two evils.[74]

Anna's boyfriend did not want her to continue the pregnancy; they argued and the lack of support she felt from her boyfriend contributed to her stress about the decision. While the physician assistant talked to Anna and her boyfriend about the options, she described the embryo as "a blob of cells." But Anna was already envisioning the life within her as a child.[75] Anna wrestled with her decision over a few weeks of time and multiple conversations with medical providers. "I couldn't see a way to have the child as a single mom and wouldn't have this child with the broker."[76] Anna described the procedure and her recovery:

> The abortion itself was uneventful. From what I have heard from the four friends who have recounted their miscarriages to me, it went like that. To me, it seemed like the worst period I've ever had. I had to wait 24 to 48 hours after I took the first pill to take the second set. I had the world's most anxious day and night, unable to focus, eat, or sleep.[77]
>
> It wasn't until after lunch that the cramps finally started, mild at first but progressing to be more intense than normal. I had a heating pad, took some ibuprofen, and settled into the couch. When the bleeding started it was a lot. I typically have light and short periods, so this amount of blood was new to me. There was also tissue, and with every trip to the bathroom I checked to see if I could see a fetus—by seven and a half weeks I was told it would be nearly the size of a blueberry. I never saw anything, and wondered what I would do if I did. The reality that whatever that life was, was ending in our sewage system was a difficult thought to bear. I was relieved I never saw anything more distinct than some clots of blood.[78]

Anna recognized something negative in the experience of abortion itself but was also grateful and relieved afterward.[79] Anna's healing process led her to find a middle way between celebration and grief. She writes of the conflicting ideas, thoughts, and feelings that haunted her: "I didn't feel like a murderer. I knew I had stopped *something* in its tracks. *I'm a monster. No one knows how bad I really am.*"⁸⁰ Anna's abortion was a turning point in her life, and yet the emotional aftermath included shame and grief; she found she needed the help of her mother, friends, and a therapist to process her thoughts and emotions about the experience. Doing so helped her to name the shame she felt and take time to understand it.

> While I was still learning to forgive myself for the circumstances of getting pregnant, I had a much better understanding of where the shame around it came from—that it was more from society and less from myself. The deep thinking and wrestling with my decision not only freed me up from shame, but ultimately, it reminded me of the preciousness of life.⁸¹

Anna did not feel that she could go to a priest to talk about her experience of grief after abortion.⁸² But she wanted to find a way to ritualize her loss.

> Funerals usually serve as an opportunity for us to share our grief with our loved ones, and express our thoughts and emotions within the framework of our faith. But there is no funeral for an abortion, and any ceremony we may need to process what we're feeling is expected to happen quietly and alone, ideally without making a mess, or spewing our emotions on anyone who happens to come too close. I dealt with it by spending more time in my car, always my car, crying alone, usually into my scarf, often in between meetings.⁸³

With time and the support of loved ones, Anna found that she no longer felt guilt or shame about her abortion. Instead, for a time, she felt "guilty for not feeling guilty, as if carrying this heavy emotion would be a suitable penance for what I'd done."⁸⁴ In time, she was able to also let go of the need to punish herself and move toward self-acceptance.

> Instead of dwelling on what I cannot change—this has become my thing—I choose to allow my abortion to be a part of me, and I also choose to love it. Not because this somehow makes it more okay, but because I choose to love all of myself, including the experiences I wish I had not been through. I will not exile this part of me, and I will not exile this part of any other woman who has made this choice for herself and her future, either. Instead, I will keep engaging this practice of self-acceptance.⁸⁵

Lou

Lou shared her abortion story on a podcast called *Abortion, with love*,⁸⁶ eighteen months after her abortion. Lou was still grieving. Lou lives in a really small country town in Australia. She told the podcast host, Camila, that she remembers exactly where she was when she realized that her period was late.

Lou was driving home, and "not one single part of me thought maybe I'm pregnant" because she had a copper IUD and thought there was no way she could be pregnant. Upon seeing the result of the positive pregnancy test that night in her bathroom, she was shocked.

> I went to tell my partner at the time, "It's positive," and I laughed, and he, his face turned very quickly. And the first thing he said to me was "We'll make an appointment at the doctor's tomorrow, and we'll get it sorted." And I remember feeling that sense of laughter and shock completely disappeared, and I went into distraught mode. I remember just sobbing and sobbing and sobbing. I don't remember much of what happened that night. I just remember "This is what's happening, there's no going around what's going to happen." I remember going to work the next day, and something changed for me. I felt different. I felt, like part of me was excited, part of me was like "O my God, this is really great." And I was definitely wanting to keep it. I remember straight away thinking "No, I want to do this." But I knew it wasn't an option from my partner. And he had his reasons, so fair, I guess. But I remember thinking I just want to have a conversation about it.

When Lou called her friends, they offered congratulations, but then she told them that she "wasn't keeping it." When she called her mom, her mom became distraught, and Lou ended up needing to offer support to her mother, and did not get the support that Lou herself needed. "I wanted her to ask me, 'What do *you* want to do? How do *you* feel? Are *you* excited?' and my poor mom, she fell into absolute distraught mode." Lou's partner at the time said he would leave her if she were to keep the baby.[87]

> I remember thinking "I can't do this on my own." Because, I feel like society tells us we can't do it on our own. Like, nobody ever assumes that I could have this baby and do it myself. That's another whole patriarchal issue in its own right. Everyone said to me, "What does *he* want to do? What does *he* think?"

Lou's experience with abortion professionals was very negative. First Lou went to her primary physician, and in an appointment with her partner in the room, the doctor spoke directly to Lou. Lou believes that the doctor knew that Lou was feeling pressured by her partner, but the doctor did not ask the partner to leave the room so that Lou could speak to her privately. Lou felt betrayed by this doctor, who also did not offer any follow-up care after the procedure. Lou wanted the doctor to say, "Maybe you should think about it and come back in a week." For Lou, it was a "traumatic, emotional, ridiculous feeling" that she had never experienced before. "I didn't need cold and clinical, I needed a bit of sisterhood."

Chapter 5

Lou was surprised by the condition of the abortion clinic itself. Her partner drove her there, but because of visitor rules related to the COVID-19 pandemic, he could not go inside. It was a two-hour drive from her home. Lou said it was an office building, and she did not believe that she was in the right place. Lou could choose between a medical or surgical abortion. She chose to have a surgical abortion. With the medical abortion, she knew she could pass it over several days, but she was living in a share-house where she did not have a private bathroom. She thought the surgical abortion would be easier.

I desperately wanted him [my partner] to change his mind. I kick myself every day, saying "You should have spoken up, you should have spoken louder, maybe said something more." But also, he was someone I loved dearly, and his opinion mattered to me, so I thought "If that's what you think, that's probably what's best." I don't think I realized that my opinion, or my want, was being ignored. Because I trusted him so much, thinking it was the right decision.

I cried the whole way through the ultrasound and the procedure. I desperately wanted someone to look at me and ask me "Is this what *you* want to do?" I regret so much that I did not look at the ultrasound monitor. I guess it sounds bananas. She told me I was eight or nine weeks. She told me "Take your clothes off, put this gown on." It looked like a dentist chair. She pointed at the chair. "Sit down there." I have no clothes on, just the gown. In walks this man. He looks like something out of a cartoon. Six-foot-eight, gray hair, old, his covid mask was under his nose, his nose hair sticking out. It seemed unreal. I was like "What is going on?" And they start to put things in my arms. And they injected the anesthetic. Nobody was really talking to me. And I was getting visibly panicked, and the nurse asked, "Would it help if someone told you what was going on?" And I was like, "YES! Absolutely, if someone could tell me what is going on, that would be lovely." And before she finished the explanation, I was falling asleep from the anesthesia.

I remember waking up, and my feet couldn't move, and they were dragging me into another room, and I was crying, and they just dumped me on a bed in another room, and I was just sobbing uncontrollably. They came back and asked me "Are you in pain? What's wrong?" And I was asking for my partner, and she said he couldn't come in, I had to lay there for twenty minutes. Then she just came in and told me that it was time to put on my clothes and leave. And I remember thinking "This is absolutely nuts." But I didn't know that that wasn't the norm.

Lou experiences regret about her abortion decision. The evening of her abortion, she felt that her life had changed, and she sobbed in her bed. She explains why she was sobbing: "I immediately felt a sense of loss." But Lou repressed her experience. Ten months afterward, she began to process what had happened, and began to feel more strongly that she didn't have the choice she should have had. "I didn't know you could miss something you didn't even have," she says. Lou felt angry and sad. She wanted to tell people at her work what had happened to her, this awful thing, but she remembered thinking that she could not express sadness about it to others because she "chose" to do it. Lou says that she did not know that she was "allowed" to feel grief-stricken about it. She remembers previous conversations about "cells" that you can "get rid of," but after her own abortion experience, Lou felt upset, numb, and confused.

> I desperately wanted someone to recognize that I wasn't okay. My housemates at the time—who are fabulous and some of my dearest friends—but no one noticed. Everyone thought that I just wasn't the fun girl at the party anymore. And I remember thinking "I'm not okay. I can't handle this."

After the one-year anniversary of her abortion, Lou began to more deeply process her experience. Her parents remain supportive of her in her grief and healing process, encouraging her to "let it go," but Lou continues to grieve deeply. She and her partner split up. But Lou still feels a deep connection toward him. "The only thing that reminds me of the baby is him, and I can't let it go. I can't let him go. Because it feels like he's part of that for me." Lou continues, "It's peculiar, and it's weird, and I can't explain it to anybody that hasn't had an abortion."

Lou wishes that she had given herself more time to process her discernment *before* the abortion. She says there's a strong chance she would have come to the same conclusion, and maybe had she done that, she would not feel the same way now. But right now, what remains for her is that she feels like she did not have a real choice when she was going through the process. Lou says that she did not see any of it clearly at the time. Lou searched the internet as she began to process her experience and she read many testimonies of women who felt empowered by their abortion, but that was not Lou's experience. Lou was hoping to find testimonies in which women felt safe to share that they lost something, that the abortion changed them deeply.

> I feel like we, as a movement, I guess, need to change the way we talk about it so it doesn't feel so, like I have to be okay about it. I had no idea that I was allowed to be sad, which sounds so ridiculous. I had no idea that I was allowed to grieve. And looking back, I may have let down my own friends who had abortions, by not checking up on them.

Kassi

When Kassi Underwood was nineteen years old and in a relationship with a man who was a college dropout and drug dealer, she discovered she was pregnant. Kassi never thought she would have an abortion because she had always wanted to have children, but when she talked about this with her boyfriend, he said that he was not ready to be a father. When she told her parents, they told her she could move back home to raise the child. What Kassi *heard* in the conversation with her parents was that moving back home would be her only option. Neither having the baby nor terminating her pregnancy seemed like the right course of action.[88] Kassi went to church hoping for a message from God as she was discerning. But she heard nothing.[89] Kassi struggled to envision how she would parent.

> We had fifteen dollars between us. I was broke, jobless, nineteen, pregnant, 891 miles from home, with no transportation to the clinic 46 miles away. Even my foot was broken. I didn't qualify for a credit card. Bluegrass Family Health didn't cover the procedure. As far as being a "provider," Noah was the world's worst drug dealer. He had two clients: Minivan Dad and himself.[90]

Kassi struggled to find the funds to pay for her $425 abortion, feeling ashamed as she asked her parents for financial assistance and asked friends if she could borrow a car. As Kassi laid back for the abortion procedure in the clinic, she wanted to tell the nurse: "I was a good Christian, a virgin until last year. This was not supposed to be happening to me."[91] After the procedure, Kassi was physically healthy, but overcome with sadness.[92] "Having an abortion did not break me," Kassi later wrote. "It revealed the ways I was already broken."[93]

Kassi experienced years of heartache, soul-searching, and grief. She thought she would go to hell, and she avoided prayer because she "was afraid that God would say that I had murdered my own child."[94] Kassi's abortion had been a "big deal" in her life, but she found that when she disclosed her experience to feminist friends, they often tried to minimize her experience or tell her that she was wrong to think that it was a big deal at all.[95] Kassi found this unhelpful and confusing. Kassi came to realize that the mental anguish she experienced reflected our culture's inability to talk about the messiness of real life and sex. She felt that in our culture, women are given two options: either feel guilty after murdering your baby, or don't feel anything because abortion is no big deal, it was your "choice."[96] For Kassi, her complex grief and coming to terms with the reality of her life helped her to find a middle way.[97] She found that the binary of pro-life/pro-choice did not explain her experience.[98] She wrestled with guilt and shame even though she knew she had done the right thing.[99] For years, she dreamed of babies, thought about her "child" and what "could" have been. Ultimately, she came to see her decision as an act of love in a situation of constraint.[100]

Kassi searched for people who could help her in her healing journey. Kassi attended a Catholic retreat for women who have experienced abortion. Named *Rachel's Vineyard*, the retreat name references Jeremiah 31:15: "Rachel is weeping for her children."[101] Kassi tried to keep an open mind at the retreat, but found the approach of the retreat leaders to be spiritually and emotionally manipulative, especially as they discussed "postabortion syndrome," and the requirement of sacramental confession in order to repair one's relationship with God.[102] Kassi did not feel a deep sense of trust in the retreat leaders. Instead, she felt judged and shamed.[103] This made Kassi less likely to want to disclose her story in a way that made her feel vulnerable. "I wouldn't sit in a confessional with a man who carried a plastic fetus in his pocket to try to guilt me into telling him my secret thoughts about my dead baby," she explained.[104] Kassi struggled to keep an open mind during the retreat, especially as the leaders moved from the testimony phase into the ritual phase, including a "stoning" ritual and the "cup of bitterness" ritual.[105] Journaling and private prayer remained meaningful, but after the Catholic retreat Kassi found herself curious about the spiritual resources of other faith traditions. Her "journey of enlightenment" included conversations and rituals with Buddhist and Jewish leaders as well as grief counselors and other women who experienced abortion.

It was in a feminist post-abortion ritual with Jewish women that Kassi had a breakthrough moment in her spiritual journey. Kassi brought socks that were symbolic of her grandmother, of her abortion, of her shame. In the ritual, she buried the socks beneath a canopy of trees and said aloud that she was burying her anxiety, her shame, and her feeling of being alone.[106] Kassi came to understand her abortion as an "act of love," and she committed to being honest about her grief and her process of healing so that she could be a light to others.[107]

Emily

Emily Lind shared her personal experience of abortion as a way to describe the impact on her sense of self.

> In my mid-twenties, I had two abortions, twenty-two months apart. The first time I became pregnant, I was twenty-five years old, and three weeks into my first professional job. My partner and I were fighting one morning. In an effort to quickly deescalate and leave for work, I dismissed my stake in the argument, and said, "don't even listen to me. I feel really premenstrual and I must be

sensitive." He eyed me with nervous suspicion and looked in his calendar. "You sure you're only premenstrual?"[108]

Emily took a pregnancy test that day, which confirmed her pregnancy.

> I instantly went numb. My body felt empty and flushed with panic. In that moment, I felt time accelerate at an uncomfortable pace. For years, I had been anticipating my entry into parenthood. It was one of the few things I felt no ambivalence about. I yearned to parent, looked forward to pregnancy, and did not want to delay family planning much longer. Yet *this* version of pregnancy, *this* catapult into maternity felt wholly, painfully, and urgently *wrong*. It would take me years before I could articulate why, years I would spend confused and muddled in a mix of relief and regret at how the story played out.[109]

Emily found that the perplexing nature of "choice" in the reality of her life story was anything but straightforward.

> For as long as I could remember, I had been told reproductive choice was mine to claim. For as long as I could remember, I was taught that women's liberation was bound to the right to choose. No amount of fluency in second-wave political slogans prepared me for the intricacies of my decision to terminate my first pregnancy. Nothing felt less liberating than feeling trapped in my own body and confronting a contradiction for which I had no preparation: my decision to abort would have little to do with my desire to parent. I was certain I wanted to parent. I was certain I was old enough to parent. But carrying that particular pregnancy to term would lock me in a set of relationships I worried would kill me: a job I hated, a deteriorating relationship, and a spontaneous rewriting of my assumed life narrative. In this way, the first lesson I learned about abortion was that the decision to carry a pregnancy to term intersects with all facets of a person's social location.[110]

Emily discovered, as she discerned the possible paths before her, that her assumption had been that she would experience a healthy and formalized monogamous relationship, stability in her career, and then parenthood. Everything was topsy-turvy in her mind. Emily also had concerns related to her weight and body image. "I was fat, and had always been fat, and because of that, I always assumed that I had to lose weight before beginning my adult life in earnest. I had also assumed that my fat body was broken, incapable or somehow not allowed to be pregnant."[111] Emily thought that she needed to get rid of the pregnancy because the pregnancy threatened her ability to reach her personal goals. "It threatened my sense of self and my sense of my own future."[112] Almost two years after her first abortion, Emily's period was late, and she took another pregnancy test. She was still in an unhappy relationship, and her job continued to present significant stress in her life.[113] Emily felt shame about her weight, which was compounded by a visit to the doctor for an annual check-up, when her doctor told her she may struggle to conceive, and that she may be diabetic. As it turns out, she was pregnant during that appointment.

> I walked around numb for months. I now understand that I was mourning my decision to terminate my second pregnancy, not because I regretted it but because I regretted the fact that abortion presented itself once again as the best option.... To rescue my sense of self, I needed to once again terminate my pregnancy. The self I rescued, however, was not a unified sense of self, but rather the promise of a unified sense of self.[114]

Emily judged that the reasonable course of action before her was to terminate her pregnancy, even as she wished the situation were otherwise. Emily concludes her reflection on her own abortion experience by explaining that perhaps the idea of a coherent self is a problematic myth itself. She sometimes experiences regret, but also realizes how many unknowns there are as she considers not only the path she took, but the paths she did not take.[115]

Samerah

Samerah is a twenty-two-year-old woman and mother of a young son who is two years old. She shared her abortion story with journalists after Texas Senate Bill 8 limited abortion care in her home state of Texas.[116] Because of the SB-8 restrictions, Samerah traveled from Beaumont, Texas, to Oklahoma City, Oklahoma, for her abortion. Before this travel, Samerah had tried to procure an abortion in Houston. Samerah explains that since she discovered she was pregnant at five weeks gestational age, she thought she would be able to complete her abortion in Texas before the new law went into effect. However, the medical provider detected fetal cardiac activity on the day she was scheduled to terminate her pregnancy. Since fetal cardiac activity had been detected, Samerah was no longer able to access abortion care at the clinic in Texas. She was referred to a clinic in Oklahoma City. Samerah was not alone. She describes bawling in the hallway of the clinic with other women who had been told the same news.

Samerah describes her upbringing as one of six kids, and what led to her decision to terminate her pregnancy. Watching her mom parent six children through difficult times made Samerah aware of the responsibilities of motherhood. Samerah met her partner in high school, and they had a son together in 2019. Her minimum wage job did not pay for all of their bills.

> We didn't have really much anything. Kind of just started from square one, and our main goal was giving [our son] everything that he ever wanted. Everything that we ever wanted and couldn't have. I mean, lights is on, water—hot water is on. Like those are things that we were like, I want to do for him and I remember.

Samerah and her partner were thrilled when they could finally afford to move into an apartment of their own with their son. Living with family had been a struggle, but Samerah got a different job that paid $13.50/hour and allowed her to work from home. Once she and her partner saved up enough, they moved out and into their own place. When she found out she was pregnant again, Samerah explained that parenting her two-year old son was her top priority.

> And if I can't have another child right now because it'll prohibit me from taking care of him the way I want to, then I won't have another baby right now. And that was my main mindset. Like, I can afford to get him pullups at any point in time. With any of the money I have in my account, if I can spend the last cent of my money, it'll hold me over till I get paid again. I can't do that for two. So that was my main thought. I have to be able to keep taking care of my bills and my baby. And if I can't take care of my baby with the bills as well, I don't need the other child right now, because why would I bring them into that?

It was not easy to make travel arrangements to fly from Beaumont to Oklahoma City. She could not borrow money from family or friends, and had to cobble together funding from nonprofit abortion funds to make it work. Her partner took time off of work to accompany her and to watch their son during the procedure.

> I literally have a two-year-old that I like, I don't—I'm not struggling to provide for him, but I'm providing for him in a comfortable manner right now. And if I had another child, I couldn't do that for both. And I don't want to be that parent. I don't want to bring my kid into something that I can't afford to take care of, because they don't deserve that. I grew up in that kind of reality. And I know what it does to people. I know how hard it is, it can be. And I pride myself on being able to take care of my child.
>
> So it's like, people don't understand that we're real human beings and we have real lives. We cry, we get sad, we have stressful situations going on.

After the abortion procedure in the Oklahoma City clinic, Samerah tells the journalist: "It was super easy. No pain, just a little tired, but other than that." She left with her partner and son, after expressing gratitude to the staff at the clinic.

Mary

Mary Gordon described her experiences of pregnancy loss in *Commonweal* magazine after the *Dobbs* decision in the summer of 2022; she self-identifies as pro-choice and Catholic.[117] Mary describes her five pregnancies: two of which ended in abortion, one that ended in miscarriage, and two that ended in live births. Mary also describes her accompaniment of a friend and her daughter in the process of their miscarriages.

Mary's first pregnancy was the result of "what was then known as heavy petting" when Mary was nineteen and a sophomore in college.[118] "I knew that having a baby would mean the end of the life I had worked so hard to begin," she writes, offering the rationale for her decision to seek an illegal abortion.[119] A legal abortion could have been obtained for $2,000, says Mary, had she been willing to seek approval for an abortion by claiming to be suicidal, but $2,000 was unaffordable for her. Instead, she "got a number" from a classmate, was picked up outside of a movie theatre, and blindfolded for the drive to the illegal clinic run out of an apartment in New York City, where the "excruciating procedure" took place.[120] That night, a friend offered support and comfort. "She held me in her arms as I wept from the memory of the pain and the awareness that I could have died. I was also angry that if I'd had more money, I would not have had to put myself in danger. But not for a moment did I regret what I had done."[121]

Six years later, Mary was twenty-five years old and enrolled in a doctoral program; Mary discovered she was pregnant soon after her boyfriend had ended the relationship.[122]

> I knew that I wanted to have an abortion; I knew that I very much wanted to have children, but not in this way, and not at this time. I saw that the path to a career as a writer and college teacher would be greatly complicated, if not rendered impossible, if I had a baby.[123]

Her second abortion was a very different experience than the first because in the intervening years, the *Roe v. Wade* decision had created the opportunity for safer and legal abortions for women in her situation.

> I went to my local Planned Parenthood. Everyone was more than kind; I was tested and found to be nine weeks along. I wrote to my former lover, informing him. He was remorseful and said he would help me pay for an abortion. I informed him that Planned Parenthood only charged $200 and he needn't bother. He sent me $100 the next day.
>
> The Planned Parenthood facility was welcoming, clean, and cheerful. The friend who accompanied me was invited to stay until the procedure was done. I was

given an anesthetic; the doctor explained the procedure. I will remember the wonderful nurse all my life. She was probably in her sixties, small, compact, with tight gray curls and a reassuring touch. "I was retired," she said, "but I came back to work because I wanted to be part of the new world, where women could have abortions safely."[124]

Mary felt cared for and supported at the legal abortion clinic in 1974. Mary felt relieved as she was treated with dignity. In contrast to her first abortion, in the second she experienced only "mild discomfort" and was informed that she could call if she had any questions afterward. She received follow-up care from a physician who offered reassurance as she recovered. As Mary reflects on her second abortion, she explains: "Certainly, I wished that what had happened had not happened, but I never thought I had made the wrong decision."[125]

Mary's third pregnancy was very much welcomed; Mary was "joyously married" and they were "very eager" to have children.[126] The morning sickness she experienced in the first trimester was deeply unpleasant, but bearable. When her daughter was born, Mary says: "I can say without reservation or hesitation that it was the greatest moment of my life."[127] Mary was overwhelmed with gratitude as she held her newborn daughter, remembering the way that she was "brimming over with peaceful love" and reflecting on the "miracle in which I had somehow participated."[128]

A year later, Mary was called to her neighbor's house to help her while the neighbor experienced miscarriage when she was nine weeks pregnant. Her neighbor asked Mary to retrieve the bloody tissue from the toilet so that they could take it to the doctor's office as requested.

> I took a cup and scooped what I could into it. Floating in the bloody water was something gelatinous around the size of a large postal stamp. Was this the fetus? I couldn't know. It seemed so much more like the kind of heavy period I'd sometimes had than anything like a human child that I was tempted to flush it down the toilet. But I obeyed my friend's wishes.
>
> The doctor told us that it was in fact a fetus, that she had miscarried, and would need procedures to remove whatever remains she was still carrying. "Do you want to take it home?" the doctor asked, and my friend looked at him in anger and said, "Of course not. Please dispose of it in any way that you normally do."[129]

Mary reflected afterward about how her friend, also Catholic, "had no impulse to bury, baptize, to name what had been lost."[130]

The next year, Mary and her husband were delighted when they discovered Mary was pregnant again. But her pregnancy ended in miscarriage at nineteen weeks, after her water broke and she was confined to bedrest for ten days in the hopes of saving the pregnancy. She delivered in the hospital, and asked her husband to look at the fetus and describe it to her. He said, "It was very tiny. It was like a baby but not like a baby. All I could think of was how pathetic it looked, how unable for life."[131] Mary felt "despair," "that I had failed this creature."[132] Mary was not comfortable describing her miscarriage loss as a "baby," but mourned in her confusion and anger anyway.[133] A few months later, she discovered she was pregnant again, and felt nervous throughout the pregnancy, worried that it too would end in miscarriage. In the fourth month, she was "seized with terror" when she began spotting, and after it was explained to her that she had an "incompetent cervix," Mary opted for bedrest for the remaining duration of her fifth pregnancy.

> Once again, I lay dreading the dire consequences of any false move, but in fact I carried to term and gave birth to my son—although the cord was around his neck, and he required a forceps delivery in the course of which my vaginal walls were nicked, and I had to be wheeled to another room to be stitched up. So it was only after that recovery that my little boy was brought to me and the same sense of miracle, of unspeakable love, was mine.[134]

Almost thirty years later, Mary accompanied her daughter through a difficult miscarriage, and then welcomed with joy two grandsons, for whom she would "in a second, give my life."[135] As she reflects upon her experiences of pregnancy loss and of parenthood and the joy of being a grandparent, Mary says that "abortion is a serious issue" because it "raises large questions."[136] But she also makes a distinction between "a fetus" and "a baby," rooted in her own experiences of the differences between her five pregnancies.[137]

COMPLEXITY AND AMBIGUITY

I have chosen to bring together women's testimonies of miscarriage, stillbirth, and abortion here because all of these are examples of pregnancy loss and they share some common features. Pregnancy loss is a profoundly embodied experience that contains ambiguity and complexity. Despite similarities across narratives, the *meaning* of each event is subjective, and the circumstances and woman's feelings about the pregnancy contribute to the woman's determination of the meaning of the pregnancy loss. Whether she was seeking care because of miscarriage, stillbirth, or abortion, each woman wanted access to medical care that would safeguard her life and respect her decisions, and the space to process what she was experiencing without judgment and shame imposed by others. Christian ethicist Rebecca Todd Peters explains that "paying attention to the actual moral situations that people face is a necessary first step in creating meaningful ethical responses to real problems."[138]

Catholic magisterial teachings claim universal knowledge but have been crafted by men, leading to "a situation in which men (male human beings) reflected upon the whole of life on behalf of the whole community of men and women, young and old."[139] Protestant ethicist Christine Pohl complained that "in the construction of the public debate [about abortion], women's actual lives and experiences have figured very little."[140] Natalia Imperatori-Lee explains that in the Roman Catholic Church, "women have not been considered reliable witnesses to their own lives, or faith, or the faith of the church that they love."[141] There are, of course, serious implications when women are not given the opportunity to contribute meaningfully to the development of Catholic teachings. By sharing stories of pregnancy loss—even stories that make one uncomfortable—women can reshape the community's imagination and practices. Such speaking up and speaking out carries risk but can also be deeply affirming if such sharing leads to solidarity among women.

These testimonies reveal that "choice" is an inadequate category. Choice implies moral freedom—meaning that one freely chooses to do what one believes to be right within the present circumstances, and experiences no constraint in that self-determining action. But testimonies of pregnancy loss challenge this category. Women who miscarry during a wanted pregnancy report a dramatic loss of control, and profound conflict between their desires and the reality of their body's limitations. Similarly, women who experience stillbirth often report *aspects* of choice within their narrative (for example, they may have the choice between vaginal delivery or Caesarian delivery; induction of labor or waiting for labor to begin naturally); but women do not say that they "choose" stillbirth. Even with the decision to terminate a pregnancy, the language of choice is not used consistently, and is even experienced as a barrier by some women. Of the testimonies I have cited, Viva describes her abortion decision without regret, but acknowledges that abortion is not an ideal situation (comparing it to a painful tooth extraction). Lou describes her abortion story, focusing on the pressure she felt to abort, and wishing that she had felt she had a choice. Anna, Kassi, Emily, and Mary describe in various ways feeling stuck in unhealthy relationships when they discerned that abortion was the best way forward in the particularities of their lives at the time. Anna even invoked the principle of toleration when she called her abortion the "lesser evil." Samerah, Anna, Kassi, and Lou reported feeling constrained by their financial situations, though with varying emphases. Their testimonies align with the statistics cited in the introduction of the chapter, which indicated that among the women interviewed, forty percent had said that they were not financially prepared to have a child. The description of procuring an abortion because one *has* to instead of doing it because one *wants* to is a part of many women's testimonies about pregnancy termination. Anna, Kassi, and Emily consented to their abortion in the sense that they sought care from a medical professional who offered them options, and they signed consent forms, and followed through with the medical or surgical abortion; they were not coerced by other people but still felt stuck by the circumstances. Pro-life authors who accuse women of ending their pregnancies out of "convenience" misunderstand the complexity of everyday dilemmas and mischaracterize how pregnant women think through the many values at stake in their decisions to seek an abortion. We will continue to unpack these women's testimonies in the next chapter, in which I defend the moral agency of pregnant women.

NOTES

1. Yolanda Pierce, *In My Grandmother's House: Black Women, Faith, and the Stories We Inherit* (Minneapolis: Broadleaf, 2021), xvii.

2. Pierce, *In My Grandmother's House*, xvii.

3. Jael Silliman, Marlene Gerber Fried, Loretta Ross, and Elena R. Gutiérrez, eds., *Undivided Rights: Women of Color Organize for Reproductive Justice* (Chicago: Haymarket, 2016), ix.

4. Guttmacher Institute, "Induced Abortion in the United States" (September 2019), 1, https://www.guttmacher.org/fact-sheet/induced-abortion-united-states.

5. Guttmacher Institute, "Number of Abortions in the United States Likely to Be Higher in 2023 than in 2020" (January 17, 2024), https://www.guttmacher.org/news-release/2024/number-abortions-united-states-likely-be-higher-2023-2020.

6. Guttmacher Institute, "Induced Abortion," 1.

7. Jeff Diamant and Besheer Mohamed, "What the Data Says About Abortion in the U.S.," Pew Research Center (January 11, 2023), https://www.pewresearch.org/short-reads/2023/01/11/what-the-data-says-about-abortion-in-the-u-s-2/.

8. Guttmacher Institute, "Number of Abortions" (2024).

9. Diane Greene Foster, *The Turnaway Study: Ten Years, A Thousand Women, and the Consequences of Having—or Being Denied—an Abortion* (New York: Scribner, 2020), 35.

10. Guttmacher, "Induced Abortion," 1.

11. Serene Jones, "Hope Deferred," in *Trauma and Grace: Theology in a Ruptured World*, 2ed. (Louisville: Westminster John Knox, 2019), 127–50, at 129.

12. Elise Erikson Barrett, *What Was Lost: A Christian Journey through Miscarriage* (Louisville: Westminster John Knox, 2010), 12–13. See also Masha Sukovic and Margie Serrato, "Communicating Miscarriage: Coping with Loss, Uncertainty, and Self-Imposed Stigma," in Emily R. M. Lind and Angie Deveau, eds., *Interrogating Pregnancy Loss: Feminist Writings on Abortion, Miscarriage, and Stillbirth* (Bradford, ON: Demeter Press, 2017), 21–39; Nancy Gerber, "Grief, Shame, and Miscarriage," in Lind and Deveau, *Interrogating Pregnancy Loss*, 47–60; Robin

Silbergleid, "Missed Miscarriage," in Lind and Deveau, *Interrogating Pregnancy Loss*, 150–56; Shannon Gibney and Kao Kalia Yang, eds., *What God Is Honored Here? Writings on Miscarriage and Infant Loss by and for Native Women and Women of Color* (Minneapolis: University of Minnesota Press, 2019); and the testimonies published in Dorothy E. McBride and Jennifer L. Keys, eds., *Abortion in the United States*, second ed. (Santa Barbara: ABC-CLIO, 2018).

13. Barrett, *What Was Lost*, 14.
14. Barrett, *What Was Lost*, 15.
15. Barrett, *What Was Lost*, 15–16.
16. Barrett, *What Was Lost*, 15–16.
17. Barrett, *What Was Lost*, 21.
18. Barrett, *What Was Lost*, 22.
19. Barrett, *What Was Lost*, 22.
20. Barrett, *What Was Lost*, 23.
21. Barrett, *What Was Lost*, 23.
22. Barrett, *What Was Lost*, 24.
23. Barrett, *What Was Lost*, 19.
24. Jessica Zucker, *I Had a Miscarriage: A Memoir, A Movement* (New York: Feminist Press, 2021), 45, xi.
25. Zucker, *I Had a Miscarriage*, 4.
26. Zucker, *I Had a Miscarriage*, 6.
27. Zucker, *I Had a Miscarriage*, 7–8.
28. Zucker, *I Had a Miscarriage*, 9.
29. Zucker, *I Had a Miscarriage*, 11.
30. Zucker, *I Had a Miscarriage*, 10.
31. Zucker, *I Had a Miscarriage*, 12.
32. Zucker, *I Had a Miscarriage*, 14–15. Jessica was not prosecuted for her bleeding, but scholars of law and criminal justice report that some women have been investigated and prosecuted for violating fetal protection laws or laws regarding disposal of human remains. Steve Marshall, Attorney General of Alabama, strategically uses child abuse or endangerment statutes to prosecute cases involving fetuses in order to punish pregnant women. See Michele Goodwin, *Policing the Womb: Invisible Women and the Criminalization of Motherhood* (New York: Cambridge University Press, 2020), 195.
33. Zucker, *I Had a Miscarriage*, 27.
34. Zucker, *I Had a Miscarriage*, 27.
35. Zucker, *I Had a Miscarriage*, 31.
36. Zucker, *I Had a Miscarriage*, 84.
37. Soniah Kamal, "The Face of Miscarriage," in *What God Is Honored Here?*, 177–86.
38. Kamal, "The Face of Miscarriage," 177.
39. Kamal, "The Face of Miscarriage," 179–80.
40. Kamal, "The Face of Miscarriage," 181–82.
41. Kamal, "The Face of Miscarriage," 182–83.
42. Kamal, "The Face of Miscarriage," 184–85.

43. Kamal, "The Face of Miscarriage," 185.
44. Kamal, "The Face of Miscarriage," 186.
45. Susan Reynolds, "Vigil-Keeping," in Kate Williams, ed., *Of Womb and Tomb*, 23–26. This book contains valuable resources for rituals that may contribute to healing after pregnancy loss.
46. Reynolds, "Vigil-Keeping," 24.
47. Reynolds, "Vigil-Keeping," 26.
48. Reynolds, "Vigil-Keeping," 26.
49. Janet Lee Ortiz, "Kamali's Stillbirth," in *What God Is Honored Here*, 149–70, at 151.
50. Lee-Ortiz, "Kamali's Stillbirth," 152.
51. Lee-Ortiz, "Kamali's Stillbirth," 153.
52. Lee-Ortiz, "Kamali's Stillbirth," 156.
53. Lee-Ortiz, "Kamali's Stillbirth," 158.
54. Lee-Ortiz, "Kamali's Stillbirth," 164.
55. Lee-Ortiz, "Kamali's Stillbirth," 165.
56. Lee-Ortiz, "Kamali's Stillbirth," 166.
57. Lee-Ortiz, "Kamali's Stillbirth," 170.
58. Taiyon J. Coleman, "Tilted Uterus: When Jesus Is Your Baby Daddy," in *What God Is Honored Here?*, 45–65.
59. Coleman, "Tilted Uterus," 60–61.
60. Coleman, "Tilted Uterus," 61.
61. Coleman, "Tilted Uterus," 61.
62. Coleman, "Tilted Uterus," 63–64.
63. Viva Ruiz, *Shout Your Abortion*, ed. Amelia Bonow and Emily Nokes (Oakland, CA: PM Press, 2018), kindle location 662.
64. Viva Ruiz, *Shout Your Abortion*, kindle location 670.
65. Viva Ruiz, *Shout Your Abortion*, kindle location 670.
66. Viva Ruiz, *Shout Your Abortion*, kindle location 678.
67. Viva Ruiz, *Shout Your Abortion*, kindle location 696.
68. Viva Ruiz, *Shout Your Abortion*, kindle location 696.
69. Viva Ruiz, *Shout Your Abortion*, kindle location 705.
70. Wood, *I've Had One Too*, 51.
71. Wood, *I've Had One Too*, 29.
72. Wood, *I've Had One Too*, 29.
73. Wood, *I've Had One Too*, 29–30.
74. Wood, *I Had One Too*, 32, 44.
75. Wood, *I've Had One Too*, 12–13.
76. Wood, *I've Had One Too*, 47.
77. Wood, *I've Had One Too*, 48.
78. Wood, *I've Had One Too*, 49.
79. Wood, *I've Had One Too*, 50.
80. Wood, *I've Had One Too*, 53.
81. Wood, *I've Had One Too*, 69.
82. Wood, *I've Had One Too*, 119.

83. Wood, *I've Had One Too*, 118–19, 123–24.
84. Wood, *I've Had One Too*, 142.
85. Wood, *I Had One Too*, 143–44.
86. "Lou's Abortion Story," *Abortion, with Love*. Season 2, episode 24 (December 14, 2021), https://www.abortionwithlove.com/episodes/lous-abortion-story. *Abortion, with Love* is a podcast that aims to change the way we talk about abortion and to honor the experiences of each person. It is a project started by Camila Ochoa Mendoza in December 2020, in order to create spaces for people to speak from the heart. In the introduction to each episode, Camila explains that each abortion story is valid, and encourages listeners to have an open heart when listening. "Some things may be hard to hear, and you may not relate to everything she says, and that's okay," says Camila. See also *The Abortion Diary* podcast created by Melissa Madera, https://www.theabortiondiary.com/.
87. Lou admits when telling her story that she does not remember if he said this before or after her abortion procedure. "Lou's Abortion Story," 9:00–9:17.
88. Kassi Underwood, *May Cause Love: An Unexpected Journey of Enlightenment After Abortion* (New York: HarperOne, 2017), 32–35.
89. Underwood, *May Cause Love*, 38.
90. Underwood, *May Cause Love*, 39.
91. Underwood, *May Cause Love*, 41.
92. Underwood, *May Cause Love*, 41.
93. Underwood, *May Cause Love*, 62.
94. Underwood, *May Cause Love*, 75.
95. Underwood, *May Cause Love*, 80–81.
96. Underwood, *May Cause Love*, 198–99.
97. Underwood, *May Cause Love*, 201–2.
98. Underwood, *May Cause Love*, 212.
99. Underwood, *May Cause Love*, 119, 151.
100. Underwood, *May Cause Love*, 259.
101. Underwood, *May Cause Love*, 134.
102. Underwood, *May Cause Love*, 127–47.
103. Underwood, *May Cause Love*, 157.
104. Underwood, *May Cause Love*, 145.
105. Underwood, *May Cause Love*, 152–53.
106. Underwood, *May Cause Love*, 256–59.
107. Underwood, *May Cause Love*, 259–64.
108. Emily R. M. Lind, "Fatphobia, Pregnancy Loss, and My Hegemonic Imagination: A Story of Two Abortions," in *Interrogating Pregnancy Loss: Feminist Writings on Abortion, Miscarriage, and Stillbirth*, eds. Emily R. M. Lind and Angie Deveau (Bradford, ON, Canada: Demeter Press, 2017), 141.
109. Lind, "Fatphobia," 141.
110. Lind, "Fatphobia," 139–49, at 142.
111. Lind, "Fatphobia," 143.
112. Lind, "Fatphobia," 144.
113. Lind, "Fatphobia," 144–45.

114. Lind, "Fatphobia," 146.

115. Lind, "Fatphobia," 148.

116. Sabrina Tavernise, "They Don't Understand That We're Real People," *The Daily* (October 1, 2021), https://www.nytimes.com/2021/10/01/podcasts/the-daily/texas-abortion-law-oklahoma.html.

117. Mary Gordon, "This Pregnancy," *Commonweal* vol. 149, no. 10 (November 2022): 14–18.

118. Gordon, "This Pregnancy," 15.

119. Gordon, "This Pregnancy," 15.

120. Gordon, "This Pregnancy," 15.

121. Gordon, "This Pregnancy," 16.

122. Gordon, "This Pregnancy," 16.

123. Gordon, "This Pregnancy," 16.

124. Gordon, "This Pregnancy," 16.

125. Gordon, "This Pregnancy," 16.

126. Gordon, "This Pregnancy," 16.

127. Gordon, "This Pregnancy," 16.

128. Gordon, "This Pregnancy," 16.

129. Gordon, "This Pregnancy," 17.

130. Gordon, "This Pregnancy," 17.

131. Gordon, "This Pregnancy," 17.

132. Gordon, "This Pregnancy," 17.

133. Gordon, "This Pregnancy," 17.

134. Gordon, "This Pregnancy," 17.

135. Gordon, "This Pregnancy," 18.

136. Gordon, "This Pregnancy," 18.

137. Gordon, "This Pregnancy," 14.

138. Rebecca Todd Peters, "Listening to Women: Examining the Moral Wisdom of Women Who End Pregnancies," *Journal of Religious Ethics* 49:2 (2021): 290–313, at 309.

139. Mercy Amba Oduyoye, "Doing Theology from Third World Women's Perspective," in *Feminist Theology from the Third World: A Reader*, ed. Ursula King (Eugene: Wipf & Stock, 1994), 29. See also Rosemary Radford Ruether, *Sexism and God-Talk* (Boston: Beacon, 1983), chapter 1.

140. Christine D. Pohl, "Abortion: Responsibility and Betrayal," *Bioethics and the Future of Medicine* (Grand Rapids, MI: Eerdmans, 1995), 212–23.

141. Natalia Imperatori-Lee, "Father Knows Best: Theological 'Mansplaining' and the Ecclesial War on Women," *Journal of Feminist Studies in Religion* vol. 31, no. 2 (2015): 89–107, at 90. See also Margaret Farley, "The Role of Experience in Moral Discernment," in *Christian Ethics: Problems and Prospects*, ed. Lisa Sowle Cahill and James F. Childress (Cleveland: Pilgrim Press, 1996), 134–45; Laurie Johnston, "Christian Ethics and Experience," in *T&T Clark Handbook of Christian Ethics*, ed. Tobias Winright (London: Bloomsbury, 2021), 27–35.

Chapter 6

The Full Humanity and Moral Agency of Pregnant Women

A Key Claim for Reproductive Justice

Catholic feminist theologian Barbara Hilkert Andolsen wisely wrote in 1992 that "one feminist criterion for evaluating the church's sexual ethic is a requirement that the church's teachings must acknowledge and enhance the moral agency of women."[1] Andolsen seeks to move away from a discourse in which women are objects and toward an ecclesial culture that honors women as subjects. What would it mean, though, to acknowledge and enhance the moral agency of gestating women?[2] Moral agency means that one has the power to do what one knows is right; the person is an agent who makes decisions out of a sense of inner freedom and responsibility. Surely, many cases of pregnancy today result from just this category of freedom—women who *wanted* to be pregnant, and accept the bodily changes that inevitably come with such a decision.[3] Even in the best of circumstances, a decision to celebrate and continue a pregnancy can be a difficult process, requiring moving through new identities and responding to challenges as they arise.[4] But as we listen carefully to a broad account of women's narratives of pregnancy loss and of reproductive injustice, we see that gestating women often feel constrained by social forces beyond their control. Enslaved women did not experience bodily autonomy.[5] Human trafficking and sexual slavery are still an everyday reality for many people today, and disproportionately for young women.[6] Philosopher Jennifer Banks explains that motherhood is venerated in the United States "except when it comes time to pay the bill from the maternity ward, offer maternity leave, feed a mother's children, or come up with solutions to the childcare conundrum."[7] Moral tragedy resulting from structural sin and unfreedom is a thread in many women's testimonies of abortion today. Samerah's testimony in chapter 5 revealed that economic constraints were part of the backdrop to her abortion decision. Anna described a toxic relationship with "the broker," and recognized that abortion was the best way forward. Chapter 4 focused on the structural supports that gestating women need, and advocated for particular policies that advance reproductive justice. But in this chapter, I defend the priority of gestating women in decision-making about their pregnancies. I articulate ways in which this argument can find support in the Catholic moral tradition, and note where the tradition needs to be further developed to better account for respect for women. A better way is possible, but it will remain complex because it requires a straightforward recognition that gestating women are human persons, and that their decisions made in conscience should be respected even while it is also true that their judgments may be in error. The Catholic tradition's reluctance to respect the decisions of gestating women displays an unacceptable misogyny that must be challenged head-on. An important part of this argument entails a nuanced description of the intrinsic value of prenatal life, and the justification for asserting the gestating woman's right to make decisions that can lead to harm for the prenate; that part of the argument comes later in the chapter.

WOMEN ARE HUMAN PERSONS

Women are human persons. Such a claim is both obvious and radical. To say that women are part of the human species is simply factual; but the claim is radical because of its implications, namely, that the basic respect for bodily autonomy that men take for granted in the Catholic theological tradition (and in US culture) must be extended to women. Recognition of the full humanity of women has emerged in magisterial teachings as an affirmation,[8] but the implications of this claim remain an important topic of investigation in theology and ethics because women continue to be treated differently in Church teachings on the basis of their difference from men.

For much of Catholic history, women were either invisible in Church teachings or assumed to be naturally inferior to men. The Bible can be used to justify patriarchy by reference to the control that male heads of household asserted over their property, including wives and children.[9] Depending on how they are interpreted, passages from the New Testament requiring female submission (Eph 5:22–24), veiling (1 Cor 11:6), silence (1 Tim 2:12), and salvation through procreation (1 Tim 2:15) can be disempowering for contemporary female readers. Even in the much beloved social teachings of the modern era, explicit patriarchal assumptions are clear. For example, in 1931, Pius XI declared a woman's proper place to be the home in a submissive relationship to her husband, and argued that women's work outside the home for wages was "unfortunate."[10]

That the Church today officially teaches women's inherent dignity and equality is in fact a *theological development* influenced by cultural forces outside the Church and shaped by the intellectual labor of Christian feminists. But problems remain. Pope Francis, more than any other pontiff, has acknowledged the long-standing misogyny present in culture;[11] but even the pope does not adequately reflect on how the Church perpetuates gender injustice in ecclesiology, canon law, and theology of marriage.[12]

Catholic feminist theologian Margaret Farley has been a leading voice in shaping an understanding of the problem of sexism in Catholicism as well as shaping what it means to respect persons as *ends in themselves*.[13] Farley insists that a just love must take into account the *concrete reality* of the person.[14] Equal dignity and unjust power differentials exist simultaneously. It is not enough, then, to cite evidence of magisterial teachings that affirm the equal dignity of all human persons. Attention must also be paid to the disproportionate and unjustifiable burdens some people are expected to bear.[15] Women do not just have innate dignity; women also seek a dignified life. Are there resources within the Catholic tradition for defending the moral agency of gestating women, particularly those facing unwanted or dangerous pregnancies?

The English translation of *Dignitatis Humanae*, the Second Vatican Council's Declaration on Religious Freedom, promulgated by Pope Paul VI, begins with this claim:

> A sense of the dignity of the human person has been impressing itself more and more deeply on the consciousness of contemporary man, and the demand is increasingly made that men should act on their own judgment, enjoying and making use of a responsible freedom, not driven by coercion but motivated by a sense of duty.[16]

The lack of inclusive language is certainly problematic in this translation, but the teaching is inclusive of women, who are fully human and should be able to act on their own judgment, out of responsible freedom, not driven by coercion but motivated by a sense of duty. Too many pregnant women are not given space to deeply discern and to act on their own judgment; but *Dignitatis Humanae* invites the Church to think more concretely about the harms of coercion.

Further, respect for the dignity of persons means respect for *embodied* persons.[17] One notable feature of our embodiment is the limit that our body imposes on our will. Catholic medical ethics has a deep appreciation for the limits we experience in the context of disease, aging, and death. Our messy, human lives are enmeshed in particular experiences of bodily limitations and relational vulnerability.[18] In addition, Catholic teachings on the person acknowledge the historical and contextual nature of the person. The reality of the human person must be understood not in the abstract but rather as situated in the particularity of time and space and influenced by language, culture, gender, family, and one's environment. Recent popes have emphasized this contextual approach to personalism.[19]

Catholic social teachings have utilized the language of human rights discourse since the mid-twentieth century, explaining that each person has entitlements to claim from the human community as well as obligations to the human community. Pope John XXIII explained in *Pacem in Terris* in 1963:

> Man has the right to live. He has the right to bodily integrity and to the means necessary for the proper development of life, particularly food, clothing, shelter, medical care, rest, and, finally, the necessary social services. In consequence, he has the right to be looked after in the event of ill health; disability stemming from his work; widowhood; old age; enforced unemployment; or whenever through no fault of his own he is deprived of the means of livelihood.[20]

The lack of inclusive language in this English translation should not lead us to believe that bodily integrity is a right only granted to men. Women, too, should have the right to live, the right to bodily integrity, the right to medical care, and more. Pope John XXIII explained that "human beings have also the right to choose for themselves the kind of life which appeals to them: whether it is to found a family—in the founding of which both the man and the woman enjoy equal rights and duties—or to embrace the priesthood or the religious life."[21] Here John XXIII rejects the norm of compulsory motherhood, indicating that women should be able to "choose for themselves the kind of life which appeals to them." Equal rights for women and men within the Church remains, unfortunately, an aspirational commitment; Synod listening sessions around the world indicate that Catholics continue to see gender injustice in the Church itself as a moral concern.[22]

If the gestating woman is an *end* in herself, and not merely a *means* for reproduction, it follows that she may freely choose to accept the burdens of pregnancy, but it would be immoral for others (Church, partners, state) to engage in coercion (that is, to force her to remain pregnant against her will). Respecting the full humanity of gestating women demands that women themselves decide the fate of their pregnancies. For too long, pregnancies have been described as wonderful blessings and beautiful gifts from God without sufficient attention to the very real burdens that pregnancy demands, burdens that cannot always be shared by others in the Church community.

In other medical cases, there are safeguards in place to prevent the exploitation of patients. Catholic teaching forbids scientific and medical experimentation that is not "at the service of the integral good of the person," experimentation that involves "disproportionate risks to the life and physical and psychological integrity of the subject," and experimentation that does not result from informed consent.[23] Catholic teachings declare that organ donation "is morally acceptable with the consent of the donor and without excessive risks to him or her."[24] Acts that are deemed "contrary to respect for the bodily integrity of the human person" include "kidnapping and hostage taking, terrorism, torture, violence, direct sterilization," and "amputations and mutilations" that are not strictly for "therapeutic medical reasons."[25] Is there evidence to support the claim that pregnancy does not involve "disproportionate risks to the life and physical and psychological integrity" of the gestating woman? What are we to make of the way that informed consent is crafted as central to the evaluation of a moral case of medical experimentation or organ transplant, but not also to pregnancy?

PREGNANCY IS BURDENSOME

Human creatures do not just *have* bodies; we *are* bodies. The self is an embodied creature; what happens to one's body happens to the self. Growing a prenate inside of you is demanding, difficult, and in some cases dangerous. The human reproductive system does not stand alone within the person's body but is integrated into every other system within the human body including the skeletal, muscular, nervous, endocrine, cardiovascular, lymphatic, respiratory, digestive, and urinary systems. For example, the gestating woman's *circulatory system* undergoes major changes during pregnancy. Maternal blood volume increases by 30 to 50 percent, so that the uterus can support prenatal growth. The gestating woman's heart must pump more blood per minute and a gestating woman's heart rate increases. Oxygen and nutrients from the gestating woman's blood are transferred across the placenta to the prenate through the blood vessels of the umbilical cord. Waste products and carbon dioxide from the prenate are sent back through the umbilical cord and placenta to the gestating woman's circulation system to be eliminated.[26] The gestating person's *respiratory system* undergoes major changes during pregnancy. Hormones and physical changes due to the growing prenate can affect the upper and lower respiratory tracts. A pregnant person may experience reduced lung capacity and increased oxygen use. When lung diseases develop or there is a preexisting condition, such as asthma, the lungs may have difficulty compensating.[27] Pregnancy also affects the *digestive system*. Due to hormonal changes, digestion slows during pregnancy and absorption of nutrients can diminish. As the uterus grows, it can put pressure on the bowel.[28] Pregnancy has an obvious impact to the *skeletal system*, as hormones loosen joints to enable the uterus to grow as the ribcage expands.

Pregnancy is also associated with deterioration of bone mass in the pregnant woman.[29] Her mechanics of walking will be affected, and lower back pain is common.[30] The *urinary system* experiences profound changes to accommodate the prenate as well. Pregnancy affects all aspects of kidney physiology; the volume of kidneys during pregnancy increases up to 30 percent.[31] Further, the bladder is compressed as the uterus expands, which means that the gestating woman will feel the urge to urinate more often, even as emptying of the bladder may be incomplete.

Pregnant women with mental illness often face additional hurdles during pregnancy. Sometimes providers will recommend that the pregnant patient stop taking psychiatric medications that were effective prior to the pregnancy, because of the potential dangers to the fetus including birth defects, behavioral teratogenesis, and perinatal syndromes.[32] Antidepressant medication and medications prescribed for anxiety disorders also carry some risk to the prenate, although the data is disputed. Medications to treat bipolar disorder have known risks for the prenate. The postpartum period is one of high risk for the development of a depressive episode, particularly for women with a history of depression. Hormonal changes are known to cause complex changes in brain functioning, and some pregnant women experience cognitive impairment and brain fog (also known as "baby brain") both during and after pregnancy. Hormonal changes can also lead to headaches, including migraines, which are difficult to treat in pregnant patients because of the adverse risks of medications to the prenate. The anxiety associated with being pregnant can contribute to psychotic or depressive episodes as well as to tension and migraine headaches.[33] Mental health and physical health are equally important aspects of overall health,[34] and her mental health is just as relevant to a pregnant woman's discernment before and during pregnancy as her physical health.

Every pregnancy is different, but even from the beginning the symptoms a gestating woman experiences can be disruptive to her everyday life and—in extreme cases—deadly.[35] Typical symptoms one can read about in a book for pregnant women include nausea, vomiting (including dry heaves), fatigue, constipation, heartburn, indigestion, flatulence, bloating, headaches, dizziness, nasal congestion, nosebleeds, ear stuffiness, sensitive gums that may bleed when you brush, leg cramps, backache, achiness in the lower abdomen, swelling of ankles and feet, hemorrhoids, itchy belly, protruding navel, stretch marks, shortness of breath, difficulty sleeping, clumsiness, and enlarged and sore breasts.[36] Most pregnant women experience a majority of these symptoms, which are deemed "natural" for the pregnant body.

Bodily changes may be welcome (for example, the joy of fetal movement felt by an expecting parent), or they may be disruptive (vomiting in the workplace or canceling of plans to visit friends or family due to nausea); but they are not nothing. The bodily changes that occur during pregnancy are not always visible to the pregnant person, and the way they present may be confusing for her. She may feel winded after walking up a flight of stairs without knowing that her lung capacity is diminished and her heart is working overtime. She may feel frustration with her body, ambivalence about its changes, or anxiety about symptoms that are difficult to interpret. All of these realities complicate the sense of control that a pregnant woman experiences during pregnancy. Further, she may experience contradictions: for example, a desire to continue the pregnancy, but resentment about feeling exhausted by fatigue every afternoon, when she has other important obligations worthy of her attention and energy. After any experience of pregnancy loss or difficult complications during pregnancy, future pregnancies will likely seem more precarious and may provoke additional anxiety.

While pregnancy may be a natural biological process, the experience of pregnancy is subjective, and the *meaning* of each pregnancy depends in part on how the gestating woman feels about the pregnancy itself. A practical and sensitive discourse about pregnancy and morality must be able to wrestle coherently with the actual burdens that real pregnant people experience. The way that moralists talk about decisions and choices must account for both variability and subjectivity. My position in this chapter departs from the sexual ethics of magisterial teachings and some leading scholars of Catholic theology and philosophy, described in detail in the second chapter. Such Christian pro-life arguments tend to be fatalistic; that is, they claim that the obvious moral choice is to continue every pregnancy. Pregnancy, they argue, is a wonderful gift from God, enabling the pregnant woman to cooperate with God's plan for life. This position assumes that the pregnant woman is a willing host to the prenate. But women's testimonies reveal that *sometimes* pregnancy is experienced as a good gift from God, but *sometimes* pregnancy is not. And pregnancy is *always* burdensome. A moral account of pregnancy, then, does not begin from the assumption that pregnancy is always a purely good end. Pregnancy can contain disvalue and even death.

A MORAL VOCABULARY FOR PREGNANCY

Because of the disconnect between magisterial teachings and women's actual testimonies of their experiences of pregnancy loss, we need to update our moral vocabulary. Some helpful options to consider have been forwarded by Christian feminist theologians: Rebecca Todd Peters describes pregnancy as a *liminal space*; Patricia Beattie Jung describes pregnancy as a *gift relation*; Margaret Kamitsuka argues for a framework of *gestational hospitality*; and Christine Gudorf articulates a framework of *bodyright*. Here I will briefly explain each and demonstrate how each sheds light on the importance of moral agency for the pregnant person.

Liminality for the Human Becoming

Presbyterian feminist ethicist Rebecca Todd Peters explains the importance of imagining pregnancy "outside the male gaze and from the perspective of the pregnant woman and her body."[37] She elaborates:

> The pregnant body is ontologically different from both the male body and the not-pregnant female body. Similarly, the prenatal body is also ontologically different from the bodies of newborns, infants, or children. Both the pregnant body and the prenate defy the strict logic of individualism and exist instead within a liminal space defined by the potential for creation of new life. But potential is not actuality; many things can happen between conception and birth.[38]

Peters explains that pregnancies are "chapters in a larger life story," and should be interpreted within the longer horizon of a woman's reproductive life.[39] Peters demonstrates that sonography obscures the fact that the prenate is radically dependent on the pregnant person. In US culture, ultrasound images have formed us to see the prenate as an individual life housed inside the mother,[40] but the ultrasound image does not indicate the ways that the pregnant woman's body is actively working to sustain life in the womb. "That we think we see the truth or reality of pregnancy once we take the pregnant woman literally out of the picture is one of the most damning examples of misogyny I can imagine," writes Peters.[41] In fact, the two exist together—woman and prenate, united and separate, two in one.[42]

Peters draws on the concept of liminality in order to explain both what *is* and what *is not* happening in a pregnancy. Liminality means inhabiting the in-between, "on the threshold of becoming something new and different."[43] Scholars of religious studies have demonstrated the importance of this concept for practices such as pilgrimage and ritual studies.[44] Peters applies the concept to pregnancy to argue for the in-between-ness of pregnancy itself. Peters asks readers to consider calling the prenate "human becoming," instead of a "human being," since "becoming" recognizes the "not-yet-ness" that characterizes the liminal state of gestation and the dynamic process of human development in the womb.[45] Pregnancy is the liminal space of intersubjectivity during which time the gestating person's body provides life support to the prenate. Childbirth marks the transition from the liminal state of intersubjectivity to the recognition of the child's entrance into the human community; the cutting of the umbilical cord is a richly symbolic moment whereby the two subjects are identified as separate for the first time.[46] In the womb, the prenate was entirely dependent on the gestating woman; outside the womb, other subjects often assume at least some responsibility for the care of the child.[47] Our moral vocabulary, then, must address the differences between the moral relations during pregnancy and the moral relations that emerge after the cutting of the umbilical cord.

Bodily Life Support and Gift Relations

Catholic feminist theologian Patricia Beattie Jung has also contributed significantly to the discourse on pregnancy by analyzing gestation as "bodily life support," and defending the claim that both organ donation and pregnancy are "gift relations."[48] Jung defines bodily life support as "any form of assistance that entails an invasion of the giver's body to sustain another's life."[49] A kidney transplant is an example of a form of assistance that entails the surgical removal of a healthy kidney from one patient, that is then transplanted into a patient suffering from kidney failure. The sacrifice of the patient with the healthy kidney can prolong the life of the patient suffering from kidney failure. In search of a moral vocabulary to describe pregnancy, Jung describes the very real burdens of pregnancy and the reality of human embodiment as relevant in her analysis. "An optimal pregnancy involves the massive (though temporary) physical modification and the minor (permanent) bodily transformation of the mother—all for the sake of and in support of fetal life."[50] But the conditions placed on the morality of bodily life support for organ donation—consent and without excessive risks—are not also present in Catholic magisterial teachings about pregnancy. Jung identifies the double standard, noting the disparity between what is demanded of women who are pregnant and what those same persons "view as obligatory in regards to other forms of bodily life support, which not incidentally can be offered by men."[51]

Jung argues that both organ donation and childbearing should be thought of as gift relations.[52] Childbearing should be identified in the category of "acts of charity," not as a moral obligation or duty but as a supererogatory act of love.[53] Framing pregnancy as gift relation helps Christians refuse to "endorse that long tradition which regards women's bodies as objects to be controlled by others, if not by their fathers or husbands, then by the state."[54] Such a view also acknowledges the very real difference between giving of one's property and giving of one's body. "Bodily life support cannot be required precisely because the human body is not like the other goods of creation which an agent can objectify without distortion. The body is not like other possessions. One does not have a body—one is embodied."[55] Jung's retrieval of the category of gift relation for pregnancy enables her to argue forcefully against the coercion of pregnant people even as she celebrates consent to pregnancy as a supererogatory gift.

Jung further situates the responsibility of securing the welfare of children as a properly communal task. "The life support of children is a *joint* parental responsibility as well as a communal one," writes Jung.[56] Pregnant people should not be forced to "carry a genuinely communal burden," although their consent to do so can be celebrated by the moral community.[57]

The right of the prenate to survival can be in conflict with the pregnant woman's right to bodily integrity. Naming this conflict is an act of honesty in debates about reproductive agency and the intrinsic value of prenatal life as well as of the pregnant woman's life and moral agency. But we need not conclude, as some do, that the prenate's right to life imposes an absolute obligation on the pregnant woman to gestate.[58] Jung situates the prenate's "right to life" within a context in which others' rights are also relevant. Conflicting claims of human rights must be negotiated in the moral community.[59]

Conceiving of pregnancy as a gift relation—the pregnant person's gift of bodily life support to the prenate (personal gift) and contribution to human reproduction for the species (social gift)—retains respect for the pregnant person's moral agency and bodily integrity. The pregnant woman must then engage in robust deliberation in order to determine the right course of action in *this* particular pregnancy. But use of her body is *her* gift to give, or to deny.[60] In other words, the category of gift relation for pregnancy reaffirms the human dignity of the pregnant woman; it does not foreclose discernment or impose a particular action on her. A woman's experience of a positive pregnancy test initiates an active discernment about how best to respond in the particularities of her experience.

Gestational Hospitality

Presbyterian feminist ethicist Margaret Kamitsuka argues that the paradigm of *gestational hospitality* would be helpful; such a paradigm describes pregnancy as an experience in which a pregnant woman can choose to serve as host to a prenate. Hospitality in the Christian theological tradition involves a more-powerful host generously welcoming and attending to the needs of a less-powerful guest. Hospitality is encouraged within Christian discipleship, but Christian ethicists have also named very real limits to the virtue of hospitality in light of Christian claims about justice.[61] Christians are permitted to lock the doors to their home, and can refuse to house a homeless neighbor, while also advancing efforts to address the needs of the unhoused community through structural supports. Kamitsuka interprets the parable of the Good Samaritan (Lk 10:25–37) to construct a "paradigm for gestational hospitality that encourages virtues of care but also supports a pregnant woman's choice to refuse her fetus the hospitality of her womb."[62] Kamitsuka is critical of the way that pro-life discourse tends to apply the parable of the Good Samaritan in such a way as to demand that pregnant women continue a pregnancy. As she reads the parable, Kamitsuka notes that Jesus does not relate this story to pregnancy. Further, the comparison does not seem to fit neatly. Kamitsuka explains that pro-life authors will typically associate the pregnant person with the Good Samaritan, and the fetus with the wounded man. But after listening carefully to actual stories of pregnant women who face unwanted pregnancies, she finds that what the Good Samaritan does in the parable is dissimilar from what pregnant women are asked to do. Kamitsuka explains:

> [The Good Samaritan] is generous but in a monetary and not a corporeal self-gifting way.... The Samaritan did not say that he would stay and take care of all the wounded man's daily bodily needs for the next nine months, breast-feed him for months, or support him the next eighteen years of his life. The Samaritan aided the wounded man but did not thereby become so emotionally attached to him that he could not consider relinquishing him to another's care; in fact, the Samaritan leaves him with the innkeeper and departs.[63]

The analogy does not fit, for the kind of sacrifices that the Samaritan makes are considerably less invasive and less costly than the burdens and risks of pregnancy and parenthood. Moreover, the parable sets up a binary distinction: one is either "the helper" or "the wounded." Kamitsuka finds it noteworthy that pro-life authors do not recognize the pregnant woman herself as a wounded person in need of assistance.[64] The pregnant woman is cast, instead, in the role of "the beast—that is, she must be made to carry the wounded man (fetus) to safety at the inn."[65] Black feminists have been especially critical about this framing in light of the history, previously recounted in chapter 1, of chattel slavery, Jim Crow laws, and the persistence of institutional racism. A particularly poignant scene can be found in Zora Neale Hurston's *Their Eyes Were Watching God*, in which the wise grandmother figure explains to Janie that "white man is de ruler of everything," and when he gives work to Black men, the Black man "hand it to his womenfolks," who become "de mule uh de world."[66] Surely part of what Christians are called to do today is to resist the ways that women of color—especially poor women of color—are expected to bear disproportionate burdens and suffering.

How might Christians today resist such a dehumanizing discourse—one that casts women in roles of labor, submission, and sacrifice for others, while failing to prioritize a woman's own agentic response? Kamitsuka argues that gestational hospitality is a more helpful paradigm because it "insists on fairness in the ethics of corporeal self-gifting"[67] and resists the implication that a woman's body is "expendable."[68] A paradigm of gestational hospitality describes the self-gifting of gestation as a generous act of hospitality, freely chosen; but just as persons are not morally obligated to give their home to every unhoused neighbor, hospitality is a virtuous response and not an absolute duty. "People are finite and society is unjust," Kamitsuka argues; the reality of finitude and life's ambiguities means that it is not possible always to respond to every neighbor, including every prenatal neighbor.[69] Kamitsuka is clear about the social implications of her argument, saying that what must be in place, politically, for hospitality not to be an oppression for women, is "legal choice."[70]

Kamitsuka draws on the work of womanist theologian Chanequa Walker-Barnes, whose work pushes back against dangerous messages about expectations for Black women to sacrifice themselves for the good of the family or community. Walker-Barnes finds in the parable of the Good Samaritan a reassuring message in that the man whose actions are praised—the Samaritan—finished his journey.

> The Samaritan encounters the beaten man while traveling. Presumably, then, he has a destination and a goal in mind. By caring for the wounded man, he has delayed his journey. But he does not allow caring for another to bring his own journey to a halt. Neither does he assume that the man has become his long-term responsibility.[71]

Jeanne Stevenson-Moessner explains that "the Samaritan finished his journey while meeting the need of a wounded and marginal person. The Samaritan did not give everything away. He did not injure, hurt, or neglect the self."[72] Kamitsuka argues that the most appropriate interpretation of the Good Samaritan parable today must include a note of caution: "It is good to help the needy fetal neighbor in your womb, but make sure you can finish your journey."[73] Gestational hospitality *invites* pregnant women to undertake the burdens of pregnancy, but does not *coerce* such a response; it refuses to treat pregnant women as "mere beasts of burden without a choice."[74]

Bodyright

A fourth framework for reconceiving of pregnancy in light of the radical claim that women are human persons can be found in the work of Catholic feminist theologian Christine E. Gudorf.[75] She develops the category of bodyright in conversation with scholarship of sexual violence, and attributes the lack of bodyright in Western Christianity to the influence of patriarchy, citing as evidence the Christian practice of a husband exercising control over his wife's body.[76] Sanctioning of wife abuse and the development of the tradition of the husband's "conjugal rights" were not only central to Christian marriage traditions but to civil laws on marriage in US history.[77] The history of patriarchal control can be summarized as follows:

The purpose of women in patriarchies is both sexual and reproductive—as sexual object for the male, and as reproductive source of his heirs. To this end, women have not historically been allowed to control completely either their sexual or their reproductive functions. In our society until very recently, there was no legal recognition of marital rape, since sexual consent was permanently conferred with a woman's consent to marriage.[78]

Gudorf finds in testimonies of sexual violence a clear violation of bodyright and long-lasting traumas that distort the survivor's self-concept, worldview, and affective capabilities.[79] She proposes that bodyright become a guiding framework in the continuing development of Christian sexual ethics. Bodyright means the moral right to control one's body and therefore the ability to become a responsible moral agent.[80] While Gudorf's analysis predates the #MeToo movement and the widespread media reporting of clergy sexual abuse, the realities of sexual violence were already well documented in academic literature and featured prominently in her ethical analysis of bodyright. For Gudorf, God does not demand or require the continuation of a particular pregnancy against the will of the pregnant person; such a framework would be abusive. Gudorf problematizes images of divine domination in the Christian tradition because of how such God-talk undermines the healing of survivors of sexual abuse.[81] Instead, relationship with "a God who both knows vulnerability and shares power, directing it toward justice and healing," would enable survivors of violence to find healing comfort in the loving embrace of God.[82] Summoning a God who knows vulnerability and who celebrates the inherent worth of the pregnant woman would foster healing and liberation in difficult pregnancy discernments.[83] It is past time for Christians to let go of—in the words of womanist theologian Yolanda Pierce—the "wrathful God, a God lurking around every corner waiting to punish me for any infraction, and [begin instead] to embrace a loving God."[84]

Gudorf argues that implementing bodyright would mean "for ordinarily competent individuals to be understood to have complete control over their own bodies, and for such individuals to understand themselves as part of an integral human community and a common biosphere."[85] Such a framework rejects the "instrumentalization" of women by securing women's reproductive bodyright. Gudorf argues that limiting women's access to contraception and abortion are violations of bodyright, as are forced sterilization campaigns.[86] Elsewhere, Gudorf joins others in articulating the implications for abortion in particular:

> This notion of the right to control one's own body is a key element in the position that sees abortion as an option. Those who hold this position argue that in order for women to take control of their lives and to construct a meaningful life

plan, they must have the capacity to break the link between sex and procreation. Otherwise their bodies, or whoever controls their bodies, will control them, and pregnancy will interrupt all possible plans except mothering.[87]

Importantly, bodyright in Gudorf's analysis is not a call to support rampant individualism; it is, instead, "a call to accept responsibility for preparing self and world to cooperate with God's saving action in history."[88] Human dignity, for Gudorf, means "the fact that human beings were made in the image and likeness of God's own self."[89] Bodyright is the first condition of moral agency and therefore of responsible decision-making. Importantly, bodyright does not preclude self-sacrificial love; freely chosen sacrifices can be life-giving.[90] Ghanaian Methodist feminist theologian Mercy Amba Oduyoye makes a helpful distinction between voluntarily sacrificing and "being sacrificed."[91] Christian sacrifice should advance the dignity of the agent, even if that person also accepts voluntary suffering. For Gudorf, bodyright means that pregnant women will be the ones making decisions about what kinds of sacrifices are morally appropriate and possible for them to make.

Together, these feminist articulations of pregnancy provide practical considerations for our treatment of pregnant women as moral agents. When we see pregnancy as a *liminal space*, we honor both the ways that the pregnant body is like and is not like a non-pregnant body. When we see pregnancy as *bodily life support*, we can reflect on the ethical dangers of requiring bodily life support without the free consent of the giver. When we see women's choices through the framework of *gestational hospitality*, we recover the important distinction between a gift relation and a forced coercion. Seeing pregnancy as an act of gestational hospitality calls to mind the power and decision-making of the host, who retains at least some sense of appropriate control in the process. We also have an expanded vocabulary to ask about the broader context in which hosts are asked to offer hospitality, and appropriate moral limits of a host's giving. If we find the claims of *bodyright* compelling for human subjects, and then extend human subjectivity to pregnant women, we can hold together both the difficulties of pregnancy and the moral agency of the pregnant woman, who has a moral right to exercise control over how her body is used. If, in contrast to these claims, a pregnant woman is told that her coercion contributes to the common good, she has resources for identifying that claim as dehumanizing. Women should not *be sacrificed for* the good of others because women are human persons. Christian feminists provide vocabulary for an approach that honors the pregnant woman's genuine discernment in context. If she is a means by which God acts in the world, a just and loving God would not force her actions beyond her understanding of her real limits.

A MORAL VOCABULARY FOR ABORTION

What vocabulary about abortion would foster greater attention to the gestating woman's moral agency while also honestly naming the value of prenatal life? In chapter 2 I explained authoritative Church teachings on abortion and identified the problems of a framework rooted in moral absolutism. I also explained that describing women as murderers is not only inflammatory but unfair. Another way forward is possible—a way that seeks to describe abortion with attention to the subjective experience of the pregnant woman and her situation. The moral categories that we use to describe an experience of abortion can have significant implications for the spiritual well-being of the woman. There are at least four possibilities worthy of consideration: withdrawal of life support, return of a liminal creature to God, tragic dilemma, and premoral disvalue. Taken together, these point toward new possibilities for responding to the testimonies of women with reassurance and hope.

Abortion as Withdrawal of Life Support

When we recognize the hard work of gestation, and the way that pregnancy can be described as a gestating woman's gift of life support to prenatal life, we can construct an understanding of abortion as the withdrawal of life support to prenatal life. Such a framing carves out a space of genuine moral discernment for the pregnant person, who must determine the best way forward within her particular situation. Describing abortion as withdrawal of life support would mean that the prenate's right to life does not necessarily override the pregnant woman's will. The pregnant woman does not, in every situation, have an absolute duty or moral obligation to continue the pregnancy; instead, she has a duty to engage in robust discernment about the best course of action given her particular situational needs.

Church teachings already recognize cases in which it is morally legitimate to withdraw life-sustaining treatments that are deemed extraordinary, disproportional, or that involve "a grave burden for oneself or another."[92] If a patient has a lethal disease (e.g., cancer), they are not obligated to accept harmful or disproportionate treatments for their disease. When a patient is incompetent, then the patient's surrogate makes the decision. Withdrawal of life support for proportionate reason is not described as "murder" within hospital settings. The wisdom of this moral reasoning within medical ethics has not been applied to abortion.[93]

Considering abortion as a case by which the prenate's surrogate (the pregnant woman) makes a decision to withdraw life-sustaining care could be defensible for proportionate reasons. The process by which medication abortion works aligns with this understanding of withdrawing life support. Mifepristone works by blocking progesterone, a hormone essential to the development of a pregnancy.[94] A pregnant woman who takes mifepristone is not necessarily engaging in the act of killing, but rather is withdrawing hormones from the environment that is nurturing prenatal life.[95] By taking mifepristone, she is preventing the pregnancy from progressing. She is withdrawing life support from the prenate.

Abortion as Return of Potential Life to God

Another way to conceive of abortion is to describe the gestating person returning the liminal creature's prenatal existence to the loving embrace of God. Such a vocabulary holds together the absolute beneficence of God, the liminality of prenatal life, and the embodied limitations of the pregnant person. It honors the experiences of women who report that their abortions cannot be truthfully described as murder; in their subjective awareness, their love and affection for the potential human life within them were genuine commitments that nevertheless did not impose on them a duty to gestate and parent. This position is stated in a "love letter" from Emelia to her "seedling," when Emelia writes that as a result of her abortion, her seedling "returned to the magical dust of the universe." Emelia's partner, Olle, writes that they loved their seedling and wanted to prevent further suffering.[96] Christian feminist theologian Serene Jones draws upon Trinitarian God-language to describe the experience of miscarriage in the womb of God: God experiences death within the God-self and continues to live.[97] Such a framework recognizes both the stability and dynamism of God in Christian theology. It also suggests that prenates, if not brought to birth, continue to bear meaning in the mind of God and in the universe. Many women who have experienced miscarriage or stillbirth have found this language to be deeply healing;[98] I advocate for expanding this category to abortion as well.[99] Entrusting the liminal becoming to the source of all life and love can be an act of faith in God's loving embrace as well as an honest recognition of one's own bodily limits.

Abortion as Tragic Dilemma

Christian ethicist Kate Jackson-Meyer describes a tragic dilemma as a particular kind of moral dilemma. A moral dilemma is when "a moral agent cannot fulfill all of her obligations."[100] A tragic dilemma is "a moral dilemma that involves tragedy of some sort."[101] The agent in a tragic dilemma recognizes an "ought" that cannot be fulfilled. Jackson-Meyer, drawing on the work of philosopher Lisa Tessman, distinguishes between negotiable and nonnegotiable moral requirements, arguing that Christians have "nonnegotiable commitments to protect the vulnerable and to protect human life."[102] When such a moral requirement must go unfulfilled, the moral agent commits a wrong and bears some responsibility; but in constrained circumstances, according to Jackson-Meyer, "blame is mitigated when the agent acts reluctantly—that is, with repugnance of the will."[103] Jackson-Meyer does not treat abortion decisions in her analysis, but one can readily see how valuable these distinctions can be for pregnant people who face such moral dilemmas, feeling that there are competing nonnegotiable moral requirements that they must choose between. Examples of such discernments abound—from the pregnant woman told that her prenate threatens her life, to expecting parents who reason that another child would severely harm their marital stability and ability to care for already-born children, to parents with a wanted pregnancy facing a diagnosis of fetal anomaly.[104] In chapter 5 we saw that Anna sought a way out of an unhealthy relationship and sought a stable financial life; she did not see how it would be possible to achieve these life goals while continuing the pregnancy. Anna was motivated by fear and by love; she persisted despite doubts; she experienced both regret and relief. In such cases, Jackson-Meyer wisely notes that the inability to fulfill Christian commitments "sparks lament in moral agents."[105] When agents perceive themselves to be in a moral quandary, the Christian community must find ways of supporting and assisting them in their discernments, and acting after their decision in such a way that contributes to their genuine healing.

Abortion as Physical Evil or Premoral Disvalue

A central maxim for the Christian moral life is to "do good and avoid evil." In practice, it can be difficult to determine how this maxim translates to the complicated everyday realities that we face. In the renewal of moral theology that preceded and followed the Second Vatican Council, moral theologians expanded analysis with regard to the *acting person*, situating complex moral judgments within the many dimensions of what it means to live a moral life in a fundamentally unjust world.[106] Since the evaluation of a *moral* act depends on an understanding of the act in itself, the intention of the agent, and the circumstances of the action, we cannot establish that a particular act is *morally* good or evil unless we know what the agent thinks she is doing. Moralists thus make a distinction between a *moral* judgment and a *premoral* judgment. Before one identifies the intention of the agent and the circumstances of the action, any evaluation of the act is a *premoral* judgment (that is, the judgment does not reference the subjective elements of the act including the intent of the agent and the circumstances of the action).

In the manualist tradition of Catholic moral theology, evil is classified as *malum morale* (moral evil) or *malum physicum* (physical evil).[107] To engage in *moral evil* means that one intentionally causes the unjustified suffering of another; to do so constitutes a *sin* for the agent when one acts with sufficient knowledge and consent.[108] *Physical evil* is distinct from moral evil. Physical evil describes the disvalue that is contained in the action apart from the agent's intention.[109] For example, physical evil results when a particular action is undertaken because the agent believes it is the best course of action in a complex situation even though it will have some negative consequences. As one Catholic moralist explains: "To choose against any good or for any evil is *ipso facto* a premoral disvalue."[110] We are not perfect creatures and we do not live in a perfect world. Physical evil is a category that assists moralists in describing "the moral ambiguity of the universe," including natural disasters, accidental harms, and the negative effects of human actions that proceeded from good intentions.[111] Catholic moralist Louis Janssens explains:

> Human acting means being engaged with reality. If that reality is material—because of our corporeality and the material realities of the world—then our activity is characterized by ambiguity. We can use the material things of the world in keeping with their specific nature and laws in order to achieve our goals, but we do not sufficiently control the consequences of this process to avoid disadvantageous effects for ourselves, other persons, and the community. . . . These facts make an appeal to proportionality unavoidable for evaluating the morality of human acts.[112]

Proportionalism is a method of moral reasoning whereby one considers how an action affirms value and/or disvalue, and seeks through one's actions to increase value while minimizing disvalue.[113] Sometimes it is not clear how one can "do good" without participating in some evil. The question is whether one participates in *moral evil* (that is, intentionally willing the disvalue or evil effect) or *physical evil* (that is, recognizing but not willing the disvalue or evil effect of one's action). In order to evaluate the *morality* of an action, we would ask: Does the moral agent desire the disvalue in itself? Does the moral agent welcome the disvalue? Jesuit moralist Edward C. Vacek posits the following: "If I could achieve an enhancement of value without going against a value, would I do so? If the negative effect is also desired, then I am acting directly for it, whether or not it precedes, accompanies, or follows other effects."[114]

One way to think about pregnancy loss, then, is to say that pregnancy loss contains *premoral disvalue* or *physical evil*. Prenatal demise is not a value (that is, good in itself, contributing to the perfection of the universe). Prenatal demise, or the inability to bring the prenate to birth, is a disvalue. But in some cases, the decision not to bring the prenate to birth, which carries disvalue, can be tolerated because of the weight of other values at stake.

If we adopt the language that proportionalists in the Catholic tradition have used, we would say that physical evil is sometimes inevitable and can be willed for proportionate reason.[115] In a virtuous life, a disvalue is experienced as something to be avoided and/or overcome when possible. As one strives to do good and avoid evil, one finds oneself wading through the murky waters of disvalue when one cannot achieve a purely good end. When deliberating in a complex situation, one should always seek the greater good. When one acts in favor of the greater good, one is not engaging in immoral action even if the act contains *premoral disvalue*. Regret is appropriate when "the good without qualification could not be realized," even though one did not engage in *moral* (that is, intentional) evil.[116]

Until we have more information about the agent's intentions we would be unable to assess whether an abortion decision contained *moral evil* in addition to *physical evil*. To categorize a particular abortion decision as a moral evil would mean that the pregnant woman intends to cause harm to the prenate and/or accepts prenatal demise without proportionate reason. Today we must ask how other aspects of the pregnant woman's well-being can factor into the determination that accepting the disvalue of prenatal demise is proportionate. It is now well established that in cases in which the pregnant woman's life is in danger, a medical procedure to save her life that also ends the pregnancy is widely considered proportionate (moralists describe this as an indirect abortion or therapeutic abortion). There are ongoing debates among thoughtful Christians about what other reasons might licitly be considered proportionate to accept the disvalue of prenatal demise; in the contexts of building a moral community such debates are important.

But critics argue that these debates can also undermine women's flourishing. In effect, this framework of moral reasoning renders all abortion decisions suspicious unless a woman can "justify" her decision.[117] Kenya Martin is among those who are openly critical of their formation in Catholic spaces, including the excessive "Catholic guilt" she experienced.[118] While these authors make excellent points about the dangers of scrutinizing women's intentions before and after a determination of abortion, I think the justification paradigm remains valuable for Christians engaging in normative ethics when discussing the morality of abortion (though it does not apply in the same way in legal discourse).[119] At the heart of the justification paradigm is a conversation about justice. As a feminist theologian I seek justice for women while recognizing appropriate power of the pregnant woman over the prenate. Justice for prenates requires respect for their liminal human becoming and the life force within them; a pregnant woman should have proportionate reasons for ending that life and returning the liminal creature to God. In this way we avoid a moral callousness about fetal demise while also empowering pregnant women to think critically about their reasons for seeking to end a pregnancy.

Formation in Christian community could provide robust tools for discerning in a particular situation whether one's reasons for procuring an abortion are proportionate. Each woman must determine whether her reasons—perhaps including that she is "not emotionally or mentally prepared," that she "needs to focus on other children," that she "wants a better life for the baby than she could provide," or that she is "not independent or mature enough for a baby"—are proportionate.[120] To the young woman who explains that she "wants a better life for the baby than she could provide," it is not self-evident that she desires the disvalue of prenatal demise in itself. Instead, she might be placing the well-being of the prenate at the very center of her moral reasoning, and realistically recognizing her own limits. It is possible to explain her situation not as "desiring the disvalue" (employing Vacek's terminology) but rather as "accepting the disvalue in order to seek the greater good."

If an otherwise healthy (physically, mentally, emotionally) woman freely seeks an abortion with the primary intent of causing harm to the prenate—that is, willing only the disvalue in itself—she may find after honest self-reflection that she engaged in moral evil, and that she is in a state of serious sin. Women, as fully human persons, are certainly as capable of sinning as men are. In other cases (perhaps most cases of abortion today), abortion could be described as a moral act that contains disvalue. Since the pregnant woman alone knows her intentions and the particularities of her circumstances, external observers should not accuse her of serious sin. It is also the case that an agent can experience different and competing intentions, intentions that cannot all be honored in a particular act. For example, not every abortion is against pregnancy per se, but against *this* pregnancy, *right now*; the abortion may in fact be regrettably accepted with the goal of creating opportunities for parenting in the future, or parenting others now. Recall Kassi's testimony in chapter 5, in which she described her abortion as an act of love even as she grieved afterward. When we take seriously women's stories of abortion, we see many testimonies of moral agents who discerned that their duties to "God, themselves, their families, and human society" led them to the decision not to continue the pregnancy.[121]

The agent's degree of moral freedom (or experiences of serious and inescapable unfreedoms) must influence our moral vocabulary about the action. In general, the more moral freedom an agent has, the greater her sense of responsibility and culpability for any harm resulting from the moral act. Moral freedom can be experienced on a spectrum given the structural injustices women face. These realities form the circumstances of her decision.

While some feminist theologians do assert that abortion can be a moral good,[122] I am inclined to resist such a framing, in order to name straightforwardly the disvalue present when any pregnancy cannot be continued.[123] At the same time, the availability of abortion is necessary, and participation in the delivery of reproductive health care for patients should not be identified as a *moral* evil. Even if every abortion cannot be described as a value in itself, it is sometimes a right course of action in order to affirm other values. The woman in need of that necessary abortion requires trained providers and a legal framework that recognizes her moral decision as legitimate.[124] Providers need not share the agent's viewpoint but should offer respectful care. In pro-life literature, such discernments often ascribe selfish motivations to the pregnant person, saying that a rejection of motherhood reveals immaturity, selfishness, or a woman's desire not to be inconvenienced. But when we look at the testimonies of moral anguish that many pregnant people report, such dismissals ring hollow. The Christian community must find the vocabulary to encourage the pregnant person to engage in honest analysis of her situation even as we affirm a hopeful response.

THE INTRINSIC—NOT ABSOLUTE—VALUE OF PRENATAL LIFE

Christians who accompany women who have experienced abortion should be open to naming what is lost in a way that makes sense to the women who have themselves experienced it. But here, too, words fail. Usually when we discuss death, we are talking about human persons who are born and then die. In the case of pregnancy loss, we are talking about creatures who are never born. Whether we call it prenatal demise or death in the womb, pregnancy loss is real, and carries disvalue. But the loss of prenatal life is not equivalent to the loss of infant life. My position is that the prenate's life has intrinsic, but not absolute, value. Intrinsic (or inherent) value means value-in-itself, while absolute (or ultimate) value means value-above-all-other-values. My position is that the bodily integrity of already born persons outweighs the bodily integrity of the prenate (before and after viability). The prenate's intrinsic value (or right to life) does not at any point outweigh the pregnant woman's consent or bodily integrity. Here I advocate for a development of Catholic teachings, in order to make it clear that women are human persons whose dignity and self-determination must be respected—privileged, even—especially in cases of constraint when multiple competing values are at stake.

My position, then, differs from scholars who argue that a preembryo or fetus should be treated as a person because of its intrinsic potential.[125] Some Catholic leaders and moral theologians forward the argument that justice for prenates demands that the gestating person continue a pregnancy at all cost; at the heart of this argument is the claim that prenates are human persons and that they have a "right to life."[126] But "personhood" is a moral category, not a biological one.[127] And it is not lost on women that the argument for fetal personhood leads to inevitable restrictions on women's maternal agency.[128] Some argue that the principle of "the sanctity of human life" should be privileged. But bioethicist David Albert Jones points out that such a principle is a recent invention; it does not occur either in the Hebrew Bible or the New Testament, has no fixed meaning, and became prevalent in official Catholics teachings only in the late twentieth century.[129] When theologians and philosophers argue that the prenate's life has absolute value, this means that the prenate's life "exceeds all other values" so that "no other value overrides the value of life."[130] Jones explains: "If it is absolutely prohibited to end the life of an innocent human being, irrespective of the circumstances, and irrespective of the consequences of refraining from doing so, this seems to imply that life is being granted infinite value."[131] But if the prenate's life has absolute value, that either means that it has more value than the pregnant woman, or that no conflict between these two lives, each with absolute and infinite value, is possible. Women's testimonies counter both claims. A better way forward advances the claim that both prenatal and maternal lives have intrinsic value, and that reverence and respect for both is required. When a conflict between the two emerges, the principle of reverence for life cannot—on its own—solve the moral dilemma. Other principles must be invoked to navigate the dual claims, and that requires the virtue of prudence in a proportionate judgment. An approach that minimizes the pregnant person's role in gestation is also insufficient and instrumentalizes her body in the service of another.[132] Thus, privileging the bodily integrity and decision-making of the pregnant woman is necessary, even if this leads to tolerating prenatal demise (the disvalue of which is lamented but accepted).

Building on the earlier analysis of the dignity and agency of the pregnant person as well as the liminality of pregnancy in the human reproduction cycle, I argue that prenatal life bears intrinsic value at every stage of development; but it has value precisely in its context—that is, not as a born person but as a prenatal becoming (to use Peters's term) dependent on a born person for its nourishment. Accurate descriptions of prenatal life must attend to the inherent dependency of the prenate on the gestating person, and demark a significant difference between potential life in the womb and human life at birth, when the umbilical cord is severed and the baby breathes on its own outside the womb. With Kamitsuka, I argue that value inheres for the prenate throughout pregnancy, and that the gestating person "retains the moral authority to decide about abortion, whether early or late in the pregnancy."[133] The prenate's development is a value in itself, but the prenate's development does not exist apart from the human realities of moral conflict and legitimate constraints.[134]

Some feminist theologians take other positions: for example, arguing that fetal personhood is dependent on the mother's act of love;[135] or that fetal personhood claims get stronger as the pregnancy continues,[136] restricting the gestating person's choices post-viability.[137] Some bioethicists argue that the moral status of the fetus changes with its developmental stages.[138] It is possible, however, to claim that prenatal life is a sacred potential human life, valuable in itself, while at the same time positioning the power of the pregnant woman over the prenatal becoming she carries. Kamitsuka describes this as a "tensive, dual claim." The prenate has value, "but that value does not override the maternal authority of the pregnant woman."[139] Such a claim has very real practical implications for women today. The pregnant woman should be the one who determines whether to continue a pregnancy.

THE DUTY TO DISCERN

Let me state clearly where I see the pregnant woman's moral obligation: she does not (necessarily, in every case) have a *duty to gestate*; she does, in every case, have a *duty to discern* how best to proceed. The Catholic moral tradition has long identified discernment in the moral life as an essential component of discipleship, and discernment has been a key theme in the pontificate of Pope Francis. We are broken and imperfect people in a broken and imperfect world. Discernment happens precisely in the midst of that brokenness and imperfection.

While it is her decision to make, she need not make it alone. Genuine discernments provide mechanisms for the discerning person to seek wisdom from the community before a decision is made, and to reflect on that decision afterward in an ongoing self-reflection about the direction of one's life.[140] In cases of miscarriage, the discernment may focus on whether and how to seek medical intervention. Should she wait for the tissue to pass on its own? Should she take a medication that will cause the tissue to pass out of the womb? Or should she schedule a medical procedure so that a medical professional can remove the contents of her uterus? In cases of stillbirth, the discernment may focus on a decision to induce labor or begin a dilation and evacuation procedure. In both cases, women may consult medical professionals, family members, and trusted friends as they try to figure out the right course of action. The pregnant woman's feelings about her pregnancy, details of her physical and emotional health, ability to access medical care, and details of the responsibilities of her everyday life all shape her decision-making in obvious ways. If she faces an unwanted pregnancy, she may ask herself if she has the physical and emotional strength to gestate and relinquish the baby through adoption; or question whether she could reasonably rethink her plans for education, career, and/or family life. She may wonder if there are resources of support available to her that she has not yet considered, or she may feel that this pregnancy is threatening to her very sense of self, that to continue would risk overstepping her very real embodied limits. The Catholic tradition's awareness of moral struggle and growth over time present a vision of the human person as one in process, never static, but always situated in a context of dynamism.[141] Discernments are often non-linear, and can include confusing thoughts and feelings. Framed in the language of virtue ethics, the moral subject asks: What is the most loving way forward? What would the prudent person do in this situation?[142]

The Catholic moral tradition contains a wealth of resources on discernment, including resources created by women. Religious orders have developed distinctive modes of prayerful discernment practices that can be individual, interpersonal, or communal;[143] examples include Benedictine spirituality, Franciscan spirituality, Ignatian spirituality, Society of the Sacred Heart spirituality, Immaculate Heart of Mary spirituality, Mercy spirituality, and so forth. For example, in Ignatian spirituality, discernment requires attunement to the presence of God in everyday life. Through practice, one develops "spiritual wisdom that involves learning how to understand which of our spiritual impulses (or desires) are life-giving and which are destructive."[144] Put another way, discernment is "the art of distinguishing what leads to God from what does not."[145] St. Madeleine Sophie Barat, foundress of the Society of the Sacred Heart of Jesus, explained to her sisters that "the spirit is always speaking to us deep in our hearts, if only we listen."[146] Cultivating an interior life and seeking out conversation partners about one's prayer life can help one to understand what leads to God and what does not. Feminist theologian Anne E. Patrick reminds us that "the church gives us saints to inspire us, friends to support us, spiritual guides to assist us, and teachers to challenge and instruct us."[147]

In a society characterized by "structures of sin"[148]—sexual inequality, racism, lack of access to the basic goods of sexual and reproductive healthcare—pregnant women today discern how to carve out some agentic response to the complex realities in which they find themselves. Often, there is no perfect solution to the quandaries they face. Every possible way forward contains disvalue. As people who journey with pregnant women, then, we are called to walk in solidarity with them, aware of the planks in our eyes, and reluctant to condemn before we ourselves have walked in their shoes.[149]

Catholic teachings on conscience can be of particular assistance in this discourse. But conscience claims also raise additional thorny questions. Conscience has received significant treatment in the Catholic moral tradition, not only in contemporary debates about morality but also in the moral manuals.[150] Conscience is described as a faculty, as a process of discernment, and as a decision. In the Catholic tradition, a person is obliged to both form and follow their conscience.[151] *Dignitatis Humanae* states:

In all his activity a man is bound to follow his conscience in order that he may come to God, the end and purpose of life. It follows that he is not to be forced to act in manner contrary to his conscience. Nor, on the other hand, is he to be restrained from acting in accordance with his conscience, especially in matters religious.[152]

Thus, according to authoritative Catholic teachings, a pregnant woman is bound to follow her conscience. But Catholic teachings also affirm that conscience can err. If the person could have known better, they are held culpable; if, however, the person is in a state of "invincible ignorance" (meaning that they are not responsible for their lack of knowledge), then they are not culpable for the moral evil of the wrong action.[153]

This leads some people, especially in situations of conflict about life and death, to seek to coerce moral agents. After all, if conscience can err, should we not use power over moral agents in order to make them comply with what we think is right? Does not such action facilitate the common good and human flourishing? Abortion bans at the state level have this function in civil law. A key problem with these bans, from the perspective of fundamental moral theology, is that they restrict the legitimate choices that moral agents should have, and therefore coerce patients and providers alike. Catholic theologian Richard McBrien has claimed that, "as a general rule, a person should not be prevented from following even an erroneous conscience, unless the action is seriously injurious to himself/herself, to others, or to the common good."[154] A respectful dialogue with a pregnant woman in the spirit of accompaniment and discernment is very different than an attempt to force her to act in a certain way.

There is a "helping" impulse that many Catholics seem to have, by which they want to prevent pregnant women from making the "wrong" choice, and thus are comfortable with abortion bans that provide legal restrictions. But here I want to question whether that impulse to prevent someone from making what you think is the "wrong" choice reflects correctly the Catholic moral tradition on conscience and moral freedom. A desire to "help" someone else can express a very good and loving motivation to reduce harm and to promote human flourishing. But it can also mask other motives, including a desire to control the outcomes for someone else. When we operate in a discourse of control instead of persuasion, we are adopting a power dynamic whereby the moral agent is no longer making their own decision in conscience. Instead, they are being directed, manipulated, and even coerced. Such actions then do not flow from true moral freedom for the agent.

Feminist authors have been especially suspicious of this dynamic because of the ways that misogyny and racism have functioned in Church and in society.[155] The role of the person who accompanies a pregnant woman today should not be to force her to act in a certain way, but rather to accompany her in her discernment and decision-making process. Sometimes pregnant women will not make the decision that you want them to make. Can we stand alongside women in this process, supporting them, without undermining their own discernment and decision-making? If we rob someone of the opportunity to discern based on their own situation and its inevitable constraints, we are in effect saying that they should not trust their own conscience. Such a claim undermines their human dignity. An individual pregnant woman's decision may not align with your values, but if you try to stop someone else from "sinning," or try to protect them from "falling," you take away their own opportunity to discern the good in their circumstances and reflect upon it afterward in light of their faith. Moral agents who engage in difficult discernments learn from those actions, even if they later describe them as "mistakes" on their journey. If each of us thinks with a growth mindset about our own journey of Christian discipleship, we will undoubtedly name mistakes we have made along the way. But often those mistakes help us to learn and grow. What I am advocating here is a Christian community that does not try to control the outcomes of a pregnant woman's discernment, but instead walks alongside her as she discerns and after her decision, no matter what that decision is. I am advocating for a Christian community that refuses to harass or coerce pregnant women. Showing pregnant women respect means being present on their journey, not taking away their own power to decide.[156] Pope Francis has repeatedly focused on the role of the Christian to accompany others on the journey.[157]

CONCLUSION

In this chapter, I have sought to move away from an abortion discourse rooted in moral absolutism and instead have identified resources from the Christian tradition to describe pregnancy in a way that holds together both complexity and ambiguity. I have argued that women are human persons; that pregnancy is naturally burdensome; and that in order to respect both gestating women and prenates, Catholic communities should develop a more adequate moral vocabulary to describe pregnancy and prenatal life. Drawing on feminist theologians, I described four helpful frameworks: liminality, gift relation, gestational hospitality, and bodyright. These, in turn, can shape a better moral vocabulary for abortion discourse, which can include descriptions of abortion as withdrawal of life support, return of potential life to God, tragic dilemma, and premoral disvalue. But changing the way we talk about abortion is only one part of the solution. This approach to a new vocabulary must be seen in tandem with new efforts to seek structural change in society—change that is needed because too many pregnant women are constrained by their circumstances.

We need realism now even as we strive for a better world. Christian communities should take into account a realistic understanding of what is possible for moral agents in a sinful world. A wise theologian, drawing on Thomas Aquinas, reminds readers that "No one is morally obligated to do what he or she is incapable of doing."[158] A major challenge of Christian discipleship, then, is to do the best one can in the circumstances in which one finds oneself, cultivating both hope and honesty simultaneously.[159]

Throughout his ministry, Jesus employed a method of persuasion, not of coercion, honoring the moral agency of his followers and challenging them without forcing their actions. As Catholic social teaching notes, "The truth cannot impose itself except by virtue of its own truth, and it makes its entrance into the mind at once quietly and with power."[160] In order to more faithfully witness to the intrinsic value of prenatal life and the human dignity of women, Christians should affirm women's agency and address the structural injustices that form the context in which pregnant women discern whether they can continue their pregnancy. Scholars of reproductive justice defend the moral agency of pregnancy women as a key component of the interrelated rights to have a child, to not have a child, and to parent children in safe and healthy conditions. This chapter has demonstrated that frameworks developed by feminist Christian theologians can strengthen support for women's moral agency in the Church and world. The Catholic moral tradition has developed over time, and further developments are needed in order to live out the Church's teaching on the full humanity and dignity of women.

NOTES

1. Barbara Hilkert Andolsen, "Whose Sexuality? Whose Tradition? Women, Experience, and Roman Catholic Sexual Ethics," in *Readings in Moral Theology, no. 9: Feminist Ethics and the Catholic Moral Tradition*, eds. Charles E. Curran, Margaret A. Farley, and Richard A. McCormick, SJ (New York: Paulist, 1996), 207–39, originally published in *Religion and Sexual Health: Ethical, Theological, and Clinical Perspectives*, in 1992.

2. In this chapter I use the terms "gestating woman," "gestating person," "pregnant woman," and "pregnant person." The modifier "gestating" conveys that growing a prenate in one's body is an ongoing, naturally burdensome activity.

3. According to the United Nations Population Fund, about half of pregnancies worldwide are planned. Forty-eight percent of pregnancies worldwide are unintended. This does not necessarily mean they are unwanted. An unintended pregnancy occurs to a woman who was not planning to have any (more) children, or that was mistimed (a pregnancy that occurs more than two years before a woman wanted to

be pregnant). An unwanted pregnancy is a pregnancy that a woman does not want to have. Researchers have documented that women's attitudes toward getting pregnant fall on a spectrum. The current rate of 64 unintended pregnancies per 1,000 women means that roughly 6 percent of the world's women experience an unintended pregnancy each year. Sixty-one percent of unintended pregnancies ended in abortion in 2019. UNFPA, *Seeing the Unseen: The Case for Action in the Neglected Crisis of Unintended Pregnancy* (Geneva: UNFPA, 2022), 6–7, 17, 26–30.

4. Catholic theologian Nichole Flores has described some of these experiences from her two pregnancies. Nichole M. Flores, "Rihanna's Super Bowl Performance Put the Power of Pregnancy Center Stage," *America* (February 14, 2023), https://www.americamagazine.org/faith/2023/02/14/rihanna-super-bowl-halftime-pregnant-244721.

5. Dorothy Roberts, *Killing the Black Body: Race, Reproduction, and the Meaning of Liberty, 20th Anniversary Edition* (New York: Vintage, 2017), 22–49. Yolanda Pierce tells the story of Margaret Garner and the many unfreedoms and traumas she experienced as an enslaved woman in Yolanda Pierce, *In My Grandmother's House: Black Women, Faith, and the Stories We Inherit* (Minneapolis: Broadleaf, 2021), 27–32.

6. UN researchers explain that trafficking in persons is a modern form of slavery and that more than 700,000 persons are trafficked each year across international lines. United Nations Population Fund, *Trafficking in Women, Girls, and Boys: Key Issues for Population and Development Programmes* (Geneva: UNFPA, 2003), 3–5, https://www.unfpa.org/sites/default/files/pub-pdf/Trafficking.pdf. California has the most reported cases of human trafficking in the United States, with 1,300 reported in 2021. A recent law enforcement case in San Diego, "Operation Better Pathways," resulted in 48 arrests and the identification of 16 people as victims of trafficking, including 8 children. Lyndsay Winkley and Karen Kucher, "48 Arrested in Human Trafficking and Sexual Exploitation Investigation," *San Diego Union Tribune* (February 21, 2023), https://www.sandiegouniontribune.com/news/public-safety/story/2023-02-21/38-arrested-in-human-trafficking-and-sexual-exploitation-investigation-in-san-diego-national-city. If you or someone you know is a victim of human trafficking, call the National Human Trafficking Hotline at (888) 373–7888.

7. Jennifer Banks, *Natality: Toward a Philosophy of Birth* (New York: Norton, 2023), 22.

8. Thomas Massaro, *Living Justice: Catholic Social Teaching in Action* (Lanham, MD: Rowman & Littlefield, 2016), 169–71. John Paul II affirms the "dignity" of women and the "essential equality of man and woman in their humanity" in *Mulieris Dignitatem* (August 15, 1988), 1, 6, https://www.vatican.va/content/john-paul-ii/en/apost_letters/1988/documents/hf_jp-ii_apl_19880815_mulieris-dignitatem.html. Francis affirms the "equal dignity of men and women" in Francis, *Amoris Laetitia* (2016), 54, https://www.vatican.va/content/dam/francesco/pdf/apost_exhortations/documents/papa-francesco_esortazione-ap_20160319_amoris-laetitia_en.pdf.

9. Gareth Moore explains, for example, that the Exodus version of the Decalogue "enshrines an extreme inequality of the sexes." See Gareth Moore, "Some Remarks on the Use of Scripture in *Veritatis Splendor*," in Joseph A. Selling and Jan Jans,

eds., *The Splendor of Accuracy: An Examination of the Assertions Made by Veritatis Splendor* (Grand Rapids: Eerdmans, 1995), 71–98, at 90.

10. Pius XI, *Quadragesimo Anno* (May 15, 1931), 71, https://www.vatican.va/content/pius-xi/en/encyclicals/documents/hf_p-xi_enc_19310515_quadragesimo-anno.html.

11. Francis, *Fratelli Tutti* (October 3, 2020), 23, https://www.vatican.va/content/francesco/en/encyclicals/documents/papa-francesco_20201003_enciclica-fratelli-tutti.html.

12. Emily Reimer-Barry, "*Amoris Laetitia* at Five," *Theological Studies* 83:1 (2022): 109–32.

13. Margaret A. Farley, "A Feminist Version of Respect for Persons," in *Readings in Moral Theology, no. 9: Feminist Ethics and the Catholic Moral Tradition*, 164–83, at 177.

14. Margaret A. Farley, *Compassionate Respect: A Feminist Approach to Medical Ethics and Other Questions* (New York: Paulist, 2002), 79. See also Margaret A. Farley, *Personal Commitments: Beginning, Keeping, Changing* (San Francisco: Harper and Row, 1986), 81–85; Margaret A. Farley, *Just Love: A Framework for Christian Sexual Ethics* (New York: Continuum, 2006), xi.

15. Farley, *Personal Commitments*, 82.

16. Paul VI, *Dignitatis Humanae* (1965), 1, https://www.vatican.va/archive/hist_councils/ii_vatican_council/documents/vat-ii_decl_19651207_dignitatis-humanae_en.html

17. Paul VI, *Gaudium et spes* December 7, 1965), 14, https://www.vatican.va/archive/hist_councils/ii_vatican_council/documents/vat-ii_const_19651207_gaudium-et-spes_en.html.

18. Cristina L. H. Traina, "Feminism, Finitude, and Flourishing," 2023 Madeleva Lecture (Mahwah, NJ: Paulist Press, 2024).

19. John Paul II, *Centessimus Annus* (May 1, 1991), 11–12, https://www.vatican.va/content/john-paul-ii/en/encyclicals/documents/hf_jp-ii_enc_01051991_centesimus-annus.html; Benedict XVI, *Spe Salvi* (November 30, 2007), 14–16, https://www.vatican.va/content/benedict-xvi/en/encyclicals/documents/hf_ben-xvi_enc_20071130_spe-salvi.html; Francis, *Evangelii gaudium* (November 24, 2013), 55, https://www.vatican.va/content/francesco/en/apost_exhortations/documents/papa-francesco_esortazione-ap_20131124_evangelii-gaudium.html; Francis, *Laudato si'* (May 24, 2015), 66, https://www.vatican.va/content/francesco/en/encyclicals/documents/papa-francesco_20150524_enciclica-laudato-si.html.

20. John XXIII, *Pacem in Terris* (April 11, 1963), 11, https://www.vatican.va/content/john-xxiii/en/encyclicals/documents/hf_j-xxiii_enc_11041963_pacem.html.

21. John XXIII, *Pacem in Terris*, 15.

22. The documents from the continental stage of the Synod provide examples from around the world of how Church communities seek greater attention to gender justice and inclusion of women in ecclesial leadership. See "Final Documents of the Continental Assemblies," Synod on Synodality (Vatican 2023), https://www.synod.va/en/synodal-process/the-continental-stage/final_document.html.

23. United States Conference of Catholic Bishops (USCCB), *Compendium of the Catechism of the Catholic Church* (Washington, DC: USCCB, 2020), 475.

24. USCCB, *Compendium of the Catechism of the Catholic Church*, no. 476.

25. USCCB, *Compendium of the Catechism of the Catholic Church*, no. 477.

26. Children's Hospital of Philadelphia, "Blood Circulation in the Fetus and Newborn," 2014, https://www.chop.edu/conditions-diseases/blood-circulation-fetus-and-newborn#:~:text=Through%20the%20blood%20vessels%20in,mother's%20circulation%20to%20be%20eliminated. See also John David Gordon, Jan T. Ryfors, Maurice L. Druzin, Yona Tadir, Yasser El-Sayed, John Chan, Dan Lebovic, Elizabeth Langen, and Katherine Fuh, *Obstetrics, Gynecology, and Infertility: Handbook for Clinicians*, seventh ed. (Arlington, VA: Scrub Hill Press, 2017).

27. "The Lungs in Pregnancy," Stanford Children's Health (2023), https://www.stanfordchildrens.org/en/topic/default?id=the-lungs-in-pregnancy-85-p02468.

28. "Yes, Pregnancy Affects Your Digestion," Gastrova (2023), https://www.gastrova.com/article/pregnancy-and-your-digestion/#:~:text=In%20the%20beginning%20of%20pregnancy,bloated%2C%20gassy%2C%20and%20constipated.

29. Mary Lloyd Ireland and Susan M. Ott, "The Effects of Pregnancy on the Musculoskeletal System," *Clinical Orthopaedics and Related Research*, vol. 372 (March 2000): 169–79. DOI: 10.1097/00003086-200003000-00019.

30. Mohamed Nabih El Gharib and Amro D. Aglan, "Changes in Skeletal System during Pregnancy," *Interventions in Gynaecology and Women's Healthcare* 2:1 (May 14, 2018). DOI, http://dx.doi.org/10.32474/IGWHC.2018.02.000127.

31. Katharine L. Cheung and Richard A. Lafayette, "Renal Physiology of Pregnancy," *Advances in Chronic Kidney Disease* 20:3 (May 2013): 209–14. DOI, https://doi.org/10.1053%2Fj.ackd.2013.01.012.

32. Randy K. Ward, MD, and Mark A. Zamorski, MD, MHSA, "Benefits and Risks of Psychiatric Medications During Pregnancy," *American Family Physician* 66:4 (2002): 629–637, https://www.aafp.org/pubs/afp/issues/2002/0815/p629.html. Pregnant patients should not stop taking any medications without first consulting their doctor; instead, these authors recommend that pregnant patients talk to their provider as soon as possible. The provider will review the patient's psychiatric history and current challenges and make a recommendation based on the patient's history and current assessment of risks for both the patient and the prenate.

33. Dr. Chandrima Biswas, ed., *The Pregnancy Encyclopedia: All Your Questions Answered* (New York: Dorling Kindersley, 2016), 118–47.

34. Centers for Disease Control and Prevention, "About Mental Health" (2023), https://www.cdc.gov/mentalhealth/learn/index.htm.

35. The UN reports that every two minutes, a woman dies during pregnancy or childbirth. There have been alarming setbacks for women's health in the past decade as maternal deaths either increased or stagnated in nearly every region of the world. See United Nations Population Fund, "A Woman Dies Every Two Minutes Due to Pregnancy or Childbirth," See UNFPA, *Trends in* Maternal Mortality *2000–2020* (February 23, 2023), https://www.who.int/publications/i/item/9789240068759. According to the Centers for Disease Control and Prevention, the US pregnancy-related mortality ratio was 17.6 per 100,000 in 2019, up from 7.2 per 100,000 in 1987. The

pregnancy-related mortality ratio is highest for Non-Hispanic Native Hawaiian or Other Pacific Islander women (62.8) and Non-Hispanic Black women (39.9). See CDC, "Trends in Pregnancy-Related Death" (March 23, 2023), https://www.cdc.gov/reproductivehealth/maternal-mortality/pregnancy-mortality-surveillance-system.htm#trends.

36. Heidi Murkoff and Sharon Mazel, *What to Expect When You're Expecting*, fifth ed (New York: Workman, 2016).

37. Rebecca Todd Peters, *Trust Women: A Progressive Christian Argument for Reproductive Justice* (Boston: Beacon, 2018), 153.

38. Peters, *Trust Women*, 153.

39. Peters, *Trust Women*, 154.

40. Peters cites the *Life* photography of Lennart Nilsson as an example of the cultural impact of sonography. Lennart Nilsson, "Drama of Life Before Birth," *Life* (April 30, 1965); Lennart Nilsson, "First Days of Creation," *Life* (August 1, 1990). See also Barbara Duden, *Disembodying Women: Perspectives on Pregnancy and the Unborn*, trans. Lee Hoinacki (Cambridge, MA: Harvard University Press, 1993), 18.

41. Peters expresses gratitude to Ann Cahill for this observation. Peters, *Trust Women*, 155, n9.

42. Peters, *Trust Women*, 156.

43. Peters, *Trust Women*, 157.

44. Victor Turner and Edith Turner, "Introduction: Pilgrimage as a Liminoid Phenomenon," in *Image and Pilgrimage in Christian Culture* (New York: Columbia University Press, 1978), 1–39; Arnold van Gennep, *The Rites of Passage* (Chicago: University of Chicago Press, 1960).

45. Peters, *Trust Women*, 159.

46. Peters explains that the two separate subjects remain marked by their prior experience of connection—the baby's belly button is a symbol of their connection to the birth mother, and the birth mother will retain cells that crossed the placenta during the pregnancy and integrated themselves into her tissues. See Peters, *Trust Women*, 162. Other scars of postpartum recovery can include sutures, weakened pelvic floor muscles, hemorrhoids, sore nipples, engorged breasts, uterine wall prolapse, and other bodily changes (even in a "typical" and "healthy" childbirth experience).

47. Sometimes this happens through co-parenting, but there are also cases in which the birth mother does not take on parenting responsibilities. Examples include placement of children with adoptive parents, surrogacy, or tragic cases of maternal death in which others assume care for the child.

48. Patricia Beattie Jung, "Abortion and Organ Donation: Christian Reflections on Bodily Life Support," in *Readings in Moral Theology, no. 9: Feminist Ethics and the Catholic Moral Tradition*, eds. Charles E. Curran, Margaret A. Farley, and Richard A. McCormick, SJ (New York: Paulist, 1996), 440–80.

49. Jung, "Abortion and Organ Donation," 442.

50. Jung, "Abortion and Organ Donation," 442–43.

51. Jung, "Abortion and Organ Donation," 444.

52. Jung, "Abortion and Organ Donation," 443.

53. Jung, "Abortion and Organ Donation," 452,

54. Jung, "Abortion and Organ Donation," 457.

55. Jung, "Abortion and Organ Donation," 455.

56. Jung, "Abortion and Organ Donation," 452.

57. Jung, "Abortion and Organ Donation," 452.

58. Nicholas Ramirez argues that because a prenate has a right to life, the prenate has a right to use the bodily organs of another in order to survive. See Nicholas Ramirez, "Teleology and the Problem of Bodily-Rights Arguments," *National Catholic Bioethics Quarterly* 23:1 (Spring 2023): 83–97, https://doi.org/10.5840/ncbq20232318. The woman's value is not intrinsic but instrumental in this account.

59. On human rights that conflict, see James Griffin, *Human Rights* (New York: Oxford, 2008), chapter three, https://doi.org/10.1093/acprof:oso/9780199238781.003.0004.

60. Catholic scholarship on right of access to one's body has been shaped largely by women's experiences of sexual assault and of growing awareness of the traumas of the sexual abuse of minors, including by Catholic clergy. See, for example, Tina Beattie, "Theological (De)Formations? The Sex Abuse Crisis in the Context of Nuptial Ecclesiology and the Theology of Priesthood," *Journal of Moral Theology* 3 (CTWEC Book Series, No. 3, 2023): 195–212. https://doi.org/10.55476/001c.72065; Karen Peterson-Iyer, *Reenvisioning Sexual Ethics: A Feminist Christian Account* (Washington, DC: Georgetown University Press, 2022), 21–80.

61. Jessica Wrobleski, *The Limits of Hospitality* (Minneapolis: Liturgical Press, 2012).

62. Kamitsuka, *Abortion and the Christian Tradition*, 155.

63. Kamitsuka, *Abortion and the Christian Tradition*, 168.

64. Kamitsuka, *Abortion and the Christian Tradition*, 171.

65. Kamitsuka, *Abortion and the Christian Tradition*, 171.

66. I am grateful to my colleague Jamall Calloway for sharing his expertise with me and helping me to understand this pattern in literature and poetry. See Zora Neale Hurston, *Their Eyes Were Watching God* (originally published in 1937); Joshua Bennett's *Being Property Once Myself: Blackness and the End of Man* (Cambridge, MA: Belknap Press, 2020), 114–39; Zakiyyah Jackson's *Becoming Human: Matter and Meaning in an Antiblack World* (New York: NYU Press, 2020); Dolores Williams, *Sisters in the Wilderness: The Challenge of Womanist God-Talk* (Maryknoll, NY: Orbis, 2013); Monica A. Coleman, "Sacrifice, Surrogacy and Salvation: Womanist Reflections on Motherhood and Work," *Black Theology* 12:3 (2014): 200–12.

67. Kamitsuka, *Abortion and the Christian Tradition*, 182.

68. Kamitsuka, *Abortion and the Christian Tradition*, 185.

69. Kamitsuka, *Abortion and the Christian Tradition*, 189.

70. Kamitsuka, *Abortion and the Christian Tradition*, 189.

71. Chanequa Walker-Barnes, *Too Heavy a Yoke: Black Women and the Burden of Strength* (Eugene, OR: Cascade Books, 2014), 152–54.

72. Jeanne Stevenson-Moessner, "From Samaritan to Samaritan: Journey Mercies," in *Through the Eyes of Women: Insights for Pastoral Care*, ed. Jeanne Stevenson-Moessner (Minneapolis: Fortress Press, 1996), 323, quoted in Chanequa Walker-Barnes, *Too Heavy a Yoke,* 154.

73. Kamitsuka, *Abortion and the Christian Tradition*, 190.

74. Kamitsuka, *Abortion and the Christian Tradition*, 191.
75. Christine E. Gudorf, *Body, Sex, and Pleasure: Reconstructing Christian Sexual Ethics* (Cleveland: Pilgrim Press, 1994).
76. Gudorf, *Body, Sex, and Pleasure*, 163–64.
77. Gudorf, *Body, Sex, and Pleasure*, 165.
78. Gudorf, *Body, Sex, and Pleasure*, 165.
79. Gudorf, *Body, Sex, and Pleasure*, 173. See also Daniel Fleming, James F. Keenan, SJ, and Hans Zollner, SJ, eds., *Doing Theology and Theological Ethics in the Face of the Abuse Crisis* (Catholic Theological Ethics in the World Church Book Series) *Journal of Moral Theology* 3:3 (2023): i–374, https://doi.org/10.55476/001c.72042.
80. Gudorf, *Body, Sex, and Pleasure*, 161.
81. Gudorf, *Body, Sex, and Pleasure*, 200.
82. Gudorf, *Body, Sex, and Pleasure*, 201. See also Toinette M. Eugene and James Newton Poling, *Balm for Gilead: Pastoral Care for African American Families Experiencing Abuse* (Nashville: Abington, 1998).
83. Examples abound in feminist theologies. See, for example, the Madeleva Lecture Series at St. Mary's College, published by Paulist Press, https://www.paulistpress.com/Products/CategoryCenter.aspx?categoryId=MFSP!MADL. A classic text is Catherine M. Lacugna, ed, *Freeing Theology: The Essentials of Theology in Feminist Perspective* (New York: HarperOne, 1993).
84. Pierce, *In My Grandmother's House*, 40.
85. Gudorf, *Body, Sex, and Pleasure*, 201. She explains implications for the military, the workplace, and parenting.
86. Gudorf, *Body, Sex, and Pleasure*, 166–67.
87. Robert L. Stivers, Christine E. Gudorf, Alice Frazer Evans, and Robert A. Evans, *Christian Ethics: A Case Method Approach* (Maryknoll, NY: Orbis, 2006), 280. This describes in more detail what Gudorf herself articulates about bodyright in her single-authored book.
88. Gudorf, *Body, Sex, and Pleasure*, 213.
89. Gudorf, *Body, Sex, and Pleasure*, 215.
90. Emily Reimer-Barry, *Catholic Theology of Marriage in the Era of HIV and AIDS: Marriage for Life* (Lanham, MD: Lexington Books, 2015), 91.
91. Mercy Amba Oduyoye, "Church-Woman and the Church in Contemporary Times: A Study of Sacrifice in Mission," *Bulletin de Theologie Africaine* 6:12 (1984) 259–72.
92. Pius XII, "The Prolongation of Life," address to an International Congress of Anesthesiologists (November 24, 1957), in *National Catholic Bioethics Quarterly* 9.2 (Summer 2009), 327–22; Congregation for the Doctrine of the Faith, *Declaration on Euthanasia* (May 5, 1980), 4, https://www.vatican.va/roman_curia/congregations/cfaith/documents/rc_con_cfaith_doc_19800505_euthanasia_en.html. See also Christopher Kaczor, "Philosophy and Theology: Notes on the Human Embryo Debates," *National Catholic Bioethics Quarterly* 9:2 (Summer 2009): 369–75. Catholic moralist Louis Janssens identifies the *Declaration on Euthanasia* as an example

of proportionate reasoning in "Teleology and Proportionality: Thoughts about the Encyclical *Veritatis Splendor*," in Selling and Jans, *The Splendor of Accuracy*, 99–102.

93. Chapter 2 explains that authoritative Catholic teachings on abortion defend the obligation to safeguard human life from conception, and describe pregnancy as a natural process even though it is burdensome for the pregnant woman. While the Catholic tradition broadly understood does distinguish between killing and murder, John Paul II's *Evangelium Vitae* (1995) described direct abortion as murder.

94. Kaiser Family Foundation, "The Availability and Use of Medication Abortion" (June 1, 2023), https://www.kff.org/womens-health-policy/fact-sheet/the-availability-and-use-of-medication-abortion/.

95. M. Cathleen Kaveny, "Intentional Killing or Right to Bodily Integrity: Can We Bridge the Moral Languages of Abortion?" *Journal of Moral Theology* 12:1 (2023): 97–100, at 99.

96. Emelia and Olle, "Dear Seedling," *Abortion, with love* podcast. Avaialble online, https://www.abortionwithlove.com/abortionloveletters/dearseedling.

97. Serene Jones, "Hope Deferred," in *Trauma and Grace: Theology in a Ruptured World*, second ed. (Louisville: Westminster John Knox, 2019), 127–50, at 129.

98. Elise Erikson Barrett, *What Was Lost: A Christian Journey Through Miscarriage* (Louisville: Westminster JohnKnox Press, 2010); Serene Jones, "Hope Deferred."

99. Anne Eggebroten, ed., *Abortion: My Choice, God's Grace: Christian Women Tell Their Stories* (Pasadena: New Paradigm, 1994); Maureen Walsh, *Grief and Healing after Pregnancy Loss: Stillbirth, Miscarriage, and Abortion in Japanese Buddhism and American Catholicism* (New Brunswick, NJ: Rutgers University Press, 2023).

100. Kate Jackson-Meyer, *Tragic Dilemmas in Christian Ethics* (Washington, DC: Georgetown University Press, 2022), 1.

101. Jackson-Meyer, *Tragic Dilemmas*, 1.

102. Jackson-Meyer, *Tragic Dilemmas*, 162.

103. Jackson-Meyer, *Tragic Dilemmas*, 163.

104. Examples of testimonies can be found in Rebecca Todd Peters, "Listening to Women: Examining the Moral Wisdom of Women Who End Pregnancies," *Journal of Religious Ethics* 49:2 (August 18, 2021): 290–313, https://doi.org/10.1111/jore.12352; Hallie Gould, "Five Honest, Personal Stories from Women Who Have Gotten Abortions Byrdie (May 4, 2022), https://www.byrdie.com/abortion-stories; Melissa Madera, *The Abortion Diary Podcast* (2020), https://www.theabortiondiary.com/; Meera Shah, *You're the Only One I've Told: The Stories Behind Abortion* (Chicago: Chicago Review Press, 2020); Diana Greene Foster, *The Turnaway Study: Ten Years, a Thousand Women, and the Consequences of Having—or Being Denied—an Abortion* (New York: Scribner, 2020); Lori Frohwirth, Michele Coleman, and Ann M. Moore. "Managing Religion and Morality Within the Abortion Experience: Qualitative Interviews with Women Obtaining Abortions in the U.S.," *World Medical & Health Policy* 10, no. 4 (2018): 381–400. doi:10.1002/wmh3.289; Rachel K. Jones, Lori F. Frohwirth, and Ann M. Moore, "'I Would Want to Give My Child, Like,

Everything in the World': How Issues of Motherhood Influence Women Who Have Abortions," *Journal of Family Issues* 29:1 (2008).

105. Jackson-Meyer, *Tragic Dilemmas*, 163.

106. Landmark texts in Catholic moral theology that emphasize the moral agent's striving include Bernard Häring's *The Law of Christ: Moral Theology for Priests and Laity* (Westminster: Newman, 1964); and *Free and Faithful in Christ: Moral Theology for Priests and Laity* (Slough: St. Paul, 1966); Klaus Demmer, MSC, *Shaping the Moral Life: An Approach to Moral Theology,* trans. Roberto Dell'Oro, ed. James F. Keenan, SJ (Washington, DC: Georgetown University Press, 2000).

107. James T. Bretzke, SJ, *Handbook of Roman Catholic Moral Terms* (Washington, DC: Georgetown University Press, 2013), 83.

108. Bretzke, *Handbook*, 83.

109. Louis Janssens preferred the term "ontic evil" to "physical evil" because he argued that the contemporary meaning of "physical" corresponds to the meaning of "material." See Louis Janssens, "Ontic Evil and Moral Evil," *Louvain Studies* 4 (1972): 115–156, at 133. My summary here is unable to address the nuances of the important debates among revisionists theologians in the 1970s and 1980s as they developed this approach to ambiguity in the moral life, nor to their critics.

110. Edward Collins Vacek, SJ, "Proportionalism: One View of the Debate," *Theological Studies* 46 (1985): 287–314, at 310.

111. Nadia Delicata, "Ontic Evil," in A. L. C. Runehov and L. Oviedo, eds., *Encyclopedia of Sciences and Religions* (Dordrecht, Switzerland: Springer, 2013).

112. Louis Janssens, "Teleology and Proportionality: Thoughts about the Encyclical Veritatis Splendor," in Selling and Jans, eds, *The Splendor of Accuracy,* 99–113, at 100.

113. A detailed summary of this debate would be beyond the scope of this chapter. However, the interested reader can trace the arguments in these publications: Richard A. McCormick, *Notes on Moral Theology 1965 through 1980* (Washington, DC: University Press of America, 1981); Richard A. McCormick, *Notes on Moral Theology 1981–1984* (Washington, DC: University Press of America, 1984); Lisa Sowle Cahill, "Teleology, Utilitarianism, and Christian Ethics," *Theological Studies* 42 (1981): 601–629; Lisa Sowle Cahill, "Contemporary Challenges to Exceptionless Moral Norms," in Donald G. McCarthy, ed., *Moral Theology Today: Certitudes and Doubts* (St. Louis: National Catholic Bioethics Center Publications, 1984), 121–35, 193–209; Josef Fuchs, SJ, *Moral Demands and Personal Obligations* (Washington, DC: Georgetown University Press, 1993); Aline H. Kalbian, "Where Have All the Proportionalists Gone?" *Journal of Religious Ethics* 30:1 (2002): 3–22.

114. Vacek, "Proportionalism," 310.

115. Vacek, "Proportionalism," 301.

116. Richard McCormick, SJ, and Paul Ramsey, eds. *Doing Evil to Achieve Good: Moral Choice in Conflict Situations* (Chicago: Loyola University Press, 1988), 43. For a sophisticated analysis of the distorted view of proportionalist debates presented in *Veritatis Splendor,* see Joseph A. Selling, "The Context and Arguments of *Veritatis Splendor,*" in Selling and Jans, *The Splendor of Accuracy,* 11–70.

117. Peters describes this as the justification paradigm, and her own work seeks to move beyond this paradigm and instead toward an understanding of reproductive autonomy as a human right. See Peters, "Listening to Women," 290–92.

118. Kenya Martin, "Damned If You Do, Damned If You Don't," *Conscience* 43:1 (2022), 9–11.

119. To say that prenatal demise is a premoral evil is not to say that abortion should be illegal; moral discourse within the Catholic community does not determine the appropriate legal codes for a pluralist democracy.

120. Foster, *The Turnaway Study*, 35.

121. Paul VI, *Humanae Vitae* (July 25, 1968), 10, https://www.vatican.va/content/paul-vi/en/encyclicals/documents/hf_p-vi_enc_25071968_humanae-vitae.html. The document goes on to describe that direct contraception, direct sterilization, and direct abortion are morally illicit. While I take issue with some of those moral norms as they are employed in a reductionist and physicalist framework, I want to raise up for further scrutiny here the fact that even the birth control encyclical contains within it seeds of a broader personalist (and even feminist) approach to deliberation rooted in responsible fertility, as the agent considers one's duties to God, themselves, their families, and human society. Regarding the physicalist approach to the natural law in *Humanae Vitae*, see Charles Curran, "Physicalism and a Classicist Methodology in the Encyclical," in Charles E. Curran and Robert E. Hunt, *Dissent in and for the Church: Theologians and Humanae Vitae* (New York: Sheed and Ward, 1969), 156–72. Curran's significant contributions to Catholic moral theology include *Christian Morality Today: The Renewal of Moral Theology* (Notre Dame: Fides Press, 1966); *Tensions in Moral Theology* (Notre Dame: University of Notre Dame Press, 1988); *Loyal Dissent: Memoirs of a Catholic Theologian* (Washington, DC: Georgetown University Press, 2006); *The Catholic Moral Tradition Today: A Synthesis* (Washington, DC: Georgetown University Press, 1999); *The Development of Moral Theology: Five Strands* (Washington, DC: Georgetown University Press, 2013).

122. See Peters, *Trust Women*, 203–6.

123. It is worth noting that the pro-choice movement is increasingly willing to recognize the moral ambiguity of reproductive decision-making as well as the grief women experience after abortion. See Katey Zeh, *A Complicated Choice: Making Space for Grief and Healing in the Pro-Choice Movement* (New York: Broadleaf Books, 2022). Rebecca Todd Peters, "Abolishing the Pro-Life/Pro-Choice Binary," *Conscience* (July 26, 2022), https://www.catholicsforchoice.org/resource-library/abolishing-the-pro-life-pro-choice-binary/. It is also important to note that Catholic proportionalist arguments do not ascribe guilt to the moral agent. Vacek explains: "Once the decision in favor of the greater good has been made, there is no moral regret for having realized premoral disvalue, since one has acted on the whole (morally, therefore) in favor of the good. Still . . . there is regret that the good without qualification could not be realized, and even the good realized wears tattered clothes." Vacek, "Proportionalism," 312.

124. On the fiduciary responsibilities of health care providers, see Carolyn McLeod, *Conscience in Reproductive Health Care: Prioritizing Patient Interests* (New York: Oxford University Press, 2020). We saw in chapter 2 that the *Directives*

privilege the principle of cooperation in this case, but there are other options that should be explored.

125. Richard A. McCormick, "Who or What Is the Preembryo?" *Kennedy Institute of Ethics Journal* 1:1 (March 1991): 1–15, doi: 10.1353/ken.0.0028. Reprinted in *Corrective Vision: Explorations in Moral Theology* (Kansas City: Sheed & Ward, 1994), 176–88.

126. USCCB, *Compendium of the Catechism of the Catholic Church*, 500. See also John Paul II, *Evangelium Vitae* (March 25, 1995), https://www.vatican.va/content/john-paul-ii/en/encyclicals/documents/hf_jp-ii_enc_25031995_evangelium-vitae.html.

127. Beverly Wildung Harrison, as quoted by Kamitsuka, *Abortion and the Christian Tradition*, 140. A discussion of fetal protection laws and legal personhood debates is beyond the scope of this chapter. For a helpful way forward that aligns with my proposal in this chapter, see Amanda Gvozden, "Fetal Protection Laws and the 'Personhood' Problem: Toward a Relational Theory of Fetal Life and Reproductive Responsibility," *Journal of Criminal Law & Criminology* 112:2 (2022): 407–38.

128. Kamitsuka, *Abortion and the Christian Tradition*, 138. Brent Waters and Ronald Cole-Turner, eds., *God and the Embryo: Religious Voices on Stem Cells and Cloning* (Washington, DC: Georgetown University Press, 2003); John F. Kavanaugh, SJ, *Who Count as Persons? Human Identity and the Ethics of Killing* (Washington, DC: Georgetown University Press, 2001); Jason T. Eberl, *The Nature of Human Persons: Metaphysics and Bioethics* (Notre Dame, IN: University of Notre Dame Press, 2020).

129. David Albert Jones, "An Unholy Mess: Why the 'Sanctity of Life Principle' Should Be Jettisoned," *The New Bioethics: A Multidisciplinary Journal of Biotechnology and the Body* (19 January 2017): 185–201.

130. Jones, "An Unholy Mess," citing Suber (1996), 196.

131. Jones, "An Unholy Mess," 194–97. Jones notes that Pope Benedict XVI spoke, in a general audience in 2009, of "the sacred respect for human life, which always possesses an infinite value."

132. Catholic philosopher Christopher Kaczor claims that pregnancy is not supererogatory because "the burden need only involve nine months of pregnancy; the woman can put the child up for adoption." Christopher Kaczor, *The Ethics of Abortion: Women's Rights, Human Life, and the Question of Justice* (New York: Routledge, 2014), 170. Catholic theologian Charles Camosy does not describe a politics of coercion as morally repugnant, explaining "we simply cannot reflect and respect all points of view in our law and public policy," adding further that "it is up to those who would like to see our set of values prevail to convince others of our point of view," even "via raw imposition of power." See Charles C. Camosy, *Beyond the Abortion Wars: A Way Forward for a New Generation* (Grand Rapids: Eerdmans, 2015), 91, 181n10.

133. Kamitsuka, *Abortion and the Christian Tradition*, 138. The term "late-term abortion" is not a medical term but a term used by pro-life activists to stigmatize abortions later in pregnancy (including after viability). Abortions after twenty weeks represent a very small percentage of overall abortions in the United States, and many

are tragic choices by women who described their pregnancies as wanted. Fewer than 2 percent of abortions are past twenty weeks, according to Foster, *Turnaway Study*, 4. Abortions after thirteen weeks can result from late recognition of the pregnancy as well as obstacles to abortion within one's community (waiting periods, abortion bans that necessitate travel, the cost of the procedure, and so forth). See Foster, *Turnaway Study*, 87–77, 144–45, 249–50, 306.

134. Lloyd Steffen, *Ethics and Experience: Moral Theory from Just War to Abortion* (Lanham, MD: Rowman & Littlefield, 2012), 177–92.

135. Marjorie Reiley Maguire, "Personhood, Covenant, and Abortion," *American Journal of Theology & Philosophy* 6:1 (1985): 37–43.

136. Tina Beattie, "Catholicism, Choice, and Consciousness: A Feminist Theological Perspective on Abortion," *International Journal of Public Theology* 4:1 (2010): 51–75; Carol A. Tauer, "Abortion: Embodiment and Prenatal Development," in *Embodiment, Morality, and Medicine*, ed. Lisa Sowle Cahill and Margaret Farley (Dordrecht: Kluwer Academic Publishers, 1995), 75–92; Carol A. Tauer, "Personhood and Human Embryos and Fetuses," *Journal of Medicine and Philosophy* 10:3 (1985): 253–266; "The Tradition of Probabilism and the Moral Status of the Early Embryo" *Theological Studies* 45:1 (1984): 3–33.

137. Lisa Sowle Cahill, "Abortion and Argument by Analogy," *Horizons* 9:2 (1982): 271–87; "Abortion, Sex, and Gender: The Church's Public Voice," *America* 168:18 (1993): 6–11; Karen Houle, "Abortion as the Work of Mourning," *Symposium* 11:1 (2007): 141–66.

138. Thomas A. Shannon and Allan B. Wolter, OFM, "Reflections on the Moral Status of the Pre-Embryo," *Theological Studies* 51 (1990): 603–26, at 625.

139. Kamitsuka, *Abortion and the Christian Tradition*, 122.

140. Anne E. Patrick, *Conscience and Calling: Ethical Reflections on Catholic Women's Church Vocations* (London: Bloomsbury, 2013).

141. On gradualism, see Kevin T. Kelly, *New Directions in Sexual Ethics: Moral Theology and the Challenge of AIDS* (London: Geoffrey Chapman, 1998), 187; Richard M. Gula, *Moral Discernment* (New York: Paulist, 1997), 106–11.

142. Joseph Selling explains that the moral act is "an act motivated by the love of God and neighbor," and that Jesus himself prioritizes the love commandment (Mt 22:34–40). But virtue develops over time. "One lives virtuously by appropriating and interiorizing attitudes that will lead to virtuous action. One's fundamental or basic intention becomes the source of one's activity." See Joseph A. Selling, "The Content and Arguments of Veritatis Splendor," in Selling and Jans, eds., *The Splendor of Accuracy*, 11–70, at 55.

143. Maria Cimperman, RSCJ, defines communal discernment in the context of religious life as "the way in which a community or congregation hears the Spirit's voice calling and responds." Maria Cimperman, *Religious Life for Our World: Creating Communities of Hope* (Maryknoll, NY: Orbis, 2020), 153.

144. Phillip Sheldrake, *Spirituality: A Very Short Introduction* (Oxford: Oxford University Press, 2012), 74.

145. Katherine Dyckman, Mary Garvin, and Elizabeth Liebert, *The Spiritual Exercises Reclaimed: Uncovering Liberating Possibilities for Women* (New York: Paulist, 2001), 247–48.

146. Kathleen Hughes, RSCJ and Therese Fink Meyerhoff, *Seeking the One Whom We Love: How RSCJs Pray* (St. Louis: Society of the Sacred Heart, 2016), 75.

147. Anne E. Patrick, *Liberating Conscience: Feminist Explorations in Catholic Moral Theology* (New York: Continuum, 1996), 38.

148. John Paul II explains that "the sum total of negative factors working against a true awareness of the universal common good, and the need to further it, gives the impression of creating, in persons and institutions, an obstacle which is difficult to overcome." John Paul II, *Solllicitudo rei socialis* (December 30, 1987), 36, https://www.vatican.va/content/john-paul-ii/en/encyclicals/documents/hf_jp-ii_enc_30121987_sollicitudo-rei-socialis.html. Latin American liberation theologians pressed the Church to recognize the structural dimensions of poverty, colonialism, and political corruption. See Bishops of Latin America, "The Medellín Statement," *New Blackfriars* 50:582 (November 1968): 72–78, https://doi.org/10.1111/j.1741-2005.1968.tb07710.x.

149. Matthew 7: 3–4. Catholic ethicist Richard Gula writes, "we need to refrain from making an absolute and final judgment not only about our own moral status before God but also about someone else's." Richard M. Gula, *Reason Informed by Faith: Foundations of Catholic Morality* (Mahwah, NJ: Paulist, 1989), 85.

150. Anthony Marinelli, *Conscience & Catholic Faith: Love and Fidelity* (New York: Paulist, 1991); Kathryn Lilla Cox, *Water Shaping Stone: Faith, Relationships, and Conscience Formation* (Minneapolis: Liturgical, 2015); Brian V. Johnstone, "Erroneous Conscience in *Veritatis Splendor* and the Theological Tradition, in Joe Selling and Jan Jans, eds., *The Splendor of Accuracy*, 114–35.

151. *Catechism of the Catholic Church*, no. 1790. Thomas Aquinas treated this in *Summa Theologica* I–II Q. 19, articles 5–6. See also Elizabeth Sweeny Block, "White Privilege and the Erroneous Conscience: Rethinking Moral Culpability and Ignorance," *Journal of the Society of Christian Ethics* 39:2 (Fall/Winter 2019): 357–74.

152. Paul VI, *Dignitatis Humanae*, 3.

153. Libreria Editrice Vaticana, *Catechism of the Catholic Church*, second ed., no. 1793, https://www.usccb.org/sites/default/files/flipbooks/catechism/442/.

154. Richard P. McBrien, *Catholicism: A New Study Edition* (New York: HarperOne, 1994), 973.

155. Classic feminist theological texts that discuss the misogyny in Christian traditions include Mary Daly, *Beyond God the Father* (Boston: Beacon, 1973); *Gyn/Ecology: The Metaethics of Radical Feminism* (Boston: Beacon, 1978); Rosemary Radford Ruether, *Sexism and God-Talk: Towards a Feminist Theology* (Boston: Beacon, 1993); Elizabeth A. Johnson, *She Who Is: The Mystery of God in Feminist Theological Discourse* (New York: Herder & Herder, 2017); Delores S. Williams, *Sisters in the Wilderness: The Challenge of Womanist God-Talk* (Maryknoll, NY: Orbis, 1993).

156. I am grateful for the conversation between Molleen Dupree-Dominguez and Elizabeth Bowler in *On a Mission Podcast* Episode 29 at 16:00–19:00, which helped

me to clarify my own thinking on this issue. In addition, activists who focus on birthing justice describe the hegemony of medicalized childbirth and the importance of honoring birthing women's decisions. See Barbara Gurr, *Reproductive Justice: The Politics of Health Care for Native American Women* (New Brunswick, NJ: Rutgers University Press); Julia Chinyere Oparah, ed., *Birthing Justice: Black Women, Pregnancy, and Childbirth* (New York: Routledge, 2016).

157. Francis, *Evangelii Gaudium*, 169–72.

158. Gula, *Reason*, 84. Thomas Aquinas, *Summa Theologica* I–II, 13.5, https://www.newadvent.org/summa/2013.htm.

159. Kathryn Lilla Cox's retrieval of Klaus Demmer's call for "moral personalities" is particularly helpful moving forward. Lilla Cox summarizes Demmer: "Moral personalities have courage, critically reflect on their decisions, acknowledge omissions/failures, identify with ideals and concepts that demand striving for something beyond the self, call attention to forgotten or ignored goods, and live with hope." See Kathryn Lilla Cox, "Gnoseological Concupiscence, Intersectionality, and Living Truthfully: Insights into How and Why Moral Theology Develops," *Journal of Moral Theology* 10:2 (2021): 212–38, at 230.

160. Paul VI, *Octogesima Adveniens*, 25, quoting *Dignitatis Humanae*, 1.

Chapter 7

Pragmatic Solidarity and Spiritual Supports

Enacting Reproductive Justice as Church

"But what should I do?" The answer to this question will not be the same for all, because in order to answer the question of what one should do, one must understand one's own positionality and power. I hope that all readers will engage in robust discernment about how they can use their own power to address the multi-layered problems that make up reproductive injustice in our world today. Enacting reproductive justice must be a collective effort. At the same time, each individual can contribute to this important collective effort. In this concluding chapter I articulate a way forward that focuses on structural and spiritual supports for pregnant women.

PRAGMATIC SOLIDARITY: A CATHOLIC APPROACH TO REPRODUCTIVE JUSTICE

In the Catholic tradition, collective action for social change is guided by solidarity. Solidarity recognizes human interdependence and the collective responsibility to improve the conditions of life for all. The ethic of solidarity has developed over time in the Catholic tradition; solidarity has been described as an attitude, a duty, and a virtue.[1] While solidarity is a firm commitment the good of the other, it must go beyond prayers and good wishes. The term "pragmatic solidarity" was described by physician Paul Farmer and means to go beyond the virtue of solidarity by actually *providing* "the goods and services that might diminish unjust hardship."[2] Pragmatic solidarity, then, requires much more than piety or promises; pragmatic solidarity provides actual help to those who are vulnerable. Pragmatic solidarity takes action to address human suffering. Farmer explained that "to those in great need, solidarity without the pragmatic component can seem like so much abstract piety."[3] In the face of complex and interrelated injustices, pregnant women need much more than abstract piety.

Christian communities are uniquely positioned to enact pragmatic solidarity with pregnant women. Thus, reframing the mission of the Church is a key aspect of Catholic reproductive justice work today. Such a mission would include specific structural and spiritual supports for pregnant and birthing women and their children. Thinking about the Church as a community of disciples who work together to foster justice may seem radical today, but it is actually a very traditional understanding of Church. Based on an interpretation of Matthew 25:40 ("Whatever you do for the least of these, you do unto me"), followers of Jesus have sought to address situations of suffering as if they were attending to the wounds of Christ himself. In the biblical account of Pentecost—often described as the birthday of the Church—the disciples "had all things in common; they would sell their possessions and goods and distribute the proceeds to all, as any had need" (Acts 2:44). While scholars debate whether this account is factually accurate or idealistic,[4] the witness of an ecclesial communion that lives out distributive justice and experiences "the goodwill of all the people" (Acts 2:47) privileges action for justice as constitutive of ecclesial mission. From the earliest records, scholars note that ministries of social justice by Christians prioritized the needs of abandoned infants, as well as community members who faced hunger and housing insecurity.[5] In the medieval world, parents who could not care for their children could surrender them to convents through a "foundling wheel," so that vowed religious could provide care.[6] But the same solutions from the past will not fit today's needs. Instead, today's solutions must be rooted in the complex systems and structures in which we find ourselves. On every level of US society, there is room for growth toward justice. In some cases, federal solutions are needed, while in other cases a robust parish-based ministry will be more helpful.

STRUCTURAL SUPPORT FOR REPRODUCTIVE JUSTICE

A Catholic approach to reproductive justice seeks to effect structural change in order to address the root causes of injustice. Increased criminalization of abortion exacerbates women's suffering and contributes to a racist carceral system. Instead, Catholics need to create the structures of support that would enable women facing unplanned pregnancies to imagine a "good life" inclusive of parenting responsibilities, while at the same time supporting pregnant women in their discernment and affirming their agency. Church institutions have an important role to play here, but we should not underestimate the difficulty of working for structural solutions.

Bishops are uniquely positioned to enact substantive reforms within the Church that would reorient our work in the world to nurture and support reproductive flourishing instead of simply asserting truth claims and expecting pregnant women (and their health care providers) to obey. But ultimately, living out the mission of the Church is a task for the whole People of God. The laity have an active and indispensable role in living out the principles of social justice, not only in parish life but in every aspect of our lives in families, workplaces, and communities.

Chapter 4 argued that in order to foster reproductive justice today, significant changes in US culture are needed, including worker justice, safe and affordable housing, nutrition, health care, childcare, just adoption programs, quality public education, increased support for raising children with special needs, freedom from sexual and relationship violence, and more. While such a list can be overwhelming, it can also signal the many different opportunities that people of faith have for effecting long-term structural change that would make significant impacts in the lives of pregnant women as they discern whether to continue a pregnancy.

PRAGMATIC SOLIDARITY WITH PREGNANT WOMEN

The circle of praxis in Catholic social teaching empowers each person within the Church—lay and ordained—to share responsibility for social analysis and action.[7] Attributed to Belgian Catholic priest Joseph Cardijn, the circle of praxis in Catholic ethics involves a process of seeing, judging, acting, and reflecting; Cardijn encouraged people to "observe situations, to evaluate them based on the Gospels, and to act in ways that respond to observed injustices."[8] Whenever possible, it would be wise to implement an approach rooted in a community-asset mindset that seeks to build on existing strengths within a community, instead of a deficit model that focuses on what is wrong in a community.[9] As we consider how to apply an asset-based circle of praxis framework to reproductive justice activism today, the following provide suggested paths for reflection and action.

Begin Where You Are

Each of us is already embedded in particular relationships, tethered to particular places, and enmeshed in particular institutions. The first step, then, is to pay attention to the dynamics that already shape one's lived realities. Who are the wisdom-keepers in your community? What existing networks of support could be strengthened? What resources are available for pregnant women discerning whether to continue a pregnancy? What are the policies for pregnant people in your school or workplace? What challenges do new mothers face in your particular context? What are the conditions of children in foster care in your community? Are there enough infant day care centers? Each of us must observe and analyze the situation around us. In doing so, we must also interrogate the degree of privilege we have in relation to the experiences of those most vulnerable. In the words of Jesuit priest and author Gregory Boyle, SJ, we seek "a compassion that can stand in awe at what the poor have to carry rather than stand in judgment at how they carry it."[10] Compassion and pragmatic solidarity go hand in hand. The first step in the circle of praxis requires that we see the complexity of pregnancy discernments and recognize the structural constraints in which women make decisions about their pregnancies.

Commit to Listening

If we are to truly center the needs of vulnerable populations, we have to commit to listen to those most impacted by sexism, racism, poverty, and related structural injustices. Pope Francis has begun to center synodality in his approach to ecclesiology. In synodality, listening is a central task and posture. Francis explains: "A synodal Church is a listening Church, aware that listening is more than hearing. It is a reciprocal listening in which each one has something to learn."[11] Our task is to become a listening Church so that we can better understand the everyday struggles of those around us as well as the way that the Spirit is already moving in our community. Faith communities have a special role to play in fostering social trust and in creating brave spaces in which people can recognize multiple sides of an issue and learn from one another.

In their landmark study on Americans' attitudes about abortion, sociologist Tricia Bruce and her team of scholars suggest that we need a new conversation about abortion in America today. "A different kind of conversation on abortion," they write, "can clarify and complicate personal views, generating opportunities for more common ground."[12] Further, "The occasion for conversation is an occasion for reflecting upon one's thinking, and for listening to that of another. Bringing abortion conversation out from the quiet and away from the shouting is in itself a way forward."[13] Entering into brave conversations that are inclusive, intentional, and focused on listening instead of debating may expose areas of common ground even across parishioners' partisan affiliations. Such conversations—especially when they are part of a broader discernment about how a community can foster social change within their contexts—can give rise to initiatives that focus on supporting long-term outcomes for pregnant women and to reducing the circumstances that lead to abortion decisions. When people of good will enter into brave dialogues about messy moral topics, shared commitments can lead to decisive action for change.

Join Existing Movements

If one is committed to justice for pregnant women, one need not reinvent the wheel in order to make a difference. Plugging into an organization near you may be the best approach. But remember that the goal is not to dictate the direction of the organization from your perspective; we must avoid what Jordan Flaherty calls "saviorism." Flaherty explains:

> The prototypical savior is a person who has been raised in privilege and taught implicitly or explicitly (or both) that they possess the answers and skills needed to rescue others, no matter the situation. . . . The savior mentality means that you want to help others but are not open to guidance from those you want to help.[14]

Instead, Flaherty explains that the best way to combat the savior mentality is to "act collectively for systemic change in a way that is accountable to the communities affected."[15] Religious communities can be hubs of support but religious people can also partner fruitfully with organizations that bring people together across faith traditions. Given the ways that reproductive justice intersects with other issues of structural injustice, one need not focus exclusively on abortion-related activism in order to make a positive impact for pregnant women. Among the many organizations that work on reproductive justice-related activism are SisterSong, Native Youth Sexual Health Network, Colorado Organization for Latina Opportunity and Reproductive Rights (COLOR), and National Asian Women's Health Organization. Organizations that focus on anti-racism include Black Lives Matter, Showing Up for Racial Justice, and Southern Poverty Law Center.[16] Some organizations focus on lobbying for social justice and voter education and mobilization; for example, NETWORK Lobby for Catholic Social Justice[17] and Faith in Public Life Action are important faith-based organizations that center the needs of vulnerable populations in advocating for social justice.[18] A coalition-building approach is important, as many complex issues are beyond the scope of one organization's or movement's ability to address.

Virtuous Voting

One of the important ways that people of faith can impact social change is through political participation. Political engagement is not limited to voting, but voting is one important way that one can live out a commitment to the common good. A Catholic feminist approach to responsible voting is rooted in the virtue of prudence. Prudence enables one to "know how to act in the midst of the contingencies of particular situations."[19] Given that no candidate is perfect and no party aligns exactly with Catholic values, every opportunity to vote requires prudential discernment and the weighing of values and disvalues. Virtuous voting is not about securing one's own self-interest but rather it is about supporting the common good. One can ask such questions as: Which party platform charts a way forward for addressing the social conditions that lead to unjust suffering for so many people today? Which candidates demonstrate wisdom, courage, compassion, justice, and fitness for office? Theologian and legal scholar Cathleen Kaveny explains that voters have "multifaceted obligations" and that "voters must select among candidates, not among issues."[20] This is an important caution as voters form their conscience and seek out information about both candidates and relevant issues.

SPIRITUAL SUPPORTS FOR REPRODUCTIVE FLOURISHING

There is much for faith communities to do to foster social change and to create a culture welcoming of new life and supportive of struggling parents. In addition to outward-seeking coalition-building within local communities, there is work to be done within the Church and especially within parish life.

The 2023 synod invited Catholics to think about what it would mean to adopt an ecclesiology of radical inclusion.[21] In order for parishes to be places of radical inclusion, we need to welcome the messiness that comes in ordinary human encounters. We need a new way of appreciating the grace present when people of diverse backgrounds, abilities, and ages celebrate together the mystery of God-with-Us. Holiness is too often constructed as reverence to clerical power requiring silence and submission. But holiness is also found in shared communion and intentional community. When we welcome messy, ordinary moments of grace—the outburst of a parishioner with cognitive disabilities, the questions of young children, the cries of infants—we construct spaces in which we are welcomed for who we are. We come as we are, needing to be fed and in search of a community that will bolster our faith, just as our own presence bolsters the faith of those around us in the pews who know they are not alone on their faith journey. Creating these spaces is not just important for the people in the pews today. Such spaces of radical inclusion would also demonstrate to the woman facing unplanned pregnancy that if she risks childbirth and takes on the challenge of parenting, she will find in this community a place of refuge and support. It can also communicate to her that even if she cannot take on that responsibility, this parish welcomes her then too. To say that "all are welcome" really must mean that all are welcome.[22] Living that claim in parish life is not easy but it is possible.

Parishes can demonstrate radical inclusion in very practical ways. These include:

- spaces that are accessible for members with disabilities and wide enough for walkers and strollers;
- changing tables and free diapers in all restrooms;
- inviting participation of children in music, as lectors, and in liturgical dance;
- sign language interpretation for the deaf community;
- Greetings and Prayers of the Faithful that speak meaningfully to the particular prayers and needs of the community;
- children's Liturgy of the Word;
- robust youth ministry programs for middle-school and high-school youth that maximize fun and include age-appropriate conversations about healthy relationships;
- bereavement ministries, including after pregnancy loss;
- programming for young adults and for new parents;
- ministries for families who have special needs related to their immigrant status, substance abuse, food and/or housing insecurity;
- adult formation programs that provide ongoing education about Catholic social teachings and antiracist practices;
- signage in women's restrooms alerting women to anti-trafficking and domestic violence assistance resources;
- increased opportunities for women's leadership and participation in every level of Church leadership;
- affordable infant day care and after-school programs on site;
- voter education programs that provide space for communal discernment about complex moral issues, the community's needs, and the virtues and vices of particular candidates;
- and other needs-based-ministries specific to the community's situation.

If parish life itself is not genuinely supportive of children's lives, the Church will lack credibility when teaching about the value of children's lives, born and unborn.[23]

Breaking bread together in the sacrament of Eucharist is an opportunity to worship God, remember sacred stories of faith, and repair broken relationships, including our relationship with God. But a first step must be honesty about the ways that the body of Christ is experiencing brokenness and alienation. On the feast of the Body and Blood of Christ, Pope Francis explained that "Eucharist is meant to nourish those who are tired and hungry along the journey," and that the "Eucharist is not the reward of saints, but the bread of sinners."[24] Such an approach signals the importance of being spiritually nourished in parish life.

BEYOND EUCHARIST: NEW RITUALS NEEDED FOR HEALING AFTER PREGNANCY LOSS

When Katherine Brown experienced her third pregnancy loss, female colleagues at the Catholic school where she worked wrote touching letters of support and gave her books that had helped them during their own losses. But Katherine found nothing within her parish or diocese to help her and her family during their time of grief.[25] A growing number of feminist theologians in the Catholic tradition have argued that new rituals are needed to facilitate spiritual healing after pregnancy loss. Kate Williams, in *Of Womb and Tomb: Prayer in a Time of Infertility*, begins by reflecting on the wisdom of the book of Ecclesiastes, in which we hear that there is a season for everything: "a time to be born, and a time to die; a time to plant, and a time to pluck up what is planted; a time to kill, and a time to heal; a time to break down, and a time to build up; a time to weep, and a time to laugh; a time to mourn, and a time to dance."[26] Williams continues:

> We eagerly welcome the opportunities to laugh and dance, but outside the regular parish funeral, we can struggle to make equal room in our communities for openly acknowledging the times for weeping, for mourning, for dying. Those who struggle with the inability to conceive, those who know the pain of losing a child before birth, and those who have faced their infant's death at the time of birth know that this season of mourning is often held inside, hidden and unseen.[27]

Claire Nicogossian has experienced such loss firsthand, and explains the importance of rituals that enable women to have closure after pregnancy loss. "Women need permission—they need to know that they can name a baby. Sometimes we need to put something concrete on our grief. The ritual piece can be helpful, along with talking about it and knowing that grieving is an ongoing process."²⁸ In a beautiful reflection on Christian hope after the death of Jesus and the celebration of the empty tomb at Easter, Kate Williams explains that Christians profess belief in a God "who remains with us through all seasons of life," and that the parish community can be a space where together we "bear witness to the Christian mystery—that new life is born of the womb and the tomb."²⁹ Rituals that hold together the ambiguity and complexity that women feel about prenatal death in the womb are needed so that grieving families have space to name their experiences and feel accompanied on their journey during and after pregnancy loss.

Maureen Walsh describes "liturgical and memorial practices" as a growing trend in US Catholicism in order to acknowledge and commemorate pregnancy losses (miscarriage, stillbirth, and abortion).[30] Memorials can range from rituals that honor pregnancy loss to public monuments at which one can mourn pregnancy loss to post abortion ministry retreats.[31] An example of a memorial during Mass can be found in Fr. Thomas Turner's "A Rite for Miscarriage."[32] Turner invited people who had experienced pregnancy loss to light votive candles, one for each child who died in the womb, with the goal of affirming two distinct realities: "the full Church membership of these unborn children and the mothers' pain."[33] An example of a ritual during the Rachel's Vineyard post-abortion retreat involves the participant carrying around a rock representing the emotional baggage that they carry with them as a result of their abortion experience. During the retreat, they are invited to discard the rock when they feel ready to let go of their burdens. The sacrament of reconciliation is often a space in which participants are encouraged to do so.

The structural problems of clericalism can contribute to women's pain, especially when male ritual leaders lack pastoral sensitivity and have difficulty relating to grieving families. In light of the structural problems of clericalism and sexism, greater attention to pregnancy loss is an important component of seminary curricula.[34] But I do not advocate for new rituals that maintain male clerical privilege. Instead, our parishes should have a variety of new rituals that include the possibility of women who serve as presiders of rituals that remember the dead and offer hope to grieving families. Karen Girolami Callam, who experienced miscarriage during a Sunday Mass, yearned afterward for "a way to recognize the pain and the process within my own faith community," and described the importance of "a safe, spiritual space for women and their families, friends, and community to say and know, 'Yes, this happened. Yes, God is here too. Yes, I am whole.'"[35] The poems, hymns, blessings, and rites that Williams collected serve as a very helpful starting point. Another important resource for adult spiritual formation could be retelling of and discussion of stories of the saints as they relate to themes of gender justice, pregnancy, parenthood, and pregnancy loss. A litany of saints inclusive of Brigid of Kildare, Hildegard of Bingen, and Gianna Beretta Molla would encourage Catholics today to provide compassion and accompaniment for women who are in the midst of difficult pregnancy discernments.[36] Maintaining flexibility and encouraging rituals that meet the particular needs of a parish community will be important, even as scholars continue to advocate for new and official (Vatican-sanctioned) rites and feminist rituals outside of mainstream Catholic liturgical practice.[37]

CONCLUSION

Scholars of reproductive justice explain the importance of shifting the conversation "from abstract rights to everyday justice."[38] The reproductive justice framework "engages people in their everyday lives and centers the people who need help the most."[39] This approach refuses to see pregnancy discernments as simple, straightforward, or easy. Instead, it recognizes that pregnant woman are embedded in complex social structures over which they do not have complete control. A key insight of reproductive justice is that the way forward must focus on social justice. Enacting reproductive justice as Church will require both internal reforms and outward-facing social change activism. I remain hopeful that as a synodal Church we will work to foster greater justice for pregnant women, families grieving reproductive loss, and vulnerable children. Moving away from an ecclesiology in which we expect the institutional Church to have all of the answers to our problems, we need to instead pivot to a synodal Church in which we collaborate together at every stage of discernment, learning, teaching, and implementing reforms. I close by describing this book's key takeaways as well as its limitations.

This book set out to show the limitations of a pro-life/pro-choice binary for discussing the complexity of women's experiences of reproductive loss and parenting in an unjust world. US history is replete with examples of reproductive injustice, especially for poor women and women of color. Remembering the legacies of enslavement, forced sterilizations, forced migrations, and family separations remains a key aspect of truth-telling today, and situates today's struggles for reproductive freedom in a long history of abuses of women of color. When women today claim their bodily integrity, moral agency, and the right to parent in safe and healthy conditions, they do so against the backdrop of reproductive oppressions in US history.

Unfortunately, the so-called successes of the pro-life movement from 1973–2022 have yielded increased suffering and alienation for women in the pews. Abortion bans celebrated by the pro-life movement have not addressed the dangers of pregnancy and birthing, and have created new barriers to health care that exacerbate existing inequalities. Abortion bans and increased legal restrictions create "mechanisms for the state to enforce those restrictions," which "brings the carceral system into the exam room."[40] We face increased polarization in US politics, but in order to achieve social justice we must move beyond culture war polemics and the MAGA extremism that now exemplifies the dominant voice in the political party that calls itself pro-life.

Reproductive justice provides a way forward that holds together both the human dignity of women and the disvalue of prenatal demise experienced in any pregnancy loss (miscarriage, stillbirth, and abortion). Catholics need greater opportunities for naming and grieving that loss, but in ways that do not shame, stigmatize, or exclude the very women whose bodies most suffered. Additionally, we need to recognize how stigmatizing language and theologies of sin have contributed to the harm many women have experienced. Catholic magisterial teachings can be turned into "stones to throw at people's lives,"[41] in contradiction to the gospel's invitation to accompany and support in order to bring spiritual growth, healing of deep wounds, and structural justice. It might be challenging to recognize that for many women who have experienced abortion, they believe the Church has harmed them by unjustifiably labeling them as sinners when in fact many others also bear responsibility for prenatal death, and that for true healing to happen, a recognition of this harm cannot be avoided.

I have suggested that in order to adequately address reproductive injustice we must focus on structural change. I have articulated the ways in which a Catholic feminist vision for social change aligns with the key goals of the reproductive justice movement. I have also highlighted the themes of ambiguity and complexity that emerge in women's testimonies of pregnancy loss. Respect for women demands that we recognize the complex decision-making processes women are engaged in when they decide whether to continue a pregnancy. Instead of doubting their moral judgments, we should respect women's decisions and work to address the constraints pregnant women report.

Reclaiming women's human dignity is key in the abortion debates because it recognizes that women have intrinsic, not just instrumental, value. That some women report abortion as "good" for them and as empowering in context can be interpreted as a failure of our society and Church to have created a culture of life and support systems for all women. Accompanying women is a different model than "teaching to" and "preaching at" women. But naming the loss of prenatal life as a disvalue is not equivalent to advocating for legal protections of the unborn. Women must be recognized as fully human agents with control over their reproductive choices, bodies, and vocational futures. If we cannot persuade a woman to remain pregnant and offer her genuine life-giving choices and a future that is as empowering with a child as without one, then we should support her decision made in conscience, and continue to work for a day when fewer women make that difficult decision.

New spiritual resources are needed so that women facing complex discernments have the tools to reflect adequately on the competing values at stake in their decisions and on the seemingly impossible choices they face. In the wake of those choices, new rituals are needed that can restore a sense of belonging in the communion of the Church and foster spiritual healing. But women need more than the Church's mercy—women demand justice.

An action plan for reproductive justice can be summarized by specific do's and don't's:

Do respect women.
Do put pregnant women at the center.
Do address the root causes of injustice.
Do consider how your privilege and positionality may distort your perception.
Do seek common ground across partisan divides to advance structural change.
Don't shame women who procure abortion.
Don't criminalize reproductive health care.
Don't participate in political extremism.
Don't lose hope or succumb to apathy.

Reproductive flourishing encompasses much more than one book could hope to address. This book could not address all possible relevant issues related to reproduction and social justice, including infertility, surrogacy, sterilization, health care for transgender youth, contraception, pornography, teen pregnancy, prison policies, sex work, paternal rights and responsibilities, sexual education, child abuse, birthing justice, and emerging information about how climate change is influencing pregnant women's discernments around the world. I am grateful for my colleagues who are taking up these related issues in their own work.

Some readers may not be persuaded by the arguments in this book. But a synodal Church is one in which disagreement signals the need for continued dialogue and communal discernment. During his journey to Portugal for World Youth Day in 2023, Pope Francis encouraged an audience of Jesuits by telling them not to be "backward-looking." Francis explained that "we need to understand that there is an appropriate evolution in the understanding of matters of faith and morals." He added that "our understanding of the human person changes with time, and our consciousness also deepens."[42] Francis captures well the nature of theological discourse today, as teachings must evolve in order to account for the ways in which our understanding of the full dignity of women necessitates a new approach to discourse regarding sexuality, reproduction, and respect for women's lives. I urge the Church, my

Church, to pursue opportunities for ecclesial dialogue and discernment that will lead to greater recognition of the full dignity of women.

NOTES

1. Meghan J. Clark, "Pope Francis and the Christological Dimensions of Solidarity in Catholic Social Teaching," *Theological Studies* 80:1 (2019): 102–22, at 102–5.

2. Paul Farmer, *Pathologies of Power: Health, Human Rights, and the New War on the Poor* (Berkeley: University of California Press, 2005), 146.

3. Paul Farmer, "Health, Healing, and Social Justice," in *In the Company of the Poor: Conversations with Dr. Paul Farmer and Fr. Gustavo Gutiérrez*, edited by Michael Griffin and Jennie Weiss Block (Maryknoll: Orbis, 2013), 44.

4. Richard B. Hays, *The Moral Vision of the New Testament: A Contemporary Introduction to New Testament Ethics* (New York: HarperCollins, 1996), 122–24, 302. See also Raymond E. Brown, *An Introduction to the New Testament* (New York: Doubleday, 1997), 283–89.

5. Christine Schenk, *Crispina and Her Sisters: Women and Authority in Early Christianity* (Minneapolis: Fortress, 2017).

6. Christine E. Gudorf, "Contraception and Abortion in Roman Catholicism," in Daniel C. Maguire, ed., *Sacred Rights: The Case for Contraception and Abortion in the World's Religions* (New York: Oxford, 2003), 55–78.

7. Erin M. Brigham, *See, Judge, Act: Catholic Social Teaching and Service Learning* (Winona, MN: Anselm Academic, 2013), 9.

8. Brigham, *See*, 9; Joseph Willke, "The Worker-Priest Experiment in France," *America* (April 1984), 253.

9. John McKnight and Peter Block, *The Abundant Community: Awakening the Power of Families and Neighborhoods* (Oakland, CA: Berrett-Koehler Publishers, 2012).

10. Gregory Boyle, *Tattoos on the Heart: The Power of Boundless Compassion* (New York: Simon & Schuster, 2010), 127.

11. Cindy Wooden, "Pope Calls for 'Synodal' Church that Listens, Learns, Shares Mission," *National Catholic Reporter* (October 17, 2015).

12. Tricia C. Bruce, *How Americans Understand Abortion: A Comprehensive Interview Study of Abortion Attitudes in the U.S.* (Notre Dame, IN: McGrath Institute for Church Life, 2020), 52.

13. Bruce, *How Americans*, 52.

14. Jordan Flaherty, *No More Heroes: Grassroots Challenges to the Savior Mentality* (Chico, CA: AK Press, 2016), 17–18.

15. Flaherty, *No More Heroes*, 199.

16. Cf. chapter 1, n. 122.

17. Mara D. Rutten, *Called to Action: NETWORK's 50 Years of Political Ministry* (Washington, DC: NETWORK Advocates for Catholic Social Justice, 2023). See also "NETWORK Lobby for Catholic Social Justice," https://networklobby.org/.

18. "Faith in Public Life Action Fund," https://www.fplaction.com/ (2024).

19. Aquinas, *Summa Theologica*, II–II, 47,5; Stephen J. Pope, "Overview of the Ethics of Aquinas," in *The Ethics of Aquinas* (Washington, DC: Georgetown University Press, 2002), 40.

20. Cathleen Kaveny, *Law's Virtues: Fostering Autonomy and Solidarity in American Society* (Washington, DC: Georgetown University Press, 2012), 212.

21. XVI Ordinary General Assembly of the Synod of Bishops, *Instrumentum Laboris* (October 2023): B 1.2 (p. 29), citing DCS 30.

22. In the Welcome Ceremony for World Youth Day 2023 in Lisbon, Portugal, Pope Francis repeated that "in the Church, there is room for everyone." Francis, Apostolic Journey of His Holiness Francis in Portugal on the Occasion of the 37th World Youth Day (2 to 6 August 2023), Welcome Ceremony at the Parque Eduardo VII, August 3, 2023. https://press.vatican.va/content/salastampa/en/bollettino/pubblico/2023/08/03/230803c.html.

23. Ethna Regan, "Barely Visible: The Child in Catholic Social Teaching," *Heythrop Journal* 55, no. 6 (2014): 1021–32, at 1030. See also Mary M. Doyle Roche, "Children and Youth: Forming the Moral Life" *Journal of Moral Theology*, vol. 7, no. 1 (2018): 1–12.

24. Carol Glatz, "Eucharist Is Bread of Sinners, Not Reward of Saints, Pope Says," *Catholic News Service* (June 7, 2021). https://catholicreview.org/eucharist-is-bread-of-sinners-not-reward-of-saints-pope-says/.

25. Katherine Brown's story is told in Julie Schwietert Collazo, "The Quiet Grief of Miscarriage," *U.S. Catholic* (October 18, 2016). https://uscatholic.org/articles/201610/the-quiet-grief-of-miscarriage/.

26. Ecclesiastes 3: 1–4b.

27. Kate Williams, ed., *Of Womb and Tomb: Prayer in Time of Infertility, Miscarriage, and Stillbirth* (Chicago: GIA Publications, 2019), 1.

28. Claire Nicogossian, as quoted in Julie Schwietert Collazo, "The Quiet Grief of Miscarriage," *U.S. Catholic* (October 18, 2016). https://uscatholic.org/articles/201610/the-quiet-grief-of-miscarriage/.

29. Williams, *Of Womb and Tomb*, 3–4.

30. Maureen L. Walsh, Emerging Trends in Pregnancy-Loss Memorialization in American Catholicism," *Horizons* 44 (2017): 369–98.

31. United States Conference of Catholic Bishops, *Project Rachel Ministry: A Post-Abortion Resource Manual for Priests and Project Rachel Leaders* (Washington, DC: USCCB, 2009). See also Rachel's Vineyard Ministries, http://www.rachelsvineyard.org.

32. Thomas Turner, "A Rite for Miscarriage," *Modern Liturgy* 13, no. 9 (December 1986/January 1987): 18–19. See also Lauren Markoe, "Church Offers Place to Mourn Pregnancy Loss, Infant Death," *The Christian Century*, May 7, 2015.

33. Turner, "A Rite for Miscarriage," 18–19.

34. United States Conference of Catholic Bishops Committee on Clergy, Consecrated Life and Vocations, *Program of Priestly Formation*, sixth ed. (Washington, DC: USCCB, 2022).

35. Karen Girolami Callam, "Yes, I Am Whole," in Kate Williams, ed., *Of Womb and Tomb*, 33–38, at 36.

36. Cf. Introduction, n. 8.

37. Rosemary Radford Ruether, *Women-Church: Theology and Practice of Feminist Liturgical Communities* (San Francisco: HarperRow, 1985), 161–63. See also Diann L. Neu, *Women's Rites: Feminist Liturgies for Life's Journey* (Cleveland, OH: Pilgrim Press, 2003) and *Stirring Waters: Feminist Liturgies for Justice* (Collegeville, MN: Liturgical Press, 2020).

38. DeShawn Taylor, *Undue Burden: A Black, Woman Physician on Being Christian and Pro-Abortion in the Reproductive Justice Movement* (Charleston, SC: Advantage, 2023), 105.

39. Taylor, *Undue Burden*, 105.

40. Taylor, *Undue Burden*, 184.

41. Francis, *Amoris Laetitia*, 305: https://www.vatican.va/content/dam/francesco/pdf/apost_exhortations/documents/papa-francesco_esortazione-ap_20160319_amoris-laetitia_en.pdf.

42. Antonio Spadaro, SJ, "The Water Has Been Agitated: Francis in Conversation with Jesuits in Portugal, August 5, 2023," *La Civiltá Cattolica* (August 28, 2023), https://www.laciviltacattolica.com/the-water-has-been-agitated/.

Appendix

Poems and Prayers for Reproductive Justice

Praise the LORD!
How good it is to sing praises to our God;
    for he is gracious, and a song of praise is fitting.
The LORD builds up Jerusalem;
    he gathers the outcasts of Israel.
He heals the brokenhearted,
    and binds up their wounds.
He determines the number of the stars;
    he gives to all of them their names.
Great is our Lord, and abundant in power;
    his understanding is beyond measure.
The LORD lifts up the downtrodden;
    he casts the wicked to the ground.

Psalm 147: 1–6 (NRSV-CE)

The Beatitudes

"Blessed are the poor in spirit, for theirs is the kingdom of heaven.
Blessed are those who mourn, for they will be comforted.
Blessed are the meek, for they will inherit the earth.
Blessed are those who hunger and thirst for righteousness, for they will be filled.
Blessed are the merciful, for they will receive mercy.
Blessed are the pure in heart, for they will see God.
Blessed are the peacemakers, for they will be called children of God.
Blessed are those who are persecuted for righteousness' sake, for theirs is the kingdom of heaven.
Blessed are you when people revile you and persecute you and utter all kinds of evil against you falsely on my account. Rejoice and be glad, for your reward is great in heaven, for in the same way they persecuted the prophets who were before you."

Matthew 5:3–12 (NRSV-CE)

The Spirit of the Lord is upon me,
because he has anointed me
to bring good news to the poor.
He has sent me to proclaim
release to the captives
and recover of sight to the blind,
to let the oppressed go free,
to proclaim the year of the Lord's favor.

Luke 4:18–19 (NRSV-CE)

Paul's Thanksgiving after Affliction

Blessed be the God and Father of our Lord Jesus Christ, the Father of mercies and the God of all consolation, who consoles us in all our affliction, so that we may be able to console those who are in any affliction with the consolation with which we ourselves are consoled by God. For just as the sufferings of Christ are abundant for us, so also our consolation is abundant through Christ.

2 Corinthians 1:3–5 (NRSV-CE)

Excerpt, "The Second Letter to Agnes of Prague"

What you hold, may you always hold.
What you do, may you always do and never abandon.
But with swift pace, light step and unswerving feet, so that even your steps stir up no dust,
may you go forward securely, joyfully, and swiftly,
on the path of prudent happiness,
not believing anything,
not agreeing with anything
that would dissuade you from this resolution
or that would place a stumbling block
for you on the way,
so that you may offer your vows to the Most High
in the pursuit of that perfection to which
the Spirit of the Lord has called you.

St. Clare of Assisi
Reprinted with permission. All rights reserved.

Prayer for Times of Reproductive Loss

Mother God,

> You birthed all living things from the waters of your womb,
> Guide me as I breathe and labor in the space between
> the beginning and the end,
>> Life and death,
>> Body and spirit,
>> Grief and hope,
>> Relief and hurt,
>> Control and surrender,
>> Peace and confusion.
>
> Though I may never comprehend the rhythms and cycles of your creation, I sit in awe of their power, and of that same power within me.

Midwifing Spirit,

> Hold me as I cradle my tender and aching body,
> Anoint me with healing oils of nourishment and warmth,
> Cleanse me with refreshing water,
>
> And support me with gentle touch throughout the contractions and expansions of my pain.
> Breathe in me the strength to rise again, the courage to turn towards my body with love, and the resiliency to face the unknown roads of my journey.

Sister Mary,

> You trembled in fear and hope as you learned the news of your pregnancy, during a time of great danger and personal vulnerability.
> Walk with me through the difficult paths and uncertain circumstances of my own reproductive story,
> Grieve with me at the foot of my own crosses,
> And fight with me for my sisters around the world whose bodies are being violated, and whose flesh cries out for justice.

May we who hold the great power to create and release life in our bodies hold one another in solidarity and love, singing together a song of resurrection hope.
Amen.

Karen Ross, PhD
Used with permission. All rights reserved.

i carry your heart with me(i carry it in
my heart)i am never without it(anywhere
i got you go,my dear;and whatever is done
by only me is your doing,my darling
                      i fear
no fate(for you are my fate,my sweet)i want
no world(for beautiful you are my world,my true)
and it's you are whatever a moon has always meant
and whatever a sun will always sing is you

here is the deepest secret nobody knows
(here is the root of the root and the bud of the bud
and the sky of the sky of a tree called life;which grows
higher than soul can hope or mind can hide)
and this is the wonder that's keeping the stars apart

i carry your heart(i carry it in my heart)

—e.e. cummings
Reprinted with permission. All rights reserved.

the mother

Abortions will not let you forget.
You remember the children you got that you did not get,
The damp small pulps with a little or with no hair,
The singers and workers that never handled the air.
You will never neglect or beat
Them, or silence or buy with a sweet.
You will never wind up the sucking-thumb
Or scuttle off ghosts that come.
You will never leave them, controlling your luscious sigh,
Return for a snack of them, with gobbling mother-eye.

I have heard in the voices of the wind the voices of my dim killed children.
I have contracted. I have eased
My dim dears at the breasts they could never suck.
I have said, Sweets, if I sinned, if I seized
Your luck
And your lives from your unfinished reach,
If I stole your births and your names,
Your straight baby tears and your games,
Your stilted or lovely loves, your tumults, your marriages, aches, and your deaths,
If I poisoned the beginnings of your breaths,
Believe that even in my deliberateness I was not deliberate.
Though why should I whine,
Whine that the crime was other than mine?—
Since anyhow you are dead.
Or rather, or instead,
You were never made.
But that too, I am afraid,
Is faulty: oh, what shall I say, how is the truth to be said?
You were born, you had body, you died.
It is just that you never giggled or planned or cried.

Believe me, I loved you all.
Believe me, I knew you, though faintly, and I loved, I loved you
All.

Gwendolyn Brooks
Reprinted with permission. All rights reserved.

In the Swirl of Discernment

God of Wisdom,
I come to you in my hour of need.
Confusing thoughts and feelings disturb me, unsettle me, and swirl around me.
I long for peace.
I thirst for justice.
Break these chains so that I may be free:
    free to love,
    free to serve,
    free to be the person you created me to be.
Help me to hear your call
    today,
    tomorrow,
    always.

Emily Reimer-Barry

Wise Women Also Came

Wise women also came.
the fire burned
in their wombs
long before they saw
the flaming star
in the sky.
They walked in shadows,
trusting the path
would open
under the light of the moon.

Wise women also came,
seeking no directions,
no permission
from any king.
They came
by their own authority,
their own desire,
their own longing.
They came in quiet,
spreading no rumors,
sparking no fears
to lead
to innocents' slaughter,
to their sister Rachel's
inconsolable lamentations.

Wise women also came,
and they brought
useful gifts:
water for labor's washing,
fire for warm illumination,
a blanket for swaddling.

Wise women also came,
at least three of them,
holding Mary in the labor,
crying out with her
in the birth pangs,
breathing ancient blessings
into her ear.

Wise women also came,
and they went,
as wise women always do,
home a different way.

Jan Richardson
Reprinted with permission. All rights reserved.

A Prayer of Accompaniment

God of care,
   be with me
   as I enter this clinic
   knowing what I need.
God of love,
   steady my hands
   smile down through those
   who love me
   and the abortion providers
   whom you have called
   to walk with me today.
Spirit of God,
   be with me now
   on this day
   and in those to come.
   Amen.

Catholics for Choice
Reprinted with permission. All rights reserved.

"A Prayer for Those Denied Abortion Care"

May you be safe—may a canopy of safety and peace, health and care cover you, despite everything you are now forced to endure.

May you find ways to own your body, your agency, and your dignity despite everything the government has taken from you.

May you be surrounded by a community of caring hands and loving hearts, who can hold you.

May you always know that you are holy, sacred, and your will—your autonomy—matters, should be respected as such.

May you be protected in all ways, able to weather the material, physical, emotional and spiritual hardships that come your way.

May you find within yourself resilience, strength, and bravery.

May you know that you are not alone.

National Council of Jewish Women
Reprinted with permission. All rights reserved.

From the Nursery

After a while, I stopped asking whether my child would survive,
although everything I asked in its stead
could be heard as this question.

Her body, not ready for the bare earth,
and like a nude soul, suffered each thing
with an intuition impossibly more acute
than what her body could carry out
in practice.

I must have seemed, at times, almost unconcerned
by what the clinicians said—
each small, survivable diagnosis touched me only as the sleeve
of a passing stranger.

When I looked up from her hospital crib
to see the wider world, could I help it
if I saw a war?

I can sense you are poised to accuse me now
of that sentimental watershed we call new motherhood:

Because my child was threatened, I too quickly conclude
from my single-mindedness that no one should be threatened,
that we shouldn't kill
those asleep in their bedclothes
somewhere we haven't heard of, somewhere
foreign, a desert—an infant, a mother, many cousins.

I concede, it was an emotional time.
I felt I had been dropped from a considerable height
where the future remained, as it always had been,
stridently unknown; it was simply the pitch that had changed.

Now I look out from the nursery window—
first a birch tree, then rowhomes, the city, the country, the world—
still the war widens, wide as prehistoric mouth,
wide as desperate slander.

If you wish, call me what the postpartum have long been called:

tired mother, overprotective bear,
open sore,
a body made sensitive
to the scent of fire or fume,
just as your mother would have been
when you were born, you who are alive
to read this now.

Katie Ford
Reprinted with permission. All rights reserved.

St. Brigid, Pray for Us

You were a woman of peace.
You brought harmony
where there was conflict.
You brought light to the darkness.
You brought hope to the downcast.

May the mantle of your peace cover
those who are troubled and anxious,
and may peace be firmly rooted in our
hearts and in our world.
Inspire us to act justly and
to reverence all God has made.

Brigid, you were a voice for
the wounded and the weary.
Strengthen what is weak within us.
Calm us into a quietness
that heals and listens.
May we grow each day into greater
wholeness in mind, body, and spirit.
Amen.

Catholics for Choice
Reprinted with permission. All rights reserved.

Bibliography

Administrative Board of the United States Catholic Conference. *Political Responsibility: Reflections on an Election Year.* Washington, DC: United States Catholic Conference, 1976.
Alexander, Michelle. *The New Jim Crow: Mass Incarceration in the Age of Colorblindness.* New York: New Press, 2010.
Annett, Anthony M. *Cathonomics: How Catholic Tradition Can Create a More Just Economy.* Washington, DC: Georgetown University Press, 2022.
Arkes, Hadley. "Killing Abortionists." *First Things.* December 1994. https://www.firstthings.com/article/1994/12/killing-abortionists-a-symposium.
Atwood, Margaret. *The Handmaid's Tale.* New York: Anchor Books, 2020.
Bachiochi, Erika, ed., *Women, Sex, and the Church: A Case for Catholic Teaching.* Boston: Pauline, 2010.
Balmer, Randall. *Bad Faith: Race and the Rise of the Religious Right.* Grand Rapids: Eerdmans, 2021.
Banks, Jennifer. *Natality: Toward a Philosophy of Birth.* New York: Norton, 2023.
Barrett, Elise Erikson. *What Was Lost: A Christian Journey through Miscarriage.* Louisville: Westminster John Knox, 2010.
Beattie, Tina. "Catholicism, Choice, and Consciousness: A Feminist Theological Perspective on Abortion." *International Journal of Public Theology* 4 (2010): 51–75.
Bednar, Gerald J. *Mercy and the Rule of Law: A Theological Interpretation of Amoris Laetitia.* Collegeville, MN: Liturgical, 2021.
Beisel, Nicola and Tamara Kay. "Abortion, Race, and Gender in Nineteenth-Century America." *American Sociological Review* 69:4 (2004): 498–518.
Bernardin, Joseph. *Consistent Ethic of Life.* Kansas City: Sheed & Ward, 1988.
Bonow, Amelia and Emily Nokes, ed., *#ShoutYourAbortion.* Oakland: PM Press, 2018.
Bretzke, James T., SJ, *A Morally Complex World: Engaging Contemporary Moral Theology.* Collegeville, MN: Liturgical, 2004.
———. *Handbook of Roman Catholic Moral Terms.* Washington, DC: Georgetown University Press, 2013.
Bruce, Tricia, et al., *How Americans Understand Abortion.* McGrath Institute for Church Life, University of Notre Dame, 2020.

Cahill, Lisa Sowle. "Teleology, Utilitarianism, and Christian Ethics." *Theological Studies* 42 (1981): 601–29.

———. "Abortion and Argument by Analogy," *Horizons* 9:2 (1982): 271–87.

———. "Contemporary Challenges to Exceptionless Moral Norms," in *Moral Theology Today: Certitudes and Doubts*, edited by Donald G. McCarthy. St. Louis: National Catholic Bioethics Center Publications, 1984, 121–35.

———. *Between the Sexes: Foundations for a Christian Ethics of Sexuality*. Philadelphia: Fortress Press, 1985.

———. "Abortion, Sex, and Gender: The Church's Public Voice," *America* 168:18 (1993): 6–11.

Callahan, Daniel. *Abortion: Law, Choice, and Morality*. New York: Simon & Schuster, 1970.

Callahan, Daniel and Sidney Callahan, eds., *Abortion: Understanding Difference*. New York: Plenum Press, 1984.

Callahan, Sidney. "Abortion and the Sexual Agenda: A Case for Pro-Life Feminism," *Readings in Moral Theology, No. 9: Feminist Ethics and the Catholic Moral Tradition*, edited by Charles E. Curran, Margaret A. Farley, and Richard A. McCormick, SJ. New York: Paulist, 1996, 422–39.

Camosy, Charles C. *Beyond the Abortion Wars: A Way Forward for a New Generation*. Grand Rapids: Eerdmans, 2015.

———. "The Consistent Ethic of Life under Pope Francis," *Crux*. October 4, 2016.

———. *Resisting Throwaway Culture: How a Consistent Life Ethic Can Unite a Fractured People*. New York: New City Press, 2019.

Camosy, Charles C. and David McPherson. "Consistent-Life-Ethics Catholics Can and Should Treat Abortion as Today's Preeminent Priority," *America*. July 8, 2021.

Clark, Meghan J. *The Vision of Catholic Social Thought: The Virtue of Solidarity and the Praxis of Human Rights*. Minneapolis: Fortress, 2014.

Clifford, Anne M. *Introducing Feminist Theology*. Maryknoll, NY: Orbis Books, 2000.

Congregation for Catholic Education. *Male and Female He Created Them: Towards a Path of Dialogue on the Question of Gender Theory in Education*. Vatican City: Libreria Editrice Vaticana, 2019.

Cloutier, David. "Intrinsic Evil and Public Policy." *Commonweal*. October 31, 2012.

Congregation for the Doctrine of the Faith. *Declaration on Euthanasia*. May 5, 1980.

———. *Donum Vitae*. Vatican City: Libreria Editrice Vaticana, 1987.

———. *Dignitas Personae*. Vatican City: Libreria Editrice Vaticana, 2008.

Connery, John R. *Abortion: The Development of the Roman Catholic Perspective*. Chicago: Loyola University Press, 1977.

Coolman, Holly Taylor. "Adoption and the Goods of Birth." *Journal of Moral Theology*, vol. 1, no. 2 (2012): 96–114.

Copeland, M. Shawn. *Enfleshing Freedom: Body, Race, and Being*. Minneapolis: Fortress, 2010.

Cox, Kathryn Lilla. *Water Shaping Stone: Faith, Relationships, and Conscience Formation*. Minneapolis: Liturgical Press, 2015.

———. "Gnoseological Concupiscence, Intersectionality, and Conversion of Heart: Insights into How and Why Moral Theology Develops." *Journal of Moral Theology* vol. 10, no. 2 (2021): 212–38.

Crenshaw, Kimberlé. "Demarginalizing the Intersection of Race and Sex: A Black Feminist Critique of Antidiscrimination Doctrine, Feminist Theory, and Antiracist Politics." *University of Chicago Legal Form* 1, art. 8 (1989): 139–67.

Curran, Charles E. *Christian Morality Today: The Renewal of Moral Theology*. Notre Dame: Fides Press, 1966.

———. *Tensions in Moral Theology*. Notre Dame: University of Notre Dame Press, 1988.

———. *Loyal Dissent: Memoirs of a Catholic Theologian*. Washington, DC: Georgetown University Press, 2006.

———. *Catholic Moral Theology in the United States: A History*. Washington, DC: Georgetown University Press, 2008.

———. *The Development of Moral Theology: Five Strands*. Washington, DC: Georgetown University Press, 2013.

Curran, Charles E., Margaret A. Farley, and Richard A. McCormick, SJ, eds., *Readings in Moral Theology, no. 9: Feminist Ethics and the Catholic Moral Tradition*. New York: Paulist, 1996.

Curran, Charles E. and Robert E. Hunt. *Dissent in and for the Church: Theologians and Humanae Vitae*. Kansas City: Sheed and Ward, 1969.

Davis, Cyprian. *The History of Black Catholics in the United States*. New York: Crossroad, 1990.

DeCosse, David E. and Thomas A. Nairn, OFM, eds., *Conscience & Catholic Health Care: From Clinical Contexts to Government Mandates*. Maryknoll, NY: Orbis, 2017.

Dombrowski, Daniel A. and Robert Deltete. *A Brief, Liberal, Catholic Defense of Abortion*. Urbana, IL: University of Illinois Press, 2000.

Eberl, Jason T. *The Nature of Human Persons*. Notre Dame: University of Notre Dame Press, 2020.

Eggebroten, Anne, ed., *Abortion: My Choice, God's Grace: Christian Women Tell Their Stories*. Pasadena: New Paradigm, 1994.

Ellison, Marvin. *Making Love Just: Sexual Ethics for Perplexing Times*. Minneapolis: Fortress Press, 2012.

Eugene, Toinette M. and James Newton Poling, *Balm for Gilead: Pastoral Care for African American Families Experiencing Abuse*. Nashville: Abington, 1998.

Evans, Shannon K. *Feminist Prayers for My Daughter: Powerful Petitions for Every Stage of Her Life*. Grand Rapids: Brazos, 2023.

Farley, Margaret A. "Feminist Theology and Bioethics," in Barbara Hilkert Andolsen, Christine E. Gudorf, and Mary D. Pellauer, eds., *Women's Consciousness, Women's Conscience: A Reader in Feminist Ethics*. Minneapolis: Seabury, 1985.

———. *Personal Commitments: Beginning, Keeping, Changing*. San Francisco: Harper and Row, 1986.

———. "The Role of Experience in Moral Discernment," in *Christian Ethics: Problems and Prospects*, edited by Lisa Sowle Cahill and James F. Childress. Cleveland: Pilgrim Press, 1996, 134–45.

———. "Liberation, Abortion, and Responsibility," in *On Moral Medicine: Theological Perspectives in Medical Ethics*, second ed., edited by Stephen E. Lammers and Allen Verhey. Grand Rapids: Eerdmans, 1998, 633–38.

———. "The Church in the Public Forum: Scandal of Prophetic Witness?" *Proceedings of the Catholic Theological Society of America* 55 (2000): 89–101.

———. *Compassionate Respect: A Feminist Approach to Medical Ethics and Other Questions*. New York: Paulist, 2002.

———. *Just Love: A Framework for Christian Sexual Ethics*. New York: Continuum, 2006.

Ferraro, Barbara, and Patricia Hussey with Jane O'Reilly. *No Turning Back: Two Nuns' Battle with the Vatican over Women's Right to Choose*. New York: Poseiden, 1990.

Fleming, Julia. *Defending Probabilism: The Moral Theology of Juan Caramuel*. Washington, DC: Georgetown University Press, 2006.

Flores, Nichole M. "A Response to Emily Reimer-Barry's 'Another Pro-Life Movement Is Possible'—Power, Politics, and the Pro-Life Movement." *Proceedings of the Catholic Theological Society of America* 74 (2019): 42–45.

———. "Rihanna's Super Bowl Performance Put the Power of Pregnancy Center Stage," *America* (February 14, 2023).

"Final Documents of the Continental Assemblies," Synod on Synodality. Vatican City: Libreria Editrice Vaticana, 2023.

Finn, Daniel K. *Consumer Ethics in a Global Economy: How Buying Here Causes Injustice There*. Washington, DC: Georgetown University Press, 2019.

Foster, Diane Greene. *The Turnaway Study: Ten Years, A Thousand Women, and the Consequences of Having—or Being Denied—an Abortion*. New York: Scribner, 2020.

Francis, *Evangelii gaudium*. Vatican City: Libreria Editrice, 2013.

———. *Amoris laetitia*. Vatican City: Libreria Editrice, 2016.

———. *Gaudete et exsultate*. Vatican City: Libreria Editrice, 2018.

———. *Fratelli tutti*. Vatican City: Libreria Editrice, 2020.

Freeman, Philip. *The World of Saint Patrick*. New York: Oxford, 2014.

Fried, Marlene Gerber, ed., *From Abortion to Reproductive Freedom: Transforming a Movement*. Boston: South End Press, 1990.

Frye, Marilyn. *The Politics of Reality: Essays in Feminist Theory*. Freedom, CA: Crossing Press, 1983.

Fuechtmann, Thomas, ed., *Consistent Ethic of Life: Joseph Cardinal Bernadin*. Kansas City: Sheed & Ward, 1988.

Fullam, Lisa A. "Abortion in the Catholic Conscience: The Truth about Catholic Teaching," *Conscience* 44:1 (2023): 12–17.

Furton, Edward J. ed., *Catholic Health Care Ethics*, third ed. Philadelphia: The National Catholic Bioethics Center, 2020.

Gehring, John. *The Francis Effect: A Radical Pope's Challenge to the American Church*. Lanham, MD: Rowman & Littlefield, 2015.

Genovesi, Vincent J. *In Pursuit of Love: Catholic Morality and Human Sexuality*, second ed. Collegeville, MN: Liturgical Press, 1996.

Gibney, Shannon and Kao Kalia Yang, eds., *What God Is Honored Here? Writings on Miscarriage and Infant Loss by and for Native Women and Women of Color*. Minneapolis: University of Minnesota Press, 2019.

Gillman, John. *What Does the Bible Say About Life and Death?* Hyde Park, NY: New City Press, 2020.

Goodwin, Michele. *Policing the Womb: Invisible Women and the Criminalization of Motherhood.* Cambridge: Cambridge University Press, 2020.

Gordon, Mary. "This Pregnancy." *Commonweal* vol. 149, no. 10 (November 2022): 14–18.

Gudorf, Christine E. *Body, Sex, and Pleasure: Reconstructing Christian Sexual Ethics*. Cleveland: Pilgrim Press, 1994.

———. "To Make a Seamless Garment, Use a Single Piece of Cloth." *Conscience* 17:3 (1996): 10–21.

———. "Contraception and Abortion in Roman Catholicism," in Daniel C. Maguire, ed., *Sacred Rights: The Case for Contraception and Abortion in the World's Religions*. New York: Oxford, 2003, 55–78.

Gula, Richard M. *Reason Informed By Faith: Foundations of Catholic Morality*. New York: Paulist, 1989.

———. *Moral Discernment*. New York: Paulist, 1997.

Guttmacher Institute. "Induced Abortion in the United States." September 2019.

———. "Fact Sheet: Unintended Pregnancy and Abortion Worldwide." March 31, 2022.

———. "Interactive Map: US Abortion Policies and Access After Roe." July 25, 2023.

———. "Abortion Rights and Access in the Post-Roe Era." July 25, 2023.

Gurr, Barbara. *Reproductive Justice: The Politics of Health Care for Native American Women.* New Brunswick, NJ: Rutgers University Press, 2015.

Gvozden, Amanda. "Fetal Protection Laws and the 'Personhood' Problem: Toward a Relational Theory of Fetal Life and Reproductive Responsibility." *Journal of Criminal Law & Criminology* 112:2 (2022): 407–38.

Haas, John M. "Moral Theological Analysis of Direct versus Indirect Abortion," *Linacre Quarterly* 84:3 (2017): 248–60.

Haigh, Jennifer. *Mercy Street*. New York: Harper, 2022.

Haker, Hille. *Towards a Critical Political Ethics: Catholic Ethics and Social Challenges*. Basel: Schwabe Verlag, 2020.

Hamel, Ron. "Early Pregnancy Complications and the ERDs [Ethical Religious Directives]," *Health Care Ethics USA*. St. Louis: Catholic Health Association: February 10, 2014.

Häring, Bernard, CSSR, *Christian Renewal in a Changing World*. New York: Desclee, 1964.

———. *Medical Ethics*. Notre Dame, Fides, 1973.

Hayes, Diana L. and Cyprian Davis, eds., *Taking Down Our Harps: Black Catholics in the United States*. Maryknoll, NY: Orbis, 1998.

Heyer, Kristin E. "Enfleshing the Work of Social Production: Gender, Race, and Agency," *Journal of Moral Theology*, vol. 12, special issue 1 (2023), 81–107.

Hill, Mark A. *Embryology & Embryonic Development*. University of New South Wales Medicine, 2021.

Hinze, Christine Firer. *Glass Ceilings and Dirt Floors: Women, Work, and the Global Economy*. Mahwah, NJ: Paulist, 2015.

———. *Radical Sufficiency: Work, Livelihood, and a US Catholic Economic Ethic*. Washington, DC: Georgetown University Press, 2021.

Imperatori-Lee, Natalia. "Father Knows Best: Theological 'Mansplaining' and the Ecclesial War on Women," *Journal of Feminist Studies in Religion* vol. 31, no. 2 (2015): 89–107.

Iozzio, Mary Jo. *Disability Ethics and Preferential Justice: A Catholic Perspective*. Washington, DC: Georgetown University Press, 2023.

Jackson-Meyer, Kate. *Tragic Dilemmas in Christian Ethics*. Washington, DC: Georgetown University Press, 2022.

Jennings, Willie James. *After Whiteness: An Education in Belonging*. Grand Rapids: Eerdmans, 2020.

John Paul II, *Mulieris Dignitatem*. Vatican City: Libreria Editrice Vaticana, 1988.

———. *Centessimus Annus*. Vatican City: Libreria Editrice Vaticana, 1991.

———. *Evangelium Vitae*. Vatican City: Libreria Editrice Vaticana, 1995.

Johnson, John and Mike Schmitz, *Pocket Guide to the Sacrament of Reconciliation*. West Chester, PA: 2021.

Jones, David Albert. "An Unholy Mess: Why the 'Sanctity of Life Principle' Should Be Jettisoned." *The New Bioethics: A Multidisciplinary Journal of Biotechnology and the Body* (2017): 185–201.

Jung, Patricia Beattie, "Abortion and Organ Donation: Christian Reflections on Bodily Life Support," in *Readings in Moral Theology, No. 9: Feminist Ethics and the Catholic Moral Tradition*, edited by Charles E. Curran, Margaret A. Farley, and Richard A. McCormick, SJ. New York: Paulist, 1996, 440–80.

Kaczor, Christopher. *The Ethics of Abortion: Women's Rights, Human Life, and the Question of Justice*. New York: Routledge, 2014.

Kalbian, Aline H. "Where Have All the Proportionalists Gone?" *Journal of Religious Ethics* 30:1 (2002): 3–22.

———. *Sex, Violence, and Justice: Contraception and the Catholic Church*. Washington, DC: Georgetown University Press, 2014.

Karrer, Robert N. "The National Right to Life Committee: Its Founding, Its History, and the Emergence of the Pro-Life Movement Prior to *Roe v. Wade*," *Catholic Historical Review* 97, no. 3 (2011): 527–57.

Kaveny, Cathleen. "Toward a Thomistic Perspective on Abortion and the Law in Contemporary America," *The Thomist* 55, no. 3 (1991): 343–96.

———. *Law's Virtues: Fostering Autonomy and Solidarity in American Society*. Washington, DC: Georgetown University Press, 2012.

———. "Intentional Killing or Right to Bodily Integrity: Can We Bridge the Moral Languages of Abortion?" *Journal of Moral Theology* vol. 12, no. 1 (2023): 97–100.

Kamitsuka, Margaret D. *Abortion and the Christian Tradition: A Pro-Choice Theological Ethic*. Louisville: Westminster John Knox Press, 2019.

Kavanaugh, John F. *Who Counts as Persons? Human Identity and the Ethics of Killing*. Washington, DC: Georgetown University Press, 2001.

Keenan, James F., SJ. *Goodness and Rightness in Thomas Aquinas's Summa Theologiae*. Washington, DC: Georgetown University Press, 1992.

———. *Ethics of the Word: Voices in the Catholic Church Today*. Lanham, MD: Sheed & Ward, 2010.

———. *A History of Catholic Theological Ethics*. New York: Paulist, 2022.

Kellerman, Christopher J., SJ. *All Oppression Shall Cease: A History of Slavery, Abolitionism, and the Catholic Church*. Maryknoll, NY: Orbis, 2022.

Kim, Grace Ji-Sun, and Susan M. Shaw. *Intersectional Theology: An Introductory Guide*. Minneapolis: Fortress, 2018.

Kissling, Frances. "Religion and Abortion: Roman Catholicism Lost in the Pelvic Zone," *Women's Health Issues* 3, no. 3 (Fall 1993): 132–37.

———. "Abortion Rights Are Under Attack, and Pro-Choice Advocates Are Caught in a Time Warp," *Washington Post*. February 18, 2011.

Kluger-Bell, Kim. *Unspeakable Losses: Healing From Miscarriage, Abortion, and Other Pregnancy Loss*. New York: Harper, 1998.

Leath, Jennifer. "Out of Places, Please! Demystifying Opposition to Procreative Choice in Afro-Diasporic Communities in the United States" *Journal of Feminist Studies in Religion* 30:1 (2014): 156–65.

Leo XIII, *Rerum Novarum*. Vatican City: Libreria Editrice Vaticana, 1891.

Lind, Emily R. M. and Angie Deveau, eds., *Interrogating Pregnancy Loss: Feminist Writings on Abortion, Miscarriage, and Stillbirth*. Bradford, ON: Demeter Press, 2017.

Lorde, Audre. "Learning from the 60s," (1982), Black Past Digital Archives.

Lysaught, M. Therese. "Moral Analysis of Procedure at a Phoenix Hospital," *Origins* vol. 40, no. 33 (2011): 537–52.

Lysaught, M. Therese, ed., "Dialogue After Dobbs: Toward Reasoned Dialogue and Constructive Conversation on Abortion," *Journal of Moral Theology* vol. 12, no. 1 (January 2023): 89–144.

Lysaught, M. Therese, Joseph Kotva, Stephen E. Kammers, and Allen Verhey, eds. *On Moral Medicine: Theological Perspectives on Medical Ethics*. Grand Rapids: Eerdmans, 2012.

Lysaught, M. Therese, Michael McCarthy, and Lisa Sowle Cahill, eds., *Catholic Bioethics and Social Justice: The Praxis of US Health Care in a Globalized World*. Collegeville, MN: Liturgical, 2019.

Maguire, Daniel C. "Abortion: A Question of Catholic Honesty," *The Christian Century*. September 14–21, 1983.

Mahoney, John. *The Making of Moral Theology: A Study of the Roman Catholic Tradition*. Oxford: Clarendon, 1987.

Manne, Kate. *Entitled: How Male Privilege Hurts Women*. New York: Crown, 2020.

Massa, Mark S., SJ. *The Structure of Theological Revolutions: How the Fight Over Birth Control Transformed American Catholicism*. New York: Oxford, 2018.

Massingale, Bryan. *Racial Justice and the Catholic Church*. Maryknoll, NY: Orbis, 2010.
———. "A Parallel that Limps: The Rhetoric of Slavery in the Pro-Life Discourse of U.S. Bishops," in *Voting and Holiness: Catholic Perspectives on Political Participation*, edited by Nicholas Cafardi. Mahwah, NJ: Paulist, 2012, 158–77.
Martin, James SJ. "Why I Am Pro-Life," *America Magazine* (January 10, 2019).
Mason, Carol. *Killing for Life: The Apocalyptic Narrative of Pro-Life Politics*. Ithaca, NY: Cornell University Press, 2002.
McBride, Dorothy E. and Jennifer L. Keys, eds., *Abortion in the United States*, second ed. Santa Barbara: ABC-CLIO, 2018.
McLeod, Carolyn. *Conscience in Reproductive Health Care: Prioritizing Patient Interests*. New York: Oxford University Press, 2020.
McCormick, Richard A., SJ. "Rules for Abortion Debate," *America* (July 22, 1978).
———. "Abortion: A Changing Morality and Policy?" *Catholic Mind* 77 (October 1979): 42–59.
———. "Who or What Is the Preembryo?" *Kennedy Institute of Ethics Journal* 1:1 (March 1991): 1–15.
McCormick, Richard, SJ, and Paul Ramsey, eds. *Doing Evil to Achieve Good: Moral Choice in Conflict Situations*. Chicago: Loyola University Press, 1988.
McDonagh, Eileen L. *Breaking the Abortion Deadlock: From Choice to Consent*. New York: Oxford, 1996.
McGann, Anthony J., Charles Anthony Smith, Michael Latner, and Alex Keena. *Gerrymandering in America: The House of Representatives, the Supreme Court, and the Future of Popular Sovereignty*. New York: Cambridge University Press, 2016.
Mescher, Marcus. "Toward a Taxonomy of Moral Injury: Confronting the Harm Caused by Clergy Sexual Abuse," *Journal of the Society of Christian Ethics*, vol. 43, issue 1 (Spring/Summer 2023): 75–91.
Millies, Steven P. *Good Intentions: A History of Catholic Voters' Road from Roe to Trump*. Minneapolis: Liturgical, 2018.
Mistry, Zubin. *Abortion in the Early Middle Ages, 500–900*. Woodbridge, Suffolk: York Medieval, 2015.
Mohr, James C. *Abortion in America: The Origins and Evolution of National Policy, 1800–1900*. New York: Oxford University Press, 1978.
Morgan, Jennifer. *Laboring Women: Reproduction and Gender in New World Slavery*. Philadelphia: University of Pennsylvania Press, 2004.
Munson, Ziad W. *The Making of Pro-Life Activists: How Social Movement Mobilization Works*. Chicago: University of Chicago Press, 2008.
Murkoff, Heidi and Sharon Mazel. *What to Expect When You're Expecting*, fifth ed. New York: Workman, 2016.
Nairn, Thomas, ed., *The Consistent Ethic of Life: Assessing Its Reception and Relevance*. Maryknoll, NY: Orbis, 2008.
Neu, Diann L. *Stirring Waters: Feminist Liturgies for Justice*. Collegeville, MN: Liturgical, 2020.

Noonan, John T., Jr., "Abortion and the Catholic Church: A Summary History," *The American Journal of Jurisprudence* 12, no. 1 (1967): 85–131.

———. "An Almost Absolute Value in History," in *Vice and Virtue in Everyday Life*, seventh ed., edited by Christina Sommers and Fred Sommers. Belmont, CA: Wadsworth, 2006.

Oduyoye, Mercy Amba. "Church-Woman and the Church in Contemporary Times: A Study of Sacrifice in Mission," *Bulletin de Theologie Africaine* 6:12 (1984): 259–72.

Owens, Emily A. *Consent in the Presence of Force*. Chapel Hill: University of North Carolina Press, 2023.

Parker, Willie. *Life's Work: A Moral Argument for Choice*. New York: 37 Ink/Simon & Schuster, 2017.

Parsons, Margaret Sammon. "Abortion and Religion: The Politics of the American Catholic Bishops," PhD. diss. Catholic University of America, 2011.

Patrick, Anne E., SNJM, *Liberating Conscience: Feminist Explorations in Catholic Moral Theology*. New York: Continuum, 1996.

———. "Framework for Love: Toward a Renewed Understanding of Christian Vocation," in *A Just & True Love: Feminism at the Frontiers of Theological Ethics: Essays in Honor of Margaret A. Farley*, edited by Maura A. Ryan and Brian F. Linnane, SJ. Notre Dame: University of Notre Dame Press, 2007, 303–37.

———. *Conscience and Calling: Ethical Reflections on Catholic Women's Church Vocations*. London: Bloomsbury, 2013.

Paul VI, *Gaudium et spes*. Vatican City: Libreria Editrice Vaticana, 1965.

———. *Dignitatis humanae*. Vatican City: Libreria Editrice Vaticana, 1965.

———. *Humanae vitae*. Vatican City: Libreria Editrice Vaticana 1968.

Perlstein, Rick. *Nixonland*. New York: Scribner, 2008.

———. *Reaganland*. New York: Simon & Schuster, 2020.

Peters, Rebecca Todd and Margaret D. Kamitsuka, eds., *Abortion and Religion: Jewish, Christian, and Muslim Perspectives*. New York: T&T Clark/Bloomsbury, 2023.

Peters, Rebecca Todd. *Trust Women: A Progressive Christian Argument for Reproductive Justice*. Boston: Beacon, 2018.

———. "Listening to Women: Examining the Moral Wisdom of Women Who End Pregnancies," *Journal of Religious Ethics* 49:2 (2021): 290–313.

Peterson-Iyer, Karen. *Reenvisioning Sexual Ethics: A Feminist Christian Account*. Washington, DC: Georgetown University Press, 2022.

Pew Research Center, "Religious Landscape Survey: Views About Abortion Among Catholics," 2023.

Picarello, Anthony R., Jr., General Counsel, United States Conference of Catholic Bishops, *Brief Amici Curiae of USCCB and Other Religious Organizations in Support of Petitioners*," No. 19-1392, *Dobbs v. Jackson Women's Health*. July 28, 2021.

Picoult, Jodi. *A Spark of Light*. New York: Random House, 2018.

Pierce, Yolanda. *In My Grandmother's House: Black Women, Faith, and the Stories We Inherit*. Minneapolis: Broadleaf, 2021.

Pius XI, *Quadragesimo anno*. Vatican City: Libreria Editrice Vaticana, 1931.

Pohl, Christine D. "Abortion: Responsibility and Betrayal," in *Bioethics and the Future of Medicine*, edited by John F. Kilner, Nigel M. de S. Cameron, and David L. Schiedermayer. Grand Rapids: Eerdmans, 1995, 212–23.

Polgar, Nenad and Joseph A. Selling, eds., *The Concept of Intrinsic Evil and Catholic Theological Ethics*. Lanham, MD: Lexington, 2019.

Pontifical Council for Justice and Peace. *Compendium of the Social Doctrine of the Church*. Vatican City: Libreria Editrice Vaticana, 2004.

Powell, Lisa. *The Disabled God Revisited: Trinity, Christology, and Liberation*. London: T&T Clark, 2023.

Rambo, Shelly. *Spirit and Trauma: A Theology of Remaining*. Louisville: Westminster John Knox Press, 2010.

Ramirez, Nicholas M. "Teleology and the Problem of Bodily-Rights Arguments," *National Catholic Bioethics Quarterly* (Spring 2023): 83–97.

Reimer-Barry, Emily A. "On Women's Health and Women's Power: A Feminist Appraisal of *Humanae Vitae*," *Theological Studies* 79:4 (2018): 818–40.

———. "Another Pro-Life Movement is Possible," *Proceedings of the Catholic Theological Society of America* 74 (2019): 21–41.

———. "*Amoris Laetitia* at Five," *Theological Studies* 83:1 (2022): 109–32.

———. "Miscarriage of Justice," in *Disturbing the Foundations: Feminist Ethicists Respond to the Dobbs Decision*. Catholic Re-Visions Series, Political Theology Network, July 22, 2022.

———. "Wisdom from a Reproductive Justice Framework," *Journal of Moral Theology* 12:1 (2023): 131–34.

———. "A Year after *Dobbs*: What about Maternal Life?" *National Catholic Reporter*. June 29, 2023.

Reisinger, Doris. "Reproductive Abuse in the Context of Clergy Sexual Abuse in the Catholic Church," *Religions* 13: 198 (2022): 1–21.

Rice, Charles E. *The Vanishing Right to Life: An Appeal for a Renewed Reverence for Life*. Garden City, NJ: Doubleday, 1969.

Riddle, John M. *Contraception and Abortion from the Ancient World to the Renaissance*. Cambridge: Harvard University Press, 1992.

Roberts, Dorothy. *Killing the Black Body: Race, Reproduction, and the Meaning of Liberty*, twentieth anniversary ed. New York: Vintage, 2017.

Ross, Loretta J., Lynn Roberts, Erika Derkas, Whitney Peoples, and Pamela Bridgewater Toure, eds., *Radical Reproductive Justice: Foundations, Theory, Practice, Critique*. New York: Feminist Press, 2017.

Ross, Loretta J. and Rickie Solinger. *Reproductive Justice: An Introduction*. Oakland: University of California Press, 2017.

Rubin, Eva R. *Abortion, Politics, and the Courts: Roe-Wade and Its Aftermath*. Westport, CT: Greenwood Press, 1982.

Rubio, Julie Hanlon. *Hope For Common Ground: Mediating the Personal and the Political in a Divided Church*. Washington, DC: Georgetown University Press, 2016.

Ruether, Rosemary Radford. *Sexism and God-Talk*. Boston: Beacon, 1983.

———. *Women-Church: Theology and Practice of Feminist Liturgical Communities.* San Francisco: HarperRow, 1985.

Salzman, Todd A. and Michael G. Lawler, *Pope Francis and the Transformation of Health Care Ethics.* Washington, DC: Georgetown University Press, 2021.

Sasser, Jade S. *On Infertile Ground: Population Control and Women's Rights in the Era of Climate Change.* New York: New York University Press, 2018.

Schenk, Christine, CSJ, *To Speak the Truth in Love: A Biography of Theresa Kane, RSM.* Maryknoll: Orbis, 2019.

Schlesinger, Kira. *Pro-Choice and Christian: Reconciling Faith, Politics, and Justice.* Louisville: Westminster John Knox Press, 2017.

Seabrook, Nick. *One Person, One Vote: A Surprising History of Gerrymandering in America.* New York: Knopf, 2022.

Segers, Mary C. and Ted G. Jelen, eds., *Wall of Separation? Debating the Public Role of Religion.* Lanham, MD: Rowman & Littlefield, 1998.

Selling, Joseph A. and Jan Jans, eds., *The Splendor of Accuracy: An Examination of the Assertions Made by Veritatis Splendor.* Grand Rapids: Eerdmans, 1995.

Shah, Meera. *You're the Only One I've Told: The Stories Behind Abortion.* Chicago: Chicago Review Press, 2020.

Shannon, Thomas A. and Allan B. Wolter, OFM, "Reflections on the Moral Status of the Pre-Embryo," *Theological Studies* 51 (1990): 603–26.

Steffen, Lloyd, ed., *Abortion: A Reader.* Cleveland: Pilgrim Press, 1996.

———. *Ethics and Experience: Moral Theory from Just War to Abortion.* Lanham, MD: Rowman & Littlefield, 2012.

Shapiro, Thomas. *The Hidden Cost of Being African American: How Wealth Perpetuates Inequality.* New York: Oxford University Press, 2004.

———. *Toxic Inequality.* New York: Basic Books, 2017.

Silliman, Jael and Marlene Gerber Fried, Loretta Ross, and Elena R. Gutiérrez. *Undivided Rights: Women of Color Organize for Reproductive Justice.* Boston: South End Press, 2004.

Simmons, Paul D. "Biblical Authority and the Not-So-Strange Silence of Scripture about Abortion," *Christian Bioethics* vol. 2, no. 1 (1996): 66–82.

Smith, Andrea. "Beyond Pro-Choice Versus Pro-Life: Women of Color and Reproductive Justice," *National Women's Studies Association Journal*, vol. 17, no. 1 (2005): 119–40.

Smith, Janet E. and Christopher Kaczor, *Life Issues, Medical Choice: Questions and Answers for Catholics.* Cincinnati: Servant Media, 2016.

Solinger, Rickie. *Pregnancy and Power: A Short History of Reproductive Politics in America.* New York: New York University Press, 2008.

Steffen, Lloyd. *Ethics and Experience: Moral Theory from Just War to Abortion.* Lanham, MD: Rowman & Littlefield, 2012.

Stasiak, Kurt, OSB, *A Confessor's Handbook: Revised and Expanded.* New York: Paulist, 2010.

Sullivan-Dunbar, Sandra. "Catholic Abortion Discourse and the Erosion of Democracy," *Journal of the Society of Christian Ethics*, vol. 43, issue 1 (Spring/Summer 2023): 55–73.

Tauer, Carol A. "The Tradition of Probabilism and the Moral Status of the Early Embryo," *Theological Studies* 45:1 (1984): 3–33.
———. "Personhood and Human Embryos and Fetuses," *Journal of Medicine and Philosophy* 10:3 (1985): 253–66.
Tavernise, Sabrina. "They Don't Understand That We're Real People," *The Daily*. October 1, 2021.
Tentler, Leslie Woodcock. *Catholics and Contraception: An American History*. Ithaca, NY: Cornell University Press, 2004.
Townes, Emilie M. *Womanist Ethics and the Cultural Production of Evil*. New York: Palgrave Macmillan, 2006.
Traina, Cristina L. H. "Papal Ideals, Marital Realities: One View from the Ground," in *Sexual Diversity and Catholicism*, edited by Patricia Beattie Jung and Joseph A. Coray. Collegeville, MN: Liturgical Press, 2001, 269–88.
———. *Feminist Ethics and Natural Law: The End of the Anathemas*. Washington, DC: Georgetown University Press, 1999.
———. "Between a Rock and a Hard Place: Unwanted Pregnancy, Mercy, and Solidarity." *Journal of Religious Ethics* 46:4 (2018): 658–81.
———. "Feminism, Finitude, and Flourishing: On 'Being Mortal, Like Everyone Else' (Wis 7:1)." Madeleva Lecture, St. Mary's College, South Bend, IN. April 13, 2023.
Turner, Thomas. "A Rite for Miscarriage," *Modern Liturgy* 13, no. 9. December 1986/January 1987, 18–19.
Underwood, Kassi. *May Cause Love: An Unexpected Journey of Enlightenment After Abortion*. New York: HarperOne, 2017.
United Nations Population Fund. *Seeing the Unseen: The Case for Action in the Neglected Crisis of Unintended Pregnancy*. Geneva: UNFPA, 2022.
———. *Trends in Maternal Mortality 2000–2020*. February 23, 2023.
United States Catholic Conference. *Pastoral Plan for Pro-Life Activities*. Washington, DC: United States Catholic Conference, 1975.
———. *Many Faces of AIDS: A Gospel Response* (November 14, 1987).
United States Conference of Catholic Bishops. "Living the Gospel of Life: A Challenge to American Catholics." Washington, DC: USCCB Publishing, 1998.
———. "A Matter of the Heart: On the 30th Anniversary of *Roe v. Wade*." Washington, DC: USCCB Publishing, 2002.
———. *Project Rachel Ministry: A Post-Abortion Resource Manual for Priests and Project Rachel Leaders*. Washington, DC: USCCB, 2009.
———. *Ethical and Religious Directives for Catholic Health Care Services*, sixth ed. Washington, DC: USCCB, 2018.
———. *Open Wide Our Hearts: The Enduring Calling to Love, A Pastoral Letter Against Racism*. Washington, DC: USCCB, 2018.
———. *Forming Consciences for Faithful Citizenship*. Washington, DC: USCCB, 2019.
———. *Compendium of the Catechism of the Catholic Church*. Washington, DC: USCCB, 2020.
———. "Abortion Is Not Healthcare." Washington, DC: USCCB, 2021.

———. "USCCB Statement on U.S. Supreme Court Ruling in *Dobbs v. Jackson*," Washington, DC: USCCB, 2022.
U.S. Supreme Court. *Roe v. Wade*. 410 U.S. 113 (1973).
Vacek, Edward Collins, SJ, "Proportionalism: One View of the Debate," *Theological Studies* 46 (1985): 287–314.
Verhey Allen. *Reading the Bible in the Strange World of Medicine*. Grand Rapids: Eerdmans, 2003.
Wagner, Teresa R. *Back to the Drawing Board: The Future of the Pro-Life Movement*. South Bend, IN: St. Augustine's Press, 2003.
Walker-Barnes, Chanequa. *Too Heavy A Yoke: Black Women and the Burden of Strength*. Eugene, OR: Cascade Books, 2014.
Walsh, Maureen. "Emerging Trends in Pregnancy Loss Memorialization in American Catholicism," *Horizons* 44 (2017): 369–98.
Ward, Kate. *Wealth, Virtue, and Moral Luck: Christian Ethics in an Age of Inequality*. Washington, DC: Georgetown University Press, 2022.
Washington, Harriet A. *Medical Apartheid: The Dark History of Medical Experimentation on Black Americans from Colonial Times to the Present*. New York: Anchor, 2006.
Weaver, Darlene Fozard. "Freedom in a Morally Diverse World." *Catholic Theological Society of America Proceedings* vol. 77 (2023): 18–30.
Weschler, Toni. *Taking Charge of Your Fertility: The Definitive Guide to Natural Birth Control, Pregnancy Achievement, and Reproductive Health, 20th Anniversary Edition*. New York: William Morrows/Harper Collins, 2015.
White, Christopher. "Francis Says, 'Pro-Life' Means Supporting Immigrants, Others Disagree," *Crux* September 12, 2017.
———. "Pope Francis Says He Has Never Denied Communion," *National Catholic Reporter*. September 15, 2021.
White, Sophie. *Voices of the Enslaved: Love, Labor, and Longing in French Louisiana*. Chapel Hill: University of North Carolina Press, 2019.
Williams, Daniel K. *Defenders of the Unborn: The Pro-Life Movement Before* Roe v. Wade. New York: Oxford University Press, 2016.
———. *God's Own Party: The Making of the Christian Right*. New York: Oxford, 2010.
Williams, Kate, ed., *Of Womb and Tomb: Prayer in Time of Infertility, Miscarriage, and Stillbirth*. Chicago: GIA Publications, 2019.
Williams, Shannen Dee. *Subversive Habits: Black Catholic Nuns in the Long African American Freedom Struggle*. Durham, NC: Duke University Press, 2022.
Wilson, Jeff. *Mourning the Unborn Dead: A Buddhist Ritual Comes to America*. New York: Oxford University Press, 2009.
Winright, Tobias, ed., *T&T Clark Handbook of Christian Ethics*. London: Bloomsbury, 2021.
Wood, Anna. *I've Had One Too: A Story of Abortion and Healing*. Los Angeles: Numinous Books, 2021.
Zeh, Katey. *A Complicated Choice: Making Space for Grief and Healing in the Pro-Choice Movement*. New York: Broadleaf Books, 2022.

Ziegler, Mary. *Abortion and the Law in America:* Roe v. Wade *to the Present.* Cambridge: Cambridge University Press, 2020.

———. *Dollars for Life: The Anti-Abortion Movement and the Fall of the Republican Establishment.* New Haven: Yale University Press, 2022.

Zucker, Jessica. *I Had A Miscarriage: A Memoir, A Movement.* New York: Feminist Press, 2021.

Index

abortion:
    bans, 2, 5, 43, 62, 217, 234, 242;
    craniotomy, 46, 78n21;
    direct, 21, 45–46, 57, 69, 112;
    in *Ethical and Religious Directives*, 65;
    as evil, 48, 73;
    as economic issue, 23–24, 129–45;
    as gender justice issue, 24;
    as human rights issue, 23, 57;
    and liturgy, 5, 240–42;
    intrinsically illicit, 48;
    indirect, 21, 46, 65, 69–71, 78n21, 211;
    as killing, 46–47, 65;
    as legal issue, 22;
    as medical issue, 23;
    medication, 20, 208;
    as moral good, 15, 212, 243;
    as non–negotiable moral issue, 86n115, 112;
    as partisan issue, 105–11;
    as personal issue, 21–22, 145;
    as philosophical issue, 25;
    as preeminent issue for voters, 15, 32n1, 59, 106, 117;
    as premoral disvalue, 209–14;
    as public health issue, 24;
    as racial justice issue, 24;
    rates of, 162;
    and reproductive justice, 1–2, 145;
    as return of life to God, 208–9;
    as sinful, 48, 73;
    social responsibility for, 144–47;
    and spiritual well–being, 207;
    spontaneous abortion (miscarriage), 164;
    surgical, 20;
    testimonies of, 43–44, 172–88, 212–14, 226n105;
    therapeutic, 2, 43–44, 70–71, 211;
    as tragic dilemma, 208–9;
    and US history, 2;
    as withdrawal of life support, 207–8
accompaniment, 215–19, 243
adoption, 138
Afiya Center, 29
agency, 161
ambiguity, 7, 186–68
Amoris Laetitia, 50, 67, 220n8
Andolsen, Barbara Hilkert, 193
Annett, Anthony M., 130–33
anthropology, 195–99, 216
anti-abortion. *See* pro-life
Aquinas, 66–67, 219

Baby in womb. *See* prenate
Balmer, Robert, 107
Banks, Jennifer, 193
Barrett, Elise Erikson, 163–65
Bednar, Gerald J., 75
Benedictine spirituality, 216
Benedict XVI, 45, 96, 146
Bernadin, Joseph, 14–15, 95, 111–12,
Birthmark Doula Collective, 29
bishops. *See* United States Conference of Catholic Bishops (USCCB)
Black, Indigenous and People of Color (BIPOC), 7
Black Mamas Matter Alliance, 29
bodily integrity, 197
bodily life support, 201, 207
bodyright, 204–6, 214
Bretzke, James T., 227nn108–9
Brooks, Gwendolyn, 257
Bruce, Tricia, 236

Cahill, Lisa Sowle, 122n78, 153n78, 227n114, 230n138
Camosy, Charles C., 51
cancerous uterus, 70–71
care work, 130
casuistry, 66
Catechism of the Catholic Church, 48
Catholic Answers, 116
Catholic Democrats, 111
Catholics for Choice, 59, 260, 264
Catholic health care, 62–65, 70–74
Catholic social teaching. *See* Church teachings and social justice
childbirth, 14, 27, 60, 200, 239;
    and cost, 136–37;
    and complications, 166, 222n36;
    and racism, 232n157
childcare, 56, 130, 137–38, 144, 193, 235–36
    Child Tax Credit, 130
circle of praxis, 235
choice, 16, 61–62, 72–75, 106, 112, 130, 138, 145, 174, 178–79, 181, 187–88

Christian nationalism, 28
Church, 193, 195–96, 219, 233–6, 241–5
Church teachings, 4, 6, 32n6, 45–49, 54, 243;
    and abortion, 45–49, 54, 58;
    and bodily integrity, 196;
    and clericalism, 238, 241;
    and common good, 7, 30, 62, 238;
    and conscience, 217;
    and contraception, 48, 60, 62, 100–101, 228n122;
    and development needed, 194–95, 199, 207, 213, 219, 244;
    and health care, 15, 23, 45, 60, 62–65, 71, 112, 137, 196–7, 207–8, 235, 242;
    and listening, 236;
    and neocapitalism, 132, 145;
    and organ donation, 197, 201–2;
    and patriarchy, 59, 161, 187, 194, 204–5;
    and public square, 57–58, 74, 108;
    and slavery, 25–26;
    and social justice, 145–47, 219;
    and women as breeder, 49–52;
    and women as fully human, 194
circumstances, 73, 186
Clark, Meghan J., 245n1
Coleman, Taiyon J., 171–72
Colorado Organization for Latina Opportunity and Reproductive Rights (COLOR), 29
Committee for Abortion Rights and Against Sterilization Abuse, 29
common ground, 97
communion wars, 53–55, 115
Communities Against Rape and Abuse (CARA), 29
community asset model, 235
compassion, 236
complementarity, 49
complexity, 7, 66, 73, 186–88
conception, 47, 57

conscience, 62, 194, 216–17
control, 217
Copeland, M. Shawn, 27
Cordileone, Salvatore, 53–54
Cox, Kathryn Lilla, 222n26, 231n151, 232n160
crisis pregnancy centers, 98–99
cummings, e.e., 256
Curran, Charles E., 56

dark money, 115
deficit model, 235
delayed hominization, 107
Dignitatis humanae, 195, 216–17
Dignitas personae, 47–49, 79n34
Dilation and Curettage (D&C), 20. See also Abortion, surgical
Dilation and Evacuation (D&E), 20. See also Abortion, surgical
disability, 141–42, 238
discernment, 62, 74–75, 131, 202, 209, 212, 215–17, 233
Dobbs vs. Jackson Women's Health, 5, 8, 23, 43, 61, 96, 117,
Donum vitae, 47, 79n30
double standard, 201

ectopic pregnancy, 70–71
education, 139–41
embryo, 17–18
embodiment, 195
Eternal Word Television Network, 116
Ethical and Religious Directives. See Catholic health care
Eucharist, 53–55, 115, 240
Evangelium vitae, 46–47, 56–57, 112

family values, 109
Farley, Margaret A., 195, 221nn13–14
Farmer, Paul, 233–34
feminism, 6, 147;
    and Catholic, 6, 161, 193, 211, 217, 243;
    and pro-life, 32n5, 51–52, 81n66;
    and pro-choice, 15, 54, 114;
    as threat to family, 108
fertility awareness, 18–19;
    and Church teaching, 228n122
fetus. *See* prenate
Firer Hinze, Christine, 99–100, 130
Flaherty, Jordan, 237
food insecurity, 135–36
foster care, 138–39, 236
freedom, 28, 187, 193, 195, 212
Francis, 6, 46–47, 54, 67, 96, 146, 195, 220n8, 244
Franciscan spirituality, 216
Frye, Marilyn, 31

Gaudium et spes, 48–49
gender complementarity
gerrymandering, 110–11
gestation. *See* pregnancy
gestational age, 17
God–talk, 205–6, 208
Good Samaritan, 202–3
Gordon, Mary, 184–86
grave matter, 48
Greene Foster, Diana, 8, 162
grief, 138, 164, 166, 168–70, 174, 178–80, 240, 254
growth mindset, 218
Gudorf, Christine E., 204–6
Guttmacher Institute, 162

Hamel, Ron, 71
health care, 1, 7, 14, 23, 29, 31, 44, 56, 71–72, 97, 136–37, 142, 173, 213, 244
Heyer, Kristin, 130
hospital closures, 44
housing, 133–35
Hyde Amendment, 25, 106
human life:
    as sacred, 48, 57;
    not absolute value, 73
human reproduction, 17–18;
    as site of violence, 25;
    as social good, 25
Humanae vitae, 55, 101

Hurston, Zora Neale, 203

Ignatian spirituality, 216
Imperatori–Lee, Natalia, 187
incarceration, 25, 144, 147, 234
Indian women. *See* Indigenous women
Indigenous women, 27
Indigenous Women Rising, 29
In Our Own Voice, 29
intrinsic evil, 48–49, 65, 90n169

Jackson–Meyer, Kate, 208–9
Janssens, Louis, 210
Jennings, Willie James, 28
Jesus, 3, 30, 74–75, 172, 219, 234, 250–51
John XXIII, 196
John Paul II, 45, 47, 52, 71, 96, 146, 220n8
Jones, David Albert, 214
Jung, Patricia Beattie, 199–202
justification paradigm, 211
just war theory, 72–75

Kamal, Soniah, 167–68
Kamitsuka, Margaret, 9n7, 19, 199, 202–4, 214
Kaveny, M. Cathleen, 238, 226n96
killing:
    abortion as. *See* Abortion;
    of abortion providers, 113–14;
    in just war theory, 72–75

latae sententiae excommunication, 49
Life Site News, 116
liminality, 214
Lind, Emily, 180–82
listening, 161, 236
liturgy after pregnancy loss, 168–70, 240–42
Lorde, Audre, 31
Lou, 175–78
Lysaught, M. Therese, 46

magisterium. *See* Church teachings

manualism, 66
maternal mortality, 25, 222n36
McBrien, Richard, 217
McElroy, Robert, 54, 59
Medicaid, 25
memorials, 241
midwifery, 9n7
Mifepristone, 20, 208.
    See also Abortion, medication
Millies, Steven P., 60
miscarriage, 19–21;
    early, 19;
    incurs no guilt, 21;
    testimonies of, 163–69
misogyny, 194–95, 217
Misoprostol, 20.
    See also Abortion, medication
Mohr, James, 101
moral absolutism, 7, 45, 52, 60, 73–75, 112, 116, 218
moral act, 56, 65–66, 69, 209
moral agency, 193
moral dilemmas, 43, 45, 214
moral evil, 209–10
moral injury, 20
moral striving, 227n107
moral tragedy, 193
motherhood, 5, 15, 30, 50, 53, 72, 193, 196, 213;
    as sacred duty, 49–51, 72.
    See also women as breeders
Munson, Ziad, 97–99

National Association for the Repeal of Abortion Laws, 110
National Organization for Women, 110
National Right to Life Committee, 103
Native American Women. *See* Indigenous Women
Native Youth Sexual Health Network, 29
natural law, 57, 67, 72, 209, 228n122
neoliberalism, 130
New Deal, 100
New Testament, 194

New Voices, 29
nutrition, 135–36

Oduyoye, Mercy Amba, 206
Ortiz, Janet Lee, 170–71

parenting, 23–24
Parker, Willie, 20
parish life, 52–53, 113–14, 238–39, 241
Pastoral Plan for Pro-Life Activities, 103–5
Patient Protection and Affordable Care Act, 60
patriarchy, 161, 187
Patrick, Anne E., 216
Pelosi, Nancy, 53
personalism, 196
personhood, 19, 25, 47, 213–14
Peters, Rebecca Todd, 9n7, 186–87, 199–201, 214
Peterson-Iyer, Karen, 10n11, 224n61
physical evil, 209–11
Pierce, Yolanda, 161, 205, 220n5
Pius XI, 194
Pius XII, 225n93
Planned Parenthood Federation of America, 110, 116, 184
plantation power, 25–29.
　　See also slavery
Pohl, Christine, 187
policing, 135
political lobbying, 57
political parties, 58;
　　Democratic party, 58, 97, 100, 102, 106, 109–10, 114–16;
　　Republican party, 58, 102, 105, 109–11, 115–17
positionality, 7, 233, 244
praxis, 235
prayer, 53, 168, 179–80, 216, 233, 239–40, 254–55, 258, 260–61, 264
preferential option for the poor and vulnerable, 30
pregnancy:
　　as blessing, 26, 196;
　　as bodily life support, 201–2;
　　as burdensome, 197–99;
　　complications, 43–44;
　　as dangerous, 197;
　　as gestational hospitality, 202–4;
　　as gift relation, 201–2;
　　as liminality, 200–201;
　　and medical science, 17–18;
　　and moral authority over, 214–15;
　　and moral vocabulary, 199–206;
　　subjective experience of, 19, 193;
　　symptoms, 198;
　　termination of, 65, 69, 172–86, 188
pregnancy loss, 20–21, 161–88, 243
premoral disvalue, 209–11, 218, 228n120, 228n124
prenate, 14, 19;
　　absolute (ultimate) value, 213–15;
　　inherent value of, 8, 19, 194, 213–15;
　　innocence, 46–47;
　　and prenatal justice, 51, 211, 213
principles, moral theology, 65, 214;
　　cooperation, 65, 68;
　　double effect, 65, 68–70;
　　gradualism, 65, 216;
　　toleration of the lesser evil, 65, 67–68, 174, 187
prisons. *See* incarceration
privilege, 3, 5;
　　and reproductive privilege, 10n10
pro-choice, 7, 15–17, 242;
　　and eugenics, 16;
　　movement, 15–16;
　　and racial bias, 16;
　　and recognition of post-abortion grief, 228n124
pro-life, 7, 13–14, 50–51, 57, 116–17, 242;
　　consistent ethic, 14–15, 32n6, 111–13;
　　as discourse of control, 28;
　　label, 3;
　　harassment as strategy, 113–14;

movement, 57–58, 95–118, 242–43;
　opposition to feminist movement, 100;
　and political violence, 16, 113–14;
　rhetoric of, 117;
　and shame, 16;
　streams, 97–99
proportionalism, 65, 69, 73, 207, 210–13, 226n93
prudence, 62, 214, 238

Rachel's Vineyard, 180, 214, 216, 238, 241
racism, 28, 132, 217, 234
realism, 219
reconciliation, 56
relationship violence, 142–44, 204–6
reproductive justice 1, 7, 13, 17, 25, 29–31, 56–57, 117, 144–47, 233–45;
　critique of choice, 16;
　focus on social conditions, 129, 147;
　founders, 8n1, 29;
　as human rights framework, 30;
　movement, 29, 114;
　organizations 29, 237;
　right to have a child, 30;
　right to not have a child, 30;
　right to parent in safe and healthy conditions, 16, 30, 34n22, 242;
　as unwieldy, 31
Reproductive Rights National Network (R2N2), 29
Reynolds, Susan, 169
　right to life, 112, 202, 213, 224n59
Roberts, Dorothy, 26–27, 220n5
Roe vs. Wade, 2, 43, 45, 60, 96, 98, 102–3, 107, 117
Ross, Karen, 254–55
Ross, Loretta J., 1, 25, 31
Ruether, Rosemary Radford, 11n20, 231n156, 247n37

Ruiz, Viva, 172–73

sacraments, 52–57.
　See also communion wars
sacrifice, 206
saints, 2, 216, 241–42
Samerah, 182–83
sanctity of life, 57, 64, 96, 214
saviorism, 237
seamless garment. *See* pro-life
settler colonialism, 27
sexual violence. *See* relationship violence
shame, 20, 73–75, 138, 173, 175, 179–80, 182, 186, 243–44
sin, 55, 243;
　mortal, 56, 212;
　social, 56, 193, 216
Sister Love, 29
SisterReach, 29
SisterSong, 29
slavery, 24–29;
　and plantation logic, 25–28;
　and woman as breeder, 26
Society of the Sacred Heart of Jesus, 216
social justice, 242
solidarity, 233–45
Solinger, Rickie, 1, 27, 31
spirituality, 216
Spiritual Alliance of Communities for Reproductive Dignity (SACReD), 29
spontaneous abortion. *See* miscarriage
Steffen, Lloyd, 73–74
sterilization:
　coerced, 24–25, 144
Stevenson-Moessner, Jeanne, 204
stigma, 138, 142, 161–62
stillbirth, 5, 170–72, 186–87, 208, 215, 241
structural supports, 118, 129–47, 218, 235, 243
Sullivan-Dunbar, Sandra, 19, 36n43, 93n204, 117, 148n9
synod, 236, 238, 242

Tessman, Lisa, 208
trafficking, 193
trauma-informed supports, 144
Trump, Donald J., 116–17
Turner, Thomas, 241

umbilical cord, 166, 197, 200–201, 214
unborn child. *See* prenate
Underwood, Kassi, 179–80
United States Conference of Catholic Bishops (USCCB), 6, 8, 45, 111;
    and abortion, 53, 102–5;
    and *Dobbs*, 8, 45, 61;
    and HIV and AIDS, 104–5;
    political action and lobbying, 57–60, 95, 115–16;
    and peacemaking, 104;
    and poverty, 145–47;
    and racism, 28–29, 101.
    See also Catholic health care

Vacek, Edward C., 210
Vatican II, 48–49, 55, 58, 72, 195, 209
Veritatis splendor, 49
virtue ethics, 216
voting, 16, 98, 109, 238

wages, 131
Walker-Barnes, Chanequa, 204
Ward, Kate, 133
Walsh, Maureen, 241
Washington, Harriet A., 27
welfare policy, 15, 96, 100, 114, 116–17, 130
White supremacy, 25–26, 29, 101, 107
Williams, Daniel K., 100–101, 105
Williams, Kate, 240–41
wisdom-keepers, 236
Wood, Anna, 173–75
Womanist commitments, 30, 145, 161
women:
    as breeders, 26, 28, 49–52, 73, 161, 196;
    as human persons, 193–97, 219, 243;
    instrumentalization of, 73, 205, 214, 224n59, 243;
    as subjects, 161, 193
Women of African Descent for Reproductive Justice, 29

Zucker, Jessica, 165–67

About the Author

Emily Reimer-Barry, PhD, is associate professor in the Department of Theology and Religious Studies at the University of San Diego. She teaches undergraduate courses in theological ethics utilizing feminist and antiracist pedagogies. Dr. Reimer-Barry's research explores themes in fundamental moral theology, including the role of experience in theological method, as well as topics that probe the relationship between social justice and sexuality, including HIV-prevention, birth control, gender justice in marriage traditions, and reproductive justice. Her articles have appeared in *Theological Studies*, *Theology and Sexuality*, *Proceedings of the Catholic Theological Society of America*, the *Journal of Moral Theology*, and the *Journal of the Society of Christian Ethics*. She is a contributor to the Catholic Moral Theology blog and The Forum blog for Catholic Theological Ethics in the World Church. Her first book, *Catholic Theology of Marriage in an Era of HIV and AIDS: Marriage for Life*, was published by Lexington Books in 2015. She is a graduate of the University of Notre Dame (BA), Weston Jesuit School of Theology (MTS), and Loyola University Chicago (PhD). Dr. Reimer-Barry lives in Chula Vista, California, with her family. More information, including links to publications, can be found on her website: https://emilyreimerbarry.com/.

www.ingramcontent.com/pod-product-compliance
Lightning Source LLC
Chambersburg PA
CBHW021851230426
43671CB00006B/342